To the Islands

To the Islands

White Australians and the Malay Archipelago since 1788

Paul Battersby

LEXINGTON BOOKS
A division of
ROWMAN & LITTLEFIELD PUBLISHERS, INC.
Lanham • Boulder • New York • Toronto • Plymouth, UK

LEXINGTON BOOKS

A division of Rowman & Littlefield Publishers, Inc.
A wholly owned subsidary of The Rowman & Littlefield Publishing Group, Inc.
4501 Forbes Boulevard, Suite 200
Lanham, MD 20706

Estover Road
Plymouth PL6 7PY
United Kingdom

British Library Cataloguing in Publication Information Available

Library of Congress Cataloging-in-Publication Data

Battersby, Paul, 1961-
  To the Islands : White Australians and the Malay Archipelago since 1788 / Paul
Battersby.
    p. cm.
  Includes bibliographical references and index.
  ISBN-13: 978-0-7391-2051-4 (cloth : alk. paper)
  ISBN-10: 0-7391-2051-4 (cloth : alk. paper)
  1. Malay Archipelago—Relations—Australia. 2. Australia—Relations—Malay
Archipelago. I. Title.
  DS603.B37 2007
  305.82′405951—dc22   2007017912

Printed in the United States of America

ed in this publication meets the minimum requirements of
l Standard for Information Sciences—Permanence of Paper for
aterials, ANSI/NISO Z39.48–1992.

To Carmel

Table of Contents

List of Tables

List of Figures

Acknowledgments

To the Islands began as an undergraduate paper in 1991 in the then School of History and Politics at James Cook University in Townsville. While researching potential honors thesis topics, I learned of a race riot in 1888 in the Queensland frontier town of Normanton that involved several people of "Malay" origin. Both the riot and the date intrigued me because it was then generally believed that Australia had little contact with Asia before the outbreak of war in the Pacific in 1941. Reading through newspaper reports on the Normanton Riot and its political aftermath I came across short travel articles written by people from North Queensland who provided vignettes of life in the Netherlands Indies, Malaya, Singapore, the Philippines and even Siam. The shipping pages of major Australian metropolitan daily newspapers furnished more proof of the extent of the economic and social interconnections between Australia and Asia and confirmed my belief that this line of inquiry was worth pursuing.

It quickly became apparent that "ordinary Australians" from all walks of life had ideas about where they and the Australian colonies stood, culturally and geographically, in relation to Asia. Further research uncovered an established tourist trail through the Indies sustained by limited but important trading and transport linkages between Australian port cities, Batavia (Jakarta), Singapore and Manila. The work of Francis Birch, Jennifer Cushman and Phuwadol Songprasert led me to take an interest in Australian mining investment in South East Asia and the role of mining investors in the development of diplomatic ties between Australia and its regional neighbors. It was obvious, to me at least, that all these stories were connected by a common thread, namely Australia's discovery and gradual rediscovery of the economic value of its geographical proximity to Asia.

I became engrossed in researching the social history of Australia's discovery and rediscovery of its region and the relationship between the banalities of everyday Australian holiday experiences in Asia and the grander themes of regional trade and diplomacy. Australians in the nineteenth and early twentieth centuries saw and read about many parts of Asia and knew these places by many names, but social and economic interactions were perhaps most significant in insular South East Asia which, as far as Australian mining investors were concerned, included the Malay Peninsula and Siam.

It is unfashionable for historians to claim any historical continuity let alone pronounce the discovery of long-term trends, but the events related in this book evidence trends or tendencies, of long duration, moving beneath the surface of regional economic, cultural and political affairs. My approach to this subject became "globalized" as a consequence of my exposure to the theories and practices of globalization and cultural change since joining the Bachelor of Arts (International Studies) program at RMIT University. From interpreting my research findings through the frame of world systems theory, I now think and write about Australians in Asia in "global" terms, in recognition that regional happenings are linked to broader transnational and "global" concerns. One idea that has not altered is my belief in the educative potential of international travel. This in part stems from my own life experiences after migrating from the UK to Australia in the mid 1980s. Moving from the frontier world of northwest Western Australia to Melbourne, to Townsville, to Khorat in northeastern Thailand and then back to Melbourne, my outlook on the world shifted as often as did my geographical standpoint. While many people travel the world and learn nothing, I remain optimistic that increased cultural awareness and learning gained through travel or simply exposure to different ways of life can shift entrenched parochialism and cultural chauvinism. This is the promise of globalization.

Throughout this project I have received generous assistance, advice and encouragement from many people. Rodney Sullivan guided my early career as a research student at James Cook University and to this day retains an interest in my progress. Without the confidence and support of my former head of school at JCU, Kett Kennedy, and former JCU Vice-Chancellor, Ray Golding, I could not have undertaken necessary archival research in Australia and Thailand. Research students at regional campuses depend upon funding support for essential travel and hence I am indebted to the Australian Vice-Chancellors Committee for a grant received through their Australian Awards for Research in Asia program to visit the National Library and the National Archives of Thailand and to the Chaiyong Limthongkul Foundation for providing additional and substantial financial assistance. It was an honor to become one of the Foundation's first scholarship recipients and to be taken under its wing. In the course of my research I have been fortunate to be associated with and to learn from those closely connected with the Foundation's philanthropic work, especially Sondhi and Junthip Limthongkul, Chai Anan Samudavanija, Somsakdi Xuto and Preecha Uitragool.

In more recent times, David Walker provided indispensable advice and inspiration. Anna Shnukal, Guy Ramsay and Yuriko Nagata of the Aboriginal and Torres Strait Island Unit at the University of Queensland revived my interest in Australia-Asia relations at a time when it seemed that this project would stall. I am grateful to Hank Nelson, Adrian Vickers, Joseph Siracusa, and one anonymous reviewer who generously provided feedback on earlier drafts of this book. While I have endeavored to accommodate their recommendations, I of course accept full responsibility for any remaining errors and omissions. I am particularly indebted to Joe Siracusa for his encouragement to see this book through to its completion and for his advice about seeking and gaining publication. In this regard I am grateful to Lexington Books for publishing my book and for their understanding and patience as I went through the final stages of manuscript preparation.

I have incurred substantial debts to the many scholars, including those mentioned above, who have guided my research through their published and unpublished work. Thanks are also due to librarians at the John Oxley Library, the National Library of Australia, the National Library of Thailand, the State Library of New South Wales and the State Library of Victoria, and to archivists at the National Archives in Canberra. Lastly, I thank my wife, Carmel, for without her love and support this project could never have begun.

Proud Queen of Isles! Thou sittest vast, alone,
A host of vassals bending round thy throne:
Like some fair swan that skims the silver tide,
Her silken cygnets strew'd on every side,
So floatest thou, thy Polynesian brood,
Dispersed around thee on the Ocean flood,
While ev'ry surge, that doth thy bosom lave,
Salutes thee "Empress of the southern wave."

William Charles Wentworth, *Australasia*, 1823

At that time Macassar was teeming with life and commerce. It was the point in the island where tended all those bold spirits who, fitting out schooners on the Australian coast, invaded the Malay Archipelago in search of money and adventure. Bold, reckless, keen in business, not disinclined for a brush with the pirates that were to be found on many a coast as yet, making money fast, they used to have a general "rendezvous" in the bay for purposes of trade and dissipation.

Joseph Conrad, *Almayer's Folly*, 1896.

1

Introduction

In the morning of August 27, 1883, the volcano Krakatoa, on the island of Rakata in the Sunda Strait exploded with such ferocity that two-thirds of the island vanished in a pyroclastic cloud. This apocalyptic event, in effect a succession of violent eruptions, generated a series of tsunamis the last and largest of which claimed the lives of an estimated 36,417 people, mostly from the larger, more populous islands of Java and Sumatra. The impact of this cataclysm was felt with varying degrees of intensity around the globe. Sound waves ripped across the Indian Ocean, but while people from Perth to Darwin to Alice Springs heard what seemed at first to be distant thunder, the scale of this natural disaster and the ensuing human tragedy caused barely a ripple of interest in Australia.[1]

From May onwards steamship passengers travelling between Australia and Europe through the Netherlands East Indies would have witnessed the effects of volcanic activity at Krakatoa but the changed skies in the vicinity of the smoldering mountain gave no inkling of what was to follow. In the late evening of that calamitous August day residents of the Western Australian town of Geraldton reported a strange tidal surge. According to an account published in the *West Australian* several days after the event, astonished townspeople watched as the sea receded leaving behind a windfall catch of stranded fish. As beachcombers rushed to gather a share of the bounty, they were driven back by a sudden and deafening inrush of water as the sea returned. Neither the report nor the paper's editors connected Geraldton's mini tsunami and "the strange rumbling sounds" heard earlier in the town with Krakatoa's demise.[2]

A little over a century later, on December 26, 2004, an earthquake off the south coast of Sumatra produced a deadlier tsunami that obliterated the Indonesian city of Banda Aceh and much of the south coast of Sumatra, before rushing on to destroy lives and property in island and coastal communities along the northern Indian Ocean rim, from Sri Lanka to southern Thailand. Over 300,000 people, mostly Indonesian, lost their lives in the flood. This time, with the assistance of instantaneous communications, Australians sensed the enormity of the tragedy. The "Asian Tsunami" was a tragedy shared, and Australians responded with unprecedented yet understandable generosity. The dramatic contrast in these public responses invites the conclusion that a major reorientation is occurring in Australian society towards broader acknowledgement and acceptance of Australia's geographical proximity to Asia. These events should not, however, be read as evidence that, for nineteenth-century Australians, their region mattered little.

AUSTRALIA'S ISLAND WORLD

The history of Australian engagement with its region is multilayered, complex and begins well before the Japanese attack on Pearl Harbor in December 1941, which plunged the Pacific into war and which, it is widely believed, marked Australia's awakening to Asia. Later in the year of Krakatoa's demise, the British Australian colony of Queensland annexed the southeastern corner of New Guinea. This unilateral act, reluctantly acknowledged by Britain, ushered in a brief but intense period of imperial rivalry between Australians, Germans and Dutch that marked the high tide of Australian hegemonic aspirations in the islands to the north.

Popular cartography ensures that Australians are conversant with the geography of modern Australia—a nation largely contained within continental borders. Yet for colonial Australian adventurers, writers, scientists and colonizers, the future geographical contours of the new nation that was to be founded on the Australian continent were a matter for speculation. Australian novelist Marcus Clarke foreshadowed, in terms strikingly resonant with modern theories of cultural and economic globalization, the far-reaching consequences of increasing maritime exchange across the Arafura and Timor seas in his visionary book, *The Future Australian Race* (1877). Writing of "that abolition of boundaries," brought by economic, social and technological modernization, he sensed that powerful global forces would one day lead to the transcendence of the cultural divide between Australia and Asia.[3]

Clarke envisaged a civilizational split, not between the Australian continent and the Archipelago, but at a line south of Brisbane. A "luxurious and stupendous civilisation," he wrote, would one day evolve to encompass northern Australia, New Guinea, Moluccas (Maluku) and "parts adjacent," leaving southern Australia and New Zealand to form a residual European cultural sphere.[4] His scenario captured plausible tendencies, cultural, economic and political, then pointing towards a new regional order. Steam navigation companies joined the Australia-Asia run promising new markets for Australian producers; separationism was rampant in north Queensland, entrepreneurs looked to colonial spoils across the Torres Strait, while the importation of indentured labor added to northern Australia's multi-ethnic character that rendered it a world apart from the southern colonies. Conceived before the ideal of a white Australia was elevated to an article of national faith, Clarke's narrative offers a starting point from which to fashion a different history of Australian engagement with its region.

When nineteenth-century Australian politicians declared that Australia must assert primacy in the Pacific, the Pacific region, in their understanding, incorporated much if not all the Malay Archipelago, a name made famous by the English naturalist Alfred Russel Wallace for the chain of islands reaching east to the Solomons and west to the Malay Peninsula and the kingdom of Siam, or Thailand as the country was renamed in 1939. Once known severally as the Malay Archipelago, "the Islands" and Australasia, this region is today divided into two: South East Asia and the South West Pacific, with the former nomenclature gaining currency only during the Pacific War (1941–45) as a theater of Allied military operations.[5] This level of historical complexity in Australia's regional engagement is obscured by widespread and persistent fears of the dangers lurking in Australia's near north—to the detriment of our better understanding of Australia's engagement in international or global affairs.

Australian impressions of their surrounding island world were as diverse as the names by which this region was known. Here was an area of economic opportunity, a reservoir of cheap and compliant labor, a vital defensive barrier, a playground for the affluent, a source of biological and moral contagion, a danger zone but one that was ripe for "improvement." Equally important, the Archipelago was also a "gateway" to somewhere else, to the Americas and to Europe, and a "bridge" to British India. For the well-to-do of Sydney, Brisbane and the port towns of northern Australia, the Islands were part of "their" region, an Australasian region rightfully open to Australian travel, commerce and, if not direct colonial rule, at least periodic political intervention.

SCOPE AND PURPOSE OF THE BOOK

The South West Pacific is traditionally viewed as Australia's backyard, the focus of an Australian "Monroe Doctrine," and a part of the world where Australia stands in relation to its neighbors as a major power. This book draws attention to early Australian interactions with a long-since renamed and reordered Western Pacific zone, incorporating the "Malay" world reaching west from New Guinea to southern Siam. It is not conceived as an addition to the literature on Australian bilateral or regional diplomacy, nor is it an exposition of the evolution of Australian foreign policy towards Asia although such topics are necessarily addressed, with particular emphasis on Thailand—a too often overlooked regional strategic partner. Written from an Australian perspective, and reliant upon principally Australian primary resource material, this study presents a transnational history of Australian involvement in this northwestern frontier zone of Australasia, and examines how Australians have accommodated themselves to their island region from the early years of British colonisation to the present.[6] The act of writing Australia into regional affairs is both a part of this ongoing process of accommodation and a challenge to orthodox narratives of Australian history.

There could be many starting points for such a history: the arrival of the first Australians some 40,000 years ago or the first "Malay" fishermen at least one hundred years before the celebrated English navigator Matthew Flinders mapped the Australian coastline. Here, however, we are concerned with White Australia, a term that privileges the narrative of British colonization but which is also synonymous with racial bigotry and nationalistic xenophobia, and which draws attention to the enduring power of the "race card" in Australian politics. A work of this scope must adopt a thematic approach to its subject matter, as the sheer volume of events, personalities, patterns and trends would easily fill several volumes. At the heart of this endeavor is an interest in the persistence of a regional idea throughout two centuries of Australasian colonization. Of central concern are the historical processes of regionalization and the close connections between regionalizing and globalizing patterns of economic exchange in Australia's evolving regional relations. Economic considerations weigh heavily in the analysis of these patterns but not to the exclusion of social, cultural and political interests. Indeed, the book details how the experiences of "ordinary" Australians in the Archipelago during the late nineteenth and early twentieth centuries betrayed fine cracks in the ideological edifice of White Australia and how the ongoing enmeshment of Australia in regional affairs turned these fissures into gaping chasms.

Five dimensions of Australia's regionality are addressed in the chapters which follow: Australian economic and territorial ambitions in the Archipelago, the evolution of intraregional transport connections; Australian travel experiences in "the Islands," investment relations and security. This thematic structure rests upon a simple chronological division of Australian history beginning in the nineteenth century where self-governing Australian colonies evolved within a wider region of European colonial states, each seeking to tighten their grip over dispersed territories and develop their economies through international trade and protected domestic markets, to the era from Federation to the 1930s when the Australian Commonwealth took faltering steps towards political independence and Australians developed a keener economic and strategic interest in Asia and the post–World War Two period when Australia moved slowly toward formal acceptance of its place in a region of newly independent states. While the primary focus is upon Australia's regional relations up to 1950, an entire chapter is devoted to regionalizing trends in a new "global era."

CONTINENTAL DRIFT

Australasia was first named and defined by eighteenth-century French philosophers but both the word and the geographical idea were quickly appropriated by British explorers, cartographers and empire builders. In its modern form Australasia is a much-attenuated region comprising Australia and New Zealand, although in the Australian mining industry the name and its earlier scope retain currency. Inscribed into the nineteenth-century English geographical imagination, Australasia is mapped to its fullest extent in Eneas Mackenzie's compendium, *A New and Complex System of Modern Geography* (1817).[7] The mapmaker R. Scott framed Australasia as a vast archipelagic chain incorporating Java, the Moluccas and New Zealand. Drawn without any apparent reference to the work of Flinders who circumnavigated Australia in 1802–1803, the Australian continent is clearly marked "Not Asia" but stands as the map's dominant geographical feature, drawing attention to an ambiguity that continues to plague attempts to both delineate and name "Australia's region."

Appropriated by the New South Wales explorer, writer, poet and political aspirant, William Charles Wentworth as the name for a new Australian nation, Australasia embodied his dream of a continental nation at the center of a vast island world.[8] But Wentworth's was less a vision of territorial expansion into Asia than a claim to regional primacy that would be repeated by successive generations of visionaries and leaders. Concerned the Dutch held justifiable claim to the northern and western coastal areas of Australia, Wentworth, like many of his contemporaries, believed the conquest and occupation of the Australian continent must be Britain's principle objective. Commercial opportunities rather than the promise of new imperial spoils drew his attention towards the Netherlands Indies and China.[9] Yet within a half century the rapid increase in population and industry in the Australian colonies engendered more far-reaching imperial designs, limited only by Britain's reluctance to accept new colonial burdens, especially where these might sour relations with the Netherlands.

If Australian colonists were by and large only vaguely aware of Asia, knowledge of the region was nonetheless readily available to those with the curiosity and the education to look. Arguably the nineteenth century's most widely read book on island South East Asia, Alfred Russel Wallace's *The Malay Archipelago* (1869) conferred, unintentionally, a semblance of scientific legitimacy on Australian regional aspirations. Wallace claimed that "no two parts of the world differ so radically in their productions as Asia and Australia."[10] Yet Wallace believed that the biogeographical boundaries of Asia stopped at Bali, to the east of which lay the "Austro-Malayan" subregion of the Indo-Malaysian Archipelago. Reflecting upon the geological structure of the Austro-Malayan zone, he wrote subsequently in *Australasia* (1879), the Australian continent "forms its central and most important feature."[11]

Wallace conceived of the Malay Archipelago as a subdivision of Australasia, with the island continent of Australia poised ambiguously in between.[12] The contraction of his geographical idea by the *Encyclopaedia Britannica* to encompass only Australia and New Zealand caused him dismay and might explain why he reasserted and perhaps exaggerated the integrity of his findings in his later study of Australia and New Zealand, also titled *Australasia* (1893), in which he claimed the island continent was "geographically a southern extension of Asia."[13] The Wallace Line, marking the point of separation between the Austral and Malayan divisions of the Archipelago, served as a point of reference for biogeographers and novelists alike, although the "faunal split" between Australia and Asia moved gradually eastward as different criteria of inclusion and exclusion were invoked. Confirming the elusiveness of biogeographical precision, Wallace revised his Line in 1910 to exclude the island of Sulawesi (Celebes) from the Austro-Malayan division to eliminate some of the ambiguities caused by overlapping faunal zones.[14] This divider, writes Adrian Vickers, is an enduring regional "fault line" and a point of contention about the geographical integrity of the modern state of Indonesia, which supplanted the Netherlands Indies in 1949.[15]

Weighty natural histories, travelogues, maps and almanacs were collection and distribution points for ideas and images that informed the Western experience of people and place.[16] Wallace's *Island Life* (1880) and *The Malay Archipelago* (2000) were extremely popular among Australians bound for Asia. The experience of reading natural histories and less weighty travelogues was akin to an informal lesson in applied geography, complemented by the availability of maps and charts provided in their ship's library.[17] Schoolchildren too learned of Australia's geographical proximity to Asia and of the tenuousness of Dutch and Portuguese territorial claims. W. Wilkins, former Undersecretary for Public Instruction in New South Wales, incorporated Wallace's Austro-Malayan division of the Archipelago, New Zealand and Polynesia into Australasia. Here were countries which bore a "natural relation" to Australia, the "central mass" of this geographic region, and which, he added prophetically, might one day become "either useful allies or dangerous enemies" of the British empire.[18] The western portion of New Guinea, he wrote, was only "nominally" under Dutch control and in a state of utter disorder while in Timor the Dutch and Portuguese "had done nothing towards developing the resources of the country or civilizing the inhabitants."[19] This was an incendiary claim in an era where mapping and naming were precursors to colonization, and where territorial rights were secured through economic advancement and the maintenance of political order.

The "naturalness" of Australia's island region persisted as a motif in the writing of Australasian geography into the twentieth century.[20] The logic of proximity remains a potent justification for the claim that Australia's future lies in the Asian Pacific. The rapid spread of international trade and investment relations in the latter half of the twentieth century has created a global economy but, despite the transcendence of the state in many fields of human interaction, geography, in particular regions, states and borders, as this book will explain, still matter.

REPOSITIONING AUSTRALASIA

"Openness to the world," writes John Tomlinson, defines the cosmopolitan attitude.[21] "Ordinary" Australians, from the affluent and leisure rich to struggling prospectors and vaudeville performers, travelled to the Archipelago in steadily increasing numbers from the beginning of white colonization and yet the cultural significance of this well-established pattern or "flow" has yet to be adequately addressed in studies of Australia's Asian engagement. Maritime travel through what Richard White terms Australia's "pleasure periphery"[22] became a comfortable leisure pursuit for the travelling classes, but the ease of movement across the northern Australian maritime frontier also heightened feelings of vulnerability to the economic and cultural challenges of globalization in its "imperial phase."[23] If British Australians thought Britain their cultural homeland, they nonetheless felt a strong attachment to the Australian continent, which they regarded as their home in a practical and emotional sense and one that must be protected from intruders.

In the imperial age of the nineteenth century Australians spoke, dreamed and on occasion planned an Anglo-Australian empire in the Archipelago. Patriotic colonizers envisaged an iron corridor of railways and steamshipping services spanning Australasia, Burma and India that would unify British possessions in Asia. Henry Copeland, New South Wales parliamentarian and mining entrepreneur, conveyed the widespread belief that the new Australian nation's geography was its destiny. The Yorkshire-born businessman-

politician alluded to lingering dreams of Imperial Federation when, echoing
Flinders, he stressed the economic advantages to be derived from Darwin's
geographical proximity to Britain's Asian empire. Copeland presumed that
economics would, if not close, at least narrow the temporal distance between
Australia and Asia.[24]

Federation heralded the stricter demarcation of Australian national space,
and anchored northern Australia to a southern axis. White Australia turned
inwards, economically and socially, but not to the extent that Australians
cut themselves off from the "near north." There has always been a current
of what John Ingleson and David Walker termed "pro-Asian sentiment"
submerged, almost subversive in the challenge that it posed to the citadel
of White Australia.[25] As debated by Adrian Vickers and other contributors
to a 1990 special edition of the journal *Australian Cultural History*, Australian travellers from many walks of life felt compelled to write about their
holiday experiences in the Archipelago. However fragmented, mundane or
"tedious" were their travel vignettes published in the Australian press, the
mere existence of so many of these Australian travellers' tales suggests a
greater degree of familiarity with Australia's geographical locale than is
commonly acknowledged.[26] Through their recorded experiences, popular
novels, travelogues and the advertisements of tour companies and government travel bureaus, the natural, cultural and moral topography of Australasia was mapped out for avid Australian readers. Importantly, as Alison
Broinowski observed, where personal encounters with Asian peoples exposed the shallowness of racial stereotypes, more enlightened forms of engagement could and did occur.[27]

Sandra Tweedie argued that the twentieth century was, for the most part,
a century of Australian missed opportunities in Asia.[28] This "failure," according to many contemporary authors, is attributable to a deep vein of
racist sentiment in Australian society, perpetuated through popular culture
and manifested in repeated official unwillingness to show regional neighbors the same level of regard given to Britain and the United States.[29] Yet
Australians could, despite decades of cultural conditioning, form mutually
beneficial business partnerships with Asian elites.[30] Attracted to the tin-rich
rivers and estuaries of the Malay Peninsula, Australian mining engineers
and their families formed small but distinguishable "expatriate" communities along the far western edge of Australasia from Malaya to southern Siam
in the early twentieth century. On the outer limits of white colonization,
Australian frontiersmen were noted for their callous disregard for life and
local culture, but, in southern Siam, Australians accepted their subordinate
position in the prevailing Thai political order. Here, Australian and British
commercial interests clashed as often as they coalesced, suggesting the
emergence of fissures in imperial relations and the cautious pursuit of a
separate economic trajectory for Australia.

The Pacific is as much a blind spot in scholarly excursions into the history of Australia's engagement with Asia as Asia is to studies of Australia's Pacific ambitions. Henry Reynolds writes in *North of Capricorn* (2003) that northern Australia in the nineteenth century "more clearly and closely reflected its geographical milieu than has been the case any time since."[31] But was this geographical "milieu" Asian or Pacific? The northward movement of Australian adventurers, traders, miners and tourists from the late nineteenth century, the early stages of which were the subject of Hank Nelson's *Black, White and Gold: Goldmining in Papua New Guinea* (1976) was a movement that spanned Wallace's Malay Archipelago.[32] Nelson recognized New Guinea's geocultural significance as a "point of balance between Asia and the Pacific."[33] As Anna Shnukal, Yuriko Nagata and Guy Ramsay reveal in *Navigating Boundaries: The Asian Diaspora in the Torres Strait* (2004), so much of northern Australia's Pacific historical experience reflects significant Asian interconnections. At least Graeme Dobell's book, *Australia Finds a Home* (2000), treats South East Asia and the South West Pacific as distinct but related spheres.[34] If we are to develop a better appreciation of Australia's adjustment to its geographical place in the world and its place in world history, we should, as Donald Denoon recommends, revisit the nineteenth-century idea of Australasia and explore the reasons, political and intellectual, for its "dismemberment."[35]

Northern Australia's multi-ethnic society evidenced the possibility of Austral-Asian coexistence both in Australia and in Asia. Northern Australia was socially, culturally and economically different from the rest of the continent. Along Australia's open northern maritime frontier cultural, social and economic exchanges between Australia and Asia were an everyday occurrence. Part of a larger Australasian maritime world, multi-ethnic pearling centers at Thursday Island, Darwin and Broome were points of entry and departure for steamships and travellers moving between Australia and the Archipelago. Overlooked or treated as secondary concerns in histories of Australia's international affairs, these movements were part of much larger patterns of social, cultural and economic interchange that connected Australians to Britain's Asian empire and to Britain.

International tourism as we know it today has its origins in the industrialization of travel during the nineteenth century. New rail and maritime technologies greatly improved the accessibility of the Archipelago to Europeans and White Australians, with appreciable economic and cultural impacts. Not least, international image, or "brand," assumed importance for colonial governments eager to promote the business and travel opportunities in their respective spheres. Colonial governments, shipping companies and tourism promoters found a common interest in promoting Java, Malaya and the Philippines as peaceful, alluring and domesticated or tamed. Increased human mobility aided the economic development of colonial states but only insofar as migration met the need for capital and cheap labor. Population movements across national and colonial boundaries provoked the stricter policing of international travellers, according to criteria of wealth, class and race. This was evident no more so than in Australia at Federation, and yet tourist shipping services perpetuated the circular movement of affluent travellers between Australia and the exotic East and the "primitive" Pacific.

Crossing the Arafura to the Indies and Malaya, Australians entered the old imperial Orient of Joseph Conrad and Somerset Maugham that lingered well into the twentieth century. Australia's gradual incorporation into the "New Asia" is, despite many discontinuities, part of a longer-term secular trend with its origins in the European colonization of the Australian continent, Asia and the Pacific Islands. Much of this history of Asian engagement before the Pacific War (1941–1945) has been obscured by our dominant state-centric view of the world. Prefiguring contemporary patterns of regional and global economic relations, nineteenth-century Austral-Asian trading routes connected Australia with an evolving regional and global infrastructure for trade and travel.[36] Although Australian governments before and after Federation exhibited a tendency to react against regional drifts, Australia did not slip entirely out of its regional orbit—nor could it. Nothing is inevitable, but whether the Australian people like it or not, this trend is carried forward by decisions made largely beyond Australian shores in circumstances over which Australian governments can exert little control and in which they have no choice other than to accept. The challenge then for Australia is to earn a place in an evolving regional architecture not as a leader or as a surrogate for a powerful outsider, but as an equal partner. The starting point for such a project is not simply to reconcile Australia's history with its geography but to re-imagine them.

NOTES

1. Simon Winchester, *Krakatoa: The Day the World Exploded, 27 August 1883* (Melbourne: Viking, 2003), 157, 210–11, 242, 263, 274. Tom Simkin and Richard S. Fiske (with the collaboration of Sarah Melcher and Elizabeth Nielsen), *Krakatau 1883: The Volcanic Eruption and Its Effects* (Washington DC: Smithsonian Institution Press,1983), 67, 144–45, 197, 350–56.
2. The *West Australian*, August 31, 1883.
3. Marcus Clarke, *The Future Australian Race* (Melbourne: A.H. Massina & Co., 1877), 3.
4. Clarke, *Australian Race*, 20. John Ingleson and David Walker, "The Impact of Asia" in *Under New Heavens*, ed. Neville Meaney (Melbourne: Heinemann Educational Australia, 1989), 295. Clarke emphasised the Moluccas but his vision of Australasia extended to Singapore and Malacca.

5. Donald K. Emerson, "Southeast Asia: What's in a name," *Journal of Southeast Asian Studies* (vol. 15, no. 1, March 1984), 7–10.

6. Sections of this book appear in *Navigating Boundaries: The Asian Diaspora in the Torres Strait*, ed. Anna Shnukal, Guy Ramsay and Yuriko Nagata (Canberra: Pandanus, 2004) and Robert Cribb (ed) *Asia Examined: Proceedings of the 15th Biennial Conference of the Asian Studies Association of Australia*, June 29– July 2, 2004, <http://coombs.anu.au/ASAA/conference/proceedings/asaa-2004-proceedings.html.> Material about Ambrose Pratt and Australia-Thailand relations after the Pacific War appear in journal articles published in the *Journal of the Royal Australian Historical Society*, the *Australian Journal of International Affairs*, and *Pacific Affairs*.

7. Eneas Mackenzie, *A New and Complex System of Modern Geography*, (London: Mackenzie and Dent, 1817).

8. William Charles Wentworth, *Australasia* [1823] (Sydney: University of Sydney, 1997), 12.

9. William Charles Wentworth, *A Statistical Account of the British Settlements in Australasia: Including the Colonies of New South Wales and Van Dieman's Land*, vol. 1 (London: P. Whittaker, 1824), 321–22, 460–61.

10. Alfred Russel Wallace, *The Malay Archipelago: The Land of the Orang-Utan and the Bird of Paradise* [1879] (Singapore: Oxford University Press, 1986), 25.

11. Alfred Russel Wallace, *Australasia*, (London: Edward Stanford, 1879), 2. Penny van Oosterzee, *Where Worlds Collide: The Wallace Line* (Melbourne: Reed Books, 1997), 23–27.

12. Tony Ballantyne, "Empire, Knowledge and Culture: From Proto-globalization to Modern Globalization," in *Globalization in World History*, ed. A. G. Hopkins, (London: Pimlico, 2002), 129.

13. Alfred Russel Wallace, *Australasia*, vol. 1., *Australia and New Zealand, Stanford's Compendium of Geography and Travel* (London: Edward Stanford, 1893), 2.

14. Michael Shermer, *In Darwin's Shadow: The Life and Science of Alfred Russel Wallace* (Oxford: Oxford University Press, 2002), 122–23. van Oosterzee, *Where Worlds Collide*, 34–38.

15. Adrian Vickers, "Indonesia in Australian Writing Before C. J. Koch," in *Representations of Indonesia in Australia*, ed. Nathalie Mobini-Kesheh, (Melbourne: Monash Asia Institute, 1997), 23.

16. Victor Savage, *Western Impressions of Nature and Landscape in Southeast Asia* (Singapore: National University of Singapore Press, 1984), 15. W. H. Sherman, "Stirrings and Searchings (1500–1720)," in *The Cambridge Companion to Travel Writing*, ed. Peter Hulme and Tim Youngs (Cambridge: Cambridge University Press, 2002), 19.

17. Australian travel writers like William Brackley Wildey drew extensively from Wallace to inform their readers and expand and enhance their travel narratives. William B. Wildey, *Australasia and the Oceanic Region* (Melbourne: George Robertson, 1876).

18. W. Wilkins, *Australasia: A Descriptive and Pictoral Account of the Australian and New Zealand Colonies, Tasmania, and the Adjacent Lands*, (London: Blackie, 1888), v.

19. Wilkins, *Australasia*, 238–39, 251–52.

20. According to Henry Frei, the Japanese author Iimoto Noboyuki, influenced by German political geography in the inter-war period, perceived Australasia as an 'Australasiatic Mediterranean,' culturally diverse but geologically unified and forming an island counterbalance to the Far East after the Pacific War; Australia's 'Indonesian Mediterranean,' according to the New Zealand geographer Kenneth Cumberland, was a mirror image of the northern hemisphere Mediterranean area; a geographical fact that defined Australia's strategic interests. Henry P. Frei, *Japan's Southward Advance and Australia: From the Sixteenth Century to World War II*, (Melbourne: Melbourne University Press, 1989), 184–86. Kenneth Cumberland, *Southwest Pacific: A Geography of Australia, New Zealand and Their Pacific Island Neighbourhoods*, (Christchurch, NZ: Whitcombe and Tombs Limited, 2nd edition, 1968), 17.

21. John Tomlinson, *Globalization and Culture* (Cambridge: Polity, 1999), 199.

22. Richard White, *On Holidays: A History of Getting Away in Australia*, (Sydney: Pluto Press, 2005), 173.

23. A. G. Hopkins, "The History of Globalization—and the Globalization of History," in *Globalization*, ed. Hopkins, 21–27.

24. Henry Copeland, *A Few Weeks with the Malays* (Singapore: Straits Times Press, 1883), 5.

25. Ingleson and Walker, "Image of Asia," 290, and David Walker, *Anxious Nation: Australia and the Rise of Asia, 1850–1939* (Brisbane: Queensland University Press, 1999), 227.

26. Adrian Vickers, "Kipling Goes South: Australian Novels and South-East Asia, 1895–1945," *Australian Cultural History* (no. 9, 1990), 66.

27. Alison Broinowski, *The Yellow Lady: Australian Impressions of Asia*, (Oxford: Oxford University Press, 1992), 36, 50–51.

28. Sandra Tweedie, *Trading Partners: Australia and Asia, 1790–1993* (Sydney: UNSW Press, 1994).

29. See for example, J. Vin D'Cruz and William Steele, *Australia's Ambivalence towards Asia* (Melbourne: Monash University Press, 2003), 259–88, esp. chapter 6, "The Politics of Turtle Beach." Alison Broinowski, *About Face: Asian Accounts of Australia* (Melbourne: Scribe, 2003).

30. Phuwadol Songprasert, "The Development of Chinese Capital in Southern Siam, 1868–1932." PhD Thesis, Monash University, 1986. Jennifer Cushman, *Family and State: The Formation of a Sino-Thai Tin-Mining Dynasty, 1797–1932* (Oxford: Oxford University Press, 1991).

31. Henry Reynolds, *North of Capricorn* (Sydney: Allen & Unwin, 2003), ix.

32. Hank Nelson, *Black, White and Gold: Goldmining in Papua New Guinea*, (Canberra: Australian National University Press, 1976).

33. Hank Nelson, *Papua New Guinea: Black Unity or Black Chaos?* (Harmondsworth: Penguin, 1972), 55.

34. Graeme Dobell, *Australia Finds a Home: The Choices and Chances of an Asia Pacific Journey* (Sydney: ABC Books, 2000).

35. Donald Denoon, "Re-Membering Australasia: A Repressed Memory," *Australian Historical Studies*, 122 (2003), 297–300.

36. David Held, Anthony McGrew, David Goldblatt and Jonathan Perraton, *Global Transformations: Politics, Economics and Culture* (Cambridge: Polity, 2000), 16–20.

2

Empress of the Southern Wave

NINETEENTH-CENTURY AUSTRALIAN AMBITIONS IN THE ARCHIPELAGO

Commercial considerations have always been significant in the definition of Australia's regional aspirations. Nineteenth-century Australian colonizers looked to the Archipelago as much for their own economic survival as for potential military threats. These islands promised tradable commodities, markets and labor needed by fledgling Australian colonies to spur autonomous economic development. In an age when European colonial spheres were vaguely mapped, the islands to the immediate north and east of the Australian continent also seemed ripe for British Australian colonization. Throughout the nineteenth century, the Australian colonies, the Netherlands and later Germany vied to capture a share of the natural wealth of the East Indies and the Western Pacific. Intensified economic exchanges throughout the Archipelago hastened the territorial expansion of colonial states. For the Dutch, this involved the assertion of a sphere of influence spanning a vast island chain that lay astride vital maritime trade routes linking the main strategic nodes of Britain's eastern empire. Colonial Australians for their part coveted a British-ruled island corridor linking Australia to Malaya through New Guinea and the Moluccas.

TRACKING NORTH

In human terms, interconnections between the Australian continent and the Archipelago predate the arrival of Captain Arthur Philip and the First

Fleet by tens of thousands of years. Indigenous Australians were the first "accidental" navigators to reach the Australian continent through the Archipelago.¹ At the end of the last Ice Age, rising seas widened the gap between northern Australians and their ancestral geography, but maritime communication remained salient in localized economic and cultural interactions between island and coastal communities along the northern shores of Greater Australia. From localized beginnings, the maritime peoples and entrepots of island South East Asia built a vast and intricate trading system that by the first millennium CE encompassed Eastern Africa, the Persian Gulf, India and southern China. According to the South East Asianist Oliver Wolters, this system comprised a "single ocean" bound together by the propensity to trade, in which the sea was perceived as a means of communication, not a prohibitive or defensive barrier.²

In his seminal study of contact between northern Australia and the Malay world, Campbell MacKnight asserted the centrality of sea voyages in Australian and South East Asian history.³ Northern Australia reconnected with the Australasian maritime world as Portuguese, Dutch and British navigators landed by accident along the northwest coast. Contemporaneous with the arrival of European explorers and colonizers in the eighteenth century, the commercial reach of fishing fleets from Makassar on the island of Sulawesi slowly extended down towards northern Australia. A pivotal maritime people in the *beche-de-mer* (trepang) trading chain reaching northward to China, the Bajau Laut roamed the eastern Indo-Malaysian Archipelago harvesting their catch for sale in the port of Makassar. As trepang stocks declined they and other seafarers from southern Sulawesi probed southward in search of new fishing grounds to Ashmore Reef in the early 1700s and the Coburg Peninsula by 1780 at the very latest according to anthropologist, James Fox.⁴ From the Kimberley coast, *kayu jawa* in Malay, to the north Australian coast and from the Coburg Peninsula to the western Gulf of Carpentaria, known to the trepangers as *marege,'* Aboriginal and South East Asian cultural spheres overlapped for more than a century until Australian fisheries law, part of an alien and inflexible British politico-legal regime, forced them apart.⁵

Maritime linkages between colonial Australia and island South East Asia can be traced back to the 1790s. As early as 1792 with the settlement at Sydney Cove on the brink of starvation, Captain Arthur Philip sent a ship to procure precious supplies of meat and flour from Batavia (Jakasta), the center of Dutch commercial and military power in the East Indies, in a desperate bid to stave off a human tragedy.⁶ Necessity stimulated the deepening of regional trade links. Early trade routes were circuitous and return voyages lengthy with merchants anxiously waiting for up to a year for the arrival of their cargoes. Ships plying between Sydney, Canton and Calcutta sailed north outside the Great Barrier Reef through the Saint George's Channel separating New Ireland and New Britain. China-bound vessels sailed on around the northern tip of Luzon in the Philippines while those bound directly for the Indies and India passed along the north coast of New Guinea to Batavia, continuing on through the Straits of Malacca and across the Bay of Bengal.[7] Return voyages from Calcutta were made along the south coast of New Holland. Once a shipping channel was mapped through the Torres Strait that divided the tip of Cape York Peninsula from New Guinea, many captains risked passage through this hazardous reef-strewn waterway to shave thousands of miles and precious days off their round-trip journey.[8] Following the cancellation of the British East India Company's shipping monopoly in 1813 the number of vessels employed in the incipient regional trade gradually increased, focusing British attention on the exposed northern Australian coastline.[9]

Looking far beyond the expanding frontiers of British colonization, the Admiralty, the Colonial Office and governors of New South Wales appreciated the potential for a British entrepot in northern Australia. Prompted by an encounter with one part of a sixty-vessel Bajau fishing fleet in 1803, Matthew Flinders hinted at the strategic importance of the northern coastline from the Gulf of Carpentaria to Melville Island in his account of his circumnavigation of Australia.[10] France rather than the United Provinces, or Netherlands as it was known after 1815, challenged British naval supremacy, and in an era when exploration and mapmaking usually presaged colonial expansion, Jean Baudin's geographical interest in the southern coast persuaded Governor Philip Gidley King (1800–1806) to protect Bass Strait, even though the Torres Strait lay closest to Australia's most important regional markets.[11] With the quickest passage from England lying through the Roaring Forties along the Great Circle route to Sydney, the decision ensured a southern bias in the future pattern of Australasian colonization. The north coast seemed less at risk of encroachment by a hostile European power until the United Provinces fell to Napoleon in 1810. British occupation of the Dutch East Indies from 1811–1815 eliminated the possibility of a French threat from the north, but with the return of the former colonial power Dutch ambitions became a cause for concern.

Overlapping spheres of geopolitical interest exacerbated the intense commercial rivalry between the British and Dutch in Asia. The Netherlands was, according to John Barrow, Second Secretary at the Admiralty, "our greatest Commercial Enemy in the East."[12] British occupation of the Indies opened new markets for British merchandise but did not result in a lasting British presence in the eastern Indo-Malaysian Archipelago. Upon their return, the Dutch signaled their determination to turn a profit from their Asian colony by imposing duties on foreign trading vessels carrying goods to and from Dutch ports in the Indies. Eager to outmaneuver their Dutch competitors, British East India merchants persuaded the Admiralty of the urgency for a

British emporium in northern Australia to complement Singapore and arrest the westward movement of Dutch imperium. An East India merchant and former Sydney trader, Captain William Barns, is the acknowledged protagonist of British planning for a new Singapore in northern Australia. Citing blatant discrimination against foreign traders in the Indies as a serious challenge to British commercial interests, Barns argued a new British port on the Gulf of Carpentaria would open the Archipelago from Timor to the Solomon Islands to the "British Flag."[13] Recognizing the tenuousness, under international law, of British claims to the whole of Australia, the British Admiralty was also concerned that Dutch expansionism might extend into northern Australia. As Barrow wrote to Undersecretary for the Colonial Department, R. Wilmot Horton,

> From the neighboring island of Timor, it is but a step to the northern part of New Holland; and it would be well to bear in mind that they would have a justifiable plea, in planting an establishment on any part of the Northern Coast of the latter, in our own example of taking possession of the Eastern Coast and the Island of Van Diemen, the original discovery of which by the Dutch is not disputed. Indeed I believe it is admitted . . . that Occupancy is a stronger title than priority of discovery; but be this as it may, in the present instance our own Conduct might be quoted against us.[14]

The Anglo-Dutch Treaty of 1824 recognized the Indies as a Dutch sphere of interest, but importantly, at that time the Dutch barely controlled the island of Java and parts of Sumatra. Britain naturally adopted a very narrow definition of what constituted the Dutch sphere in the Archipelago while the Netherlands unsurprisingly preferred a broader interpretation. It is generally accepted that Fort Dundas (1823–29), Fort Wellington at Raffles Bay (1827–29) and later Port Essington (1838–49) in what is now the Northern Territory were established to secure British sovereignty over northern Australia and link New South Wales through maritime trading networks to Britain's far eastern empire.[15] Inadequately prepared, and only intermittently resupplied, these early experiments failed. Though often treated as examples of imperial folly, these bold but poorly executed experiments had the much wider purpose of drawing the eastern Archipelago within the commercial orbit of New South Wales. This much is evident in correspondence to the Colonial Department from Barns and the East India Trade Committee who predicted Batavia's significance as an entrepot would decline in the face of competition from British free ports to the north and south. Barns even presumed that Portuguese Timor might be used for coffee growing and Timor Laut for nutmeg to furnish additional commodities for the China trade, although giving no indication as to under whose direction. In addition to trepang, tortoise shell, sandalwood and pearl shell abounded in the seas of Australasia.[16] What emerges from the historical record is the geographic impression of northern Australia and the eastern Indo-Malaysian Archipelago from Timor to the Solomons as a "natural" British commercial sphere of unlimited and untapped value.

There were obvious economic motives for dividing the Archipelago into two distinct regions. George Windsor Earl, whose explorations of the northern Australian coastline and the Indies persuaded him to lobby for the establishment of Victoria Settlement at Port Essington, concluded that the western and eastern portions of the Archipelago differed in that the latter remained unsettled by Europeans and suffered from the absence of a major trading center comparable to Singapore and Batavia. Earl, like Barns before him, placed Timor at the western extremity but his eastern boundary he drew at New Guinea.[17] Working against the quick realization of such a bold vision, major Australian population centers had no need of a port so far to the northwest. An indication that Australasian trade could flourish without the aid of a far northern trading post, Asia-bound ships sailing from Sydney through the Torres Strait more than doubled in number from fifteen to forty-one per year between 1832 and 1838.[18] Canton and Calcutta remained as colonial Australia's principal export markets in the Indian and Pacific Ocean regions but a vigorous import trade emerged with the Philippines and the Netherlands Indies as both the Dutch and Spanish pursued increased market share for their tropical produce throughout Asia and the Pacific.

INDIAN PACIFIC

Regional boundaries, like nation-state boundaries, are elastic, permeable and subject to revision. While Wentworth did not entertain territorial ambitions in the Archipelago, popular geographical representations of Australia's region suggested a "natural" connection that might one day become political reality. R. M. Martin's *British Possessions in Europe, Africa, Asia and Australasia* (c1847) was a promotional pamphlet for the failed India and Australia Steam Packet Company steamer service intended to connect eastern Australia to Britain through the Archipelago. Distinguishing between the East Indian and Australasian spheres, Martin placed his readers in no doubt that the islands to the north were virgin territories waiting to be explored and exploited. Steam communication, he wrote, would help to bind together far-flung British possessions and bring "the immense, and almost untilled and unexplored regions of Australasia and the Eastern Archipelago" within the British commercial sphere to enlarge "the commerce and power of England."[19]

Proximity to islands rich in tradeable natural resources provided economic incentives for Sydney traders who built business empires on the export of sealskin and sandalwood to China and British India and the importation of tropical foodstuffs New South Wales. Entrepreneurs like Robert Towns, whose trading interests reached as far north as Canton in the 1830s, secured rich cargoes of tea, coffee, sugar and tobacco, satiated the "sweet tooth" of colonial Australian society and created a dietary dependency upon regionally sourced tropical produce.[20] Sydney's growth from a small convict colony into the third most important port in the Indian Ocean trade brought increased demand for tropical commodities. By the 1840s sugar was sourced primarily from Java and the Philippines. Mauritius remained an important sugar supplier, but purchases from Java reached 16 million pounds weight in 1842, more than three-quarters the total volume of sugar imported into New South Wales for that year.[21] The Australian colonies became the largest and second largest market for Philippine sugar and coffee respectively in 1847. A decade later they were the largest market for both commodities with the bulk of imports entering through Sydney.[22] Tropical commodities added variety to colonial Australian life and were quickly assimilated into everyday consumption patterns. Australians slept on pillows stuffed with Javanese kapok, or smoked tobacco harvested by Filipino or Javanese plantation workers, or drank "Billy tea" sweetened with sugar from Java and the Philippines.

Consumer preferences strengthened business "connectivity" between Australia and the Archipelago but imperial rivalries limited the growth of new Australian export markets. Gold rushes brought about major demographic changes in Victoria and New South Wales, increasing still further demand for Asian commodities (tables 2.1 and 2.2: figures 2.1 and 2.2). New South Wales alone imported goods from the Philippines worth £463,151 in 1857.[23] In that year colonial Australians consumed 46.17 percent of Philippine coffee exports but, while the Australian colonies accounted for one-fifth of Philippine exports, Australian goods captured less than 0.5 percent of the total Philippine market, suggesting a lack of complementarity in Australia's export profile. The development of two-way trade was retarded by the punitive tariff regime imposed by Cortes to protect Spanish commercial interests in Manila.[24] Like the Dutch in the Indies, the Spanish sought to defray the cost of colonial administration by profiting from their colonial possessions at the expense of other maritime trading powers.

To Australasian colonizers, the Dutch stood between Australia and the dream of a greater British empire in the East. The van Delden Proclamation of 1828 extended Dutch territorial claims west to New Guinea, but, as Nicholas Tarling writes, they "had to accept that their tenure in the Archipelago itself was in a sense conditional."[25] Britain exerted indirect influence over northern Borneo in the 1840s and watched on disdainfully as more islands in the eastern Archipelago were hastily incorporated into the Netherlands Indies. British policymakers, however, hesitated to extend Britain's territorial reach beyond what was deemed necessary to advance British

Table 2.1. Imports into the colony of New South Wales (including Port Phillip District), 1839–48 (£ sterling)

Year	Great Britain	Other British Colonies		South Sea Islands	Fisheries	United States	Foreign States	Total
		New Zealand	Elsewhere					
1839	1,251,969	71,709	504,828	3,863	186,212	23,093	194,697	2,236,371
1840	2,200,305	54,192	376,954	1,348	104,895	24,164	252,331	3,014,189
1841	1,837,369	45,659	286,637	24,361	97,809	35,282	200,871	2,527,988
1842	854,774	37,246	260,955	10,020	64,999	20,117	206,948	1,455,059
1843	1,034,942	15,738	211,291	22,387	42,579	12,041	211,566	1,550,544
1844	643,419	20,795	133,128	10,624	32,507	17,187	73,600	931,260
1845	777,112	34,470	203,289	40,048	43,503	7,416	128,016	1,233,854
1846	1,119,301	23,367	239,576	21,799	56,461	4,459	165,559	1,630,522
1847	1,347,241	27,159	361,565	6,919	41,557	1,550	196,032	1982,023
1848	1,084,054	9,548	254,239	2,642	73,715	2,065	130,287	1,556,550

Source: *Statistics of New South Wales from 1839–1848*, NSW Legislative Council, *Votes and Proceedings*, 1849.

Table 2.2. Imports and exports for the colony of New South Wales, 1857, 1867 & 1874 (£ sterling)

	Imports				Exports		
	1857	1867	1874	1857	1874	1867	1874
United Kingdom	3,864,901	2,303,462	4,888,725	1,987,703		3,111,108	5,737,066
Australasia†	1,953,773	3,536,079	4,980,729	1,635,440		2,730,234	5,993,993
India & Hong Kong	120,405	100,794	—	80,865		790,386	—
Mauritius	193,919	197,837	—	21,749		—	—
West Indies	—	—	—	536		—	—
China & Japan	**137,195	247,462	***262,676	**1,782		44,069	58,989
Europe	135,880	120,623	31,593	28,234		—	—
Americas	344,526	192,542	277,498	10,571		20,702	169,370
Other	28,809	1,001	—	244,372		8,010	12,363
Total	1,218,401	870,356	981,574	335,539		176,569	510,314
All Countries	6,729,408	6,599,804	11,293,739	4,011,952		6,880,715	12,345,603

Sources: Statistics of the Colony of New South Wales from 1848–1857, *NSW Legislative Council Journals*, vol. 3, 1858; Statistical Register of New South Wales, *NSW Legislative Council Journals*, vol. 116, 1868/69.
†Australian colonies, Singapore and Straits Settlements, New Caledonia, South Sea Islands, Netherlands Indies, the Philippines and New Zealand.
**China only
***Includes Formosa (Taiwan).

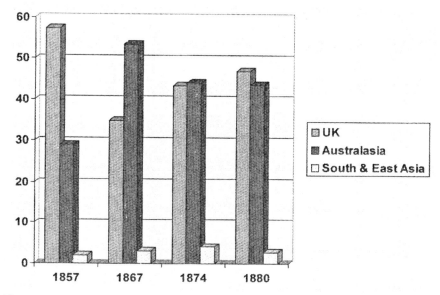

Figure 2.1.　New South Wales imports by region of origin, 1857–1880.

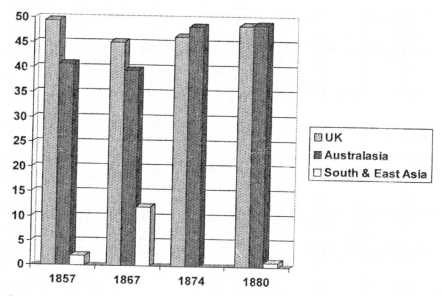

Figure 2.2.　New South Wales exports by region of destination, 1857–1880.

economic interests and protect major shipping lanes from foreign threats.[26] As Australasia emerged as a field of colonial Australian commerce the region's richness and strategic significance tempted further speculation about the future shape of the Netherlands Indies. Concern for peace and order were common justifications for British colonial interventions, lest potentially hostile powers take advantage of local political instability and establish a strategically sensitive foothold near the vital arteries of British commerce. Colonial Australians were therefore careful to address such matters when urging the northward expansion of British influence.

Eager to emulate the achievements of Thomas Stamford Raffles, Sir George Ferguson Bowen, first governor of Queensland, harbored boundaryless aspirations towards the Archipelago. He was not alone in his ambitions for an expanded Australasian commonwealth. A Queensland select committee investigating the prospects for a northern Australian emporium heard from the likes of Reverend John Dunmore Lang, a frequent and ardent advocate of northward expansion, that trade with the "Spice Islands" would open up a "new era" for the Australian colonies.[27] Claiming "destiny" as his guide, Bowen anticipated a "convergence" of Asian Pacific trade routes to Australia's north. Advocating the creation of another northern outpost at Cape York overlooking the Torres Strait, he advised the Duke of Newcastle, Secretary of State for the Colonies, that an adequately garrisoned settlement would "command the whole of the commerce between the South Pacific and the Indian Ocean." Citing Raffles as his inspiration, the Torres Strait, he envisioned, would replicate the Strait of Malacca in its commercial and strategic significance. But further,

> a station at Cape York could not fail to extend the influence and *prestige* of Great Britain over the Indian Archipelago; while it would form a link between the possessions in Australia, India, and China, [assure] the possession of the north and north-east coasts of the Australian Continent "and, as it were close the ring fence with which we have girt the fifth quarter of the globe."[28]

Consolidation of British rule on the Australian continent could, Bowen conjectured, lead to the enlargement of Britain's eastern possessions to incorporate "New Guinea, and *other portions of the Indian Archipelago.*"(emphasis added) Expressing the hope that "the Moluccas shall be freed from the trammels in which they have hitherto been bound," Bowen imagined an arc of islands from New Guinea through the Moluccas to northern Borneo shaded in imperial red on the map of Britain's empire in Asia.[29] He declared that the "tide of colonization in Queensland is sweeping onward at the rate of about two hundred miles each year."[30] Confident in the "*assimilating* powers of the Anglo-Saxon race," he echoed the sentiments expressed by Edward Gibbon Wakefield some thirty years before and embraced the prospect of Asian immigration. Branding as "Luddites" those responsible for assaults on Chinese miners at Buckland River and Lambing Flat in New South Wales, Asian migrants, he asserted, were essential to the development of tropical industries in Queensland.[31]

Bowen's claims lent intellectual justification to demands from Queensland businessmen lobbying for "the successful cultivation of a race habituated to labor in a tropical climate."[32] Their aim was to apply the template for British colonial rule in India to build a new Australasian colony in Queensland replete with bustling northern emporium, an extensive hinterland yielding tropical products for a global market, and a colored underclass of "coolie" labor ruled by a new class of White Rajahs. Enamored of British colonial "achievements" in India, the Straits Settlements, and of Rajah James Brooke's heroic adventures in Sarawak, Bowen's ambitions raced ahead of the expanding frontiers of Australian colonization.

Bowen's dream of a new Singapore proved illusory. Cut off from the hub of the Torres Strait pearling industry by a maritime boundary that restricted Queensland's maritime jurisdiction to three miles from the Cape York coast, the settlement of Somerset (1864–1877) languished. Denied the capacity to levy tax on cargoes of pearls and *beche-de-mer*, the settlement also struggled to attract passing merchant ships.[33] An eagerly anticipated steamer service to Batavia and Singapore also failed to materialize. The India and Australian Steam Packet Company (IASP), formed in 1847, successfully tendered the British Admiralty to carry mail between Sydney and Singapore through the Torres Strait but quickly proved a financial disaster and none of its mail steamers made a single voyage. In 1852 the P&O steamer *Chusan* initiated a Sydney-Singapore mail service that ran every two months by way of the south coast of Australia until mounting losses forced its abandonment in 1855.[34] In the same decade Robert Towns made an ill-fated attempt to link Sydney to Singapore through the Torres Strait.[35]

Determined to redirect northern Australia towards the Eurasian shipping networks of the Archipelago, and lessen dependence on south coast shipping routes, the government of the newly created colony of Queensland proposed a jointly run mail-steamer service through the Torres Straits with the Netherlands Indies in 1865.[36] The Woodville, Jarret & Company's tramp steamer, *Souchays*, made two voyages to Batavia from Brisbane in 1866 under contract to the Queensland government before being replaced by a faster vessel, the Bright Brothers & Company's *Hero*, which made another three voyages along the same route between 1866 and 1867.[37] High freight rates and passenger fares discouraged exporters and tourists, and together the *Souchays* and the *Hero* took a mere forty-seven passengers from Brisbane to Batavia in 1866, and the service was suspended.[38]

Compounding the difficulties of establishing regular steam navigation services, the growth of sugar industries in Queensland and New South Wales reduced demand for imported sugar from Java and the Philippines and with it the importance of the Archipelago to eastern Australia's sugar trade. Although sugar from Java was still imported into New South Wales in substantial quantities, ship owners were reluctant to bear the commercial risk of running a regular mail-steamer service through the Torres Strait. Where markets failed to serve political aspirations, mail contracts, effectively freight subsidies, were offered as an incentive but even then, shipping companies preferred to operate out of Sydney rather than Brisbane as the Queensland government would have wished.

AUSTRALIAN ADVANCES

Despite setbacks, the belief persisted that the Australian colonies, Queensland especially, had important interests to protect and advance in the Archipelago. Prospects for a northern Australian emporium were improved with two unilateral maritime border revisions in 1872 and 1879. Claiming the altruistic intention to regulate labor recruitment, protect and control shipping, and without a thought for rights of traditional landowners, the Palmer government unilaterally enlarged Queensland's maritime jurisdiction from 3 to 60 miles in 1872. The even more aggressively expansionist premiers John Douglas and Sir Thomas McIlwraith pushed the colony's northern maritime border to within half a mile of the New Guinea coast in 1879, incorporating Torres Strait islands thought to be outside British Pacific jurisdiction. Annexation delivered the necessary tax base to fund the extension of state control north to Thursday Island, which supplanted Somerset as the commercial and administrative hub in the strait.

These were the heady days of Australasian expansionism. As one self-styled "North Queenslander" wrote to the *Straits Times*, the colonization of Cape York offered the perfect opportunity to "command the commerce of a large portion of Australia, of the Indian Archipelago, and of the islands of the Pacific."[36] Riding the expansion of the pearling industry, Thursday Island became a frontier outpost of Queensland and a forward base for Australian enterprise in New Guinea and the Indies.

The islands' international significance increased with the inauguration of the Torres Strait Mail Line (TSML) in 1874, linking Sydney and Brisbane to Batavia and Singapore. The Palmer government offered a £20,000 annual subsidy as an inducement to the British-owned Eastern and Australian Mail Steam Company Limited (E&A) to connect with Peninsular & Oriental (P&O) steamers in Singapore. Former premier A. H. Palmer stood by the mail line that his government created, taking his family on a trip to Batavia in 1874, but the TSML carried a mere 101 saloon passengers from eastern Australia to Batavia and Singapore in its first year. British migrants too preferred the long-established south coast shipping routes to Melbourne and Sydney rather than tranship at Singapore and tolerate cramped steerage quarters aboard an E&A steamer and the oppressive tropical heat of the Archipelago.[40] Although E&A insisted that their service terminate in Sydney rather than Brisbane, the Queensland government persisted with the venture assuming that British migrants would eventually opt for the Torres Strait route, and because Asian emporia beckoned as potential export markets for Queensland's primary industries. But, the TSML failed to capture the public's imagination.

The incorporation of northern Australia into the transport and communications networks of the Archipelago was further advanced with the laying of a marine telegraphic cable from Banyuwangi on the island of Java to Darwin. Because this was the first of three such marine cables connecting Australia to the British imperial electronic information "nodes," colonial centers from Perth to Brisbane depended upon the integrity of this "cable network" for the fast relay of global news. A new technology that greatly reduced the time taken to send messages between metropolitan centers and colonial peripheries, these telegraphic cables gave Australians a vested interest in the security of the Archipelago. But the cables also presented a dilemma. Although managed by the British-owned Eastern Extension Telegraph Company, communications between Australian colonies and British government were more vulnerable to interception by a potentially unfriendly if not hostile state.

Low trade volumes between Australia and its immediate neighbors relative to trade with Britain need not be interpreted as proof of Australian disinterest in Asia. As evidence of a thriving kapok trade between Melbourne and Batavia in the early 1880s, Dutch growers and traders in the Netherlands Indies supplied 93 percent of Victorian bulk purchases of this sought-after natural fiber in 1886.[41] Regularized steamshipping services to Java and Singapore emerged out of a push by the Queensland government in particular to establish new connections to Britain, and to open new markets for colonial produce. As steam navigation became the preferred mode for shipping commercial freight, migrants, business and leisure travelers, British, Dutch, Japanese and German shipping companies sought a share of the nascent Australia-Asia trade (tables 2.3 and 2.4: figures 2.3 and 2.4). It was inevitable that some intrepid colonial Australians would see in these new "vectors" of engagement fresh opportunities for adventure and enterprise.

Commercial necessity dictated that durable relations were nurtured with Netherlands Indies businesspeople, but British-Australian interest in the eastern Archipelago continued to invite speculation. Acts to establish the Federal Council of Australasia in 1885 anticipated the possibility of external territorial realignment. In defining the council's terms of inclusion, "Australasia colony," the legislation read, comprised the six Australian colonies, New Zealand and "any British colonies which may be hereafter created within Her Majesty's possessions in Australasia."[42] New Guinea undoubtedly fell within the last category. Serious discussion of British-Australian colonization of New Guinea began in the 1870s with representations to the Colonial Office from Sydney businessmen and politicians looking to exploit New Guinea's natural resources. One Sydney entrepreneur, Francis Labilliere, wrote directly to the Secretary of State for the Colonies outlining his rationale for British annexation. High on the list of justifications, the defense of

Table 2.3. Imports and exports for the colony of New South Wales, 1880 (£ sterling)

| | | | Exports | |
| | | NSW | British and | |
Countries	Imports	Produce	Foreign Produce	Total Exports
United Kingdom	6,536,661	6,483,475	1,042,162	7,525,637
Australasia†	6,091,708	5,862,811	1,732,009	7,594,820
Hong Kong	228,526	103,517	34,060	137,577
Mauritius	207,107	14,538	461	14,999
China	358,129	14,488	356	14,844
France & Germany	85,028	2	142	144
United States	387,056	160,996	11,652	172,648
Other	55,860	39,955	24,514	64,469
Total	13,950,075	12,679,782	2,845,356	15,525,138

Source: Statistics of the colony of New South Wales, 1880, *NSWLA V&P.*
†Australian Colonies, Singapore and Straits Settlements, New Caledonia, South Sea Islands, Netherlands Indies and New Zealand.

Table 2.4. Maritime import and export trade for the colony of Queensland, 1874, 1880 & 1886 (£ sterling)

| | 1874 | | 1880 | | 1886 | |
	Import	Export	Import	Export	Import	Export
United Kingdom	1,015,684	1,194,386	839,790	780,808	2,692,296	1,288,851
India, China &						
Hong Kong	36,431	13,224	128,576	120,493	127,940	124,207
Australasia†	1,774,750	2,541,569	1,880,328	2,314,808	2,838,022	2,844,115
Americas	6,778	869	30,723	890	120,227	4,070
Europe	171	—	361	—	51,279	—
Other	—	—	1,777	—	1,799	24
All Countries	2,833,814	3,750,048	2,881,555	3,216,999	5,831,563	4,261,265

Sources: Statistics of the Colony of Queensland, 1882, Part 2, *QLA V&P*, 1883–84, v. 1, Statistics of the Colony of Queensland, 1892, *QLA V&P*, vol. 1, 1892.
†Australian Colonies, Singapore and Straits Settlements, New Caledonia, South Sea Islands, Netherlands Indies and New Zealand.

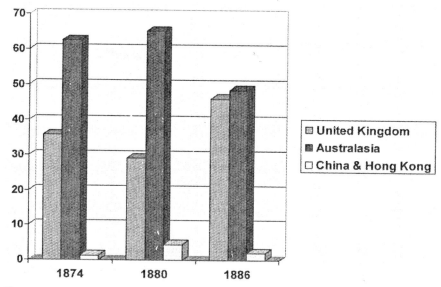

Figure 2.3.   Queensland's maritime imports by region of origin, 1874–1886

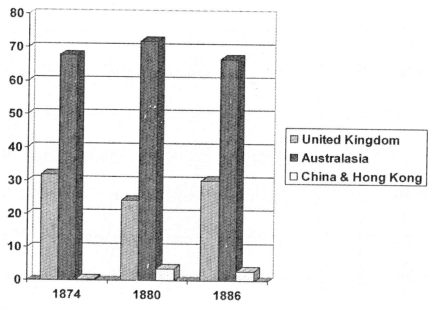

Figure 2.4.   Queensland's maritime exports by region of destination, 1874–1886.

Australia was beholden to a decaying Dutch empire whose inability to promote the economic development of its eastern islands left northern Australia
dangerously exposed. He argued that the Dutch lacked the capacity to effectively govern and develop all New Guinea, leaving Australia exposed to the
possibility of "a powerful and undesirable neighbor" moving to fill the void
and threaten Australia's economic security.[43]

In addition to the insecurities generated by the heightened perception of
geographic exposure, petitioners revealed a sense of historical destiny in
their asserting of Australia's prerogatives in the Archipelago. NSW Premier
John Robertson met a number of his colony's luminaries, including the Reverend John Dunmore Lang, to discuss the future of New Guinea. According
to Lang, Australians were particularly acclimatized in a "special manner" for
the "work of colonization" in the tropics.[44] Representatives of the self-styled
New Guinea Company advised Robertson of the "urgency" with which
colonial governments should act in the interests of empire trade and security. Their ambition driven by a splendid vision of the Torres Strait's economic significance, they reminded Robertson that this was now "the pass
through which one of the great ocean highways of the world necessarily
runs."[45]

The New Guinea Company's plans for the commercial development of
New Guinea foundered on a reef in the Torres Strait. Greater geographical
proximity and the colony's growing demand for labor resources meant the
Queensland government instead took the boldest strides towards the island's colonization. Anticipating new British territorial acquisitions in the
Pacific, and already committed to annexing the Torres Strait for Queensland, John Douglas appointed W. B. Ingham as Confidential Agent for
Queensland at Port Moresby in 1878. Writing to remind Ingham of the
delicacy of his posting, Douglas cautioned, "Discourage, let me repeat,
whenever you meet it, the idea of territorial annexation," even though from
Douglas's letter annexation was the object:

> The colonization of New Guinea must be effected with the sanction of the Na-
> tive Chiefs under their authority and in any communications you may have
> with them assure them that so far as we can, this Government will endeavour
> to give effect to this policy, a policy which I have no doubt will be found in ac-
> cordance with that of her Majesty.[46]

Douglas had reason to anticipate the incorporation of at least part of New
Guinea within the British Empire. Secretary of State for the Colonies Lord
Carnarvon countenanced the possibility of annexation, provided the Australian colonies, principally Queensland, were prepared to pay for the enterprise. At his request, the Admiralty advised of the feasibility of annexation and even prepared a provisional plan to take possession of those

"points on the mainland of New Guinea in the vicinity of the Torres Straits."[47] Disagreement between the Queensland government and the Colonial Office over who should bear financial responsibility created an impasse not broken until 1883 when, with the unequivocal support of southern colonies, McIlwraith unilaterally annexed the island's southeastern quarter. Behind the action was a carefully cultivated groundswell of public support in the eastern colonies stirred by fears of encroaching French and German colonialism in the pacific.

Less than a decade after the abolition of transportation to Western Australia, residents of the eastern colonies were alarmed by the prospect of a French penal colony in nearby New Caledonia, and the attendant danger of absconders reaching Australia and retarding the social development of White Australia. German traders in northern New Guinea were viewed as an advance guard of German imperialism in the Pacific and hence competitors in the final scramble for territories not already consumed by Britain, the Netherlands or France. Annexation was a humble and rather comical affair, but its significance lay in its impacts upon the New Guinean peoples incorporated and the signal sent to Germany and the Netherlands regarding Australian ambitions. Alleging that the German presence in northeastern New Guinea presented a threat to Australian and wider British interests in the Pacific, McIlwraith expected Britain to ratify his pre-emptive action.[48]

Already committed to the incorporation of the whole of Burma and much of the Malay Peninsula, the British government hesitated to add to its financial burdens and undertake further colonial responsibilities in what was a peripheral area of its Asian imperial sphere. Stories of depredations inflicted upon non-White laborers on the fringes of Australian colonial society gave Britain reason to treat McIlwraith's territorial ambitions with extreme caution. Demand for cheap labor in the northern Australian pearling and plantation industries promised rewards to those who could supply this need, by whatever means possible. Reports of brutalities, including kidnapping and murder by labor recruiters were commonplace if often exaggerated.[49] Calls for strict humanitarian regulation of the labor trade led to the appointment of a British Commissioner for the Pacific and the introduction of acts to protect Pacific Islanders, but the reputation of Torres Strait pearling masters and Queensland labor recruiters persisted. Living conditions for plantation workers were also a cause for public concern. For those Melanesian indents who survived the voyage to Australia, the high probability of death by disease awaited them on Queensland's sugar plantations.[50]

McIlwraith's unilateral action was intended to advance Queensland's interests ahead of other colonies. He defended annexation as a pre-emptive and defensive step to protect the interests of all, made necessary by the weakness of the Netherlands Indies and the "encroachment" of Germany into Australia's Pacific sphere.[51] But McIlwraith assumed that Queensland interests would be paramount in the new colony. Responding angrily to a report that a group of Sydney businessmen had purchased land from the indigenous inhabitants of a district in the annexed territory, McIlwraith persuaded Governor Kennedy to issue a proclamation to the effect that in this and future instances "such purchases will, so far as this Colony is concerned, be repudiated."[52] The Queensland government's aspirations went far beyond what the British Parliament would allow. Reluctantly, Britain enacted legislation to create the protectorate of British New Guinea (BNG), to be funded but not governed by the Australian colonies, and concluded a formal boundary agreement with Germany in 1885, if only to clarify German, Dutch and now British territorial claims on the island.

The extent of colonial Australian ambitions is consistently overlooked by historians who presume that Australia's Pacific region lay to the east of New Guinea. Delegates at the 1883 Intercolonial Convention clearly conceived of a Pacific Ocean region that included islands extending west from New Guinea to Java and north to the Philippines. Of principal interest were those areas without a recognized or effective sovereign, that constituted a "no-man's land" where "debasing and savage wars" were the norm.[53] A carefully worded resolution adopted by delegates called upon the Imperial Government to incorporate "so much of New Guinea, and the small islands adjacent thereto as not claimed by the Government of the Netherlands."[54] As will be discussed, commercial interests in Sydney believed that Dutch claims were not accepted by some local rulers and sought to exploit this opportunity. The London *Times* was in no doubt about the vaulting ambition of the Australian colonies, and the determination of colonial politicians to incorporate as much of the Pacific as possible into an enlarged Australasian domain, "to the furtherest limits the most thorough Australian advocate of annexation has ever imagined."[55]

TOWARD RACIAL EXCLUSION

The "waves of social progress" which Clarke argued would fashion a new Australasian civilization impacted with increasing intensity on the socio-cultural terrain of northern Australia. Histories of northern colonisation highlight the presence of Pacific Islanders, Chinese and, to a lesser extent, Japanese as the principal non-European groups employed in tropical industries. Chinese miners from the New South Wales and Victorian goldfields moved north into Queensland as new gold rushes broke out around Gympie, Ravenswood, and Charters Towers. More miners and settlers from southern China arrived by sea through the Torres Strait to Cairns and Cooktown. While Asian commodities posed no challenge to White identity and were easily assimilated into colonial consumption culture, Asian migrants were widely regarded as a biological threat to racial homogeneity. Palpable resentment towards Chinese spurred the formation of trades unions organized to protect White working men's wages and living standards against the threat of cheaper Asian workers. For plantation owners seeking competitive advantages in the Australian marketplace, imported cheap labor from Asia and the Pacific meant reduced business costs. Separationists in northern and central Queensland campaigned from the mid 1860s for the creation of a new colony, partly to liberate their taxes but, equally important, to populate the north with cheap labor recruited from as far afield as India and China. As local communities had insufficient manpower to service the expansion of pearling fleets and plantations, owners and their recruiters reached deeper into the Archipelago—under the watchful eyes of British and Dutch officials.

Hot climates, wrote Clarke, naturally induced despotism and slavery.[56] But acceptance and accommodation of Asian cultures was essential for the productive management of a multiracial workforce in northern Australia. Predominantly Muslim "Malays" were first brought into the northern pearling industry in the 1870s, in an *ad hoc* manner at first but by the early 1880s systematic recruitment through agents was in full swing.[57] Hired through local agents in Manila, Batavia and Singapore, "Malay" and Filipino pearl divers and lugger crews added to northern Queensland's growing multi-ethnic population.[58] Like their Filipino counterparts, Malays were highly regarded for their seamanship and diving skills, and were much less likely than Europeans to break the law. Entrepreneurial migrants, like the Filipino nationalist Heriberto Zarcal, became valued members of the local Australasian business community on Thursday Island. Others chose to keep their distance. Anna Shnukal found evidence of two principal Malay *kompongs* formed in the late nineteenth century, at Malaytown on Thursday Island and at Upai on the island of Badu (Mulgrave Island). The latter *kompong* was settled in a culturally appropriate way with the permission of the local custodians and served as a haven for Malays seeking to retain their cultural traditions.[59] The maritime expertise of these sea peoples from the Archipelago was highly sought after, but valued only insofar as this could be harnessed for the purpose of northern economic expansion.

Further south, inter-ethnic tensions were much more in evidence. The introduction of more stringent limitations on the recruitment of *kanaka* labor, introduced in 1885 by the government of Samuel Griffith, forced sugar planters to also look northwards to meet their labor needs. North Queensland's "Malay" community swelled from less than 300 to nearly 1,100 in 1886 as laborers, mainly from Bantam and Sunda on the island of Java, but also from Pahang on the Malay Peninsula, were brought to work on cane fields from Innisfail south to Mackay and Maryborough.[60] At Mourilyan

Plantation, Javanese were considered "cleaner in their habits than kanakas" and better suited to plantation labor.[61] Indicating the flexibility of work practices, Javanese indents were permitted to work under Javanese supervisors—"mandoors"—and when in breach of company regulations, subject to punishment according to their customary law or *adat*.[62] Admitted to the fringes of more populous districts, Javanese sugar workers more readily caught the public eye and were noted for their assertiveness. As one J. O'Halleram, manager at the Innisfail Estate, told the Queensland Royal Commission into the Sugar Industry, "They are a class of labour that, if they can best you they will best you and keep you bested."[63]

Javansese plantation workers were outside the scope of the Pacific Islanders Acts of 1880 and 1885, which imposed a government tax upon each newly indentured *kanaka* worker to recover the costs of providing adequate medical facilities in the major sugar-producing areas. Only in the most severe cases were Malays and Javanese sent to Pacific Islander hospitals for treatment at a cost of £1 per week. Others were treated on plantations provided their employer acknowledged their illness. According to one medical practitioner, Dr. William Macdonald from Ingham, Malays required six–eight months to acclimatize during which time they were especially vulnerable to bronchitis, pneumonia, pleurisy and dysentery caused by poor sanitation.[64] Neglect for the welfare of plantation workers could have contributed to the widespread unrest in the Mackay district in 1888. Regardless of the legitimacy of their protests, these and other absconders suffered the full force of the Queensland criminal justice system and were gaoled.

The *Mackay Mercury* reported in 1886 that at least ten "Malay" prisoners under sentence for absconding were forced to share a single cell in the Mackay Gaol with another seventeen prisoners in conditions that were "too disgusting to describe."[65] However sympathetic were the press in the first years of importation, the presumed visible and invisible danger, both moral and biological, arising from movement of indentured workers, goods and capital across the northern Australian frontier, became a pretext for Australian colonies to tighten border regulation.

Public debate about the "Malay" character at the time of the "Black Labour" Queensland election in 1888 highlighted the political dynamics of racial exclusion in northern Australia. Objecting to the repayment of wage advances, a legal requirement under the terms of their labor contract, fifty Javanese plantation employees protested their cause in the main street of Mackay. The *Mackay Mercury* seized upon an opportunity to mount a vigorous campaign against the importation of Javanese labour. Depicting Javanese as violent delinquents who "ran amok" and threatened "defenceless white people with their long bladed krisses," the *Mercury* invoked images of Malay savagery popularized in the writings of explorers and naturalists such as Wallace.[66] Public fears were further heightened by events at Normanton

in June 1888 where a Javanese called Sedin 'ran amuck" killing three Europeans and igniting a general riot by the town's White population. Race relations in Normanton were reportedly strained by the growing presence of
migrants from the Malay world, mostly from the transient population of
Thursday Island.[67] Such was the explosion of indiscriminate race hatred
that townspeople turned on anyone who remotely fitted their crude iden-
tikit image of a Malay, including one resident of Spanish origin who, along
with the town's Asian population, sought refuge on a prison hulk in the
Norman River. Before public order could be restored, rioters themselves ran
amok causing £5,000 in damage to non-European property in a wild orgy
of destruction.

Unsurprisingly, the fact that several Malays disarmed Sedin before police
intervened earned scant attention. The *Townsville Herald* vindicated the violent actions of the White population of Normanton as "cleansing [the
town] of its Asiatic plague."[68] Acutely conscious of Queensland's tarnished
reputation for race relations, Thomas McIlwraith described the rioters' behavior as a disgrace to the colony but promptly blocked the transportation
of another 2000 Javanese indents preparing to embark in Singapore and
Batavia.[69] Media scare-mongering provoked opposition to the recruitment
of Islander and Javanese workers, but McIlwraith's conservatives won the
Black Labour election. With the support of "liberal" parliamentarians, recruitment restrictions were relaxed to allow continuing employment of indentured labor.

Limited recruitment of Javanese and Malay workers continued in
Queensland until all non-White immigration ceased in 1901. By then an instrumental image of the savage Malay was embedded in the popular imagination alongside the Yellow Peril as a physical and moral threat to the security of White Australia. Reporting a riot by Javanese on the Mourilyan
Sugar Plantation near Ingham, the *Townsville Herald* turned the incident
into an allegory of Asian invasion:

> Making a simultaneous rush for Mr. Wiseman, the Javanese quickly got him to
> the ground, but not before one or two of the "animals" felt the sudden contact
> of a sinewy Scotch arm. However, one man against 100 was powerless.[70]

A more enduring historical image of the Malay formed around the
trepangers who from the 1880s onwards were gradually hounded from the
north Australian coast. Justification for this economic exclusion was predicated on the same invasion fears used to galvanize public opinion against
recruitment of Javanese in north Queensland. In his novel, *The Big Five*
(1910), typical of the invasion fiction genre, Australian writer and business
entrepreneur Ambrose Pratt pitted an archetypal White male bush hero,
Jim McLean, against an advance guard of "savage" seafaring Dyaks sent to

prepare the ground for a Japanese invasion of northern Australia.[71] Romanticized in Ernestine Hill's *The Territory* (1968) as "Vikings of the Arafura," the association of the Malay with brutality and the threat of invasion were confirmed. "Macassar-time was massacre-time" wrote Hill sardonically, also reviving buried memories of earlier nineteenth-century colonial invasion fears, persuading her readers that these "Macassans" were once evidence of a threatening "eastward drift" of the Netherlands Indies's commercial-imperial sphere.[74]

With the end to large-scale plantation recruitment, the number of Javanese workers quickly declined though not all were repatriated at the conclusion of their contracts.[73] Workers from Malaya and Java who entered Queensland and remained, as Rey Ileto states in relation to Filipinos, merely transferred their allegiance from one colonial power to another.[74] But the creation of the Australian nation-state severed them from their cultural roots and forced these Indo-Australians to negotiate new political identities while confronting the harsh reality of their place as cultural fringe-dwellers who were denied a voice in the politics of Australian nationalism.

BORDER SECURITY

Trusted Australian investors were welcome in the Indies. "Willie" Jack, partner in the north Queensland firm, Jack and Newell, operated a gold mine at Kuandang on the Minhassan Peninsula on the island of Sulawesi in partnership with Dutch investors from Amsterdam during the 1890s. Employing up to eighty local staff, Jack boasted to the *Cairns Argus* of both his island home's "delightful climate" and the "luxurious" cheapness of "native wages."[75] However, he admitted in the same interview that "with a similar field adjacent to Australia two or three thousand white men would readily be on it—but the Dutch are slightly conservative." Brisbane pearling magnate James Clark nonetheless secured a pearling concession near the Aru Islands with partner E. Munro in 1904. Becoming consul for the Netherlands in Queensland the following year, Clark built a new empire in tropical agriculture on the island of Ceram where his family grew cocoa, coffee, sago and rubber until 1942.[76]

Concern over Australian ambitions beyond New Guinea undoubtedly contributed to a decision by the Netherlands to ban foreign labor recruitment in its eastern islands in 1885. Captain John Carpenter of the Sydney-registered whaling barque, the *Costa Rica Packet*, was quoted in a *Townsville Herald* feature article claiming the Dutch in the Indies were "jealous and alarmed at the strides North Queensland was making and likely to make by judicious use of colored labor for field work in raising tropical produce."[77] With some justification the Netherlands remained distrustful of British and

Australian intentions and, like Germany, suspicious of Australian commercial activity in the eastern islands. Dutch and German sensitivities were undoubtedly heightened by the expanding frontiers of Australian enterprise and the cavalier attitude of many Australian maritime entrepreneurs. From the 1880s, Australian pearling fleets roamed as far afield as Labuk Bay in British North Borneo (Sabah) and the Sulu and Mergui archipelagos in search of new fishing grounds.[78] Under Captain Carpenter's command, the *Costa Rica Packet* began whaling in the Moluccas in 1887, making annual seasonal ventures into the Archipelago until the ship was abruptly sold in 1892 following Carpenter's arrest and imprisonment on a charge of piracy in the port of Ternate.[79]

Carpenter, an American-born but naturalized British subject, became the focal point of a major international controversy involving the Dutch, British and New South Wales governments. Although the issue at hand involved Carpenter's salvage, or alleged theft, of a Malay *prau* off the coast of the island of Buru in January that year, by the time a New South Wales select committee appointed to investigate the case handed down its report in 1894, the matter had attracted international media attention and broadened from concern at Carpenter's imprisonment by Dutch authorities and the conditions in which he was held, to the freedom of the seas and rights of Australians to trade in the eastern Indies.[80]

Replete with accusations of wrongful arrest, intimidation, humiliation and deprivation at the hands of captors, the *Costa Rica Packet* case exposed the fragility of relations between the Australian colonies and the Netherlands Indies. The Dutch case rested upon allegations that Carpenter and his crew had stolen a cargo of spirits from a vessel belonging to a former business associate. According to Carpenter's version of events, the cargo of *arrack* was salvaged from an abandoned and sinking Malay *prau* on the open seas, stowed aboard ship and later sold at the Moluccan port of Bacan. Although Carpenter acted with apparent probity in discharging his responsibilities in relation to the *prau* and its cargo, Dutch authorities determined to send a message to their southern neighbor. Carpenter was transported to Makassar for trial and, despite the intercessions of Sir Cecil Clementi-Smith, Governor of Singapore, appeals for consular access were repeatedly denied. He endured the squalor of an Asian gaol and, as he explained to the Committee of Inquiry in Sydney, the shocking ignominy of sharing a cell with a native prisoner under the supervision of a "half-caste" gaoler. The charge of piracy against Carpenter was subsequently dropped, leaving the Committee to conclude that his arrest was deliberate and politically motivated. As the Committee reported to the NSW Legislative Council,

> We desire to call attention to the fact that independently of the direct injury inflicted on the persons immediately concerned in this case, who are citizens of

this Colony, the whole of Australia has suffered from the attitude assumed by the Netherlands-India Government, as further enterprise by our colonists has been checked when the field of the proposed operations has been the Malayan seas or islands, even though not subject to the Netherlands-India Government.[81]

Calls from Sydney's political and business leaders for Britain to bring the Netherlands Indies to account for financial losses incurred by the ship's owners were ignored in London. The case highlighted the extent to which colonial Australian entrepreneurs were prepared to test the scope of Dutch influence in the eastern Archipelago, where potential commercial gains justified the risks of reprisal. Evidence presented to the Committee proved that Sydney business interests had in the year before Carpenter's arrest attempted to circumvent Dutch sovereignty and enter into direct trade relations with an allegedly independent rajah at Posso in the Tomini Gulf, on the island of Sulawesi. On the justifiable grounds that not all local rulers submitted to Dutch authority, the expedition sought tropical rainforest goods and planned to prospect for gold but was swiftly driven away by a Dutch gunboat. Sensitive to the tenuousness of their position in relation to the self-governing Malay rulers of northern Sulawesi, the Netherlands immediately sought treaty relations with the local rajahs in the wake of the Australian departure.[82]

The prospect of Australian colonial expansion into the eastern Indies was by that time a matter of international public speculation. Picking up on a newsworthy item published in the Australian press, the *Straits Times* reported that certain Australian business interests were openly advocating a pre-emptive Australian-led annexation of the Portuguese colony of East Timor. Fearing the Dutch were about to purchase Portuguese Timor and shut the Indies to Australian commerce, one Captain Strahan was quoted in the *Northern Territory Times* calling for the independent and "united action of the Australian colonies" with an assurance that he would personally lobby colonial governments to bring this to effect.[83] Responding to the international controversy ignited by Carpenter's imprisonment and subsequent demands for compensation from Sydney's business community, the *Cologne Gazette* was in no doubt as to Australian ambitions:

> If they could do just what they liked in Sydney, the German flag would not much longer fly in New Guinea, and on the Marshall or Bismark Islands, and in fact that the Australians wish to arrogate to themselves the right of being the "boss" in the Malayan Archipelago, has been proved by their uncouth conduct in the matter of the pearl fisheries of the Aru Islands.[84]

Despite these claims, the scope for the Australian expansion into New Guinea was diminishing rapidly. From Britain's perspective, the Netherlands Indies was an effective surrogate imperial power. In addition to shipping, trade and modest investment connections, three telegraphic cables now passed through the Netherlands Indies, bringing an oxygenating flow of vastly more immediate news from the Mother Country to Australia's expanding newspaper readership. British New Guinea stood between Queensland and the Netherlands Indies, but the Australian colonies, Queensland in particular, tended to regard the Anglo-Dutch frontier as *de facto* an Australian one.

The Queensland government was drawn into a debate about respective Dutch and British border jurisdictions after raids into British territory by the Tugeri tribe spilled over into islands in Torres Strait. The geographical origins of the tribe were disputed by both Dutch and British authorities, but British Administrator Sir William MacGregor, proposed cultural criteria to determine the Tugeris' status. "As regards personal appearance, dress, ornaments, arms, the fashion of canoes, food and habits, they are clearly Papuan" he advised.[85] It was eventually determined, however, some two years after the first reported raids, that the Tugeri originated from an area 30 miles within Dutch New Guinea territory. In order to reach final agreement over responsibility for preventing future incursions, the Netherlands accepted a refinement of the Anglo-Dutch boundary, albeit under a new international convention rather than an exchange of notes.[86]

The Tugeri were a relatively minor irritation. Australian concerns were focused increasingly upon the weightier matter of defending Australia's northern approaches. Intercolonial plans to garrison the north at Thursday Island and Darwin and west at King George's Sound reflected widespread anxieties about Australia's empty north, and the economic value of transport links with Britain's Asian empire, from the Indian subcontinent to China. Opinion differed on Australia's vulnerability to invasion. The Colonial Defence Committee in 1890 produced a seemingly complacent strategic outlook, encapsulated in the statement that "there is no British territory so little liable to aggression as that of Australia." Attempting to assure colonial governments that their regional security environment was benign, the Committee judged, somewhat dismissively, that the colonies were vulnerable only to minor naval raids designed to achieve short-term economic objectives, to secure coal supplies for example.[87]

The Defence Committee's views stressed the security of the Australian mainland, but, as a trading nation, Australia's interests extended outwards into the world's oceans. Military chiefs from the Australian colonies feared the consequences of maritime raids. As delegates to the 1894 Federal Military Conference they agreed that the Western and Northern Australian trade routes should be further secured against potential threats. King George's Sound and Thursday Island were the two principal strategic points at each end of this vast maritime arc upon which rested "the present prosperity and future commercial development of Australia."[88] Military outposts were positioned along Australia's porous northern and western perimeter, at Thursday Island, Darwin and King George Sound, in anticipation of an attack by a hostile power, be it Germany or Japan. Australia's maritime security, however, remained dependent upon Britain's ability and willingness to project naval power into the Pacific.

Biological threats required different technologies of defense. Two cases in the 1880s, both concerning ships arriving from Java, heightened public concern about the health consequences of frequent contact with unsanitary Asian cities and towns. The *SS Dorunda* arrived in Queensland from Batavia in December 1885 with what a subsequent inquiry found to be a case of cholera on board "of a sufficiently malignant type to establish its Asiatic origin."[89] The arrival of the *Ellora* in Townsville the following year carrying Javanese laborers, one of whom was suspected of having smallpox, added urgency to demands for Queenslanders to be protected from the virulent diseases of Asia.[90]

Quarantine stations were introduced to guard against such unwanted invisible arrivals. To quarantine against threats to the purity of the White race required the strict application of a racially discriminatory immigration policy and rigorous surveillance of multiracial northern communities. Sounding the alarm, future Australian Prime Minister Alfred Deakin, in many ways an intellectual progressive with a keen interest in Indian philosophy, cast Australia's region as a source of impending biological and military threat. Addressing the new Commonwealth Parliament in 1901, he justified the introduction of a racially discriminatory immigration policy by asserting that Australia was surrounded by "colored races" that were "inclined to invade our shores." The White race had to be insulated against Asian warmongers, and, by implication, all things Asian, including virulent diseases and Asian blood. Deakin left his listeners in no doubt as to the gravity of the threat, warning "nothing less than the manhood, the national character, and the national future are at stake."[91]

As Reynolds observes, the creation of a federated White Australia in 1901 weakened the commercial, social and cultural bonds between northern Australians and the peoples of the Archipelago.[92] Federation heralded the stricter demarcation of Australian national space, anchoring Northern Australia economically, politically and culturally to a southern axis. Climate, demography and the gravitational pull of established south coast shipping lanes diminished the possibilities for more vigorous involvement in the western Archipelago, but international politics also played a role. Australian regional maritime shipping activity was most intense in the South West Pacific, where Australian companies and federal and state governments vied with French and German colonial interests for commercial and territorial gains. Here opportunities were greater for Australians than in the Indies where the race for colonial spoils was all but won.

With the centrality of Melbourne and Sydney in the Australian economy confirmed, the geographic focus of the new Australian nation developed a pronounced eastward orientation, towards the Pacific. Australian states absorbed much of the commerce of New Guinea, the Solomons and Fiji. Further west, the Netherlands guarded its position in the eastern Archipelago lest these islands be drawn too closely into an enlarged Anglo-Australian sphere. Trade with Asian emporia should not, however, be dismissed as insignificant. For much of the nineteenth century, colonial Australians were open to the idea of an expanded Australasian commercial and political orbit in the eastern Indies, but, as the *Costa Rica Packet* incident demonstrated, the Dutch were prepared to defend their prerogative by force of law, and if need be, by force of arms. Suspicion and disdain lurked beneath the surface of bilateral relations, but out of necessity and convenience, Australian social and business connections with the Netherlands Indies deepened as new avenues for intraregional exchange appeared.

NOTES

1. Jim Allen, "When Did Humans First Colonise Australia?" in *Archaeology of Aboriginal Australia: A Reader*, ed. Tim Murray (Sydney: Allen and Unwin, 1998), 50–55.

2. Oliver Wolters, *History, Culture, and Region in Southeast Asian Perspectives* (Singapore: Institute of Southeast Asian Studies, 1982), 39.

3. Charles Campbell MacKnight, *The Voyage to Marege: Macassan Trepangers in Northern Australia* (Melbourne: Melbourne University Press, 1976), 9–13.

4. James J. Fox, "Reefs and Shoals in Australia-Indonesia Relations: Traditional Indonesian Fishing," in *Australia in Asia: Episodes*, ed. Anthony Milner and Mary Quilty (Melbourne: Oxford University Press, 1998), 118–19.

5. Macknight, *Voyage*, 89.

6. Geoffrey Blainey, *The Tyranny of Distance: How Distance Shaped Australia's History* (Melbourne: Macmillan, 1982), 54. Manning Clark, *A History of Australia, Volume 1: From the Earliest Times to the Age of Macquarie* (Melbourne: Melbourne University Press, 3rd edition, 1988), 121.

7. Blainey, *Tyranny of Distance*, 24–25.

8. Blainey, *Tyranny of Distance*, 55. Ships using the Torres Strait could cut up to 2000 miles from their journey to Calcutta.

9. Blainey, *Tyranny of Distance*, 62–63.

10. Matthew Flinders, *A Voyage to Terra Australis, Volume II* (London: G&W Nicol, 1814), 247–48.

11. Blainey, *Tyranny of Distance*, 83.

12. John Barrow to Undersecretary Horton, January 22, 1824, in *Historical Records of Australia* (hereafter *HRA*) (series 3, vol. 5, 1922), 753.

13. W. Barns to Undersecretary Horton, September 15, 1823, *HRA* (series 3, vol. 5, 1922), 737–39.

14. Barrow to Undersecretary Horton, January 22, 1824, 752.

15. Dora Howard, "The English Activities on the North Coast of Australia in the First Half of the Nineteenth Century," *Proceedings of the Royal Geographical Society Of Australasia, South Australian Branch* (vol. 33,1931–32), 56–57.

16. Barns to Horton, September 15, 1823 and G. G. de H. Lapent, Chairman, East India Trade Committee, to Undersecretary Horton, December 13, 1823, *HRA* (series 3, vol. 5, 1922), 742–47.

17. Howard, "English Activities," 46–49.

18. Howard, "English Activities," 103.

19. Robert Montgomery Martin, *British Possessions in Europe: Africa, Asia and Australasia*, London: W.H. Allen, 1847), 5–6.

20. Frank Broeze, "Australia, Asia and the Pacific: The Maritime World of Robert Towns, 1843–1873," *Australian Historical Studies* (vol. 24, no. 95, October, 1990), 222–27.

21. A. C. Staples, "Maritime Trade in the Indian Ocean," in *University Studies in History*, ed. Geoffrey C. Bolton and B.K. de Garis (Perth: UWA Press, 1966), 101, 114.

22. B. F. Legarda y Fernandez, "Foreign Trade, Economic Exchange and Entrepreneurship in the 19th Century Philippines," PhD Diss., Harvard University, 1955, 180–89. "Statistics of New South Wales From 1848 to 1857" New South Wales Parliament, *Legislative Council Journals*, 2nd Parliament, 1st Session, Volume 3, 1858, 427.

23. "Statistics of New South Wales from 1848 to 1857," 427.

24. Legarda, "Foreign Trade," 180, 231–32.

25. "The Van Delden Proclamation of 1828," in *Documents and Correspondence on New Guinea's Boundaries*, ed. Paul W. van der Veur, (Canberra: Australian National University Press, 1966), 2–4. Nicholas Tarling, *The Fall of Imperial Britain in South-East Asia* (Kuala Lumpur: Oxford University Press, 2nd edition, 1994), 27.

26. Tarling, *Fall of Imperial Britain*, 27–31.

27. "Queensland Committee on Settlement at the Gulf of Carpentaria," *Queensland Legislative Council Journals* (vol. 1, 1860).

28. George Ferguson Bowen to Colonial Secretary, December 9, 1861. *Letterbooks and Despatches to the Secretary of State for the Colonies*, vol. 2, November 18, 1859—December 14, 1863, QSA PRV 8226-1-2.

29. Bowen to Colonial Secretary, December 9, 1861.

30. Bowen to Colonial Secretary, November 3, 1862, *Letterbooks and Despatches*, QSA PRV 8226-1-2.

31. Bowen to Colonial Secretary, November 5, 1862, *Letterbooks and Despatches*, QSA PRV 8226-1-2. Reference to Wakefield in Walker and Ingleson, "Image of Asia," 296.

32. Sir Charles Nicholson to Governor of Queensland, Queensland Legislative Assembly, *Votes and Proceedings* (hereafter QLA V&P) vol. 1, 1861, 647–49.

33. Steve Mullins, *Torres Strait: A History of Colonial Occupation and Culture Contact, 1864–1897* (Rockhampton: Central Queensland University Press, 1994), 88.

34. John Bach, *A Maritime History of Australia* (Sydney: Thomas Nelson, 1976), 109–13. Howard, "English Activities," 141–42. Blainey, *Tyranny of Distance,* 208–9.

35. Ronald Parsons, *Steamers in the South* (Sydney: Rigby, 1979), 22.

36. "Report from the Joint Select Committee on Existing and Proposed Lines of Steam Communication," *Queensland Legislative Assembly Votes and Proceedings* (hereafter QLA V&P), 3rd Session, 2nd Parliament, 1865, 949–57.

37. John C. H. Foley, *Reef Pilots: The History of the Queensland Coast and Torres Strait Pilot Service* (Sydney: Banks Bros and Street, 1982), 25–26.

38. *Brisbane Courier,* January 1 to December 31, 1866.

39. *Straits Times,* October 10, 1874.

40. Ian H. Nicholson, *Via Torres Strait: A Maritime History of the Torres Strait Route and the Ships' Post Office at Booby Island* (Nambour: Roebuck Society, 1996), 260–61.

41. *Straits Times,* August 31, 1886.

42. Federal Council of Australasia Acts, 1886, QLA V&P, 1886, vol. 2, 1886, 1035.

43. Mr. Francis P. Labilliere to the Secretary of State for the Colonies, March 26, 1874, QSA, PRV 7192 COL/1

44. Report of the interview of the Colonial Secretary with the New Guinea Deputation at his public office, May 19, 1875 QSA PRV 7192 COL/1.

45. John Robertson, Colonial Secretary, NSW, Cabinet Minutes, May 31, 1875, QSA, PRV 7192, COL/1.

46. John Douglas, Colonial Secretary, to W. B. Ingham, Government Agent, Port Moresby, New Guinea, June 1, 1878, QSA RSI 12848 1-1.

47. Earl of Carnarvon, Secretary of State for the Colonies, to Sir A. E. Kennedy, Governor of Queensland, January 29, 1877, *Confidential Despatches from the Secretary of State for the Colonies,* QSA PRV 8231-1-1.

48. Neville Meaney, *A History of Australian Defence and Foreign Policy, 1901–1923: Volume 1, The Search for Security in the Pacific. 1901–1914* (Sydney: Sydney University Press, 1976), 17–18.

49. Mullins argues that Islander crews were in the main treated their fairly by their pearling masters. Mullins, *Torres Strait,* 60–69.

50. Patricia Mercer, *White Australia Defied: Pacific Islander Settlement in North Queensland* (Townsville Qld: James Cook University, 1995), 12–15.

51. Thomas McIlwraith to His Excellency the Administrator of Queensland, September 28, 1883, QSA PRV 7192 COL/2.

52. Minutes of the Proceedings of the Executive Council, October 24, 1883. QSA, PRV 8112-67.

53. W. Seed, Secretary of Customs, New Zealand, "Area, Population, Trade, &c., of the Principal Groups of Islands," Proceedings of the Intercolonial Convention, November–December 1883, Sydney, *New South Wales Legislative Assembly Votes and Proceedings* (hereafter NSW LA V&P), 1883–84, vol. 11, 91–105.

54. Minutes of Proceedings, Intercolonial Convention, December 5, 1883, *NSW LA V&P,* 1883–84, vol. 11, 13.

55. *The Times,* December 7, 1883.

56. Clarke, *Australian Race,* 18.

57. "Malay" was the racial term used to categorise divers and crew recruited from the Archipelago irrespective of sociocultural difference.

58. Lorraine Philipps, "Plenty More Little Brown Man: Pearl shelling and White Australia in Queensland, 1901–18," in *The Political Economy of Australian Capitalism*, vol. 4, ed. Ted Wheelwright and Ken Buckley (Sydney: ANZ Book Company, 1980), 60.

59. Anna Shnukal, "'They don't know what went on underneath': Three Little-known Filipino/Malay Communities of Torres Strait," in *Navigating Boundaries*, ed. Shnukal, Ramsay and Nagata, 85–90, 102–9.

60. *Queensland Census*, 1886, 360–65.

61. J. Gullard, Mourilyan Sugar Company to Chief Secretary, July 27, 1886, "Introduction of Javanese into Queensland," *QLA V&P*, vol. 3, 1889.

62. "Report of the Royal Commission appointed to inquire into the general condition of the sugar industry in Queensland together with minutes of evidence," *QLA V&P*, vol. 4, 1889, 84.

63. "Report of the Royal Commission," 71.

64. "Report of the Royal Commission," 223–24.

65. *Mackay Mercury*, September 21, 1886.

66. *Mackay Mercury*, March 10, 1888.

67. The *Queenslander*, July 25, 1885.

68. *Townsville Herald*, June 23, 1888.

69. Queensland Legislative Assembly, *Parliamentary Debates*, vol. 55, 1888, 296–97.

70. *Townsville Herald*, February 14, 1891.

71. Ambrose Pratt, *The Big Five*, (London: 1910), 200, 237, 290–95, 300.

72. Ernestine Hill, *The Territory*, (Sydney: Angus and Robertson, 5th edition, 1968), 31–34.

73. *Townsville Daily Bulletin*, January 26, 1912.

74. Reynaldo C. Ileto, *Filipinos and their Revolution: Event, Discourse and Historiography*, (Manila: Ateneo de Manila University Press, 1998), 122.

75. *Straits Times*, November 5, 1890, October 8, 1890, March 9, 1891. *Townsville Herald*, February 7, 1891. *North Queensland Register*, June 13, 1894. *Cairns Argus*, August 26, 1896.

76. *Townsville Daily Bulletin*, August 9, 1912. P. Mercer, "Clark, James (1857–1933)," in *Australian Dictionary of Biography*, (Hereafter ADB) vol. 8, 1891–1939, (Melbourne: Melbourne University Press, 1981), 9–10.

77. *Townsville Herald*, December 22, 1888.

78. Kennedy Tregonning, *Under Chartered Company Rule: North Borneo, 1881–1946*, (Singapore: University of Malaya Press, 1958), 95. *Straits Times*, May 27, 1892 & September 12, 1892.

79. *Townsville Herald*, October 20, 1888. "Report From the Select Committee On the 'Costa Rica Packet' Case," 217. Ken Buckley and Kris Klugman, *The History of Burns Philp* (Sydney: Burns Philp & Co, 1981), 30

80. "Report from the Select Committee on the Costa Rica Packet Case together with the Proceedings of the Committee and Minutes of Evidence," *New South Wales Legislative Council Votes and Proceedings*, vol. 51, 1893, 171–219.

81. "Report from the Select Committee on the 'Costa Rica Packet' Case," 175.

82. *Straits Times*, November 5, 1890.

83. *Straits Times*, December 14, 1892.

84. Extract from the *Cologne Gazette* quoted in the *Straits Times*, August 1, 1894.

85. Sir William MacGregor to Sir Henry Norman, Governor of Queensland, October 12, 1891, QSA, SRS 5384-1-45.

86. Memorandum, G. E. P. Hertslet, Foreign Office, June 22, 1900, QSA, PRV 5384-1-42.

87. Remarks by Colonial Defence Committee, June 4, 1890, QSA, PRV 8235-1.

88. "Report and Summary of Proceedings, Federal Military Conference" Sydney, October 1894, QSA, PRV 8235-1.

89. "Report of the Board Appointed to Inquire into the Alleged Cases of Cholera among Passengers on Board the *SS Dorunda* on the voyage between London and Brisbane," *QLA V&P*, 1886, vol. 3, 1886, 749.

90. *Mackay Standard*, September 21, 1886.

91. Alfred Deakin, Commonwealth of Australia, *Parliamentary Debates*, September 12, 1901.

92. Reynolds, *North of Capricorn*, 187.

3

Across Jeweled Seas

GLOBAL TRANSPORT REVOLUTIONS
AND THE RISE OF AUSTRALASIAN TOURISM

Steamships and rail travel epitomized nineteenth-century industrial achievement. Lacing together dispersed centers of international trade, steam navigation and railway companies provided the physical infrastructure of international travel. The emergence of leisure tourism in the Archipelago was a by-product of this global transport revolution and exemplified the power of global cultural forces to refashion local taste and practice. From Malaya to New Guinea, the growth of tourist industries was closely aligned with the imperial aims of colonial states, not least the cultivation of romantic impressions of oriental tranquillity, domesticity and contentment. Coaling stations on the major Indian Ocean and Pacific shipping routes from Batavia to Colombo and Singapore to Manila and Hong Kong were transformed into commercial hubs and celebrated tourist destinations by the expansion of steamer services. Technological advances and the proliferation of steam communications meant that voyages were no longer something to be endured for the sake of arriving at one's destination. On the Australia-Asia run, steam navigation companies strove to extend to their guests all the luxuries and conveniences expected by the modern pleasure traveller. Through the hub for a limited Melanesian shipping network, Australia was slowly enmeshed into wider Asia Pacific maritime shipping patterns and Australian tourists drawn up into the Archipelago in small but increasing numbers to savor the packaged pleasures of a mythologized and supine Orient.

A GLOBAL TIMETABLE

According to Eric Hobsbawm, the "speed, intensity, rapidity" and "range of repercussion" of nineteenth-century international economic exchange brought about a world "transformed from a geographical expression into a constant operational reality."[1] Placing the globalization debate in historical perspective, A. G. Hopkins reminds us that the world shrank rapidly in the late nineteenth century as global traveling times were substantially reduced.[2] Quickened by the introduction of new technologies to harness steam power and electricity, sprawling land and marine communications followed in the wake of European colonial expansion. Railway networks constructed in the Americas, Europe and Australia regularized the movement of goods and people across vast distances. This "compression of time and space" was aided by the development of telegraphic communications that made possible the synchronisation of intercontinental rail and transoceanic steam navigation services. Admittedly, the image of reliability conveyed in company shipping timetables did not always match reality. A forty-eight-hour delay in the arrival at Townsville of one TSML steamer in September 1874 made headline news in the *Brisbane Courier* which expressed pity for the Cleveland Bay pilots who sacrificed a good night's sleep to scour the horizon for the missing vessel.[3] Steamships might not always arrive or depart on the appointed day while the electronic transmission of information could be slowed by technical failure. The *Straits Times* gleefully lampooned the cumbersomeness of the electric telegraph, calling for the introduction of a more efficient system of "peons and bicycles" to power the world's transcontinental telegraph networks and ensure the timely and reliable conveyance of vital information.[4] Even a brief interruption in telegraphic services could upset the transcontinental movement of goods and capital. One break in the Eastern Extension Telegraph Company's service during a coffee fair in Batavia in December 1900 delayed the receipt of coffee purchase orders from Europe and the Americas through Singapore, to the immediate inconvenience and audible displeasure of Batavia's business community.[5]

Time was increasingly of the essence in international business and, embarrassing failures aside, faith in the capacity of technology to conquer time was unshakeable. Despite the limitations of ship design, steam navigation quickly achieved prominence as an alternative to sail on the north Atlantic shipping routes. Sail dominated the oceans, but a 250 percent increase in steamship tonnages on the world's trade routes between 1831 and 1861 pointed unambiguously to a new trend in maritime commerce.[6] On the Australia run, sailing ships carried goods and passengers more cheaply and, although following a more circuitous passage through the Roaring Forties, were capable of reaching Melbourne from England in sixty-three days or

less. Migrants travelled the Great Circle route around the Cape of Good
Hope to Melbourne and Sydney by sail rather than steam. But, as the cum-
bersome wooden paddles that propelled the first Atlantic steamers were dis-
carded in favor of more durable iron-screw propellers, the price advantage
enjoyed by the celebrated clipper ships was gradually eroded. Steamers became lighter and faster. New hull construction materials improved fuel efficiency while the development of more compact marine engines allowed
extra space for precious freight.[7]

Advances in technology combined with the synchronization of shipping
and rail timetables to change the nature of international trade and tourism.
In an age when commercial transactions were reliant upon seaborne traffic
in orders, contracts, receipts and bills of sale, fast, reliable mail steamship
services were attractive to businesses and governments. The opening of the
Suez Canal in 1869 meant that a journey from Southampton to Singapore
by sea took approximately thirty-four days, reduced to twenty-six days if the
train was first taken from London to the Mediterranean port of Brindisi.
Melbourne could be reached in fifty-four days or forty-six days from Brindisi along the south coast.[8] Connecting with P&O steamers in Singapore,
the E&A service brought Brisbane within forty-four days of London, only
two days faster than the south coast route. For Queensland politicians the
logic of a separate mail-steamer connection through the Archipelago was
compelling. Not only did the TSML promise faster connections to Britain
and Europe where the bulk of their colony's markets lay, the service offered
an opportunity to attract migrants ahead of southern competitors.

Almanacs and business handbooks now carried maps of Australasia in-
tricately threaded by continuous black lines marking out the major steamshipping routes that connected Australia to the British Empire in Asia. Early
examples of the packaging of the tropical travel experience for Australian
audiences appeared in travel articles published in the Queensland and Singapore press. Appealing to the romantic myth of the tropical idyll, and to a
growing concern with comfort, writers stressed the scenic beauty and the
smooth ride afforded on the Torres Strait route. "Smooth water" and the
sights of picturesque tropical scenery were considered a welcome compensation for travellers willing to endure the tropical heat of the Archipelago
and quickly became defining contours of island travel marketing. Outward-
bound steamers crossed the Arafura Sea, skirted the southern shore of
Timor and passed the islands of Sumbawa and Lombok towards the towering Gunung (Mount) Agung that announced the approaches to Bali. Ships
entered the Java Sea through either the Bali or Lombok Strait, hugging the
coastline of Java until reaching anchorage in the Batavia Roads. Land, it was
stressed, was never out of sight for more than two days on the entire journey between Sydney and Singapore. Adding to these visual attractions was
the opportunity for saloon passengers to go ashore at Batavia for a few

hours until their ship's departure for Singapore where they would await their connection to Britain.[9]

Shipowners recognized that passenger mobility and transferability of tickets were important to the wealthy, time-affluent travel consumer. Taking advantage of the demand for transferable "rights of passage," E&A provided a range of travel options for its Singapore-bound customers. From Singapore the major ports of Asia were within easy reach by P&O or Messageries Maritimes (MM) liners bound for Saigon, Hong Kong or Shanghai. Passengers, if they so chose, could sail to Marseilles with the MM. As mentioned, new maritime technology did not guarantee scheduled departure or arrival dates. Singapore stopovers for persons in transit to or from Europe varied according to the shipping line and the punctuality of ships and their captains. Transhipment between P&O and E&A steamers was scheduled to take less than a day whereas MM passengers were required to spend four to seven days in Singapore awaiting their connection to Europe or Australia. Even with the increased number and frequency of steam navigation services in the last two decades of the nineteenth century, such inconveniences continued to plague international travellers.

The "crossroads of the East," the Archipelago was also a vital thoroughfare for Australian and international shipping passing between the Pacific, eastern Asia, India and Europe. With the development of refrigeration, shipping companies found a new incentive to incorporate Australia into their global schemes and, gradually, competition for mail contracts of the Australia-Asia run became more intense. Anticipating a lucrative trade in dairy produce and frozen beef from Queensland to Britain, the British India Steam Navigation Company (BISN) wrested the Queensland mail contract from E&A in 1881, earning an increased subsidy in return for terminating their fortnightly mail service in Brisbane. Such was the urgency with which Queensland graziers and BISN directors sought to bring Australian beef to British dinner tables that BISN steamers sailed from Brisbane to Batavia by a different route than the E&A, bypassing Singapore and Colombo in favor of a more direct passage through the Sunda Strait and across the Indian Ocean to the Arabian Gulf.

The enduring need for governments to underwrite regular steam services pointed to the relative weakness of commercial links between eastern Australia and the western Archipelago. Yet a small but steady passenger traffic developed between eastern Australia, Java and Singapore in the late nineteenth century. At least 43 passengers departed Brisbane destined specifically for Batavia in the first year of operation for the BISN's Queensland Royal Mail Line (QRML), another 64 were headed for Britain. The following year 273 people left Brisbane aboard BISN steamers: 42 were bound for Batavia, 7 for Singapore and 225 for London.[10] Reverse passenger flows were greater with as many as 200 British migrants per month passing through the Archipelago to Queensland with the QRML. The association of the Archipelago with diseases such as cholera and smallpox undoubtedly diminished the attractions of Java, and Britain was a "natural" destination of choice. Viewed in a different light, however, the fact that one-fifth of outward-bound BISN passengers chose Batavia or Singapore as their primary destination suggests a stirring of interest in travel to the region, stimulated by commercial adventurism but also by the emergence of systematic tourism marketing.

Paying passengers complemented cargoes of gold, flour, tea, tobacco and Manchester haberdasheries aboard the world's expanding steam-powered merchant marine. Likened to "traveling palaces" steamers on the North Atlantic routes were global benchmarks of bourgeois status.[11] In their quest to win a share of the luxury travel market, shipping companies competed to outdo each other for opulence and comfort. The intensity of this competition was reflected less by the wording of advertisements than by the marketing of luxury services through news "reports" in daily and weekly newspapers that placed heavy emphasis upon the quality of shipboard fixtures and fittings and which sought to conjure romantic impressions of international luxury travel.[12] Ships on the Australia-Asia run were much smaller in size but, as did saloon passengers, exhibited serious pretensions to grandeur. The arrival in Brisbane of the first in a new line of steamers was accompanied by a newsworthy official function aboard ship and invariably made the front pages of the *Brisbane Courier*.

Lined with the trimmings of bourgeois success, the first-class saloon on the BISN company steamer *Meraka* closely resembled an ornately furnished "lofty room." The lofty ambitions of the captains of industry, financiers and other assorted notables, for whom such comforts were designed, were also mirrored in mahogany paneling and "birds-eye maple" moldings, layered in gold leaf. Ventilation, a major concern in an age where the miasmic theory of infection informed public perceptions of health and hygiene, was provided by portholes—two sliding mirrors and punkahs located above each of four grand dining tables, which were operated manually by saloon attendants at mealtimes. Cocooned in their floating cultural capsule, travellers were nonetheless exposed to images and tastes of the exotic Orient. Seated comfortably on their hair-cushioned settees, dinner guests were accorded the luxury of being waited upon by an "army of white-helmeted, white-robed kitmagars"—*kitmagar* meaning a servant recruited from British India.[13] Nineteenth-century equivalents of today's culturally sterile transit lounges, chain hotels, or high-speed trains—what John Tomlinson terms "non-places" of the modern global economy—these floating transit-spaces could not be sealed off from the harsh realities of the colonized worlds outside. Indeed, such shipboard distinctions of race and class as were visible were regarded as mere reflections of the natural order.

Extravagant interiors and indulgent feasting appear at odds with puritan Victorian moral values of sobriety, effort and thrift but according to Hobsbawm, the bourgeois world was rife with moral contradictions. Wealth was the just reward for hard work, and yet the late nineteenth century was also the dawn of mass international leisure travel. If one were to enjoy leisure, however, it had to serve a higher moral purpose than pleasure or mere gratification.[14] Hence the efforts of shipping companies and marine architects to provide for both the intellectual and physical health of passengers aboard ship by mimicking the socially acceptable recreational patterns of the European middle classes. Forced to endure an extended period of leisure, passengers were uplifted by inducements to be active, both out of doors and in the saloon. Deck games or a promenade in the fresh sea air along iron decks sheathed in teak were practical defenses against the moral danger of sloth engendered by lengthy confinement. Active intellects were also adequately catered for with well-stocked libraries, chessboards, draughts, and cards. Charts available in the saloon allowed the inquisitive to monitor their journey through the Archipelago. "Tiffin" was usually followed by quoits or curling, for the more athletic. In the evening tales of bravado became a focal point of male activity in the smoking room, the shipboard bastion of masculinity.[15]

Heightened interest in the Australia-Asia run brought new steamer services into the market for trade and tourism. The West Australian Stream Navigation Company (WASN) and the China Navigation Company opened new pathways to transportation hubs of Batavia, Singapore and Manila in the 1880s. Australian affluence was increasing as import substituting, mining, pastoral and transport industries made the Australian gross domestic product "one of the highest in the world," according to Dyster and Meredith.[16] The growing propensity of Australians to travel overseas is indicated by the appearance of the world's first transnational travel company, Thomas Cook and Son, well established in Australia by the 1890s. Through an international chain of offices and agencies, Thomas Cook provided modern travel services including foreign currency exchange, traveler's checks and telegraphic transfers of money, services that earned the company the title "Bankers to the World."

Although the depression of the 1890s disrupted trading relations with Asia and brought the suspension of the QRML subsidy, new shipping services connected Queensland to Asia through the Archipelago. Relying on the frozen-beef trade, BISN continued its service between London and Brisbane through the Torres Strait. The Japanese company, Nippon Yuan Kaisha (NYK), introduced a well-credentialed monthly service between Australia, Japan and Hong Kong in 1896. Boasting a British-built fleet, NYK ships were registered in London and, a condition of their Lloyds[17] Another major international line entered when the German national carrier, the Norddeutche Lloyd Company (NDL) began running a three-monthly service between Sydney and Singapore in 1900. Public concerns about German imperial ambitions in the Pacific were set aside in the interests of commerce. Reporting the official banquet aboard the *Settin,* attended by Queensland notables including Premier Robert Philp, the *Queenslander* lauded German "energy and skill," glossed over the fact of a German embargo on Australian beef, and expressed the belief that Australian trade with Germany would soon prosper.[18]

Further increases in maritime connections between Australia and the Archipelago after 1900 suggest a high level of optimism among Australian and international shipping companies about the prospects for trade. The Australian company Burns Philp concentrated its investments in shipping and trade between New Guinea and the Solomon Islands, but owners James Burns and Robert Philp sensed opportunities in the Indies and Malaya. Burns Philp inaugurated its Sydney-Singapore service through the Torres Strait in 1902 and cemented a toehold in the Indies by opening an office at Samarang in 1908. The company's "Island Line," as the Singapore service was initially called, enjoyed little competition until the Koninklijke Paketvaart Maatschappij (KPM), for whom Burns Philp was the Australian agents, entered the Australia-Asia trade. The KPM intermittently sent its steamers south to Australia from 1902, though initially only as far as Thursday Island. Buoyed by a subsidy from the Netherlands Indies government, the company set out to capture markets from Burns Philp and attract Australian tourists to sail with the KPM to the East Indies.[19]

Operating a five-weekly service between the Indies and the principal ports of eastern Australia, the KPM also took through passengers for Singapore. Stops were made at Samarang, Surabaya, Makassar, Banda and the Aru Islands in the East Indies and Thursday Island, Townsville, Brisbane, Sydney and Melbourne in Australia. During 1910 and 1911 the KPM transported approximately 222 passengers from Australia to the Archipelago; most were bound for Java and Singapore.[20]

Fares for the northern passage varied between shipping companies and by duration of voyage, but the tendency was for prices to fall over time. For passengers aboard the first E&A steamers, a first-class fare from Brisbane to Singapore one way was approximately £30 for a seventeen-and-a-half-day journey, or £35 for a twenty-and-a-half-day journey from Sydney. Through tickets covering every route section could be purchased from P&O or E&A agents in Brisbane, Sydney or Melbourne. Three decades later, a first-class NDL fare from Sydney to Singapore was £28 one way for a voyage of between thirty-two and thirty-three days.[21] The KPM charged £26 for a first-class ticket from Melbourne to Singapore with return tickets valid for one year, available at a discount of 25 percent. Return fares for the more frequent and direct Burns Philp service were competitive, costing between £44 16s and £51 4s. Similar cost reductions were also evident at the global level.

The increasing size of ships and rising standards of shipboard luxury reflected the value attached both to freight storage capacity and passenger comfort. Electric lights and fans adorned more modern interiors while steam-powered punkahs improved ventilation in first- and second-class saloons but fares remained relatively low. A one-way, first-class E&A ticket to Southampton was £113 from Brisbane in 1874. Forty years later, a return ticket from Sydney to London by Singapore and Suez with Burns Philp cost a mere £142 first class. For £166 tourists could sail around the world by way of Singapore, Hong Kong, China, Japan and the United States, returning through the Suez Canal.[22] Such improvements in efficiency, comfort and price did not bring the world of luxury international travel within reach of the majority of Australian waged workers whose leisure pursuits were governed by the frequent irregularity of employment and the pressing demands of subsistence in an era where paid holidays were not seen as essential for a healthy working life.[23]

The infrastructure of international tourism became steadily more sophisticated, pointing to the emergence of a genuinely global service industry. Discounting of return tickets to Australia began in the 1880s with the caveat that passengers made their return journey within six months. By 1900 special tourist fares were widely available. Round-trip tours from West Australia to Singapore by way of Colombo on P&O and WASN steamers could be purchased for around £50. Passengers wishing to travel in the second-class saloon aboard P&O ships to Colombo and Singapore, returning first-class with the WASN, could do so for around £38. By 1902 the Messageries Maritimes offered round-the-world tours linking Australia, China and Japan with the United States and Europe. Tourism marketing also became more innovative. First- prize winners in the Laxo-Tonic "Original Limerick" competition, featured in the *Queenslander* during 1908, were treated to an 18,000-mile round trip with the NDL to the "South Sea Islands," the Philippines, Hong Kong, China, Japan, Singapore and Penang, returning to Brisbane by Colombo and the south coast. With Burns Philp, Australians could circumnavigate the globe in both directions. Prospective tourists could make travel bookings for Singapore and Java in any company branch office and purchase "through tickets" for most other shipping lines operating worldwide.[24]

JAVA THE WONDERLAND

The appearance of Australian tourists in the Archipelago was also directly connected to the development of colonial tourist industries in Java, Malaya and the Philippines. Widening exposure to the tourist gaze forced the

Netherlands Indies government to address Batavia's international reputation as an unsanitary destination. Built by early Dutch residents in an effort to reproduce the cityscape of Amsterdam in the tropics, Batavia's poorly drained network of canals were little more than open sewers blamed for the city's high European mortality rate. The Molenvliet Canal oozed through the center of Batavia, accumulating human refuse, polluting water supplies and creating an overpowering foul stench on hot summer days. Nightly sluicing with irrigation water from rice paddies located in the hills around Batavia eased the pollution but disease was rife amongst Batavia's non-European residents. According to Susan Abeyasekere, the completion of a satellite city helped to reduce Batavia's European death rate. Weltevreden, meaning "well rested," lay a comfortable six miles distant from the "pernicious" miasma of the fever-ridden marshlands and the malodorous canals of the old port city and decaying business quarter.[25] This new city boasted Java's most popular hotels including the Hotel des Indes and the Hotel Java. Besides access to unpolluted artesian wells, the city's white pillared villas, neatly ordered parks and tree-lined streets appealed to the aesthetic tastes of European and Australian visitors alike.

Complementing government efforts to transform Java into a popular tourist destination, new rail construction gradually brought the interior within the reach of international tourists. Built in the 1800s, the Great Post Road connected Batavia, Bandung, Yogyakarta (Djokjakarta), Samarang and Surabaya. According to one Australian traveller, the road was in such good condition that the journey by mail coach from Surabaya to Samarang "at break-neck speed" took a mere three days.[26] The demands of nineteenth-century industrial development, however, required an extensive network of railway lines to reduce and regularize carriage times from inland agricultural districts to ports on the north coast. Beginning with the completion in 1871 of the first stage of the line from Batavia to the seat of Dutch Governors General at Buitenzorg, known today as Bogor, the Indies government and private investors gradually connected the island's major port cities in piecemeal, uncoordinated fashion. By 1903 tourists could travel from the easternmost port of Banyuwangi to Anyer-kidul in the west by way of Surabaya, Yogyakarta, Bandung and Batavia at a cost of one and one-quarter pence per mile first class. There was only one hitch: passengers heading east from Batavia to Surabaya had to change trains twice, at Yogyakarta and again at Solo. A consequence of non-existent coordination between government and business, the privately laid Yogyakarta-Samarang line used a 4-foot 8-inch gauge whereas the Batavia to Yogyakarta and Solo to Surabaya lines, both government projects, were built to a 1-meter gauge.[27]

Rail travel was cheap but Java in the late nineteenth and early twentieth centuries was hardly a cut-price tourist destination. Tourists were required to open their wallets at almost every turn as they snaked their way through the Javanese countryside by rail, road and mountain track. Even the most sedentary tourist required the rough standard of 9 shillings per day for hotel accommodation. Prior to the completion of the Batavia to Yogyakarta line in the early 1900s the cost of traveling from a Batavia hotel to the temples of the Dieng Plateau was £18 plus accommodation. The train from Batavia to Garut and the hill stations of West Java from Batavia was reasonably priced at a mere £1 5 shillings one way in 1893. As with steam navigation companies, tourism gave impetus to the development of sophisticated rail ticketing systems, thereby enhancing traveler mobility and convenience. By 1908 tourists were able to purchase special government rail tickets that allowed them to traverse Java by rail for the discounted price of £4 10 shillings. For the more adventurous and affluent pleasure traveler a steamship tour around the outer islands was available on board steamers of the Nederlandsch Indische Stoomvart Maatshappij (NISM) at a cost of approximately £44 in 1883, considerably more than a one-way steamer fare from Brisbane to Batavia.

A typical day for a Western sojourner residing in one of Java's many hotels was governed by the rhythms of indigenized Dutch colonial society. The complimentary rituals of leisure and hospitality began with a "morning call" of coffee or tea brought by a Javanese attendant. Washrooms consisting of bare, sometimes mirrored, walls and a marbled or tiled floor sloped for drainage were, before the early 1900s, usually situated in a courtyard away from the main hotel building. European and Australian bathers quickly learned the art of drenching or rinsing themselves with water from a large clay basin or wooden tub of cold water, poured from a jug or "dipper." A new style of bathing was only one of many minor socio-cultural modifications to behavior and routine required of the first-time visitor.

The cultural mixing of the Indies was, for many a traveler, symbolized by the *Indische* delight of *rijsttavel* or "rice table." At the Hotel des Indes the meal was served for lunch in a cool verandah facing onto the hotel gardens. Amongst tall white stone pillars diners were treated to a feast of rice which they could combine with any selection from a table replete with dishes of omelette, curry, chicken, fish, Bologna sausage, ham and beef plus a variety of sauces, pickles, preserved fruit, salt eggs, fried bananas, fish roe and young palm shoots. Beef and salad followed, and then a dessert of fruit such as pineapple, mangosteens, rambutans, and duku or langsat completed this culinary marathon.[28] Whitewashed walls and cool stone floors offered refuge from the oppressive afternoon sun and, as was the tradition, hotel guests took a siesta after lunch, rising in the late afternoon to join in the early evening colonial rituals of visiting, touring by carriage, and promenading across the Koningsplein or Waterlooplein. Concerts were prominent on the entertainment menu of European colonial society and Sunday afternoon military band concerts were a special feature in Batavia's social calendar. Military bands also provided regular music entertainment at the two elite eating establishments, the Concordia and the Harmonie Club, where guests dined from eight in the evening on more familiar fare.[29]

The appropriation, restoration and reproduction of Javanese religious sites both legitimated colonial power in the Indies and hastened the production of tourized images of Java's "classical" past. Thomas Stamford Raffles began the exhumation of the Buddhist shrine of Borobudur in 1814 and became the foremost British authority on Java of his day. But it was the Dutch who restored this and Java's many Hindu temples, giving them a new cultural role, not as religious sites but as symbols of colonial overlordship and assumed cultural superiority. Sites of local historical and cultural significance were dusted off, reconstructed, their antiquity verified by archaeologists, and then marked out as archaeological attractions for conspicuous Western consumption. Official lithographic and later photographic images marked religious sites as worthy of tourist attention, lending official sanction to the practice of gazing upon Oriental antiquity.[30] Visits to Borobudur, Prambanan, Mendut and the temples of Kalasan were popularized by a succession of Western travel writers who added to the variety of textually reconstructed historic places available to international tourists. Among them was the Englishman W. Basil Worsfold, whose travelogue, *A Visit to Java*, directed English but also Australian audiences to marvel at the architectural wonders of the East.[31]

Cultural appropriations blended with introduced cultural practices, adding to the texture of Java's nascent tourism industry. The romantic idealization of mountain landscapes inspired European travellers to appreciate mountain scenery as a manifestation of the overwhelming power of nature. Mountain environments were both exhilarating and awe-inspiring visual wonders and an attractive contrast to polluted industrial towns mushrooming in industrial Britain and industrializing Europe.[32] Western medical opinion declared mountain air pure and healthful, providing a respectable reason, or excuse, for visits to European mountain resorts, which competed for medical recommendation. Despite the renowned insalubrity of Batavia, the Dutch in the Indies were slow to adapt. For the large numbers of Dutch visitors and emigrants to the East Indies in the late nineteenth century the positive attributes of mountain retreats were already defined. Sanatoriums constructed throughout central Java, a total of eighteen from the late nineteenth century up to the Pacific War, enhanced the appeal of sightseeing excursions to the restored Hindu temples of the Dieng Plateau and the fabled Buddhist shrine of Borobudur. Yet beyond the appeal of fashion, high altitudes offered long-term residents the opportunity to escape the enervating heat of the lowlands and experience a climatic environment closer to home. The presumed restorative qualities of "Alpine" climates were harnessed to the project of Dutch colonialism in the Indies.

The popularization of hill stations marked the cultural acclimatization of Dutch colonizers to life in the tropics, more than two centuries after the first United Provinces trading posts were established in the Archipelago.[33] Beyond the relatively low-lying Buitenzorg, the two most internationally renowned mountain resorts in the late nineteenth century were Sindanglaya and Garut. Nine hours east of Batavia, at an elevation of 696 meters above sea level, Garut was one of Java's lower altitude mountain retreats but still boasted a cool mountain climate. Closer to Batavia but more isolated and less easily accessible than Garut, the Hotel Sindanglaya was, like many of Java's hill stations, originally a government sanatorium for injured servicemen. By the 1880s it was a popular tourist resort famed for its cool climate with an array of organized tourist diversions to loosen the traveller's purse strings.[34] Excursionists could take pony rides to the many surrounding lakes, hot springs, the sulphurous crater of Gunung Guntur, or the hill gardens of Cibodas at Cipanas, the site of the Governor-General's summer residence. A Saturday market at a nearby village promised the opportunity to purchase "authentic" local produce.[35] Attractions abounded at virtually every step of the tourist trail through central Java, hastening the commoditization of local and Western cultural practices in the Javanese countryside, and the incorporation of rural spaces into a global tourist itinerary.

As tourism developed into a valuable supplement to trade, tourism marketing became more professionalized and the structuring of tourist experiences more sophisticated. Colonial governments promoted travel and travel-related industries to complement the broader aim of economic development. The Netherlands Indies's Official Tourist Bureau publication, *Java the Wonderland* (c.1906) urged tourists to make most productive use of their leisure time during the early morning and after four o'clock in the afternoon. From "self-guided" early morning history and culture walks to recommended steam tram tours and recommended hotels and military clubs, the brochure imposed a busy and costly schedule on the newly arrived tourist. Introducing Java as the "Garden of the East," *Java the Wonderland*, in addition to its practical and educational information on interior hotel resorts, mountain treks, markets and scenic tours, reminded readers of the achievements of Dutch colonial rule and that all was still *"ruste en orde."* Java and later Malaya were constructed as intriguing, mysterious places where adventure and excitement could be found and where modernization made the experience of tropical nature both comfortable and relatively safe. Above all, Java's indigenous inhabitants were turned into objects in the rural landscape where they served as attractions for the Western tourist to gaze and muse upon.

The British India-born stock and station agent Edward Houghton Angelo, Labor Major of Carnarvon in Western Australia, witnessed Java's popularity as a tourist destination in the heyday of steamship travel before the First

World War. Between negotiations with British and Dutch meat traders to establish markets for Western Australian live sheep in Singapore and the Indies, Angelo sampled Java's many tourist attractions. English was everywhere spoken and both colonizer and colonized were "happy and contented" he told the *Straits Times*. Combining observations of price, with remarks about the beauty of island scenery and the antiquity of Java's culture, he listed what had become the standard Western itinerary:

> Java is quite over-num with tourists at present and all the available accommodation is taxed to the utmost. The hotels are luxurious and the charges are very moderate, 8s. 4d per day being practically the universal tariff. The scenery is superb, some of the botanic gardens being the most extensive and enchanting in the world. Majestic snow-clad mountains, active volcanoes, lovely lakes. . . Magnificent Buddhist temples and shrines are scattered throughout the island. . . Borobudur is one of the sights of the world, and alone worth the journey to Java. The railways and tourist arrangements are all that could be desired.[36]

MALAYA AND THE PHILIPPINES

A consequence of much later colonization, there were no resorts of comparable altitude or sophistication in British Malaya at the end of the nineteenth century. The absence of monuments to past civilizations left little to excite the international traveller except reputation and service. Singapore, in contrast to Batavia, acquired an image as a healthy and entertaining place to visit in the nineteenth century. A Chinese city in the heart of the tropics might be expected to provoke disparagement from the British leisure class, yet the famous English lady tourist, Isabella Bird, wrote with imperial pride that the city was remarkably free from disease and the temperature surprisingly moderate for an "equatorial metropolis." Bird identified "overpowering greenery, a kaleidoscopic arrangement of colors, Chinese predominance, and abounding hospitality," as salient markers of place and cultural space. Her initial impressions reveal a sense of rapturous enjoyment at the sights of

> vegetation rich, profuse, endless, rapid, smothering, in all shades of vivid green . . . riots in a heavy shower every night and the heat of the perennial sunblaze every day.[37]

Although the commercial and administrative center of the Straits Settlements, Singapore was home to a European population of less than 3,000 in 1881. Associations and sporting pastimes helped to transplant the institutions and conventions of British society in the tropics. The Singapore Cricket Club played its first match in 1852. Lawn tennis championships were staged yearly from 1875, increasing to twice yearly in 1884. Rugby, soccer, hockey and polo were also popular as was golf, horse racing and tiger hunting. The obligatory European amateur theatricals company was occasionally upstaged by the arrival of a theater troupe from Australia such as the Vaudeville & Specialty Company that passed through in 1901.[38] Socially but not racially exclusive, institutions such as the Penang Club, founded in 1858, encouraged British, Chinese and Malay elites to mix and share the social pleasantries of a much larger gentlemen's association, the British Empire.[39] For all its hallmarks of British culture, Singapore was a Chinese city and Malaya, though under British tutelage, a multiracial society where Europeans were in a minority.

Singapore boasted many exclusive hotels that catered to European tastes. The most celebrated were owned by the Armenian hoteliers, the Sarkies Brothers, who built an accommodation empire spanning Singapore and Penang by capitalizing upon the increased demand for European-style accommodation. The Sarkies Brothers first entered the hotel trade in the 1880s but the tourism boom of the early 1900s brought their greatest level of investment and expansion, reflecting the growing importance of Singapore and Penang to intercontinental trade and tourism. In Singapore, the Brothers owned the famed Raffles Hotel, established in 1887 and extensively renovated between 1902 and 1904, which boasted hotel suites with running water, tiled verandas, electric lights and fans, and laid claim to be the most modern hotel available. In Penang, the brothers ran the Raffles-By-The-Sea and the Eastern and Oriental Hotel, both promoted as health resorts to a less transitory clientele. Citing medical endorsement of the restorative qualities of sea air, these establishments were well patronized by British holidaymakers from across the Bay of Bengal.[40]

Colonial governments encouraged tourism as a useful adjunct to commerce and infrastructure development. A rail network connecting Singapore, Kuala Lumpur and Penang was not completed until 1909 when the last segment of the Singapore-Prai main trunk line was laid through the sultanate of Johore. The network complemented Sir Frank Swettenham's dream of a federated British Empire. Swettenham, Resident General of the Federated Malay States (FMS) and then Governor of the Straits Settlements, envisaged an imperial federation meshed together with a network of railways and steamshipping routes spanning Australasia and the Indian subcontinent. Initially in the 1880s and 1890s railway construction was funded out of state revenues in the British protectorates of Perak, Selagnor, Sungei Ujong and in the Straits Settlements. Tied principally to the economic needs of these Malay states, infrastructure development revolved around the prompt movement of tin and later rubber from their source to the nearest coastal port.[41] Political factors delayed the completion of the Singapore-Seremban segment of the main line because the Sultan of Johore believed, rightly as it transpired, that the passage of the rail line through his state would lead to the appointment of a British "Resident" to give advice on the management of economic and political affairs as was the pattern in neighboring sultanates.[42] Less than four years after the last rail was laid, Johore joined the FMS and accepted its first British advisor. Significantly, all rail lines were built to a standard one-meter gauge. Better coordinated than rail development in Java, the FMS railway was designed with the comfort of passengers in mind.[43]

Rail development opened the peninsula to travellers and tourists while tourist travel provided a valuable income supplement for the perennially debt-laden FMS rail network. Cuthbert Harrison's *An Illustrated Guide to the Federated Malay States* (1911) contained copious details about railway routes and fares, an indication that their primary purpose was to generate revenue for Malaya's struggling railway system. A return ticket to Georgetown Penang, including ferry connections at Woodlands Pier and Parit Buntar, was £6 19s 4d, considerably more expensive than the steamer voyage from Singapore to Penang, which in the 1880s cost £2 first class and only £3 by 1910. Travellers on the FMS Railway Department's special nine- or fourteen-day rail tours through the peninsula also needed to meet the cost of overnight accommodation. By the early 1900s both Malaya and Java possessed a network of metalled roads suitable for motor vehicles, an increasingly fashionable mode of transport. Car hire rates in Singapore were between 9 shillings and 14 shillings per day, plus petrol at 1 shilling 9 pence to 2 shilling 4 pence per gallon in 1911. Chauffeurs were an additional optional expense.[44] Motorized travel and a completed rail network spanning the western peninsula opened Singapore, Malacca and Georgetown and their hinterlands to the non-resident "day tripper."

Penetration of the interior was quickly followed by inland resort development, although on a much smaller scale than in Java. Only four notable hill stations evolved in British Malaya, at Penang Hill and the more elevated Fraser's Hill, Maxwell's Hill and the Cameron Highlands.[45] Before the development of peninsular road and rail networks, the only means of access to the interior was by dirt road, jungle tracks and rivers. Tourist facilities were understandably rudimentary, but harsh conditions did not completely dissuade tourists from venturing inland. Tiger and elephant hunting were popular amongst British colonial officials of whom Frederick Weld, Governor of the Straits Settlements between 1880 and 1887, was the most notable.[46] Rest houses, funded by British residents, were built on the fringes of tea and coffee plantations in Perak and Selagnor in the 1880s and available at a fixed tariff of one Straits dollar (S$) per day. By 1911 there were thirty-six such rest houses spread throughout the Federated Malay States charging S$3 per day for board and lodging.[47]

Dusan Tuah was a lowland valley resort complex, fifteen miles outside Kuala Lumpur, the administrative center of the FMS. Located close to mineral springs, Dusan Tuah had by the beginning of the twentieth century developed a reputation as a health spa.[48] The FMS-subsidized two-bungalow complex was marketed for the restorative qualities of its environs to sufferers of rheumatism, skin disease and "fatigue."[49] Guests could bathe in the specially built sulphur baths to which health-giving mineral water was fed from the nearby hot springs. For those of more robust dispositions, swimming and rafting in the Langat River were popular exertions. For the keen shooter, snipe, pigeon and pig could be hunted in nearby rice paddies. Scenic walks, cut into the surrounding jungle, allowed the traveler to savor the restorative tropical rainforest atmosphere.[50] The emergence of such inland tourist resorts in the Archipelago was a further step in the domestication of colonial hinterlands through the transformation of rugged island interiors into playgrounds for the affluent.

As in the Indies, tourism also served the ideological aims of the Malayan colonial state. Official tourist guidebooks claimed that local populations were happy with their lot, content to allow Europeans to govern, while they enjoyed nature's bounty according to their traditions. Exemplifying the tourist guide genre in its assemblage of factual advice and figurative language, Harrison promised excursionists the sight of luxuriant tropical scenery, fascinating animal life and contented "natives," grateful for the British presence. The *Illustrated Guide* exulted in the British "civilizing influence." Brilliant colors, delightful scents and placid colonized peoples were stock-in-trade in many late nineteenth- and early twentieth-century travel narratives and novels in which authors took the "exotic East" as their subject but consciously or unconsciously ignored burdensome questions as to the legitimacy of European colonial empires.[51]

Thirteen months after Admiral Dewey's humiliation of the Spanish Philippine fleet in Manila Harbor in 1898, E&A steamers called into Manila Bay followed closely by ships of the China Navigation Company and the NYK Line. American soldiers quickly acquired a taste for Australian beef. In 1899, Queensland's export trade with the Philippines leapt from zero to £40,313, the bulk of this being realized from sales of frozen meat. Beef exports to the Philippines more than doubled again in 1900 to £106,014 (See table 5.1). Steamers with refrigerated cargo space were now essential to Australian-Philippine trade and, as with shipping to Java and Malaya, paying passengers were a valuable supplementary cargo. Passengers wishing to travel to Manila from Australia could do so direct or, if preferring a more circuitous route, by way of Singapore, transferring to ships of the Norddeutche Lloyd or Blue Funnel Line bound for the Philippines. By 1907 NDL steamers were calling in at Manila en route from Sydney to Hong Kong, becoming the fourth major line to link Australia with this destination.

The American invasion heralded the transformation of the Philippines into, among other things, an Americanized tourist destination with Manila its re-invigorated center of commerce and government. Symbolic of the new colonial power's eagerness to cultivate economic modernity, electric trams were a feature of the cityscape by 1907. The *Manila Times* boasted exclusive hotel accommodation, including the city's very own Waldorf. Most tourist attractions and leisure pastimes were inherited from the Spanish era. Old Spanish churches lay within the "Intramuros," the old walled city that was an attraction in itself, although partly demolished to make way for new public buildings. Paralleling Dutch *Indische* leisure culture, in the evenings Manila's parks echoed with the sounds of brass bands on parade. Beauty spots abounded outside Manila such as at Los Banos on Laguna de Bay, accessible by steamboat along the Pasig River. Travellers with a taste for the sublime could visit Taal Lake, twelve miles overland from Calamba on Laguna de Bay, and view the "inspiring and marvelously unique" Taal Volcano. Steamers belonging to the Philippine government and the U.S. Army made round trips to Zamboanga and the Sulu Archipelago. Tourism in the Philippines, as in European colonies in Asia, was actively encouraged by the colonial state.

Acutely aware that commercial development could be enhanced by improving the colony's attributes of place, Dean Worcester, Philippine Commissioner and Secretary of the Interior from 1900–1913, oversaw the development of tourism infrastructure to international tourists, potential investors and business migrants. Worcester and W. Cameron Forbes, also a member of the Philippine Commission and from 1909-1913 Governor-General of the Philippines, upgraded tourist services and vigorously promoted the creation of an inland capital at Baguio, in northern Luzon. Concerned that long-term exposure to the lowland tropical climate of Manila would be detrimental to the health of Americans, Worcester believed that the temperate climate of Benguet Province would assist their acclimatization to the tropics and speed the process of colonization in the Philippines.[52] Similar reasons lay behind the much earlier relocation of the administrative center of the Netherlands Indies from Batavia to Buitenzorg.[53] The railroad from Manila to Dagupan was extended to within twenty-four miles of Baguio in 1907 and a state-run taxi service introduced to transport visitors and government employees from the railhead to the resort town. Forbes himself built a guesthouse and established the Baguio Country Club. By the 1920s it had grown into a thriving tourist center proclaimed "the Simla of Manila" after the popular hill station in British India.[54]

PACIFIC ASIA TOURS

Shipping activity between Eastern Australia and the Java-Singapore hub never matched the intensity of Australian maritime communications with New Zealand and the South Pacific, but this should not be interpreted as a lack of interest in the Indies, Malaya or the Philippines on the part of Australian commercial elites. Burns Philp was the principal travel company to market the Philippines as a tourist destination in Australia. The company's periodical brochure, *Picturesque Travel under the Auspices of Burns Philp*, promised travellers the sights of "beautiful islets and gardens of coral" as they sailed through the Philippine archipelago. Outside Manila, adventure tours, by then a staple of the tourism industry, gave travelers an experience of the sublime. Canoe trips down Pagsanjan Gorge to its mighty waterfalls brought the latent power of nature within touch, as did excursions to the volcanoes of southern Luzon, where tourists could view, from a safer distance, the tantalizingly active 7,900 foot Mount Mayon. On the island of Panay tourists could take a "picturesque drive" inland from the port of Ilolio, making a circle of eight or nine miles, passing through valleys, along segments of coastline, past mountain ranges, through landscapes studded with tropical trees, flowers, native huts and churches. Implying a taste for American culture, Baguio, by this time the "fun park" of Benguet Province, was singled out for special praise:

> Baguio, 160 miles north of Manila, is a delightful mountain resort, with comfortable hotels, club house, golf links, etc., besides its natural attractions. It is almost entirely American in plan and construction. There is a large amphitheatre of an unusual kind, and other places of amusement.[55]

As on Asian shipping routes, companies operating to New Guinea, the New Hebrides and Fiji also regarded tourists as useful if considered supplementary cargo. Non-tourists were more prevalent in the Pacific Islands, mainly planters, missionaries and government officers going about their business or going on leave or their sons and daughters going to school, and pregnant wives travelling to give birth on the Australian mainland. Copra was the mainstay of Burns Philp's Pacific business, augmented by a thriving agency business, and a Commonwealth subsidy to carry mails to Pacific island ports. With only two steamers on the Sydney-Singapore run in 1918, the bulk of Burns Philp's shipping serviced the arc of islands from New Guinea to Fiji.[56] Indeed, Australian shipping activity was and remains at its most intense at this eastern end of the Archipelago. Yet there were strong commercial incentives to bundle Asian and Pacific tourist services in a tropical island cruise, which could either be consumed as a single travel experience or built into a round-the-world tour. Burns Philp's South Sea Islands route offered travellers the "palm-fringed shores" of the New Hebrides, the "tropical jungles" of North Borneo, the "Ancient Spanish life and customs" of the Philippines, "contrasting with [the] ultra-modern civilization" of an Americanized Manila, to Saigon, "the Paris of the Pacific" and the "junks, sampans and teeming life" of Hong Kong.[57] Not to be outdone, Burns Philp's principal competitor, KPM, introduced cruises through the Indies to Saigon, "primitive" New Guinea and "sunny" Pacific Islands.[58]

The East and the Pacific were promoted in Burns Philp and KPM advertisements as distinct but connected geographical spheres. In the romanticized cultural space of the Philippines and East Indies, potential tourists were enticed by standardized images of an exotic Oriental paradise in which dwelled passive and contented subjects ruled by a benign imperial power. But the generic Asian paradise differed from the generic Pacific island paradise by virtue of the latter's primitiveness. During the nineteenth century the Pacific Islands also acquired a reputation as refuges for social outcasts and as places that could lead to moral and physical dereliction. A similar fate awaited those in search of wealth and dissipation in the eastern Indies of Joseph Conrad's day, but in Asia European vagrancy was hidden behind impressive colonial facades or masked by the colors and sounds of the marketplace. The creation of a new Pacific paradise brand brought about a rehabilitation of the eighteenth-century ideal of the noble savage as a marketable tourist stereotype, appealing to the industrial urge to escape into an authentic world—a state of nature but one where native savagery was restrained under the watchful eye of Western colonialism.[59]

Tourism products for international travellers to Eastern Australasia, British New Guinea, the Solomon Islands and Fiji were largely confined to island pleasure cruises until the interwar period. Australia's assumption of administrative responsibility over the Territory of Papua in 1905 coincided with a modest advertising campaign to encourage travel to New Guinea in the federal government tourist publication, *Australia To-day*.[60] As outposts of colonial tropical industries, moreso than centers of international trade and travel, small White communities catered to localized leisure needs of plantation managers, miners, commercial agents and government staff. A world away from The Raffles and the Hotel de l'Europe, New Guinea hotels, frequently managed by women, and with names such as the Cosmopolitan on the island of Samarai, vied for a share of the local and international leisure trade.[61] Scenery, not service, attracted Western tourists to New Guinea and with limited transport networks available on land, the most convenient way to view Melanesian nature was from the deck of a ship. To Australian residents, however, steamers offered the freedom to escape the tropical heat and return to Australia for a holiday.

The interwar years are seen as the golden age of ocean-going pleasure travel symbolized by the sleek silhouettes of luxury passenger liners, much more spacious and technologically advanced than their puffing and smoking nineteenth-century equivalents. Australia, too, witnessed growth in inbound tourism, and Australian tourist development tended to mirror regional patterns. Remote hill resorts attracted travelers who wished to mark their social distance by holidaying away from the masses. Tropical holidays

were made available closer to home in the Whitsundays where island resorts offered an individualistic alternative to the beach culture then emerging in Australia's coastal cities.[62] Tours through Australia and the surrounding Pacific region were thought to be educative, nation-building/promoting
activities. Published by the Australian National Travel Association, the
Walkabout magazine declared the virtue of tourist travel "so that Australians
and the people of other lands might learn more about the vast Australian
continent and the colorful islands below the equator in the Pacific."[63] Appealing to the eugenic spirit of 1930s Australia, the *Walkabout* proudly
boasted the educational and health benefits of international travel, "the
most successful of outdoor sports," with the potential to "stimulate human
vision and our powers of observation, enriching our experience, but it
should also regulate imagination by reality."[64]

Yet travellers caught a glimpse of a new era in international mobility
shortly before the outbreak of the Pacific War with the advent of international commercial airlines. Regular commercial air services were pioneered
in New Guinea in the 1930s to meet the needs of inland mining companies
and communities. International air services soon followed with a service
connecting Sydney and Rabaul.[65] Beginning with the Royal Netherlands Indies's Airways (KNILM) twice-weekly service from Batavia to Sydney in
1938, Australian encounters with the Indies acquired a new angle of elevation. The KNLIM boasted that its inaugural flight out of Sydney was fully
subscribed one week before take-off. As with the advent of steamshipping,
airlines responded to demands for faster mail and passenger services, further quickening the rate of international communication. KNILM promised
Sydneysiders the satisfaction of "dinner in Darwin, luncheon in Bali, then
Batavia for dinner," all in the space of two days at a cost of £66 10 shilling,
the equivalent of a first-class return ticket aboard a KPM steamer.[66] The new
service spurred the QANTAS Empire Airways to establish its own flying boat
service from Sydney to Singapore. Such was the demand for the service that
QANTAS doubled its passenger lists and freight load between 1939 and
1941.[67] Tragically, the Pacific War brought home the geostrategic implications of this radical technological shift.

The globalization of maritime travel opened the Archipelago to Australasian tourism. New Guinea, Java, Singapore and Manila became primary
destinations for growing numbers of Australian business travellers and
pleasureseekers. As the increasing sophistication of international transport
and commercial linkages drew Australia into closer contact with the Indies,
Malaya, the Philippines and Siam, Australia became timetabled into its region. Inspired by the promotional genius of British travel agent Thomas
Cook, travel became a socially acceptable nineteenth-century leisure pursuit. For leisure-rich "nomads of affluence," the *nouveau-riche* of the industrial age from Melbourne, Sydney, Brisbane, even Charters Towers, exotic

travel allowed for the conspicuous consumption of place that served as a marker of social status. These cultural consumption patterns remain an unaccounted for item in the shifting balance of exchange between Australia and Asia in the late nineteenth and early twentieth centuries.

NOTES

1. Eric Hobsbawm, *The Age of Capital, 1848–1875* (London: Abacus, 1985), 63, 78.

2. A. G. Hopkins, "History of Globalization," 29.

3. *Brisbane Courier*, September 26, 1874.

4. *Straits Times*, April 19, 1897.

5. *Straits Times*, December 19, 1900.

6. Hobsbawm, *Age of Capital*, 362. Blainey, *Tyranny of Distance*, 207–8.

7. Blainey, *Tyranny of Distance*. 180–81. Robin Craig, *The Ship: Steam tramps and cargo liners, 1850–1950*, (London: National Maritime Museum, 1980), 11.

8. The Australian Handbook and Almanac and Shippers and Importers Directory for 1875, (Melbourne: Gordon and Gotch, 1875), 314.

9. The *Queenslander*, December 20, 1873. *Straits Times*, September 5, 1873

10. These statistics are taken from the BI passenger lists published in the *Brisbane Courier*, January 1–December 31, 1881. *Brisbane Courier*, January 1–December 31, 1882.

11. John Malcolm Brinnin, *The Sway of the Grand Saloon: A Social History of the North Atlantic* (New York: Delacorte Press, 1971), 236–44.

12. Basil Greenhill and Anne Giffard, *Travelling by Sea in the Nineteenth Century: Interior Design in Victorian Passenger ships* (London: Adam and Charles Black, 1972), 41.

13. *Brisbane Courier*, April 26, 1881.

14. Hobsbawm, *Age of Capital*, 278.

15. *North Queensland Register*, October 10, 1894.

16. Dyster and Meredith, *International Economy*, 36.

17. *Townsville Herald*, February 7, 1891.

18. The *Queenslander*, September 15, 1900.

19. J. A. Campo, "Steam Navigation and State Formation," in *The Late Colonial State in Indonesia: Political and Economic Foundations of the Netherlands Indies 1880–1942*, ed. Robert Cribb (Leiden: KITLV Press, 1994), 19–21.

20. *North Queensland Herald*, January 1–December 31, 1910 and January 1–December 31, 1911.

21. *Sydney Morning Herald*, August 11, 1902.

22. *Picturesque Travel under the Auspices of Burns Philp and Company, Ltd.*, No. 3, 1913, (Sydney: Burns Philp and Company, 1912), 108–12.

23. White, *On Holidays*, 56–65.

24. Details of fares, routes travelled and special offers sourced from Gordon and Gotch almanacs, *Picturesque Travel* and the shipping pages of the *Brisbane Courier*, *Straits Times*, *Sydney Morning Herald* and *Queenslander*.

25. Wildey, *Australasia*, 160. *North Queensland Herald*, February 13, 1895. Susan Abeyasekere, *Jakarta: A History* (Oxford: Oxford University Press, 1989), 71–75. Savage, *Western Impressions*, 160–169.

26. *Brisbane Courier*, May 23, 1874.

27. *Straits Times*, August 8, 1903.

28. William Basil Worsfold, *A Visit to Java with an Account of the Founding of Singapore* (London: Richard Bentley and Son, 1893), 32–35. Henry Copeland, *A Few Weeks with the Malays* (Singapore: Straits Times Press, 1883), 7, *Straits Times*, March 12, 1903. Augusta De Wit, *Facts and Fancies about Java*, (London: Luzac and Co, 1900), 18–19.

29. *North Queensland Register*, February 13 & 20, 1895. Worsfold, *Visit to Java*, 35. De Wit, *Facts and Fancies*, 18–27.

30. Benedict Anderson, *Imagined Communities: Reflections on the Origin and Spread of Nationalism* (New York: Verso, 2nd edition, 1991), 179–82.

31. Worsfold, *Visit to Java*, iii. Worsfold explicitly states that his book was aimed at Australian readers.

32. J. A. R. Pimlott, *The Englishman's Holiday: A Social History* (London: Faber and Faber, 1947), 202–4.

33. Robert R. Reed, "Remarks on the Colonial Genesis of the Hill Station in Southeast Asia with Particular Reference to the Cities of Buitenzorg (Bogor) and Baguio," *Asian Profile*, (vol. 4, no. 6, December 1976), 558.

34. *Straits Times*, August 17, 1897.

35. *Java the Wonderland*, (Weltevereden NEI: Official Tourist Bureau, c. 1907), 40–49. Worsfold, *Visit to Java*, 102. *Straits Times*, August 17, 1897 & April 6, 1904.

36. *Straits Times*, April 26, 1911. Geoffrey C. Bolton, "Angelo, Edward Houghton, 1870–1948," *ADB*, (vol. 3, 1891–1939), 70.

37. Isabella Bird, *The Golden Chersonese and the Way Thither* (London: Century, 1983), 107.

38. Walter Makepeace, Gilbert E. Brooke, Roland St. John Braddell (eds) *One Hundred Years of Singapore*, Volume II (London: John Murray, 1921), 323–81. Alister Macmillan, *Seaports of the Far East*, (London: W. H. L. Collridge, 2nd edition, 1925), 436. *Straits Times*, August 15, 1901.

39. Charles Allen, *Tales from the South China Seas: Images of the British in South-East Asia in the Twentieth Century* (London: Futura, 1983), 65–75.

40. *Straits Times*, September 20, 1902, June 4, 1903, April 8 & May 17, 1904, February 28, 1911. C. Mary Turnbull, *A History of Singapore: 1819–1975* (London: Oxford University Press, 1977), 95–96, 118.

41. Chai Hon Chan, *The Development of British Malaya* (London: Oxford University Press, 2nd edition, 1967), 170–71, 194.

42. Barbara W. Andaya and Leonard Y. Andaya, *A History of Malaysia* (London: Macmillan, 1987), 198–200.

43. Frank A. Swettenham, *British Malaya* (London: John Lane, 1907), 281.

44. *Straits Times*, September 9, 1883. Cuthbert Woodville Harrison, *An Illustrated Guide to the Federated Malay States* (London: The Malay States Information Agency, 1911), i, 209–10, 311.

45. Reed, "Remarks," 562. J. E. Spencer and W. I. Thomas, "The Hill Stations and Summer Resorts of the Orient," *Geographical Review*, vol. 38, 1948, 642–45.

46. Copeland, A *Few Weeks*, 24.

47. Harrison, *Illustraed Guide*, 304.

48. *Straits Times*, February 2, 1904.

49. Harrison, *Illustrated Guide*, 100–101.

50. *Straits Times*, February 2, 1904.

51. Savage, *Western Impressions*, 203–16.

52. Rodney Sullivan, *Exemplar of Americanism: The Philippine Career of Dean C. Worcester* (Michigan: Center for South and Southeast Asian Studies, University of Michigan, 1991), 3, 143–46.

53. Reed, "Remarks," 556–59.

54. *Picturesque Travel under the Auspices of Burns Philp and Company, Ltd.* (Sydney: Burns Philp and Co., 1920), 63–64.

55. *Picturesque Travel*, 63.

56. Ken Buckley and Kris Klugman, *The Australian Presence in the Pacific: Burns Philp, 1914–1946* (Sydney: Allen and Unwin, 1983), 57, 64--67.

57. *Walkabout*, December 1, 1937.

58. *Walkabout*, November 1, 1934.

59. K. R. Howe, *Nature, Culture, and History: The Knowing of Oceania*, (Honolulu: University of Hawai'i Press, 2000), 12–23.

60. "Papua," *Australia To-day*, December 15, 1905, 6–7.

61. Jill Nash, "Paternalism, Progress, Paranoia: Patrol Reports and Colonial History in South Bouganville," in *In Colonial New Guinea: Anthropological Perspectives*, ed. Naomi McPherson (Pittsburgh: University of Pittsburgh Press, 2001), 138–40.

62. White, *On Holidays*, 90–96. Todd Barr, *No Swank Here: The Development of the Whitsundays as a Tourist Destination to the Early 1970s* (Townsville: James Cook University of North Queensland, 1990), 12–17.

63. *Walkabout*, April 1, 1935.

64. *Walkabout*, March 1, 1935.

65. Nelson, *Taim Bilong Masta*,15.

66. *Walkabout*, July 1, 1938.

67. John Gunn, *Challenging Horizons: QANTAS, 1939–1954* (Brisbane: University of Queensland Press, 1987), 8, 18–19, 42.

4

'The Whole Thing Is Very Motley Oriental'

AUSTRALIAN EXPERIENCES OF PEOPLE
AND PLACE IN THE ISLANDS

Both the lived and the remembered experience of the Archipelago altered the geographical perspective of those Australians who ventured north each year, numbering in the hundreds by the 1880s and rising to a few thousand in the decade before World War I. For London-bound saloon passengers who endured enforced stopovers at Asian coaling ports, the region's physical and cultural landscapes were little more than a fleeting if engaging novelty. However, for a large intrepid minority, traveling the Archipelago in search of riches, excitement, spontaneity or refuge, the worlds beyond northern Australia held special attractions. Commercial travelers, prospectors, scientific explorers, photographers, theatrical troupes, and holidaymakers from towns and cities as far apart as Charters Towers and Perth sojourned in Asian emporia where they experienced the exotic "East" at close quarters. Reactions were as diverse as the travelers who recorded their experiences of departure and arrival and their impressions of different peoples and places. Australian travelers relished their role as mediators of new knowledge created through their encounters with strange cultures, histories and landscapes, as much as constructed by their cultural inheritance. Through these interactions a vast geographical space was given form, its physical and cultural distance gauged and contextualized for Australians through Australian eyes.

CIRCULATION

Every Australian traveler to the Archipelago brought home cultural souvenirs in the form of observations, usually prejudiced, of local customs, manners, dress, food and of course, tropical scenery and scents. These intangible items of Australasian exchange were frequently deemed sufficiently newsworthy to warrant reproduction in the popular press. From May to September 1874 the *Brisbane Courier* ran a weekly series of travel articles detailing the tourist attractions of Asia. Written by a self-styled British-Australian who, for unspecified reasons, chose to keep his identity secret, the articles were placed to encourage Australian travel to Asia aboard E&A steamers sailing the Torres Strait route to Singapore. A British-born "Asia-hand," the enigmatic DB, or DD as he signed himself in his later articles, spent ten years running sheep in the Riverina district before taking a holiday trip to Java and Singapore in 1866. Beginning with his voyage across the Arafura Sea to Samarang aboard the *Souchays*, he assembled disparate travel experiences into a narrative of a single journey through Java, Singapore, Manila and Hong Kong. Embellished with extracts from prominent scholarly studies of history, culture and society, DB stories dramatized both himself and his subjects in a narrative laced with English pastoral motifs transposed onto oriental tropical idylls. Beyond self-dramatization and commercial inducements, DB sought to redirect the geographical focus of his readers towards Asia.

Australian exploits registered in both the Australian and regional print media. Henry Copeland traveled with his nephew to Malaya in 1882 to explore the British mining frontiers of Malaya and Lower Burma. Assuming a natural right of passage for Australian commerce through the vital sea-lanes of the Archipelago, he envisaged a network of steamshipping services and railways that would one day span Australasia and British India. This vision undoubtedly encouraged him to expand his private business interests beyond the frontier of his modest mining empire to the Malay Peninsula and Burma. Penned retrospectively on his return voyage to Australia, Copeland's impressions of the region, and valuable commercial intelligence, were serialized for the *Sydney Morning Herald* and the *Straits Times* in 1883, and then collated into a pamphlet by the Straits Times Press the following year.[1]

Copeland was one of many Australian travelers who combined mineral exploration with excursions to sights of natural and historical significance. Such was the depth of mining experience in Australia that mining expertise quickly developed into a significant knowledge export to Asia. The Reverend Julian Edmund Tenison-Woods, Catholic priest, educator and respected authority on geology, zoology and palaeontology, left Brisbane in August 1883 on what became a three-year "grand tour" of the Netherlands Indies and Malaya. Such was the level of public interest in his expeditions that his travel experiences were relayed second-hand through staff reporters at the *Straits Times* and *Brisbane Courier*. Tenison-Woods completed two mineralogical surveys of the Malay Peninsula at the invitation of Governor of the Straits Settlements Frederick Weld, a former governor of Western Australia and Tasmania, the first in 1883 and the second in 1885.[2] Even if formulated and contained within an Anglo-Celtic bureaucratic milieu, these imperial connections were no less important in drawing Australians into Asia—not least because they paved the way for Australian tourism and business investment.

Writing on gold exploration in New Guinea, Hank Nelson noted that "prospectors and miners were the foreigners most likely to go beyond the beaches."[3] Australian-owned mines became tourist attractions of a kind, drawing Australian investors into Malayan hinterlands to view the extent of their exposure to financial risk. The Raub Australian gold mine, founded by north Queensland mining personality Robert Sefton between October 1888 and June 1889, became one such celebrated attraction. Following a familiar pattern in Australian mineral exploration in Asia, Sefton allocated shares to two local Malay rajahs with claims to some derelict Chinese mine workings at Raub on the Pahang River, thereby outwitting angry British mining investors in Singapore. The Raub "discovery" attracted such public interest in Queensland that stories of the mine featured in the *Brisbane Telegraph* and the *Townsville Herald* throughout 1889. Accessible only by an arduous overland route from Port Kelang on the west coast, the Raub mine drew many eminent visitors in its early years, all members of or associated closely with the Brisbane-based Raub Australia Syndicate. Thomas Brown, Queensland grazier and mining entrepreneur, accompanied Robert Sefton on his return trip to Pahang in January 1889.[4] Interviewed some nine months later by the *Brisbane Telegraph*, Brown posed as a heroic adventurer, braving the Malayan jungle in imperial style at the head of an entourage of thirty-five Malay bearers.[5] As with Australian miners in New Guinea, Brown relished his role as *masta*, or in the Malay context, *tuan*, for the fleeting experience of power but equally so for the opportunity it afforded to wrap his adventure holiday experience in the romantic narrative of pioneer exploration.

Colonial adventure literature, a genre most commonly associated with the work of British novelist Rudyard Kipling was hugely popular in Australia well into the twentieth century.[6] Jungle adventure treks were thus understandably prominent topics in the self-dramatizing tales relayed to the Australian public by Queensland businessmen visiting the Raub. Hume Black, MLA for Mackay, and newly elected board member of the Raub Australia Syndicate, visited in 1891, following in Brown's footsteps but without such an impressive entourage.[7] There were many hundreds of prospectors, sailors, entertainers and other itinerant workers who ventured north from Australia in search of fortune and adventure, many in steerage for a few days, a few months or for more than one year. Somewhat lower on Queensland's social ladder than his contemporaries, Edward Downes, resident of

Townsville and self-proclaimed North Queenslander, spent thirteen months as a whaling hand aboard the *Costa Rica Packet*, much of it in the Moluccas. Recorded in a diary, later edited and undoubtedly supplemented, his experiences were serialized in the *Townsville Herald* between October 20, 1888 and April 20, 1889. Visiting every major port in the eastern islands, Downes, an admirer of Dutch colonial rule, spent his time ashore in the Moluccas sightseeing and prospecting for gold—such was the piecemeal fashion in which much Australian mineral exploration occurred in the Archipelago. Unlike Tenison-Woods, who had the resources of the Governor of the Straits Settlements at his disposal, Downes, like many hundreds of his Australian contemporaries, was an independent prospector. Digging their way eastward through the Louisiade Archipelago towards New Guinea and beyond, with and by whatever means they could find, their encounters with local populations were not mediated by comfortable spatial distance—they were immediate, face-to-face, tense and sometimes brutal.

In some cases leisure rather than business set the itineraries of Australian mining personalities traveling into the Indies. The Australasian mining connection led William Mowbray, Commissioner for Mineral Lands at Charters Towers, on a four-month holiday tour of Asia in early 1894. "The World," as the modest people of Charters Towers nicknamed their town, was then a major Queensland gold-mining center with a population approaching 25,000 people. Escaping dry, dusty streets, and the relentless pounding of the crushing mills, Mowbray was destined for Java, Sulawesi, Singapore, Malaya, Siam, Hong Kong, China and Japan, returning to Australia by way of Calcutta. True to the principles of outback practicality and bourgeois respectability, the trip was to be part recreation and part fact-finding tour of Asia's mineral resources and mining industries. After seeing Batavia, Mowbray planned a one-month stay in Surabaya with William Jack, and a visit to Jack's gold mine as part of an excursion to the eastern Archipelago with the NISM before moving on to Singapore and mainland Asia. Jack, like many associated with Australasian mining ventures, made the Archipelago his temporary home, commuted often between Queensland and Sulawesi and, according to Mowbray, assumed the role of guardian and guide for Australians making their first voyage beyond the "top end."[8] "New chum travelers" benefited from the advice of an "old hand" and cultural intermediary, but for those Australian entrepreneurs engaged in business in the Archipelago, it was crucial that they quickly learned how to work across cultural divides.

Expatriate lifestyles varied as widely as did experiences and impressions. While trading relations tended to be impersonal and distant, usually conducted at arm's length through intermediaries, capital investment entailed extended residence by Australian business and engineering professionals in mining areas and industrial centers. After the first pioneering wave of exploration, New Guinea, Sulawesi, Ceram, Malaya and southern Siam became second homes for Australian mine managers and their families. This entailed acceptance of a degree of personal danger by family members. Raub manager William Bibby, and his family were exposed to a simmering revolt in Pahang, ignited by the extension of British influence along the Pahang River. To the Queensland press Bibby epitomized the masculine Australian ideal of scientific practicality now engaged in the task of taming the Malayan jungle.

The jungle, like the Australian bush, was for city-dwellers a place of great beauty but also danger. Wild beasts roamed the Malayan rainforests, sometimes entering the urban fringe to the alarm of those unprepared for encounters with untamed nature. Attitudes towards the dangers of the natural environment differed according to experience and location. As in New Guinea and on the Australian mainland, frontier life gave women added opportunities to cast off their assigned roles of dutiful and dependent wife or daughter.[9] Nellie and Edie Bibby escaped the strictures of Victorian society, and the boredom of life at the Raub mine, venturing unescorted through Pahang and Terengganu. Although the independent lady traveler was by then an accepted social type, their journey caused more than a ripple of interest in polite Singapore society. Those Australians who inhabited the interior bore out, or so it would seem, the belief that the Australian type was tougher and better acclimatized than the British to life in the tropics.

For Ida Kalenski, however, the life of a society lady in Singapore was infinitely more desirable than that of a miner's wife on the Malayan tin fields. Moving from India to a bungalow overlooking the Strait of Malacca, she and her husband, a Brisbane businessman sent to supervise the construction of a cold storage works on behalf of the Queensland Meat Export & Agency Company, lived in the Straits Settlements for two years.[10] Serialized in the *Queenslander*, her vignettes of home life and holiday excursions, which she was at pains to stress were not those of a mere tourist, offered insights through Australian eyes into everyday life in Singapore at the beginning of the last century. Illustrating familiarity with Australasian playgrounds for the affluent, Asia-related holiday tales appeared with greater regularity than might be expected in this Brisbane news and lifestyle weekly. As more Australians took up temporary residence in Malaya, so the idea of a Malayan holiday became attractive to friends and relatives. One such early Australasian VFR tourist, a Miss Townley from Queensland, recorded her weekend experiences of a motoring excursion to Dusan Tuah for the same publication, replete with holiday snaps and narrative spun with romantic images of picturesque tropical nature.[11] The travel narratives of Kalenski and Townley conveyed images of Oriental domesticity and of a domesticated Orient.

A consequence of the growth of Australasian business interactions, booklength Australian traveller's tales addressing Australian audiences began to appear. Confident, self-assertive and well-educated, elite members of

Australia's mining fraternity were among the more prominent authors. Herbert Pratten's *Asiatic Impressions: A Collection of Articles by H. E. Pratten* (1908) and *Through Orient to Occident* (1911) examined the "Oriental character" as manifest in the social and economic life of the Malay Peninsula and the "Far East." The Archipelago was for Pratten a transitory space, memorable largely for the achievements of Australian mining enterprise. Practical travelers like Pratten and his contemporary Thomas J. McMahon, concerned themselves with weighty topics: commerce, politics, military affairs, and "national character" Writing on the theme of Asia's "awakening," both authors emphasized the present and future importance of Asia to Australia. In *The Orient I Found* (1926) McMahon's account of his travels through the Philippines to Japan and China was intended to awaken Australians from their ignorance and complacency about major economic and geopolitical shifts occurring in the Pacific.[12] MacMahon added to the growing number of voices warning of a Japanese threat to Australian interests in the Archipelago and at home. Both he and Pratten, as did other practical men of regional affairs, appreciated that the European colonial order would not last forever.

According to Helen Car, "All travel writing is a form of autobiography."[13] Some wrote their autobiographical accounts with greater authority and style than others whose literary work was confined to the production of one or more newspaper articles. Ambrose Pratt entered an exclusive group of Melbourne mining investors with interests in southern Siam in the 1920s. Born in 1874 into a family with a tradition of adventuring in Asia, he was nursed as a child by a Chinese *amah* at his family's comfortable Tamworth home in the country of New South Wales. Pratt's upbringing and family background gave him an open and inquisitive mind, and a fascination for Asian cultures.[14] He was a prolific novelist, journalist and vocal public commentator who wrote copious manuscripts, published and unpublished, based on impressions formed during business visits to Malaya, China and especially Siam. Although attached to the cause of White Australia in his younger days, his travel experiences and interest in Asia gradually altered his perception of Australia's relationship to its region. Pratt's shifting views and ideals exemplify the tensions and contradictions in Australian travel writing about Asia.

DEPARTURES AND ARRIVALS

The significance of tourism should not be measured simply in terms of ship or airline passenger numbers. Travel narratives, although comprised of the edited memories of lived, imagined, and sometimes vicarious experience, serve as points of contact not just with the writer's imagination but the world of popular ideas. Even the most fragmentary accounts by Australian travellers of their journeys in Asia offer insights into their cultural inheritance but also, in many cases, an occasional willingness to challenge stereotypical ideas in an era of rising economic engagement with Australia's near Orient. All travellers are challenged in some way by their overseas experiences. Movement between different cultural spaces engenders emotional reactions in the traveller, which can lead to a retreat into expatriate enclaves or the security of fellow travellers, or stimulate an interest in new places and new cultural experiences. In a state of heightened self-awareness, or mindfulness, more open-minded travellers strive to understand new cultural markers, new and physical landscapes, relying upon idealized familiar worlds as their point of reference—their familiar world back home.[15]

Inherited modes of interpretation, worldviews and frames of reference do not prevent individual reformulation of cultural influences at the level of experience or praxis. Nineteenth-century Australian travel narratives reflected the extent to which received cultural ideas furnished the Australian imagination with imagery and explanations of race. However, the parallel migration to Australia of British modes of knowing and expressing a sense of place, of British race pride, and a barely suppressed imperial covetousness, does not mean that all Australian impressions of Asia were purely derivative.[16]

Journeys create openings for cultural divides to be crossed even where there is no wish to transcend class or race. Victor and Edith Turner, drawing upon the work of Arnold van Gennep, asserted that people moving away from their everyday world pass through several transitions as they strive to come to terms with the loss of the familiar. Travellers enter a liminal state brought about by their awareness of exposure to uncertain dangers and potential social isolation. Quickly seeking new acquaintances, travellers develop feelings of communitas with others likewise removed or separated from home.[17] Turner argued that the desire for security, a major concern for persons entering unfamiliar worlds fraught with uncertainty, can lead to a breaching of conventions that force people to maintain social distance in order to reduce feelings of vulnerability.[18]

Amidst descriptions of sights and sounds, Australian experiences of place and space exhibited traces of vulnerability and of heightened mindfulness. Travelling to Asia for the first time, Australians crossed many boundaries, both physical and cultural. DB observed "a far wider space than the Arafura Sea separates us and them," implying that the geographical divide between Australia and the Archipelago was also a moral and cultural frontier.[19] Some expressed a sense of misgiving as they passed the outer markers of home—not their imagined British cultural homeland or birthplace but their lived-in Australian space of reassuring daily routines and familiar symbols.

Copeland felt a definite break with his familiar world when crossing the geographical divide between Australia and the Archipelago:

> Having availed ourselves of the two-penny postage for the last time, and spent
> the balance of our small coin, we clear from Thursday Island, feeling a genuine
> regret at leaving Australia behind us, for how long or short a period fate alone
> could decide.[20]

At sea, the curvature of the earth's surface combines with the absence of peripheral detail to distort perception of distance and shape. Viewed from the
promenade deck, the Australian coastline was noted for its flatness and mo-
notony, save for the coral islets of the Great Barrier Reef and the mountains
north of Townsville. Cast adrift in an unknown world, first-time travellers
nonetheless noticed a perceptible transformation of the land and seascape
as they crossed the Arafura Sea. Somewhere across the horizon between
Cape York and Bali travellers sensed, vaguely at first, a division between
Australia and Asia. Striking visual impressions of towering volcanoes and
lush vegetation combined with olfactory images of tropical spices to convey
the essence of DB's magical and sensuous East:

> Still, though not subdued into awe at the sight of these Asiatic shores, we were
> indeed enchanted at the scene as we sailed past beautiful islands. A sparkling
> sea, a clear atmosphere, bright heaven above us, and indeed everywhere
> around us the air rich and fragrant with the "Sabean odours" which came
> wafted to us from "spicy groves of Araby be blessed", lofty mountains in
> the distance, palm groves rising out of the richest vegetation, here and there
> skimming along with all the airy grace of living things, all this we saw passing
> before us an endless panorama in a blissful vision.[21]

Many evocative images greeted Australians as they crossed the Wallace Line. It
became the convention for travellers to register a response to repugnant or seductive smells, and to admire the abundantly "rich vegetation," as they passed
through the portals of Asia. Australian travel writing, despite embellishment,
borrowing and the possibility of total fraudulence, nonetheless offered frag-
ments of the experience of those Australians who crossed this geographical
and moral frontier. Some like DB claimed the mantle of literary traveller and
sought to emulate more distinguished British forbears. Others, like Mowbray,
captured the atmosphere of the approach to Asia with a much less pretentious
appeal to shared experience. Acknowledging his readers' familiarity with the
geography of his adventure zone, Mowbray wrote,

> The course through the Arafura Sea, the Water Pass, and the Sea of Flores, have
> so often been followed and described by Charters Towers travelers that any de-
> scription by me would be superfluous, however, we are today coasting up the
> northern shores of Flores with a fresh cool breeze, a full sail, a little spray dash-

ing over our decks, flying fish fluttering over the light sea, an occasional whale blowing in the offing, and the light smoke from a still smoldering volcano sometimes visible in the dim distance.[22]

Volcanoes, rising out of the shimmering horizon, were salient topographical details and usually the first signs of land observable from aboard ship. Brooding in the distance, they symbolized nature's latent power, notoriously unleashed at Krakatoa in 1883. New landscapes were quickly followed by the appearance of markers of new sociocultural terrain. From the comfort of their gilded traveling palaces, travellers noticed the appearance of new cultural markers. Copeland noted the "curious" lateen sails of Chinese junks that indicated the presence of a "strange people."[23] Temporarily ashore at Banyuwangi, Copeland noted the telegraph cable linking Australia to Britain surfaced at this point with the remark that he felt he had "a few shares in the place." For Copeland and many others for whom Asia was their destination, disembarkation was the beginning of a journey of self-discovery that, even for the British-born, revealed a greater depth of attachment to Australia that Australian histories admit.

The sense of sociocultural distance varied widely within a single geographical space. Copeland and nephew were detained in Java for six days awaiting a connection to Singapore. From the Hotel des Indes the pair walked through the streets of Weltevereden to view the stylish "turn-outs" of Batavian high society. An uncomfortable afternoon's riding through the cacophonous streets of Batavia in an overcrowded horse-drawn tram left them with a craving to escape the sprawling, crowded, and unsanitary city. The English traveller Basil Worsfold remarked that Australians in Batavia eventually, usually after a week, headed for Buitenzorg to escape the humidity.[24] True to Worsfold's generalization, the highlight of Copeland's island sojourn was a two-day rail excursion into the cooler climes of the Preanger Hills to Buitenzorg and Sukabumi. Racing through the countryside at twenty miles per hour, each had time to absorb the spectacle of terraced paddy fields arrayed before them in luxuriant shades of green. At the Buitenzorg markets, Copeland and some acquaintances experimented with chewing betel, the nut of the Areca palm, which is used as a mild stimulant throughout South East Asia, with no apparent effect. Adjustment to new landscapes was relatively easy, but changes in diet were much harder to digest. Recalling their introduction to the culinary delight of *rijsttavel*, Copeland wrote,

Here is a mass of heterogenous matter which any respectable pig would refuse to take on board; nevertheless, the customs of the country must be adhered to, so we deliberately fall to, and with the aid of lager beer ultimately succeed in discovering the bottom of the plate; but when this operation had been repeated twice a day for three or four days, our stomachs organized a strike, and point blank refused to load up with Dutch curry.[25]

Less concerned with personal comfort, and thankful to escape the stench and routine of life aboard a whaling boat, Downes was willing to appreciate local life ways. Celebrating the memory of his first "delicious" taste of rice table at the Bacan Plantation, he claimed that the meal was "enough to tempt a North Queenslander to sell his birth right and turn Dutch Indian."[26] But the transitoriness of the tourist stopover experience usually militated against such ready acceptance of new cultural tastes. Even some who stayed for a longer holiday found the Indies experience taxing. Hotel food and the unsanitary smells exuding from Batavia's canal system were major concerns for Australian tourists in Java in the 1880s. Dutch hospitality moved one anonymous Queensland tourist to make his complaints public. Writing for the *Brisbane Courier* about his travel experiences, the traveler complained,

> These Eastern hotels don't suit me. I have not had a good "square feed" since leaving the ship. Everything is so scrappy; breakfast is a delusion—the eggs must be boiled in cold water, indeed overnight—for they are always cold. Breakfast is from 7 to 8. I have been down sharp at 7, and found the eggs stone cold . . . The cooking is execrable at this place. At Buitenzorg it is a little better than either in Surabaya or Batavia, but between each course you have plenty of time for a nap.[27]

Downes aside, Australian dietary preferences proved resistant to the enticements of Asian cuisine. The exotic diversity of Asia's social landscapes, often vividly depicted and contrasted with those of home, proved much more palatable. Even travellers from the multiracial north of Australia were moved to acknowledge the visual diversity of cultural styles in Batavia and Singapore. The liminal experience was intoxicating, deepening traveller impressions of teeming masses, myriad cultures, added to the lexicon of topographical markers of Australasia in the Australian imaginative landscape. A heady mixture of vibrant colors and the seeming disorderliness of Batavia's business quarter greeted Mowbray on his first foray into the Dutch colonial capital:

> The first thing that struck a new chum traveler like myself was the wonderful variety of costumes people were arrayed in . . . Crowds of Javanese, Malays, Arabs, Chinese, and Hindoos [sic] thronged the narrow streets of the old town . . . dressed in all colours, vivid green, red, yellow, blue and white, turbans, caftans, sarangs [sic] and pyjamas, and bare feet or sandals only.[28]

Approaching Singapore, Copeland remarked that the island rivaled parts of Sydney Harbor for beautiful scenery, though he noted that once ashore in this Asian port city all similarities ended. Tourist impressions of Asia's cosmopolitan diversity were standard fare, with the image of the thronging marketplace serving as a microcosm of Asia. Singapore was by the time of DB's visit a bustling regional entrepot or business hub, intoxicating in its colors, shapes and sounds, especially for travellers used to the subtler pastel shades of the Australian bush and the predominantly white Anglo-Celtic complexion of Australian urban social landscapes. Situated on the Esplanade, the Hotel de l'Europe was ideally placed for tours of the city docks, Commercial Square and Singapore's residential districts. It also offered spectacular views of the harbor. Laid out before the Australian traveller's inquisitive gaze were port and roadstead that echoed Singapore's commercial success:

> You see ships from all parts of the world, from the indominable [sic] iron-clad to the frolicking sampan. Everything almost in the shape of a boat or a ship, everything that moves on the face of the water from the spidery catamaran to the graceful screw liner of the Messageries Maritimes, may be seen there.[29]

Whether viewed at a safe distance or at close quarters, Australian travellers did not recoil from Asia's cultural diversity. Yet as observers, Australians elevated themselves to a position of superiority over lower racial orders, indicated in the use of animal and insect metaphors to convey impressions of mass movement. This is exemplified in DB's description of the bustling small craft of Malay and Chinese traders, whose movements across the harbor mirrored the City's entrepreneurial mood:

> Boats of all kinds swarm like—mites—we will say. There must be at least four or five hundred of them always on the move with appropriate sounds and gesticulations. Probably they are not all quite so graceful as the Venetian gondolas, but they are a deal, oh a deal more lively; and they have all sorts of things on board—fruit and vegetables, parrots and monkeys.[30]

CLIMATE, PLACE AND RACE

The Australian cultural inheritance manifested itself in the aesthetic appreciation of architecture and nature and in the interpretation of cultural differences. Traces of romantic and neoclassical taste appear in the expressive landscapes of Australian travel narratives, betraying aspirations for picturesque rural simplicity, social order and tranquility. Visitors from a dry country, Australians gazed in wonder upon tropical nature in comparison to which, as William Brackley Wildey lamented to his readers, "The richest vegetation in Australia . . . is but arid and barren."[31] Touring the agricultural districts outside Batavia Mowbray delighted in the elimination of "useless" jungle by Javanese cultivators and its replacement with fruit-bearing "economic trees," yet appreciated the ascetic virtue of gracefully manicured environs of the Governor-General's Palace at Buitenzorg,[32] To the minds of Western travelers in Asia, nature could be improved, ordered and made more productive at the hands of colonial powers. But nature also possessed a violent though usually latent power that could never be tamed. Many Australians were inspired by the sublime grandeur of towering volcanoes, often shrouded by clouds of sulphuric vapor. Copeland, in keeping with the romantic tendency to invest the natural landscape with human qualities, mused upon the potency of nature manifest in the "gently sleeping" volcano, Gunung Salak, visible from his balcony at the Hotel Belle Vue, Buitenzorg.[33] A traveller immersed in the practicalities of business and geology, Copeland, like many other practical men from the Australian colonies, often reached for poetic language to articulate his thoughts and sentiments.

The traveller observed and pondered upon the power of nature almost at every turn. Ruins held a particular fascination because they offered halting reminders of the precariousness of civilization, and of the inevitability of decay.[34] For Australians yet to make the pilgrimage to Britain and ignorant of an indigenous heritage at home, ancient religious sites provided their first encounter with significant cultural achievements not fashioned by British or European hand. Following the overland route to Batavia from Banyuwangi, Tenison-Woods stopped to gaze upon the Hindu temples of the Dieng Plateau and the partially, at that time, reconstructed Buddhist shrine of Borobudur which served, he believed, as poignant reminders of a long-lost "high civilization" of Indian origin.[35]

Relics of a more recent era were found in Malacca where Francis Xavier's crumbling cathedral evoked solemn reflection upon the orderliness brought by Christian colonization. The peninsula lacked the Hindu and Buddhist architectural heritage of Java but in Malacca, the city's European Roman Catholic past dominated the landscape. Excited by the sight of remnants of a familiar cultural sphere in an otherwise alien Orient, Tenison-Woods marveled that "the whole place teems with ruins."[36] For the inquisitive visitor, the experience of the picturesque was enhanced through reference to officially sanctioned scholarly works such as one I. Groneman's *The Hindu Ruins in the Plain of Parambanan*, recommended by the Indies tourist bureau. Guidebooks and authoritative studies provided a frame of reference and the appropriate language with which to describe and celebrate the significance of architectural sites. As one anonymous West Australian in Central Java declared, Borobudur, with volcanoes poised to the south and east, was an "unequalled" example of Buddhist architectural perfection, and Java a "wonderland" of natural and "archaeological riches."[37]

The islands were also frequently painted as an archetypal South Seas paradise where people lived happily in a Roussavian state of nature. Of the people at Laguna de Bay in the Philippines DB wrote, "They can grow rice for next to nothing; they have bread-fruit and bananas also for next to nothing; they have fish in abundance."[38] These forest dwellers were but distant figures on an idealized landscape, enveloped by their natural surroundings into which they merged like native fauna. In such romantic accounts, nature was cast as protector and provider ensuring basic necessities without the need for soulless industry. This was the essence of the romantic idea of the wilderness as a refuge from the modern world, which added to the attraction of hill stations and health resorts in Java and Malaya. Forerunners of today's wilderness retreats, they captured the aesthetic experience of wild nature in the reassuring safety of ordered existence. Exotic localities offered an authentic experience, a sharp stimulus to the senses, and bursts of excitement privileging the pleasure of the moment. At Dusan Tuah, Townley and her companions enjoyed the adrenalin rush of riding rapids in the Langat River or splashing about in the sulphur springs. But the resort was also an idyllic "Eden-like" place, a perfect retreat where Townley could feel "at peace" amidst the nurturing protective embrace of the forest in a liminal "fairy-like" world.[39]

The apparent fecundity of tropical nature was both fascinating and disturbing. The social effects of climate were of major concern to Westerners in the Archipelago and reflected broader concerns about the relationship between nature, social order and morality in Victorian society. Contrasting the childish innocence relished by DB and Townley, luxuriance was also associated with the seduction of the senses, promiscuity and laziness. Travelogues often referred to the "intoxicating perfumes" or "delicious fragrance" of tropical foliage, which carried more than a whiff of association with opiates and other mind-altering substances. To a society which elevated the values of industry, sobriety and chastity, Australia's near Orient had the appearance of an "illicit space."[40] Everyday sights in Batavia, when viewed through the distorting mirror of bourgeois propriety, presented more than a suggestion of promiscuity—even fruit trees exhibited "promiscuous growth."[41] Clothing was a focal point for moral commentary. Appreciating the practicality of traditional Javanese costume for life in a hot climate, Copeland recognized the sense in Dutch women adopting the local style but still referred to them as being in a state of "undress."[42] The equatorial climate also changed the behavior of the resident English population of Singapore, though not to the degree that they abandoned "home etiquette" and shed their corsets.[43] Ida Kalenski was, however, shocked by the apparent impropriety and wrote disparagingly of such unladylike exposure,

The ladies [wear] the sarong and kabaya, the costume of the country. Nothing more unbecoming to a stout figure can be imagined than this short, scanty cotton skirt, tied carelessly around the middle of the body—I had nearly said waist—and the equally scanty white cotton jacket. The ladies wear no stockings and no hats.[44]

Copeland worried at the effect of climate on the moral character of British colonizers, suggesting their penchant for servants resulted from heat-induced idleness. He drew a sharp distinction between the apparent moral decay of the British in Malaya with the sturdy dependability of the stereo-typical North Queenslander. The superior adaptability of White Australians acclimatized to labor in the tropics was accepted as scientific fact by Sydney advocates of Australian colonization in New Guinea. Entertaining a vague notion that one day Australians might assume some of the White man's burden somewhere in Britain's eastern empire, the tropics, he re-flected, were suitable only for European North Queenslanders who were bi-ologically adapted to the physical stresses of an equatorial climate.[45]

The Asia represented by Australian artists had the quality of an adventure zone, a place of unbridled sensuality where Western men could seek and find consummation of their desires.[46] Fertility, seductiveness, malleability and obedience were motifs that surfaced alike in writings on the natural en-vironment and Asian peoples. For Australian adventurers, the Archipelago was infinitely penetrable space with, save for the attention of British and Dutch officialdom, abundant natural wealth there for the taking. The Philippines was not merely a playground for the visual senses. Suggesting the consummation of his own sexual fantasies, DB hinted, tactfully cog-nizant of the moral sensibilities of his respectable Brisbane audience, at the promise of sensual pleasure awaiting the adventurous Westerner in Manila who wished to be "captivated for life by dazzling signoritas who smoke cig-arettes."[47] It is both a reflection upon the writer and his audience that, like many Australian travellers before him, Pratt conjured stereotyped picture-book images of an idyllic Orient colorful, bewildering and seductive. Bril-liant colors and delightful scents were familiar motifs in many late or nineteenth- and early twentieth-century travel narratives and novels about Asia.[48] Pratt faithfully reproduced images of the "queer perfume of the East," stimulating, suffocating and as ephemeral as his personal encounters with Malaya and Siam.

Australian travellers were avid consumers of travel literature. Copeland's accounts are littered with references to McNair's *Perak and the Malays*. His-torical allusion was a common device used to convey visual images of people and places and to add creative flair to many a prosaic amateur travel narrative. The swashbuckling adventures of Francis Drake and William Dampier excited Edward Downes's nostalgia for a bygone age of British maritime exploration. The Spice Islands often appeared in Downes's ac-counts as a great historical costume melodrama, set variously in the six-teenth and seventeenth centuries, vividly revived to dramatize his experi-ence. In one diary entry, Drake's image of the Sultan of Ternate appears to Downes's readers surrounded by glittering riches and a host of subjects bowed in obeisance.[49] A republican and a northern separationist, Downes cast this fabled Oriental despot against a backdrop of "blokey" Australian egalitarianism, perpetuating impressions of an unbridgeable moral divide between northern Australia and the Archipelago.

In the same way and to the same extent that Western romantic notions of Oriental opulence and tropical luxuriance shaped Australian expectations and experiences in the Archipelago, racial ideas pervaded Australian writing about the East. Indeed, race formed part of the bedrock of common sense upon which Australians rested their impressions of people, culture and place. Ethnological theories of racial hierarchy preceded Charles Darwin, but his theory of natural selection hardened the edges of White Australian identity and shaped Australian conceptions of race and region.[50] Exhibiting a penchant for amateur scientific classification, Australians made use of Darwin's theory to frame their experiences of the Archipelago and to map racial categories onto geographical space. Downes's travel narrative of the Moluccas exemplifies the pervasiveness of racial ideas in nineteenth-century Australian perceptions of people and place and suggests an awareness of the eastern Indies as an intermediate zone between the Malay and Melanesian worlds.[51] Applying Wallace's racial taxonomy based upon a general category of the "true Malay," Downes detailed the racial markers of a biogeographical division of Australia's island region:

> The inhabitants [of Ceram] are the usual mixture of races met with in these islands, but the Alfuros and Papuan races are the predominant type in the north and eastern portion.
>
> On those smaller islands the Malay type predominates with a slight admixture of Papuan . . . The lower class of the population consists almost entirely of indigenes . . . They are a fine race, with strongly marked Papuan features and frizzly hair . . .[52]
>
> The native Amboynese . . . appear to be a mixture of three races at least . . . their hair was their pride. It was inclined to be curly not straight like the true Malay.[53]

In striving to lend intellectual weight and substance to their travel accounts, Australians understandably reached for available popular ideas to analyze the new worlds that unfolded before them. Race was used as a measure to categorize, distinguish and subordinate people according to physical features and presumed behavioral traits. Laziness, for example, was a presumed racial defect attributed by Downes to most inhabitants of the islands he visited. Copeland's concern for the moral decay of European colonizers pointed to anxiety about the corrosive effects of climate on character. The political implications of such views were far-reaching because they justified the prolongation of colonial rule. According to Syed Mohammad Alatas, images of native indolence functioned to legitimate colonial rule, be this in

Malaya, the Netherlands Indies or the Philippines where the laziness myth was well established during the Spanish era.[54] From "nature's gentlemen" to "lazy natives," indigenous inhabitants from Malaya to the Philippines were accused of environmentally induced indolence born of the availability of nature's tropical bounty and heat-induced languor. Colonial ideology, argued Alatas, maintained that Filipinos and Malays would never acquire the virtuous "habits of industry and obedience" or the capacity to govern without Western tutelage.

There were some exceptions to this orthodoxy and even Downes stumblingly acknowledged the evidence before his eyes of hardworking "industrious" island peoples. Downes went so far as to wonder for how long Malay peoples would accept Dutch overlordship, however progressive and benevolent this might be. Clinging to his faith in an idealized state of nature, DB echoed the opinion of French explorer Jean de La Perouse who blamed the Spanish for the supposed vices of indigenous Filipinos rather than any inherent weakness of character.[55] Australian poet, novelist and journalist Andrew "Banjo" Paterson, however, Filipinos were merely "little brown men, for the most part with poor physique." McMahon's contempt for presumed Filipino laziness was as palpable as Paterson's. Like Dean Worcester, an authority upon the "Filipino character," he believed that Filipinos were unfit to govern their own affairs and that their political leaders were prone to corruption and profligacy. According to McMahon, Filipinos were historically "indolent and commercially inactive," always prey to "superior races." He implied that the United States presence was "natural" as well as "necessary." Attitudes expressed about the character of Filipinos by McMahon suggest the strong influence of Worcester's Americanism:

> At present the Filipinoes (sic) are a long way off being capable of managing for themselves. They lack qualities that mark strength of character, and if left to their own devices, would, as they have done throughout their history, quickly fall into the mastership of some more active and vigorous race.[56]

Paterson's sympathies lay with "Uncle Sam," then engaged in the brutal suppression of Filipino nationalists who resisted the American invasion of their homeland. Not without relish did he describe an incident in which an American sentry shot two Filipinos, suspected of intent to commit arson, while they were running away. He lamented that the sentry "would have got some more" but for the intervention of "some Filipino woman" who obstructed the soldier's aim. Paterson himself was in no doubt that the Philippine-American War would result in the "survival of the fittest." However, Paterson's impressions of the American-occupied Philippines also betray a hint of irony as he inverts the sense of a famous Kipling phrase to portray an ignoble scramble for spoils:

Besides the Filipinos there were Chinese, Japanese, Hindoos, American soldiers and civilians, English, Australians, Spaniards, beach-combers and poor whites of every degree and of all nations taking up the white man's burden and the black man's property as fast as they can get it.[57]

Herbert Pratten in *Through Orient to Occident* condemned the "densely ignorant Joe Chinaman" as technologically backward so much so that Chinese "may perhaps show no improvement since the days of the Phoenicians."[58] Chinese miners, Pratten observed, recovered tin by luck and "sheer force of numbers" rather than by the systematic measurement of ore deposits.[59] He thought the FMS Government had created a more stable and progressive investment environment where "modern brains, experience, capital and machinery" could be applied gainfully. Praising the FMS for the probity of its officials and their promotion of economic development, he labeled Chinese capitalists "all gamblers at heart" and prone to financial speculation.[60] Despite having visited the principal emporia of Asia, he seemed unable to reconcile their geographical proximity to Australia with a yawning cultural divide. In *Asiatic Impressions*, he pessimistically described "an insurmountable barrier" between "white" and "yellow."

By nature cruel and indifferent, the suffering of others does not affect them and the only object in their life seems to be the interests of self and family. Industry, political inertia, imperturbability and ingratitude, virility, vice, dirt, disease, and that callous and passive resistance to change intensified through centuries, cannot be brought into line from any European standpoint.[61]

FOLLOWERS OF THE PROPHET

Racial caricatures ignited or inflamed prejudice by exaggerating assumed connections between race, religion and behavior. In the Australian imagination, images of Oriental domesticity, tranquility, color and social vibrancy coexisted with images of indolence, opulence, cunning, brutality, and sometimes bestiality. Inhabitants of the Archipelago were dubbed variously as "nature's gentlemen" for the Malays; "Joe" or "John Chinaman," or "the wily Chinee" for overseas Chinese, making even the complementary descriptions of Copeland and others who found reason to appreciate Chinese industry sound patronizing. Hate imagery stood at the other end of the spectrum. The "savage" Malay, used to good effect during Queensland's Black Labor election, was one variation on a theme that encompassed "bloodthirsty" pirates and the elaborately armed guards of the Archipelago's "oriental despots." Highlighting the influence of colonial myth and romance on Australian thinking about people and place, travel narratives were laced with allusions to Arabia and the stories of Arabian Nights. Displaying the common imaginative repertoire of his day, Tenison-Woods sketched the Sultan of Palawan's "Oriental Court,"

> recalling all the glories of the Arabian Nights. Silks and satins, startling contrasts in colours, gold and silver, and precious stones, made a rather dazzling display. The Sultan . . . was attended by a gorgeous sentinel with his hand on the trigger of a loaded revolver, and was surrounded by a phalanx of guards armed with crisses [sic] and spears. [62]

Muslim workers in the Torres Strait pearling industry and on the cane fields of North Queensland were tolerated, the right to prayer and the celebration of Islamic festivals respected. Yet, Islam was widely regarded as a heterodox creed and its followers at best misguided children, at worst pernicious confidence tricksters. The "Haj" is Islam's most sacred pilgrimage and those who complete the journey are entitled to the honorific "Haji." One Queenslander's image of the "Hadji," however, only served to render this badge of Muslim piety into a mark of dishonor of which Western travellers must either beware or fall foul to sharp commercial practice. As the traveller wrote for the *Straits Times*,

> If you wish to be introduced to a real aristocrat, here is one. An Arab-Musaulman, of course, and a Hadji into the bargain. He has made the pilgrimage and is a saint and a hero. What a noble looking fellow. . . What beautiful wares the Hadji displays! From Paris?—Yes. And if an Australian greenhorn, which the Hadji, with his aristocratic intuition will readily detect, he will ask for them exactly three times what they cost him as invoiced by his.[63]

Muslims were singled out for assumed weaknesses of character that led believers to perfect the dark arts of intrigue, duplicity and murder. According to Raffles, the Javanese kingdom of Majapahit gave way to a less beneficent system of government that suppressed peasant industriousness with the dead hand of extortion.[64] He was among the first English-speaking scholar/administrators to assert a violent Islamic conversion in the fifteenth century as the reason for the eclipse of this once great agricultural civilization.[65] Raffles's influence on the representation of the Malay character was as pervasive as Wallace's geography. Australian observers, as did most Western travel writers, incorporated the common association of Islam with violence. It was widely agreed that colonialism was a necessary and progressive influence in the Archipelago that would negate the regressive effects of prolonged exposure to Islam. DB accepted that Java had fallen prey to "Mohammedan conquerors" spreading outwards from Aceh in northern Sumatra. Quoting Raffles, he informed his readers that from its arrival the Muslim religion exerted a debilitating influence on industrious rice farmers and brought

about the demise of Majapahit, whose former greatness was only then being revived under Dutch tutelage.[66]

Western commentators had difficulty reconciling the presence of architectural achievements in a society that they perceived to lack the necessary industry and intelligence. Reflecting on the demise of those who built the temples of East and Central Java, Wallace wondered at "the strange law of
progress" that could permit such "a highly artistic and constructive race" to
be supplanted by one "very far its inferior." Tenison-Woods attributed the
dissipation of Java's creative Indianized civilization to the arrival of "Arab
missionaries" in the fifteenth century.[67] The "tendency of the Malay race,"
wrote Tenison-Woods, "is always to submit to the existing order of things."[68]
In Pratt's estimation, Malays were utterly inferior, enslaved for centuries by
Islam brought to the peninsula by "Mohammedan invaders from Sumatra"
and had consequently lapsed into superstition and witchcraft, weakening
their "mental texture."[69] There were different shades of opinion about the
impact of Islam, and the occasional exception to the anti-Islamic norm.
Echoing Wallace's observations of Muslims on the Moluccan island of Ambon, Edward Downes' pronounced the island's Muslim community as honest, hardworking and sober in sharp contrast to the island's Christian population.[70] Such favorable views were firmly in the minority.

Newspaper invective against the importation of Malay labor to Queensland caricatured the Malay as a bloodthirsty savage, drawing upon head-
hunter rather than Islamic stereotypes. While naturalists and scholar-
officials mused about the disappearance of a brilliant civilization, others
presumed that Malays and Javanese were once wild and savage until subdued by the civilizing forces of colonialism. Ida Kalenski's expectations of
Malayan savagery were derived from reading an adventure story about pi-
ratical "headhunters" as a child.[71] Half-human, half-animal creatures were
once part of the European imaginative landscape of the Indies. Portuguese
cartographic representations of Australasian biogeography depicted strange
beasts thought to inhabit the Archipelago, long since banished with the
transformation of cartography from imaginative art into science. Once in-
tegral to the Western mythology of an exotic Orient, carnivorous centaurs
and other half-human beasts lived in the Asia of Western imagination from
the time of Marco Polo and lived on in Mowbray's historical imagination.
After visiting the Batavia Museum he wrote that it was

> crowded with the idols and statuary of the old Javanese Brahmanical religion
> of centuries ago, before Java was over-run by the followers of Islam. Life sized
> carvings of the fabulous man-eating men and women who once dominated
> Java, with long fangs overlapping each side of their upper and lower lips;
> and similar life sized and life like representations of the diabolical torture and

disembowelments practised as a fine art in judicial punishments prior to
Dutch occupation.[72]

Exhibits were accompanied by brief descriptions for the benefit of the visitor, but as these were entirely in Dutch, Mowbray was left to his own resources to decipher the significance of the artifacts before him. His literal
translation of graven imagery from Indian and Javanese legend displayed at
the Batavia Museum is doubly ironic. Myth merged with reality in Mowbray's interpretation of Javanese religious reliquary. Images of cannibalism,
torture and human sacrifice reaffirmed Mowbray's faith in the righteous-
ness of European colonialism and the illegitimacy of Asian forms of governance. Manifest in his description of grotesque images of torture was the belief that beneath the veneer of an ordered colonial society lurked a latent
barbarism and a tendency towards savage despotism.

BETWEEN TWO CULTURES

Confronted by glaring differences in land and cityscapes, social mores and
individual appearance, the attributes of Australia were a frame of reference
against which more thoughtful travellers measured cultural distance and interpreted new environments. This did not mean that local cultures were always judged harshly by comparison. Stuart Macintyre wrote that "Australian
racism was a mass hysteria fed on ignorance and fear. When local communities had dealings with non-Australians, toleration was possible."[73] Australian society, despite its virulent racism, nurtured the facility to accept the
presence of people from strange places as long as this did not disrupt established power relations. This was as apparent in Australian-Asian encounters in the Archipelago as it was in Melbourne or Sydney. As already
stated, travel across cultural boundaries with a mind closed to the possibility of an alternative wisdom, can reinforce a sense of cultural distance from
peoples encountered and engender a desire for protection, in an exclusive
tourist resort or a culturally homogenous social group. But for those Australians who stepped out of their protected milieu to face the cultural challenges of adjustment, there is evidence that their attitudes towards their
near Orient could change.

While the contours of natural environment combined with the superfi-
cialities of cultural difference to color the experience of Asia, encounters
with the Orient at close quarters were often disturbing. Hume Black reported "disgust and revulsion" at the sight of Chinese drawing rickshaws in
Singapore, a practice which he regarded as "being entirely opposed to Australian ideas of freedom."[74] With indignation verging on outrage that such

exploitation could be permitted under British colonial rule, Black forgot the greater indignities heaped on Australia's indigenous population. Suggesting a complex relationship between Australians and the peoples of Asia, Black betrayed no resentment or revulsion towards one Rajah Impey, a fellow shareholder in the Australian-owned and -operated Raub Australia Gold Mine at Pahang on the Malay Peninsula, who greeted him on his arrival at Port Kelang. Copeland lauded Chinese merchants for their entrepreneurial flair and their bourgeois values—property, law, order and trade. Both accepted as truth the hierarchical ranking of races, but money and status were bourgeois markers of substance that, when combined with shared business interest, transcended the race divide.

Far removed from the conventions of their familiar world, Australian travellers occasionally expressed feelings of Von Gennep's communitas towards their indigenous subalterns. Finding themselves at the outer reaches of British colonial power and away from intense social pressures to maintain racial separateness, Australian travellers were likely to be more receptive to alien cultural practices. Spending a night in a Sakeis village was anything but a frightening experience for Copeland. Despite sharing the floor of the chief's house with some sixteen "natives" he commented that he felt "as safe and secure as though in a hotel in Sydney, notwithstanding the fact that not one of the people of the house had ever seen a white man before."[75] The exotic Orient formed a utopian backdrop against which travellers highlighted the deficiencies of their culture. Journeying to the source of the Perak River, Copeland expressed what can be interpreted as an affinity with his Malay boat crew. Shedding the cultural hauteur that distanced European from Malay, Westerner from Oriental, he praised their skill and dexterity as fishermen and took pleasure in their company,

> I found the boatmen a jolly set of fellows, for they used to joke with each other and laugh heartily, and when their work was done and their evening meal over they invariably commenced singing. . . . It used to be a great source of amusement to them when I, having asked the Malay name for something, would tell them the English word for it, they would repeat it over and over a score of times, laughing merrily at the idea of it being known by such a queer name.[76]

Copeland's views perpetuated a romantic stereotype of "nature's gentlemen"— child-like, innocent, amiable. Yet there is more to this scene and his subsequent reflection that suggests Copeland also experienced a moment of authentic camaraderie. Here he believed were a group people living in a pre-industrial idyll, free from the conflict inherent in the materialistic conflict-ridden society of late nineteenth-century Sydney. With heavy irony, Copeland went on to vent his anger at the vaulting ambition, corruption, selfishness and false piety that he thought so prevalent at home:

> They are a people of few wants and little or no hardships. They do not hanker after C.M.G. ships, nor go in for Darling Harbour compensation specs and then fail to pull them off. They have not many "isms" and consequently live at peace with their neighbours. . . . they get through life without being preached into eternal damnation on the one hand or sent to purgatorial punishment on the other; and they indulge in the sublime folly of enjoying this life as much as they conveniently can.[77]

Like Copeland, who used a romanticized image of Malay social life to condemn the failings of Australian society, Pratt idealized Siam between the wars, conferring upon it the status of an Asian utopia, an idea that he then used to vent his frustration with wealthy monopolists that he presumed responsible for the Great Depression.[78] Writing to the *The Spectator* he denounced the materialism that had "corrupted and infected the superficial scum of the Orient" but his vitriol was not directed towards Siam's princely elite.[79] Instead he lauded Siam, conveying an impression of a kingdom where passive happy subjects lived and enlightened and benevolent rulers alike adhered to a Buddhist religion that preached frugality, humility and pacifism. The Thai aristocracy were all "as gentle and as courtly as the fabled princes of romance." In manners and learning they approximated to a Western ideal and "lead a social life that almost exactly resembles our own."[80] Betraying his anti-Muslim prejudice, Pratt contrasted the perceived subservience of Muslim Malays with the childlike reverence of Thai villagers. Reveling in such outward gestures of social inferiority and respect as would not have been encountered on an Australian mining frontier, he wrote,

> When one meets a Siamese peasant in the jungle he will promptly fall on his knees and lift up his hands as though in prayer. But do not mistake this worshipful attitude for a gesture of servile humility! The kneeling Siamese peasant merely pays you the compliment (because your skin is white) of supposing you to be a Tuan—and therefore the social equal of any Siamese aristocrat.

Tuan is a Malay word and, ironically, Pratt referred to villagers in the tin districts of southern Siam where he visited and who were in all likelihood Malay and Muslim. While local nuances were overlooked by transient visitors, for long-term sojourners, knowledge of local cultures and cultural practicalities was essential. Australian mine managers and their families lived between two worlds, one White Australian, the other Eurasian. For them the transfer from Australian to Asian commercial centers or mining frontiers was a matter of routine. An engineer by trade, William Bibby, mine manager at Raub, spent 15 years on the north Queensland mining frontier before moving to Malaya. Chinese miners on the Queensland mining frontier most probably provided his only prior encounters with an Asian culture. And yet, in the midst of the Pahang jungle, he could at least empathize with local Malay objections to the displacement of traditional economic patterns and the swift imposition of British free trade principles. The abolition of taxing rights claimed by chiefs along the Pahang River precipitated the Pahang Revolt of 1891, which threatened Raub company staff and property. Having shipped mine equipment and provisions upstream to the Raub mine site, Bibby was familiar with, if frustrated by, the local practice of taxing riverine traffic, but he paid up to ensure security of person and company assets, as did later generations of Australian miners in the Archipelago.

The image of demoniacal savage Malays, useful in disciplining Australian public attitudes towards White Australia from the time of the Normanton Riot, did not blunt the curiosity of Australian travellers. Although residing in a Malay state still subject to periodical unrest, William's daughters Nellie and Edie Bibby were confident enough of their safety to venture away from the Raub mine. As with wives and daughters working in the New Guinea interior, necessity bred familiarity with their social environment. The Bibbys were accustomed to the presence and acquaintance of the local population employed as household servants and mine workers at Raub, and, if unable to converse, were at least familiar with the sounds of Malay and Chinese languages. It was usual for Australian managers to acquire a working knowledge of Malay, the lingua franca of labor management on the peninsula, and no doubt Edie and Nellie acquired sufficient Malay to navigate cultural barriers on their journey. Their story is more significant for the excited but casual manner in which they recounted their journey, which was less of an adventure than an outing along the tropical waterways of the eastern peninsula, visiting friends and relatives at tin mines in Kelantan and Terrengganu and attracting the curiosity of villagers along the way.[81]

Interviewed with his daughters by the *Straits Times* at the exclusive Raffles Hotel, William Bibby eased the moral anxieties of genteel colonial society with the reminder to all single women that it was "not a proper thing for two young unprotected females to go gallivanting about the Native States."[82] Fearful of Malaya's untamed interior, Kalenski by contrast endured a modest lifestyle in a rented beachside bungalow overlooking the Straits of Malacca. Occasionally, on mornings when the tide was high, she and her husband would swim in their own enclosure, keeping a watchful eye for crocodiles. Without kitchen, stove or running water, conditions hardly replicated the life of an urban *memsahib* in greater British India. Lacking basic comforts and restrained from engaging in housework by the enervating tropical heat, Kalenski's day revolved around the compensatory prestige of organizing household servants. Her "modest" contingent included a Chinese cook, a Malay gardener, one house "boy" and a *tukang ayer* or water carrier. Without the convenience of refrigeration, provisions had to be ordered every day through an errand boy for purchases from local shops or through a firm of Chinese merchants for larger orders from Singapore. Like all Edwardian ladies of the house, she organized the daily menu and entertained evening social callers as was the fashion, when she and her husband were not paying their own social calls of driving by *gharry* along the Esplanade.

The mechanical routines of life made Kalenski and her husband long for the stimulation of adventure. They agreed from the start of their Singapore sojourn to "study the myriads of Orientals" thronging the streets of their adopted home. Kalenski sought to understand Asian customs and went so far as to learn some Malay. One of Kalenski's favorite pastimes, carriage tours around the streets of Singapore, offered an opportunity to closely observe street life and was as educational as it was entertaining. She wrote,

> This is the great and unique charm of Singapore beyond any other Eastern place. One can see there almost every Oriental race—Chinese, Japanese, Malay, Hindoo, Javanese, Burmese, Siamese, Arab, Jew, Turk, Armenian, Afgan, Persian, and Cingalese, besides European, American and African types, and a ride, or better still, a walk through the native quarters gives one endless amusement.[83]

A passion for sightseeing took both beyond the city itself to Johore and Batavia and the eastern Archipelago to Banda, Amboyna and Macassar. Intrepid as they liked to think themselves, the Brisbanites remained within the protected spaces of the colonial city, first-class railway car and shipboard saloon. Excursions therefore followed the pattern and timetable of imperial infrastructure and communications. From Woodlands Pier, the terminus for this rail service, the ferry journey took less than ten minutes to cross to Abu Bakar Pier in Johore Bahru. To her surprise, Kalenski found the Johore of 1906 quite a modern place. Even the rickshaws had rubber tires!

Rituals of British culture endured even the most sapping equatorial climates. Driven by carriage from the pier to a fort in the town, they enjoyed "tiffin" with an acquaintance, a British officer in charge of the Sultan's personal guard. From the fort they were able to cast their inquisitive gaze over a magnificent view of Singapore Island and the Straits of Malacca. Through their connections Kalenski and her husband were able to go inside the Sultan's *istana* after dinner. Eager to find traces of Oriental opulence, inside the palace they were dazzled by the display of royal treasure:

> We stood and marvelled at the rooms full of treasures which were disclosed to us by a shrivelled Malay attendant. About six small rooms on the ground floor hold the collection, which includes everything possible for table use, with ornaments, salvers, bowls &c [sic] of solid gold. Heaps of magnificent silver . . . gold krises [sic], and swords with jewelled hilts and scabbards.[84]

Australian relations with British officialdom in Asia, and with British colonizers in general, were often cool. Kalenski noted that she and her husband's "free and easy" manner of communicating with peoples of different cultures set them apart from the resident English. Europeans were supposed to maintain distance and hauteur when dealing with natives but Kalenski did not wish to remain "pukka." She felt that her attitude distinguished her as an Australian and expressed a sense of wishing to distance herself both socially and culturally from "English friends," preferring the cacophony of Singapore's busy streets. While official visitors from the Australian colonies were greeted cordially, those engaged in mineral exploration were looked down upon. Australians and British shared the same language but Australians were not accepted a social equals in Britain's colonial possessions in Asia, or for that matter in Britain. As the Australian mining investor and federal politician Herbert Pratten remarked,

> They have seen but little of us, and do not so far seem to have been very favourably impressed, for the remarks they pass upon the Australian types they have become acquainted with are not always complimentary.[85]

RE-ORIENTATIONS

Beyond their grumbling acquiescence to a diet of "stone cold eggs and Dutch curry," the experiences of Australian travellers reflected deeper processes of national identification. Many consciously mapped their country's geography, invested their nation's territory with symbolic meaning, and conferred a distinctive identity upon the White society that was gradually colonizing the Australian continent. Pratten dubbed Australian mine managers, engineers and prospectors in Malaya as "patriotic sons" of Australia who "sleep for choice facing the South so that they may at night see the Southern Cross—the symbol associated by most exiles and wanderers from her shores with their sunny Austral Land."[86] Welcomed into the diaspora of independent diggers, Pratten felt a pang of national pride, made more intense by his sense of distance from his Australian home.

The experience of Asia could reinforce ideas of cultural superiority as equally as it could challenge entrenched racial orthodoxies, especially among those who approached the region with closed minds. Australian travellers like Paterson and the two Labor senators who, on returning from a trip to the East in 1905, told readers of the *North Queensland Herald* that the White Australia policy should be strengthened, hoped that their nation could be sealed from the dangers of racial miscegenation.[87] Educated travellers like the Melburnian George Meudell were capable of passing through strange places without any inclination to learn about or engage with the culture spheres through which they passed. As Meudell told readers of the *Straits Times,*

> Truly, the transient visitor to Eastern countries learns nothing of the true in-
> wardness of the places he visits. He usually learns but little of the manners, do-
> mestic existence, or views of life of the people. And the impressions on his
> mind are as fleeting and inaccurate as those on the retina of his eye. My expe-
> rience is that travel amongst colored and uncivilized peoples is neither in-
> structive nor comfortable. And it is always disappointing if the traveler paints
> beforehand pretty pictures of what he thinks he is going to see, based on his
> reading of books of travel, which are chiefly written to please and to sell.[88]

The "whole thing," Meudell concluded, "is very motley oriental." Putting
Meudell's judgement aside, the transformative potential of international
travel was evident in the recorded experiences of those Australians who
grasped the significance of changes taking place to Australia's north. Australians encountered Westernized Malayan elites that disappointed expectations of ostentatious displays and contradicted popular notions of Oriental
backwardness. Ida Kalenski remembered that Malays in Singapore con-
founded her expectations. Contrary to her preformed ideas of the Malay
character, she found the Malays of Singapore courteous and gaily dressed.
Both Kalenski and her husband were also shocked to discover that some
could even speak fluent English. Nor did Kalenski encounter any opulently
dressed Oriental potentates, as she had hoped:

> We had visions of gorgeous princes, dressed in brocades and hung with jewels,
> mounted on elephants, and attended by large retinues of slaves. . . I may say
> we did not see any princes, and our subsequent view of Sultan Ibrahim (in Sin-
> gapore) revealed a tall young man whose features gave only slight evidence of
> his Malay origin, dressed in white duck[89] trousers, tweed coat and Panama hat,
> with dark spectacles, and not, so far as we could see, any jewellery at all.[90]

From new railways to steam trams and motor cars, to the Western attire of
Asian royalty, Australians were confronted everywhere by the evidence of
confident urbanity. Comfortable with the multiracial vibrancy of Singapore's street markets, the sight of wealthy Asian businesspeople flaunting
their wealth and reveling in their superior social status was, however, dis-
concerting for Kaleneski. Observing the conspicuous consumption of one
wealthy Chinese, she wrote,

> They spend lots of money on horses and carriages and to the Australian—
> accustomed to seeing the Chinaman in the role of fruit and vegetable John—
> it comes as a double shock to see the rubber-tyred Victoria–drawn by two beau-
> tiful horses (Australian) with coachman and two footmen dressed in brilliant

liveries occupied by a portly Celestial, often bareheaded and barefooted, lolling back in a manner which is extremely annoying to the white man or woman who is riding in a rickshaw. [91]

Less confronting and much less troubling, public sanitation and urban modernization were salient topics in Australian travel writing. Copeland despaired at the practice of drawing bathing water from the Molenvliet Canal at the Hotel des Indes, a fact made all the more unappealing by the knowledge that Java was, at the time of his visit, in the grip of a cholera epidemic, although he reassured himself that this was confined to the local population.[92] Government attention to public health concerns and to good public relations ensured that images of stinking canals featured less and less in traveller accounts of Batavia. Apart from the Molenvliet, Mowbray found the city generally clean, noting that canals were drained each night, and making no reference to the foul odors that featured in earlier Australian accounts of the city. Batavia earned praise for its picturesque beauty, with its "green avenues, velvet lawns, flowered beds, white copings and artistic carvings." Even the steam trams were comfortable models of municipal cleanliness.[93]

Australians looked for evidence of social and economic progress. In the early days of American occupation Manila was a "post-conflict zone" where murderers stalked the streets after dark and where insurgent attacks were commonplace. Members of an Australian vaudeville troupe returning after a four-month season in the Philippines in January 1904 warned readers of the *North Queensland Herald* that the "smouldering embers of disaffection" felt by Filipinos towards their American occupiers meant that "murders were a startlingly frequent occurrence."[94] There seemed to be no question that, in time, the United States would bring the situation under control. Paterson, scoffing at the city's economic backwardness, mocked the use of bullock carts as the main form of heavy transport. Steamers were still coaled by hand, but he sensed a city in the throes of a cultural transformation. To his readers in the *Sydney Morning Herald*, he reported,

> There is an indescribable hurry, bustle and fuss . . . it was like Belmore Market, Sydney, on a Saturday night. The restaurants are all full, the shops are all busy, the cigar stalls and soft drink shops crowded. Money is being made here wholesale.

The character of American colonization in the Philippines was perceived as different from that of older colonial powers. Whereas in Singapore it was the Chinese who gave impetus to the thronging business mood of the marketplace, in Manila the authorities cultivated a distinctly American entrepreneurial mood. When McMahon visited Manila in 1923, the city was abuzz with "American hustle" and a haven for tourists "who pour into Manila by the hundred with every overseas steamer." Lively by day, the Philippine capital was transformed into a dazzling playground at night, with the streets, hotels and nightspots "in the fun swing of pleasure." Electric trams and motorcars made Manila's streets "a solid mass of traffic." Capturing the sights and sounds of this now thriving American metropolis in the tropics, he wrote,

> The Escolta is wonderfully animated. Pedestrians hurry along very narrow pathways, while the roadway is crowded, and the air is fined with the screech of what seems like thousands of gramophones giving forth a higgledy-piggledy of tunes . . . Flashing motor cars and motor-lorries crush side by side with strange carts and wagons.[95]

Australians sensed that material advancement must bring with it political change and an eventual redirection of Australian trade interests. Even Pratten recognized that Australia's trading future lay in Asia. Despite the overtly bigoted Australian attitude towards Chinese, shared commercial interests could, as argued by Wang Gungwu, overcome cultural barriers to trade and investment.[96] In public forums Pratten urged Australian manufacturers to respond to "the awakening of nations" in Asia where the adoption of Western ideas and tastes coupled with increasing wages and wealth had created potential and realized markets for Australian commodities. Deploying the same defensive arguments used by advocates of stricter immigration controls in the 1990s, he asserted that Asian peoples held similar chauvinistic ideas of racial homogeneity to Australians and that, therefore, the White Australia Policy should not hinder stronger regional economic ties. Where cultural barriers were breaking down, he argued, it was because "rapid strides had taken place in the Europeanising of Asiatics."[97]

Newspaper coverage of visits by Asian dignitaries conveyed the same concerns. The *Sydney Morning Herald* announced the arrival of Siam's Prince Purachatra in 1927 with the headline "Siam: Towards Western Ideals."[98] Readers were introduced to an urbane graduate of Harrow, Trinity College Cambridge and Sandhurst, entrusted with the task of "recasting his country in the Western mould." Bearing an academic pedigree the envy of many Australians, Purachatra appeared as a visionary Asian dignitary, committed to the material improvement of his country. The article credited him with adopting the best of European communications technology, emphasizing that wireless and air travel now complemented a sprawling rail network placing the country "solidly" on the path to advancement. Straddling two cultures, the prince exuded the "happy charm of the East" combined with an earnest devotion to "development." Indeed, by his accomplishments he had demonstrated that "there is more of the West in him."[99] Readers were reassured that this "picturesque" Oriental prince was "one of us."[100] Australia's salvation from Asia's "yellow hordes" lay, so it was thought, in Asia's rapid Westernization.

"Convergence" was one happy idea that encouraged the complacent view that Western culture was the developmental end-point towards which Asia was slowly but steadily progressing in the 1920s. McMahon, however, warned against such complacency and urged Australians to experience first-hand the economic and political transformation of the Orient. Australians must recognize their vital interests in Asia, he argued, adding an implicit warning that Australia may not forever be protected by Britain's imperial shield, or by the United States. While the U.S. Pacific Fleet resided in the Philippines, Australians could feel secure—but only temporarily. Western educated modern elites would lead Asian nations to prosperity and perhaps parity with the West.[101] Like his contemporary, Pratten, McMahon realized that Asian modernization was potentially of great economic benefit to Australia, but he warned Australia's racially exclusive immigration policy would as a consequence be rendered untenable:

> Much as I approve of the "White Australia" policy in its international aspect, it appears to me it will sooner or later be challenged by Oriental peoples. It is now regarded as a cause of offence, and it will be tolerated only as long as Oriental influence lacks that power which, it cannot be denied, it is rapidly gaining. A request for its abolition may probably come about in this wise: Oriental nations will need the raw products of Australia, outstanding in its resourcefulness; trade will extend as modern industries increase in the Orient, and as the Orientals demand the foods, clothing, and other necessities of modern life. With the influence of trade, and the power and wealth, which it will bring, must come the request, in some form or other, to end racial inequality. The claim may not be placed for a quarter of a century or so, but Australia, by that time or after it, can hardly have the population, the naval and military strength, to temporise, decline, or resist.[102]

McMahon echoed sentiments expressed by a growing number of Australian intellectuals in the interwar years. Academics of the stature of Griffith Taylor, Professor of Geography at Sydney University in the 1920s, and his Australian colleagues in the Institute of Pacific Relations, reasoned against social Darwinism on scientific and practical grounds.[103] There were those, like Ambrose Pratt, who, railing against the economic devastation of the Great Depression, questioned the inherent progressiveness of the West. Despite his interest in Asian philosophies and religions, Pratt was a late convert to the cause of intercultural understanding. In his early years, his admiration for China and Chinese culture coexisted with racist attachment to the ideal of White Australia. As he told a gathering of advertisers in Melbourne in 1925, racial exclusion allowed Australia's "pure" Anglo-Saxon stock the

freedom to create a "unique" and "superior" nation.[104] By the time war
erupted in the Pacific in December 1941, his attitude towards immigration
restriction had changed dramatically.

"Asia" he wrote, "had climbed to the highest peaks of philosophy, morality, psychology, art, poetry, history and religion" while Europeans "were still
painting their bodies with woad."[105] Demonstrating rare cultural awareness,
he grasped the reason why the White Australia policy was an insult to Australia's regional neighbors. Face, he noted, was a matter of "tremendous
spiritual significance . . . to every member of the Asian family." "To lose
face" he realized "is to lose all that is most valuable in life," namely the respect of one's equals and subordinates.[106] The White Australia policy, he declared to readers of the Melbourne *Age*, was sustained by nothing more than
"color snobbery."[107]

Pratt thought the processes of sociocultural evolution in Asia offered benefits for a decaying West and that Australia had much to learn from its
neighbors. Asian philosophies he believed could exert a progressive influence in Australia by teaching the next generation of leaders the cardinal
virtue of self-sacrifice for the good of the community. His upbringing undoubtedly made him more receptive to Asian influences, more inquisitive
and open-minded. Already well into middle age, and forced by illness into
semi-retirement, Pratt's travels to Siam especially during the 1930s taught
him the instrumental value of Asia-related cultural knowledge in the conduct of business negotiations. Pratt was an international celebrity, but similar ideas and sympathies were expressed by those who were not. While
Pratt praised Asian elites others questioned the fundamental justness of
colonial rule. In his unpublished diary of a round-the-world flight in 1938-
1939, Brisbane Grammar School teacher Jack Deeney voiced criticism of
Western colonialism in the Archipelago,

> Somehow the world does not think of natives as mankind and yet it is they
> who prepare the world for the invading white man who so frequently robs
> them of their hard-earned spoils.[108]

If the utopianism of Copeland and Pratt fell short of the modern cultural
cosmopolitan ideal, we should not ignore existence of such sentiments and
recognize their significance. Australian travellers were conduits for the receipt and retransmission of imperial knowledge but their writings about the
Archipelago offer brief glimpses of a different more accepting Australia.
Greater openness to the region was strangled by the disciplining ideology
of White Australia, the intellectual foundations of which were only slowly
worn down by movements of goods, ideas and people through Australasia
in the latter half of the twentieth century. The democratization of interna-

tional travel after the Pacific War would bring the region temporally much closer to Australia, but aviation would also render the experience of Asia potentially more transient and ephemeral. Compulsory confinement aboard steamers and sailing ships at least encouraged some inquisitive engagement with the peoples and landscapes through which travelers passed. From the air, people vanished into insignificance; tropical rainforests became carpets of green; towering volcanoes wide and squat. Maritime travelers had the islands thrust upon them; air travelers could pass over vast distances largely untroubled by what lay below. Closer engagement with Asia could only come with a major economic and political shift away from Britain.

NOTES

1. Copeland, *A Few Weeks*, 15. Martha Rutledge, "Copeland, Henry, 1839–1904," *ADB 1851–1890*, vol. 3, 458–59.

2. *Brisbane Courier*, November 1, 1886. *Straits Times*, January 22, 1889. D. H. Borchart, "Tenison-Woods, Julian Edmund, 1832–1889," *ADB, 1851–1890*, vol. 6, 254–55.

3. Nelson, *Taim Bilong Masta*, 141.

4. *Townsville Herald*, July 6, 1889. Francis D. Birch, "Tropical Milestones: Australian Gold and Tin Mining Investment in Malaya and Thailand, 1880–1930" (unpublished MA Dissertation, University of Melbourne), 1976, 54–57.

5. *Straits Times*, December 4, 1889. The *Straits Times* reproduced an interview with Brown from the *Brisbane Telegraph*, October 7, 1889.

6. Vickers, "Kipling Goes South," 67.

7. *Straits Times*, January 19, 1891. Geoffrey C. Bolton, "Black, Maurice Hume, 1830–1899," *ADB, 1851–1890*, vol. 2, 169–70.

8. *North Queensland Register*, June 13, 1894.

9. Miriam Dixson, *The Real Matilda: Woman and Identity in Australia, 1788 to the Present*, (Melbourne: Penguin Books Australia, Ringwood, 2nd edition, 1987), 209–13. Hobsbawm, *Age of Capital*, 279.

10. *Queenslander*, March 24 & June 17, 1906. The photographs that accompanied Kalenski's articles in *Queenslander* were taken by A. E. Allen. The date given for her departure from Australia matches that of the A. E. Allen involved with the QME & A. Kalenski could be the writer's maiden name or a pseudonym.

11. Visiting Friends and Relatives (VFR). *Queenslander*, July 3, 1909.

12. Thomas .J. McMahon, *The Orient I Found*, (London: Duckworth, 1926), 151–65.

13. Helen Carr, "Modernism and Travel, 1880–1940," in *The Cambridge Companion to Travel Writing*, ed. Peter Hulme and Tim Young, (Cambridge: Cambridge University Press, 2002), 79.

14. Raynor C. Johnson, *The Light and the Gate*, (London: Hodder and Straughton, 1964), 71–84. Diane Langmore, "Pratt, Ambrose Goddard Hesketh, 1874–1944," *ADB, 1891–1939*, vol. 11, 274–275.

15. Roger Downs and David Stea, *Maps in Minds: Reflections on Cognitive Mapping,* (London: Harper and Row, 1977), 9. Maureen Guirdham, *Communicating across Cultures at Work* (West Lafayette, In.: Ichor Books, 2005), 151, 271.

16. Paul Carter, *Living in a New Country: History, Travelling and Language* (London: Faber and Faber, 1992), 74. Carter wrote, "Whatever the origins of the terms we use, it is we who improvise out of them a world of meanings."

17. Victor Turner, Edith Turner, *Image and Pilgrimage in Christian Culture: Anthropological Perspectives* (Oxford: Basil Blackwell, 1978), 2, 13.

18. M. N. Pearson, "Pilgrims, Travellers, Tourists: The Meanings of Journeys," *Australian Cultural History* (no. 10, 1991), 125–33. Dennison Nash and Valene L. Smith, "Anthropology and Tourism," *Annals of Tourism Research* (vol. 18, 1991), 17.

19. *Brisbane Courier*, May 23, 1874.

20. Copeland, *A Few Weeks*, 5.

21. *Brisbane Courier*, May 23, 1874.

22. *North Queensland Register*, October 10, 1894.

23. *North Queensland Register*, October 10, 1894

24. Worsfold, *Visit to Java*, 103.

25. Copeland, *A Few Weeks*, 8.

26. Copeland, *A Few Weeks*, 8.

27. *Brisbane Courier*, February 10, 1881.

28. *North Queensland Register*, October 10, 1894.

29. *Brisbane Courier*, June 20, 1874.

30. *Brisbane Courier*, June 20, 1874.

31. Wildey, *Australasia*, 159.

32. *North Queensland Register*, February 20, 1895

33. Copeland, *A Few Weeks*, 10.

34. Malcolm Andrews, *The Search for the Picturesque: Landscape, Aesthetics and Tourism in Britain, 1760–1800* (Aldershot: Scholar Press,1989), 49.

35. *Straits Times*, January 22, 1889.

36. *Brisbane Courier*, November 1, 1886.

37. *Straits Times*, June 10, 1911.

38. *Brisbane Courier*, June 27, 1874.

39. *Queenslander*, July 3, 1909.

40. Broinowski, *Yellow Lady*, 39.

41. *North Queensland Register*, February 20, 1895.

42. Copeland, *A Few Weeks*, 8.

43. *Queenslander*, March 24, 1906.

44. *Queenslander*, April 6, 1907.

45. Copeland, *A Few Weeks*, 10, 29.

46. Broinowski, *Yellow Lady*, 39.

47. *Brisbane Courier*, June 27, 1874.

48. Savage, *Western Impressions*, 203–16.

49. *Townsville Herald*, March 2, 1889. Richard C. Temple, *The World Encompassed by Sir Francis Drake* (Amsterdam: N. Israel, 1926), 65–74. Dorothy Carrington, *The Traveller's Eye* (London: Readers Union, 1949), 345–60. Downes's reproduction does not precisely match Drake's impressions of the Sultan of Ternate set out in Temple's volume.

50. Ray McLeod, "The 'Practical Man': Myth and Metaphor in Anglo-Australian Science," *Australian Cultural History* (no. 8, 1989), 37.

51. *Townsville Herald*, January 5 & February 9, 1889.

52. *Townsville Herald*, January 5, 1889. Wallace, *Malay Archipelago*, 587–88.

53. *Townsville Herald*, February 9, 1889.

54. Syed Mohammed Alatas, *The Myth of the Lazy Native: A Study of the Image of the Malays, Filipinos, and Javanese from the 16th to the 20th Century and Its Function in the Ideology of Colonial Capitalism* (London: F. Cass, 1977), 7, 62.

55. *Brisbane Courier*, May 23 & June 27, 1874.

56. McMahon, *Orient*, 73.

57. *Sydney Morning Herald*, October 19, 1901.

58. Herbert Pratten, *Through Orient to Occident* (Sydney: Ferguson, 1911), 11, 30.

59. Pratten, *Orient to Occident*, 13–14.

60. Eric Rolls, *Sojourners: The Epic Story of China's Centuries Old Relationship with Australia* (Brisbane: University of Queensland Press, 1992), 352–55. Pratten, *Orient to Occident*, 15, 26.

61. Herbert Pratten, *Asiatic Impressions: A Collection of Articles by H. E. Pratten* (Sydney: Ferguson, 1908), 52.

62. *Brisbane Courier*, November 1, 1886.

63. *Straits Times*, October 24, 1874.

64. Thomas Stamford Raffles, *The History of Java*, vol. 1 (Melbourne: Oxford University Press, 1978), 110.

65. Thomas Stamford Raffles, *The History of Java*, vol. 2 (Melbourne: Oxford University Press, 1978), 126–34.

66. *Brisbane Courier*, May 23, 1874.

67. *Straits Times*, January 22, 1889.

68. *Brisbane Courier*, November 1, 1886.

69. Pratt, *Magical Malaya*, 174–79.

70. *Townsville Herald*, February 9, 1889. See also Wallace, *Malay Archipelago*, 307. Wallace's exact words were "industrious and more honest."

71. *Queenslander*, March 24, 1906.

72. *North Queensland Register*, February 29, 1894.

73. Stuart Macintyre, *The Oxford History of Australia: vol. 4, The Succeeding Age, 1901–1942*, (Oxford: Oxford University Press, 1990), 124.

74. *Straits Times*, February 24, 1891.

75. Copeland, *A Few Weeks*, 28.

76. Copeland, *A Few Weeks*, 34.

77. Copeland, *A Few Weeks*, 34.

78. Ambrose Pratt, "Production and Consumption," *Stead's Review*, 1930, 41–42.

79. Pratt to the Editor, *The Spectator*, January 19, 1931, MS6589, Box 329/5 (c), Australian Manuscripts Collection, State Library of Victoria (hereafter AMC SLV).

80. Ambrose Pratt, "An Australian in Malaya," no. 6, Pratt Papers in the John Kinmont Moir Collection, 51/1 (c), AMC SLV.

81. *Straits Times*, 19 March 1897.

82. *Straits Times*, 19 March 1897.

83. *Queenslander*, 24 March 1906.

84. *Queenslander*, 8 September 1906.

85. Pratten, *Orient to Occident*, 10.

86. Pratten, *Orient to Occident*, 11.

87. *North Queensland Herald*, June 3, 1905.

88. *Straits Times*, March 15, 1905.

89. A clothing material made from linen or cotton.

90. *Queenslander*, September 1, 1906.

91. *Queenslander*, March 24, 1906.

92. Copeland, *A Few Weeks*, 10. Although the prevailing paradigm of infection in the 1880s identified miasma as a cause of tropical disease, Copeland was aware that contaminated water played a significant role in the spread of cholera.

93. *North Queensland Register*, February 20, 1895.

94. *North Queensland Herald*, January 23, 1904.

95. McMahon, *Orient*, 61–74.

96. Wang Gungwu, "Trade and Cultural Values: Australia and the Four Dragons," in *Community and Nation: China, Southeast Asia and Australia*, ed. Wang Gungwu, (Sydney: Allen & Unwin, 1992), 301.

97. *Sydney Morning Herald*, August 1, 1913.

98. *Sydney Morning Herald*, July 19 and 20, 1927.

99. *Sydney Morning Herald*, July 19, 1927.

100. *Sydney Morning Herald*, July 19, 1927

101. McMahon, *Orient*, 151–65.

102. McMahon, *Orient*, 11–12

103. Walker, *Anxious Nation*, 190–94, 223–24.

104. *Argus*, June 30, 1925.

105. Pratt, "Racial Snobbery," unpublished manuscript, MS 6558, 327/8 Pratt Papers AMC SLV.

106. Ambrose Pratt, "What Is Wrong with the Attitude of the Australian People towards Asia," unpublished manuscript. c. 1942, Pratt Papers, MS 6556, 327/8, AMC SLV. One of the clearest examples of Pratt's interpretation of Chinese philosophy is given in A. Pratt, "A Point in Time," c. 1941, typescript, Pratt Papers, MS6507, Box 322/4, AMC SLV.

107. *Age*, January 3, 1944.

108. Jack C. Deeney, "Round the World in a School Vacation (30,000 miles in 50 Days): The Story of a Holiday trip," unpublished manuscript, John Oxley Library, OM 78–16.

5

A Share in the Place

THE POLITICS OF AUSTRALIAN
REGIONAL INVESTMENT RELATIONS

The Great War of 1914–1918 marked the end of a sustained period of world economic expansion dating from the mid-nineteenth century. International tourism remained a salient globalizing trend, but international trade and investment grew at a much slower rate in the interwar years. The White Australia policy and tariff protection were designed to shut Asia out of Australia and yet more Australians were drawn into regional economic and political affairs. Investment linkages with the Archipelago developed substance and continuity as Australian mining capital poured into Malaya and Siam. Australian investors became as sensitive to political and economic developments in Asia as they were to price movements half a world away in London. Strangely named mining companies, and the names of Thai royalty and elite Asian business people, entered the everyday conversations of Australian investors in Thai and Malayan tin stocks. As British subjects, Australians travelled and traded under the protection of the British Crown but exploited opportunities to assert an Australian identity for local commercial advantage. Members of the same imperial firm, Australian and British companies more often clashed than cooperated in their competition for Asian spoils.

COMPLEX INTERDEPENDENCIES

However much trade fluctuated from year to year, or shipping services varied their ports of call, the value of Australian exports to the Archipelago followed a long-term growth pattern, reversing the import dependence of the early 1800s. For reasons of culture, insecurity and political dependence, Australian governments strove to retain a robust preferential trading relationship with Britain, which supplied the bulk of Australia's textiles, machinery and metals. As long as Britain could supply Australian demand, then British goods were preferred. British merchants purchased Australia's wool clip, wheat, butter, frozen beef and other frozen meats, and, while Britain could absorb Australia's surplus production, Australian exporters had little reason to seek alternative markets. Such complacency contributed to the frequent dispatch of inferior quality produce to Asian buyers, resulting in the loss of useful markets. In the 1880s, sales of Australian salted beef to the Netherlands Indies army were suspended when the Commissariat deemed 97 percent of one shipment unfit for human consumption, rendering it the last in a series of poor quality consignments. However, against this must be placed the difficulty of storing perishable goods in a hot climate, and of transporting them over long distances in the early days of refrigeration. As shipping companies increased cold storage capacity aboard their mail steamers, so consumers in Malaya and Java drooled in anticipation of the arrival of Australian frozen rather than salted meat.

Frozen beef and the live cattle trade were early export success stories that seem not to have been hampered by occasionally poor quality shipments. By the 1890s, Australian meat was again a highly prized foodstuff among Netherlands Indies troops and after 1898 demand for Australian frozen beef from the American army in the Philippines was consistently strong.[1] Mayor Angelo found that the poor quality of locally produced beef and mutton gave government officials in the Straits Settlements reason to beg for supplies of Australian live sheep and cattle.[2] From being a major exporter to Australia in the 1850s, the Philippines became a major Australian meat export market. Recognizing that the absorptive capacities of British markets were diminishing, state and commonwealth governments turned their attention to independent trade promotion closer to home. In 1903 T. Suttor was appointed to represent NSW commercial interests in Asia. The following year Queensland appointed Frederick Jones as its own commercial agent in Asia.[3] By 1906 Victoria had two commercial representatives operating in Asia while South Australia had one. Businessmen in New South Wales and Queensland, eager to develop their exports of meat, coal, gold, and semi-processed foodstuffs such as flour, butter, cheese, and bacon, were peering inquisitively into Asian marketplaces

This slow drift away from reliance on British markets appears negligible in comparison to the volume and value of Australasian trade sixty years later, but it marked the beginnings of a change of tide in Australian trading patterns that preferential imperial tariff arrangements in the 1930s would fail to stem. Useful markets for Australian frozen beef, live cattle and coal opened up throughout in the Archipelago in the 1900s. Manila was an important port of call for Australian commercial agents as they travelled to Asian capitals selling Australian flour, butter, coal, jam and preserved meats "door to door." On his first visit in 1904 Frederick Jones quickly made himself known within the elite circle of American government officials. As he reported to F. Denham, the Queensland Home Secretary in April 1904, "I get more real information chatting after dinner of a night than I manage at the offices during the day."[4] Near to the end of his first tour Jones proposed an Asian trade strategy for Queensland. He ranked the major Asian markets in their order of importance to the state, advising that Queensland business interests be encouraged to direct their exports firstly towards the Hong Kong market, then Manila, Java, Singapore and the Straits Settlements. Jones even suggested in a confidential letter to the Queensland Premier in 1904 that he encourage exporters to capture Asian markets by underselling British and Dutch competitors.[5]

Criticizing both the Queensland and Commonwealth governments over trade policy, Jones shifted his attention to southern China and Manila. Talking up the worth of Asian markets and his own precarious position, he criticized Australia's failure to take full advantage of the economic opportunities presented by the American seizure of the Philippines. This might have been so, but Queensland's export trade with the Philippines grew substantially in his first year as Queensland Trade Commissioner, from £96,153 in 1904 to £170,748 in 1905, delivering a healthy balance of trade surplus for that year of £163,623 (table 5.1). On the matter of trade with the Netherlands Indies he advised Chief Secretary A. Morgan that "the neglect has simply been criminal" (table 5.2). Yet Jones realized that submerged tensions in trading relations were not simply attributable to lack of interest or the poor quality of Australian exports. In denying any possibility of Australian-Dutch antagonism in an address to the Surabaya Chamber of Commerce, Jones merely confirmed the reality of longstanding geopolitical rivalry in the eastern Archipelago:

> There is not, and cannot be, any antagonistical racial feeling between Australians and the Colonists of the Dutch East Indies. Let us endeavour then to

Table 5.1.   Queensland's balance of trade with major trading partners in maritime South East Asia, 1905 and 1913 (£ sterling).

	1905			1913		
	Import	*Export*	*Balance*	*Import*	*Export*	*Balance*
Philippines	7,125	170,748	163,623	15,894	224,158	208,264
Java	12,903	4,761	−8,142	35,671	24,531	−11,140
Straits Settlements	10,429	15,814	5,385	66,653	219,095	152,442

Source: Statistics for the State of Queensland, 1905, QV&P, Statistics for the State of Queensland, 1913, QV&P.

Table 5.2. Trade with the Netherlands Indies, 1890, 1900 & 1909 (£ sterling)

	1890		1900		1909	
	Import	Export	Import	Export	Import	Export
Queensland	260	1,625	34,600	8,410	16,245	8,205
New South Wales	122,342	50,358	103,493	86,203	607,849	183,224
Commonwealth	414,178	57,921	461,748	125,285	1,056,885	480,984

Source: J. B. Trivett, *The Official Yearbook of New South Wales, 1909–10*, (Sydney: Government Printer, 1911), QLA V&P, vol. 1, 1892, QLA V&P, vol. 2, 1901, QLA V&P, vol. 1, 1913. G. H. Knibbs, *Official Yearbook of the Commonwealth of Australia, 1901–1919*, no. 13, 1920 (Melbourne: Commonwealth Bureau of Census and Statistics, 1920), pp. 582–89. All statistics, with the exception of imports for 1909, reflect quinquennial trade values for the periods 1887–1891, 1897–1901, 1909–1913.

cement our friendship by entering into an alliance for the furtherance of commercial and industrial progress and expansion. Gentlemen, it is not military glory but prosperity, wealth, civilization and culture which are the real foundations of a nation's greatness.[6]

With an eye to his future employment, Jones argued that Australia must pursue an independent trade policy in Asia, and the Philippines in particular. Unless Australia was prepared to give preferential treatment to American goods, he predicted Australian trade with the Philippines would ultimately suffer. Unafraid to challenge entrenched orthodoxies, Jones questioned the value of Britain's diplomatic network in Asia. "Australia," he asserted "has to fight its own commercial battle in the Orient. We cannot constantly hope to rely upon British official help."[7] His NSW counterpart, Suttor, agreed and adopted a similar tone when trying to persuade his political masters to take a more active interest in trade promotion.[8]

Dogged by what he termed "spiteful" allegations that he was dishonest and bankrupt, Jones resigned as Queensland's commercial agent in 1907 complaining bitterly that his salary was unfairly low in comparison to his interstate counterparts. Commercial travellers on official or quasi-official trade missions commonly found space in their itineraries for sightseeing, leading to jibes that they combined too much pleasure with business. Queensland's improved Asian export trade from 1905 onwards reflected more bourgeoning demand for Queensland beef in the Philippines than the direct effect of state trade promotion. Returns from the NSW commercial representative were equally mixed. By 1909 NSW exports to the Philippines reached £207,464, of which more than half came from the export of coal, attributable to the growth in shipping under the American occupation. But within a decade NSW exports to the Philippines reached £490,826, three quarters of this being realized on the sale of flour. Between 1904 and 1913 the Philippines accounted for approximately 0.7 percent of the Australian Commonwealth's external trade. Yet, in 1913, the Philippines accounted for 1.81 percent of Queensland's total two-way trade. Trading partners in Asia were of greater significance to those former colonies of closer geographical proximity or with well-established trading ties than to the Commonwealth as a whole.

A similar distinction can be made between NSW and Commonwealth state trade statistics. Java provided 7.1 percent of New South Wales's imports in 1909 compared to an average 1.26 per cent of total Commonwealth imports for the period 1909–1912 with sugar remaining the chief item.[9] Australia's immigration law was a source of friction with Chinese merchants and Jones was at pains to reassure the region's Chinese business networks that the White Australia policy was not directed specifically against them. Angelo noted that Singapore's *Baba* Chinese business community was proud of their British citizenship and "well posted up in Australian affairs."[10] Australian foodstuffs reached their mainly European consumers through Asian, usually Chinese, intermediaries. Despite a litany of Australian export failures, the determination of Jones and Suttor to prolong their employment and undoubted resentment towards Australian immigration restriction, Australian businesses continued making inroads into Asian markets.[11]

The old idea of Australasia retained its appeal to those looking to justify a stronger Australian regional trade. In his commissioned report for the Commonwealth government on trade prospects with the Netherlands Indies and Malaya, Tasmanian Labor Senator James Long stressed mutual interests with neighboring states born of geographic proximity and economic complementarity that made the Archipelago a "natural outlet" for Australian exports.[12] Writing while World War I raged in Europe, he assumed an inevitable increase in the European populations to Australia's north, and anticipated greater future trading opportunities for Australian business. "The established popularity and quality of Australian goods" he advised, "should help most materially to increase the volume of our trade."[13] Long expressed concern over Australia's trade deficit with the Netherlands Indies, although the imbalance was by 1915–1916 less than 5 percent of total two-way trade, down from 37.5 percent in 1909.

Freight charges were an impediment to the growth of Australian export markets but some states fared better than others. Angelo calculated that despite the greater distances involved, flour could be supplied more cheaply from New South Wales to Singapore than from Perth.[14] A greater obstacle than the crippling freight charges imposed upon Australian exporters by British shipping cartels, Australian exports appealed to mainly European customers in Asia. The overwhelmingly Anglocentric cultural bias of the Australian economy hindered the pursuit of new trading opportunities. Export production was geared towards serving the needs of British industry and British consumer tastes, while import preferences secured markets in Australia for British manufacturers. Further, colonial governments in Asia looked to maximize consumption of domestic produce and prevent the displacement of local products by imported foods. A Queensland trade delegation to the region in the 1930s found the principal reason for the state's declining share of the Philippines's frozen beef market was a 600 percent increase in the size of the Philippines cattle herd between 1912 and 1934.[15]

Australia was surrounded by inward-looking European and American colonies seeking to promote exports and substitute imports with local produce. Comparatively small trade values consequently disguise significant Australian business promotion and investment-related activity in the Archipelago. By the 1890s, Australian prospectors and gold and tin miners could be found across an arc starting in New Guinea and stretching to the Malay state of Kelantan on the Malay Peninsula. In New Guinea, Nelson writes that "some thought they were Australian pioneers, extending the Australian frontier. Others thought they were to be civilizers in a foreign land."[16] A handful of profitable, if short-lived, Australian-owned tin-mining companies were established on the Larut tin fields in Perak but the most famous Australian Malayan venture was the Raub Australia gold mine in Pahang. Twenty years later this mining frontier extended to the tin districts of Phuket and Ranong on the west coast of Siam.

THE OUTER ISLANDS AND BEYOND

The turn towards imperial consolidation rather than expansion transformed the work of colonization into an administrative enterprise. Given formal responsibility to govern the Territory of Papua, the Australian Commonwealth looked to Eurasian models of colonial development. Staniforth Smith authored two parliamentary reports on government and development in Malaya and the Netherlands Indies that recommended, among other things, the institutionalization of research into tropical agriculture and the exchange of agricultural experts between Papua, the Netherlands Indies and Malaya.[17] The geographical and cultural origins of the Tugeri defined diplomatic exchanges between Britain and the Netherlands in the 1890s over the location of their mutual border in New Guinea. Mineral exploration hastened discussion the Anglo-German boundary. Straddling the loosely defined boundary between Papua and German New Guinea, the Waria River briefly attracted the interest of Australian gold miners in the decade before World War I. Britain and Germany agreed not to modify their land border to follow the course of the river, preferring the relative simplicity of the eighth parallel of latitude as opposed to a tangible but naturally shifting topographic feature. Without careful surveying work to position the boundary on the ground in relation to significant topographical features, miners roamed along the Waria unaware if they were passing in or out of German territory.[18]

Despite their limited numbers, the behavior of Australian miners on the Waria was a reminder of the depravity to which Australian pioneer adventurers could sink in frontier territories far removed from the gaze of European publics and the rule of British-Australian law. Lieutenant Governor of Papua Sir Hubert Murray was appalled at acts of violence perpetrated by some Australian miners towards the indigenous population, although he believed that "there has been no systematic brutality here as in Queensland and other parts of Australia." This he thought somewhat surprising given the number of "bad characters" that had migrated from North Queensland to Papua.[19] In the interior, Australians found land occupied, not by small communities of hunter-gatherers, but by populous tribes with equally complex rites of passage, of which White intruders were for the most part utterly ignorant. Nelson relates instances where miners attacked and plundered villages on the Waria in reprisal for the abduction or killing of one of their Papuan employees, or "nigs" as they were known, earning the disdain of German authorities who, though tolerant of Australian miners, were concerned by their violent tendencies.[20] For indigenous New Guineans who inhabited the area, the notion of a geopolitical land border was meaningless, but they, as with all other indigenous communities throughout the Archipelago, were powerless to prevent the slow dissection of their island world.

At home, Australians watched the expansion of German trading activity in the Archipelago with increasing alarm. Fear of a German sphere of influence from Timor to Bougainville prompted fresh calls by that militant mercantilist, Captain Strachan, for a pre-emptive invasion of Portuguese Timor.[21] Within only a few years the Anglo-German border in New Guinea became an arbitrary dividing line between two Australian-administered territories when the Australian Naval and Military Expeditionary Force seized the German capital of Rabaul following the outbreak of war in Europe. After the war, the newly formed and short-lived League of Nations granted German New Guinea to Australia as a trusteeship under a "C" class mandate. Even so, the possibility of further territorial acquisitions was not entirely discounted by Murray. Citing Dutch neglect of its portion of New Guinea, in an unofficial expression of opinion, he wrote,

It would be quite a good thing if the Commonwealth or Great Britain were to buy Dutch New Guinea and make one Govt. of the whole island. It is not too big. There is no Dutch capital invested in Dutch New Guinea, so there would be no one to compensate.[22]

In addition to Dutch New Guinea, and the British Solomon Islands Protectorate, Australian interest in Portuguese Timor resurfaced from time to time as Australian mining interests probed the island for resources. Australians were less visibly embroiled in Anglo-Siamese competition on the northern Malay Peninsula. Siamese or Thai kings who ruled a new Thai state founded on Bangkok in 1782, claimed the right to exercise authority over the Malay Peninsula and much of modern-day Laos and Cambodia. The Malay sultanates of Kedah, Perlis, Terrenganu and Kelantan were regarded by Bangkok as tributary states and during the nineteenth century became increasingly subject to the will of the Thai Court. Echoing the opinions of many in the British-Malayan mining community, Henry Copeland observed, "The Siamese native states, although safe enough to travel through if proper care is taken, are not in that stage of civilization to give a secure title to anything that might be discovered."[23] At that time, Australian mining horizons barely extended beyond Penang, leading to some confusion as to where British Malaya officially ended and Siam began. In 1900 the New South Wales Chamber of Mines expressed an interest in an exchange of mining information with the Thai government, sending a letter of introduction and an edition of their publication *Monthly Transactions* clumsily addressed to the "Minister for Agriculture, Siam, Malay Peninsula." Miraculously, the package reached its destination.[24]

There was every reason for confusion as to the extent of Thai political authority on the northern Malay Peninsula where rich deposits of highly prized alluvium had been mined commercially since at least the thirteenth century.[25] Mocking the area's political geography, a belt of alluvial tin extending from the Thai-Burma border at Chiang Rai through lower Burma and Malaysia to the islands of Bangka and Belitung (Biliton) off the northeastern coast of Sumatra, ran parallel to traditional trade routes connecting the Upper Mekong to the Bay of Bengal. Traditionally, however, elite families on the south west coast of Siam looked to the western Malay Peninsula and the Bay of Bengal for their incomes rather than to Bangkok and the Chaophraya Valley. With the encroachment of British mining interests in Malaya, economic and social links between the west coast and the Straits Settlements steadily deepened and broadened.

The vaguely defined boundary area separating Bangkok's southern territories from the Federated Malay States had developed into a pressing strategic concern for the Thai royal elite. The vast bulk of tin ore and locally smelted tin metal went to Penang for transshipment to the canneries of Britain.[26] A British sphere of influence on the northern Peninsula was acknowledged under the 1896 Anglo-French Treaty as far as Bang Saphan north of the Isthmus of Kra. The treaty was followed in 1897 by an Anglo-Siamese Secret Convention under which Bangkok agreed not to grant concessions to foreign entrepreneurs in its southern provinces and principalities without prior British approval. The agreement, which may be thought of as an appendix to the Anglo-French Treaty, did not guarantee Thai sovereignty over its Malay vassals, but rather it was designed to protect British commercial and strategic interests. Britain considered the entire Peninsula within its sphere of influence and demanded assurances that no competing foreign powers, in particular France and Germany, gain a port facility that might be used to threaten British naval supremacy in the Indian Ocean or British commerce. Bangkok feared that increased British commercial activity in the south of the country might be a precursor to further territorial demands. From the Thai point of view, state security and mining administration were inseparable.

For strategic and economic reasons, Britain was more interested in appropriating territory from Siam than either the Netherlands Indies or Germany. Malaya and Burma bordered the strategic center of Britain's Asian empire, the Bay of Bengal, while New Guinea and Australia lay at the periphery. British mining investors hungered for access to Siam's "underdeveloped" mineral-rich Malay provinces but were resisted by a suspicious Thai state. Following the familiar pattern for border demarcation and revision, defense and a "divine right" to develop natural resources were used to press Britain's advantage. The 1909 Anglo-Siamese Treaty placed the Malay states of Kelantan, Terengannu, Kedah and Perlis under British jurisdiction while Britain recognized Thai claims over the Malay majority *prathetsaraj* (principalities) of Pattani, Yala, Narathiwat and Setul, even if their traditional Malay rulers did not.[27] In return for Bangkok's acquiescence, Britain granted Siam a low-interest loan to construct a railway line connecting Bangkok with the FMS via Penang and Lopburi.[28] Rail development, of course, threatened to draw southern Siam more tightly into the economic orbit of Penang and the FMS and possibly, as was feared by the Malay state of Johore, lead to the incorporation of more of Siam's southern provinces into British Malaya.

Anglo-Thai rivalry on the Peninsula created opportunities for more adventurous Australian prospectors to gain a competitive advantage over British rivals. Unlike Malaya, where Australians negotiated access to mineral resources with British officials, in southern Siam Australians from Hobart, Melbourne and Sydney formed business alliances with prominent local Sino-Thai families. Australian capital and mining expertise were in high demand in the west coast tin-mining centers of Phuket and Ranong. The Khaw family, a prominent Sino-Thai dynasty in southern Siam, patronized by members of the Thai royal elite and incorporated into the provincial administration through the appointment of family members in key government positions, actively sought out Australian expertise. With shipping and mining interests spanning the Siam-Malaya border, the family both aided the process of state centralization in Siam while strengthening the economic linkages between the southern Thai tin-mining districts and the western Malay Peninsula. Khaws traveled from southern Siam to Penang for medical treatment, sent their children there for their education, and gathered for holidays at the salubrious Chakrabong House overlooking the harbor at Georgetown. Khaw Sim Bee, the first Superintendent Commissioner of the newly created administrative circle of Phuket, from 1899 to his assassination in 1913, held the official Thai title, *Phraya* Ratsadanupradit-mahisonphakdi, which was both a measure of the confidence placed in him by King Chulalongkorn, Rama V (1869–1910) and Siam's influential Minister for the Interior, Prince Damrong Rajanuparb, and recognition of his considerable personal influence. Testimony to the Khaw family's enduring wealth and power in the south, another three family members were simultaneously governors in Ranong, Langsuan and Krabi.[29] Access to mineral resources had to be negotiated through Khaw family mediators who were generously recompensed with allocations of free shares in Australian mining ventures.

Perhaps hoping to exploit tensions between British and Australian entrepreneurs, Sim Bee and Khaw Joo Tok, the family's "Penang director," selected a former shipping magnate, Tasmanian politician and government minister Edward Thomas Miles, as their agent of industrial modernization. Miles was taken to view tin workings on the shores of Phuket Harbor from which vantage point he assumed, correctly, that alluvial tin deposits extended far out from the shoreline. He secured leases to dredge the harbor bed and designed an offshore tin dredge to commence recovery in 1907. In addition to offloading several surplus Australian tramp steamers to Asian clients, including the Khaw-owned Koh Guan Company, Miles was also working as a commercial agent for Hobart jam manufacturers Henry Jones & Co, a company pursuing an aggressive investment strategy and looking to diversify into Malayan tin.[30] Personal considerations also affected Miles's decision to recommend offshore mining leases in Phuket Harbor to his Tasmanian sponsors. Perhaps fearing that a tarnished reputation, acquired in a public scandal concerning his dealings as harbormaster at Strahan, might hinder his progress in Malaya, Miles appreciated that in Siam he was at least not at the mercy of condescending British administrators.[31] Furthermore, as an astute businessman he could not have been entirely ignorant of the political tensions existing between British Malaya and Siam at that time.

The Hobart-registered Tongkah Harbour Tin Dredging Company Limited was the first, largest and longest surviving of the Australian tin companies formed to exploit alluvial tin in the bays and rivers of Siam's south west coast. Employing the world's first commercial offshore bucket dredge, designed by Miles, the venture proceeded with the personal blessings of Chulalongkorn, Rama V. Number 1 Dredge was launched at Pyre Dock, Penang, on 4 November 1907, in the presence of Damrong who, to mark the significance of the occasion, posed for a photograph with Miles and his entourage. Tongkah Harbour was a genuinely transnational company with a dredge built by William Simons & Co. in a Scottish shipyard using Dutch and German machine technology, re-assembled and manned by Chinese engineers, towed to Phuket by Koh Guan steamer for operation in southern Siam in the service of Sino-Thai enterprise for a Tasmanian jam maker and the Thai state. Floated on the Hobart stock exchange on 23 November 1906 with a registered capital of £150,000, the Tongkah Harbour Company proved the most successful Australian-initiated tin-dredging venture formed to operate in Siam, both in terms of its longevity and production. By 1918 the company returned £438,000 in dividends to investors.[32] Remaining in Australian hands until the late 1930s, this was an unlikely Australasian business alliance that initiated a surge of Australian mining investment into Siam.

The Thai elite appreciated the national economic benefits of increased tin production and valued the Australian contribution, both to national economic development and to the strengthening of Thai sovereignty on the peninsula.[33] Accepting that the country lacked the technology and experience to develop these resources without outside assistance, Chulalongkorn's successor, King Wachirawut, Rama VI (1910–1925), nonetheless sought tight control of the political risks associated with a potentially overpowering foreign-owned mining sector. In the context of an expanding world economy, driven largely by British overseas investment, it was understood that pressure for access from British mining companies would be difficult to resist. Minister for Lands and Agriculture, *Phya* Wongsanupraphat, set out the dilemma faced:

> We have no desire to see wild waters flood us everywhere. We must therefore plan a way to protect ourselves. But it is the nature of running water that when blocked it must be allowed to flow in another direction. We must think of a way to harness the energy of this wild water and use it to propel things that will provide benefits for our country not merely allow it to flood in and punish us.[34]

It was acceptance of harsh economic and political reality. British interests had what they believed to be treaty rights to the natural resources of peninsular Siam. The Minister warned that the government must develop a clear policy to deal with foreign investment in the rubber and mining industries. Ultimately, he believed that foreign capital investment would be to the advantage of the state.[35] Wongsanupraphat's views were not shared by other ministers or the king who transferred him to the Ministry of Communications and consented to a ban on foreign oil prospecting in 1918 lest this encourage fresh claims for a revision of Siam's southern border. [36]

CULTURE AND CAPITAL

Finding themselves in a dependent political relationship with Siam's governing classes, Australians behaved quite differently to their counterparts in
New Guinea. At a time when the currents of anti-Asian sentiment ran
strongest in Australia, Australians accepted their place in Siam's social order. Damrong twice met Miles, in Phuket and then in Bangkok, prior to the
launch of the company's tin dredge. Miles deliberately asserted an Australian identity to distance himself from British-Malayan business interests.
Recognized in Damrong's official correspondence as *"chao australia"* (an
Australian), as opposed to *"chao angkrit"* (an Englishman), Miles' ingenuity,
enthusiasm and apparent sincerity created an impression.[37] These were not
the Prince's first encounters with an Australian. He crossed paths with
Melbourne-born Earnest Morrison in Bangkok in January 1899 and again
in February 1906, when Morrison was working as a correspondent for the
London *Times*.[38] That a senior minister of a foreign country perceived a difference between Australians and British, even if the distinction was to remain vague for a long time to come, suggests the strength of Australian
identification with an emerging national ethos.

Australians formed a modestly sized but distinctive expatriate community in southern Siam. Australians and Britons did not segregate themselves
into separate enclaves; rather many Australians exhibited an ethos which
marked them out as different. Australian mine managers were more prepared to endure physical hardship than their British counterparts, were better versed in the art of mine management and more willing to get involved
in the hard physical work of mining and machine maintenance.[39] On their
site of operation they were all-powerful and ran their company's affairs like
White rajahs, albeit on the modest income of around £900 per year. The introduction of capital-intensive mining had delivered great powers of pa-
tronage to them. Dredging companies ran three shifts per day and thus
needed three crews to man the dredge. In addition, at each mine were clus-
tered workshops and ore-dressing sheds. Up to forty dredge hands and laborers, mainly Chinese, were employed on each shift, recruited directly by
the manager.[40] In his position as headman, the mine manager commanded
the respect and deference of employees and the local villagers. High wages
were paid even to unskilled workers who could earn more than double the
prevailing day rate with Tongkah Harbour while mechanics could earn as
much as five dollars per day.[41]

Mining developed into a capital-intensive industry and as a consequence
Siam became more and more dependent upon foreign capital and expertise
to develop the country's second largest source of export income.[42] While
bringing high returns to investors and increased royalty payments to the
Thai State, the benefits of these changes were unevenly distributed amongst

the population of southern Siam. High wages raised the cost of living in provinces where tin-dredging companies were concentrated. Locally recruited and trained mine engineers and dredge-hands were mostly Chinese. Thai farmers either stayed in their rice fields or else moved to a district where living was cheaper.[43] Australian mine managers and the companies for which they worked were, as in New Guinea, agents of industrial change and social dislocation in southern Siam.

Australian managers and company directors acclimatized quickly to the local commercial environment, even learning Malay, the *lingua franca* of the peninsula's tin fields. Melbourne and Sydney tin syndicates accepted the need for a local intermediary to limit political risk and consequently experienced few difficulties securing prospecting and dredging leases, provided they were willing to pay the asking price. The Australian companies Nawng Pet, Huai Yot, Nai Hoot and Haad Yai belonged to the Sydney and Taiping–based King-Munro syndicate, named after its two principal members, A. J. "Tiger" King and F. Munro. It was officially known as the Malay-Siamese group and King, a veteran of the Australian goldfields, was its colorful managing director.[44] Under King's iron leadership this group was quickest to acquire leases close to the route of the southern railway in the early 1920s. King was at the center of a bribery scandal in June 1924 involving two Thai officers in the Royal Department of Mines and Geology office in Nakhon Srithammarat, *Luang* Wimol Lohakarn and *Nai* Srisuk Thiensuwarn. Over the previous three years King dealt directly with these officials who did much to assist the establishment of a number of King-Munro syndicate companies.[45] In appreciation, King offered both a total of 2500 fully paid £1 shares in Huey Yot Tin Dredging as a gift.[46]

King's offer was declined but news of the affair reached the Minister for Lands and Agriculture, the *Chaophraya Phonlatheb*, Chalerm Na Nakhon.[47] In a strongly worded letter to directors of Huey Yot, the minister labelled King's actions "a criminal offence" and warned that they "seriously compromised the success of your company so far as operations in Siamese territory may be concerned."[48] King's fellow directors came to his defense claiming that no bribe was intended and that the share offer was merely an act of genuine gratitude on King's part. King claimed that the shares belonged to him personally and were not offered in his official capacity as a director of Huey Yot but as a friend. In his letter of defense King added that Huey Yot was located outside the jurisdiction of the Nakhon Srithammarat Mines office and that he had never been granted any official assistance from the two officers concerned.[49] This was a bare-faced lie and Chalerm had copies of King's correspondence with both officials as proof, but Huey Yot and King survived. A famed tiger hunter and polygamist, King became a celebrated character in Malayan mining circles.[50] However, the episode left the minister with a poor impression of Australian tin miners.

King's corrupt practices were merely the tip of the iceberg. Even though the extent to which Australian company directors were aware of collusion between Sino-Thai capitalists and provincial administrators cannot be known, they were enmeshed in a web of speculative land dealing that by the 1920s alarmed the central government. Working through land agents, who purchased prime tin-bearing land cheaply for later sale to eager Australian mining companies at inflated prices, Joo Tok secured shareholdings in many new Australian mining enterprises. Commissions from lease and permit sales received by the High Commissioner of Phuket, from the time of Khaw Sim Bee, were kept secret from the Mines Department and the Ministry of Lands and Agriculture. This pattern of collusion between investors and local administrators was replicated elsewhere in southern Siam, helping Australian dredging companies to secure exploration and mining leases in Songkhla and Nakhon Srithammarat. Indirectly, they were party to the extortion of local Thai residents in the south and of foreign tin companies not part of the Khaw network. Uncooperative "outsiders" engaged in exploration would be followed and the location of fresh ore deposits noted. When a new claim was lodged, the company concerned would suddenly be confronted with a bogus legal challenge brought by a Thai national to the effect that the lease infringed on a forest reserve. The same land would then later be offered at a price to a land agent either by the plaintiff or the provincial government. Another method was occupation, by Thai nationals, of land prospected and proven to be valuable but over which no mining lease was yet held. This was usually done at the instigation of local officials, often members of the Khaw family. A huge price would then be asked for the sale of surface rights over the occupied area. Part of the proceeds would go to the officials and the rest to the Tok Pun Tin syndicate.[51]

Sydney and Melbourne tin syndicates successfully negotiated a path through the maze of personalized business-government relations to form a major economic linkage between Australia, Malaya and Siam (table 5.3). Director of the Kerry group Charles H. Kerry estimated the share market value of Australian companies operating in Malaya, Burma and Siam at £25 million in 1927.[52] Total capital invested was of course much lower. Australian stock exchange records place total Australian mining investment in Malaya and Siam at £4,703,596 in 1925, rising to £7,733,820 by 1928 with £5 million of this invested in Malaya.[53] There were 54 Australian-owned mining companies operating dredges in Malaya in 1927 as opposed to 19 in Siam and consequently Australian-Malayan tin returns were much higher (table 5.4). With the exception of Tongkah Harbour and Melbourne-registered companies, the FMS was both a comfort zone and a useful regional base for Australian mining enterprise.

Rising worldwide interest in tin stocks contributed to the concentration of mining capital in the hands of tin-dredging groups. Reflecting the new

Table 5.3. The Australian share of tin metal returns in Siam (long tons), 1927–1941.

Year	Aust'n Co's*	Aust'n output	Ann. % growth (a)	Output Siam (b)	% (a) of (b)	World output	% (b) of (c)	% (a) of (c)
1927	19	1,058.4	—	7,440	14.2	153,000	4.86	0.69
1928	15	1,800	70	7,530	23.90	171,000	4.4	1.05
1929	16	3,818	112	10,517	36.31	189,000	5.25	2.02
1930	17	4,379.4	15	11,060	39.76	172.000	6.43	2.55
1931	na.	4,639.4	18.6	12,447	37.27	138,000	9	3.36
1932	12	3,423.16	−26	9,261	36.96	92,000	10	3.72
1933	12	3,317.68	−3	10,324	32.13	80,000	12.9	4.14
1934	12	2,983.83	−10	10,587	28.18	112,000	9.45	2.66
1935	12	2,850.55	14.4	9,779	29.14	129,000	7.5	2.20
1936	12	3,422.52	20	12,678	26.99	170,000	7.4	2.01
1937	12	3,851.64	12	16,494	23.35	195,000	8.41	1.97
1938	12	4,195.22	8	13,520	31.02	152,000	9.75	2.76
1939	13**	4,349.37	3	16,032	27.12	155,000	10.8	2.80
1940	13**	5,090.25	17	12,978	39.22	223,000	7.6	2.28
1941	13**	5,021.7#	−1.34	15,823	31.73	238,000	6.65	2.11

Sources: Australian Output, Birch, "Tropical Milestones", p. 221, The Stock Exchange of Melbourne *Official Record*, 1929–1941. Garnsey, *Eastern Tin Dredging Companies*. Total Output for Thailand, Sompop, *Economic Development of Thailand*, p. 219. World production statistics, Yip Yat Hoong, *Tin Mining Industry of Malaya*, pp. 392–93.

*Number of registered Australian companies in production only. Does not include Tongkah Harbour after 1931.

**Ore returns from Birch and *Official Record* converted to metal weight assuming 72 percent tin metal content.

#Tin production statistics not published after June 1941. Output to 7 Dec. 1941 for four companies included in this total is calculated on the basis of Jan.–May returns.

Table 5.4. Australian and European tin ore Production in Siam and Malaya, 1926–1931 (000 tons)

	Total Australian Production (i)*	Total European Production (ii)	Total Siam and Malaya*
1926	5.9	23.3	54.8
1927	6.0	24.5	61.8
1928	10.5	34.6	72
1929	12.2	48.8	82.3
1930	11.6	47.6	78
1931	9.6	41.7	67.1

Source: Birch, "Tropical Milestones," 229.
i) Includes dredge and non-dredge output but in the Australian case tin was almost exclusively obtained through dredging.
ii) Includes dredge and non-dredge output with as much as one-third obtained by methods other than dredging.
*Ore returns not converted to metal weight.

fashion for scientific management, the "rationalization" of ownership through the creation of registered management companies was declared to have many advantages for investors, including reduced administration costs and greater flexibility in the allocation of company resources.[54] Austral-Malay Tin Ltd., Alluvial Tin (Malaya) Ltd and Burma-Malay Tin Ltd. were registered in the FMS with head offices in Taiping, Rawang and Kuala Lumpur respectively but were still Australian-run companies with offices and share registers in Sydney.[55] In contrast, Melbourne groups preferred to keep their business relations flexible and informal. It was also a distinctive feature of the Melbourne companies that share registers were maintained solely in Victoria, unlike their Sydney counterparts which by mid-decade had all opened branch registers in the FMS.[56]

While parcels of shares in Australian tin dredging ventures were held by Chinese and British investors, the bulk of capital came from the pockets of Australians who reaped the benefits.[57] For the financial year 1913–1914 Tongkah Compound NL returned £76,460 in dividends and bonuses on an initial capitalization of £50,000. The company and its subsidiary formed in 1919, Tongkah Compound No. 2 NL, eventually worked out their government compound concessions in 1920, having paid out a total of £216,250 in dividends.[58] Although the export of Australian mining investment represented a debit to Australia's balance of payments, gross annual dividends paid to Australian shareholders indicated that, as long as tin prices remained high, capital outlays would quickly be recouped. The *Industrial and Australian Mining Standard* estimated that tin-mining companies floated on the stock exchanges of Sydney, Melbourne and Hobart were returning £1 million annually to Australian shareholders.[59] As stock market analysts Pring and Docker declared,

> The present high price of tin, and the prospect of even higher prices in the future, have focused an unusual amount of attention upon the activities of Australian tin dredging companies engaged in that form of mining in the Malay Peninsula. In one particular, at least, the industry is unique, as it is the only important enterprise carried on by Australians and financed by Australian capital, having its scene of operations entirely beyond the jurisdiction of the Commonwealth.[60]

THE DIPLOMACY OF INTERNATIONAL BUSINESS

Concern that southern Siam was being drawn too tightly into the economic orbit of British Malaya resurfaced when King Prajadhipok, Rama VII (1925–1934) called upon the Board of Commercial Development to review foreign investment regulations in 1926.[61] Chaired by Prince Purachatra, elevated by Prajadhipok to Minister for Commerce and Communications, a special sub-committee reported "the only good and sure way of driving out foreign capital . . . is by creating capital within Siam and allowing it to expand." But "certain forms of foreign capital" the report claimed, were essential to domestic capital accumulation.[62] While the Minister for Agriculture expressed reservations about profit expatriation by foreign-owned mining companies, he offered no immediate alternative. Even the government's financial adviser, Sir Edward Cook, instinctively opposed to any actions that might alarm the City of London, suggested the government compel all foreign companies to employ and give technical training to Thais, or appoint Thais to their boards of directors in return for concessions and business licences.

That these proposals were not implemented reflects Purachatra's satisfaction with the prevailing structure of ownership in the tin-mining industry as much as his attachment to *laissez faire* principles. Purachatra was, like Damrong, a patron of the Khaws and equally well disposed towards Australian mining investors linked to the Khaw family. The prince, allegedly, regarded himself as the "unofficial consul general for Australia in Siam."[63] Evidence of his predisposition, he readily accommodated requests for a review of procedures governing the issue of exploration and temporary mining permits received from Australian mining interests during a semi-official visit to Sydney and Melbourne in 1927. The Minister for Agriculture, given the task of investigating Australian complaints, remained skeptical about the long-term benefits of unrestrained foreign mining investment. Echoing the economic nationalism of Siam's independent popular press, he declared that mineral resources in southern Siam "belong to Siam yet once they are mined, they are almost entirely taken away by foreigners." Dredging, he claimed, ripped away fertile topsoil to extract the alluvium beneath "to the extent that once exhausted mining leases cannot be immediately turned over to agriculture."[64] Thais, he told the Council of Ministers, were being cheated by voracious Australian dredging companies:

> We have very few Thais engaged in mining and those that are work open-cast mines with no capital. Australian companies dig deep and clear away the surface completely. No-Liability companies change hands deceptively.[65]

No-Liability was a category of investment specific to Australian mining companies, a fact known to the ministers, hence Chalerm's accusations should be read as a direct attack upon Australian companies. In a revealing riposte, Damrong defended Australian interests, and those of Khaw Joo Tok, pointedly remarking that if "we do not accept these companies then Siam will be unable to get foreign capital."[66] In fact, Siam was attracting greater foreign interest in the wake of a tin price boom and the virtual exhaustion of available tin-bearing ground in Malaya. The Minister for Lands and Agriculture instituted a committee to vet applications with greater rigor and only issue rights to those people who "genuinely wish to bring benefit to Siam."[67]

Australian mining investment in Siam peaked at £2,733,820 in 1928, more than double the level of British investment. Because Australian tin companies had already procured the richest and most easily accessible alluvial deposits, the ban preserved the relatively strong position of Australian companies, which by 1930 contributed over one-third of Siam's annual output of tin concentrates and 68 percent of dredge production.[68] At the height of the investment surge of 1927–1928, Australian mining shares had hit an all-time low on stock markets. Australia's terms of trade were declining in the face of falling commodity prices and investment in Australian industry had slackened. Interest in the search of domestic sources of tin had all but evaporated and as a consequence Australia had ceased to be a major producer.[69] In a small but significant way, the financial fates of many Melbourne and Sydney shareholders were momentarily dependent upon the course of mining and foreign investment policy in Siam.

Australian-Sino-Thai cooperation formed part of a larger canvas of international business relations linking the economic interests of tin companies in Britain, Bolivia, the United States, the Netherlands, Malaya and Siam. With Cornish tin reserves nearing exhaustion, British mining interests were drawn to Malayan tin by the promise of high profits. Demand for tin was particularly strong in the United States and, with tin prices on the London Metal Exchange peaking at £321 per ton and averaging £291.2 in 1926, the market for tin stocks was bullish. Inevitably, demand intensified for access to Siam's tin deposits from British companies based in the FMS. Before Wall Street crashed in 1929, John Howeson, Chairman of the Anglo-Oriental Mining Corporation, told shareholders of the need for an international association of tin producers that would temporarily cap production. An investment surge in the late 1920s led quickly to an oversupply of tin metal, a problem exacerbated by the onset of global depression. Howeson bought heavily into Malayan tin after Anglo-Oriental's formation in 1928, but with the tin price spiralling downwards, his over-exposed corporation was perilously close to bankruptcy.[70]

The Wall Street Crash and the onset of the Great Depression dampened demand but did nothing to halt tin output, adding greater stridency to Howeson's appeals. In September the Tin Producers Association (TPA) was formed in London to address the crisis faced by the world tin industry. A non-governmental organization, the TPA had to work with the governments of tin-producing countries if it were to achieve its goals. The TPA was comprised of representatives of 150 mining and management companies plus another 31 individual members including Howeson, the Association's driving force, and the Bolivian mining magnate Senor Antenor Patino, who served as Honorary President. It was an organization dominated by British Empire interests and controlled from London but one, which accounted for only 20.8 percent of total world[71] production. Australian interests were represented on the TPA Council by J. Malcolm Newman, one of the founders of the Malayan Alluvial Tin group with Herbert Pratten, A. W. Palfreyman, O. T. Lampriere and Arthur Miles. Despite the strong Australian presence in the tin-mining industry in Siam, an Englishman, Sir Cyril K. Butler, a director of the Siamese Tin Syndicate, was appointed spokesman for European tin interests in Siam.[72] The Association presaged the rise of Howeson and Anglo-Oriental but it was not as all-powerful or as representative a cartel as its propaganda claimed. Beyond the British Empire the amount of pressure the TPA could bring to bear on producers and governments was acutely limited. Non-British producers especially, and Siam, were unrepresented. Also some British tin companies known as the "Goepeng group" were openly opposed to the TPA scheme. Chinese miners, who still accounted for well over one-third of tin ore output in Malaya, remained outside the association. With such limited support, the planned 20 percent reduction in world tin output in 1930 proved impossible.

Although, and for different reasons, Siam gazetted a general prospecting ban in August 1930, the Thai government was not easily convinced of the need to restrict supply. While seeking to manage the entry of foreign tin companies, Siam benefited financially from royalties realized on increased output and was thus disinclined to voluntarily diminish its revenue base. Two Melbourne company directors, A. W. Palfreyman and Ambrose Pratt took matters into their own hands.

Pratt visited Bangkok in May 1930 to lobby Thai ministers on behalf of the TPA and to plead special consideration for the plight of some tin companies operating in Siam in which he and Palfreyman had a significant interest. Tongkah Compound No.s 3, 4 and 5 had yet to equip their leases when the price of tin began to fall. In addition Tinsongkhla NL, formed in 1927, had experienced serious and costly delays caused by disputes over surface rights to land connecting Tinsongkhla's leases with a nearby river. The company did not begin production until late 1928 and by early 1930 Pratt and his fellow Australian directors reached the conclusion that in view of the price of tin it was uneconomic to continue operating. Another two companies, Rangeng Tin NL and Peninsula Tin NL, came into production in late 1929 but their monthly returns were low while Lampeh (Siam) NL barely scraped up any tin at all.[73]

While supporting the TPA, Pratt was nonetheless suspicious of the Association's principal sponsor, Howeson, and his plans for Anglo-Oriental. The *Industrial and Australian Mining Standard*, of which Pratt was once proprietor, warned Australian investors that production controls would not be sufficient to stabilize the price of tin if monopoly capitalists remained at liberty to manipulate the market:

> The price of tin has never depended for any tangible period on the balancing of consumption and production. The history of the metal proves conclusively that it has always been regulated by the speculative manipulation of two rival groups of monster operators. Sometimes these groups are in conflict, sometimes, though rarely, they operate in conjunction.[74]

The paper claimed that a "propagandist campaign" designed to alarm investors about the dangers of overproduction and effect a share-price collapse was in train but refrained from naming the protagonist.[75] The only organization capable of mounting such a campaign was Anglo-Oriental. It was the first tin company ever to gather extensive data on production and consumption on a global scale and Howeson was indeed employing his sophisticated knowledge of the world tin industry to stress the need for cartelization. Howeson and Patino planned to use the organization to take control of the world tin industry through price manipulation. Howeson's scheme for a restriction of output included the creation of a tin pool to soak up excess supply. This was to be held by the British-American Corporation created specifically to buy and store this excess until tin prices recovered.[76] If successfully implemented the plan would deliver huge profits to the Howeson-Patino syndicate at the expense of small producers.

Dominance over the world's tin resources was slowly being established by a combination of British and Bolivian capital. Melbourne and Sydney investors shared similar world economic concerns, but Melbourne tin groups valued and strove to retain their independence, unlike many of their Sydney counterparts. Australian tin-dredging companies belonging to the Pratten-Newman Alluvial Tin group were sold to the London Malayan Tin Trust Ltd., forerunner to the London Tin Corporation in 1929, increasing Howeson's share of Malayan production.[77] Alluvial Tin only held properties in Malaya, but Anglo-Oriental was vying for a foothold in Siam.[78] Pratt knew that firm action to prevent further price falls was necessary if his and other Australian companies were to avoid bankruptcy, or worse, take-over by Anglo-Oriental. Thai mining regulations compelled mining companies to begin operation within one year of obtaining surface rights and work continuously or risk heavy fines and repossession of leases which left Australian investors severely exposed. Pratt and his fellow Tongkah Compound board members feared their companies would forfeit all new properties unless the Thai government agreed to a temporary relaxation of these regulations.

Pratt's mission to Bangkok was a diplomatic success, even if the TPA's attempt to institute a global voluntary production restriction regime failed. In late May 1930, Pratt negotiated with the Thai government to waive all penalties and allow companies to suspend production until the price of tin recovered.[79] Putting his knowledge of Buddhist teaching to good effect, Pratt engaged in a more sophisticated form of cross-cultural business negotiation than his predecessors. Permission was secured to delay the equipment of Tongkah Compound leases and for his struggling companies to suspend production, although many mine managers chose to increase output in 1930. Through Pratt, Australian tin companies gained a voice in the mining policy process in Siam but Melbourne investors were far from in agreement as to how best to deal with Howeson. Even the Pratt-Palfreyman group showed signs of internal dissention.

With the TPA scheme in ruins, a new model for compulsory production restriction was put forward in the International Tin Committee (ITC), which was the brainchild of the TPA and British, Bolivian and Dutch governments through which production controls were to be enforced. Following a meeting in Phuket in late April 1931, the Australian-dominated Siamese Chamber of Mines called for Siam to ignore the newly formed ITC and remain outside the first government-sponsored International Tin Agreement.[80] Breaking ranks with their director, managers for several of Pratt's companies objected to compulsory restriction. In a written statement to the Board of Commercial Development, Chamber President and manager at Pratt's Rangeng Tin NL, J. M. White, outlined the Chamber's rationale for non-compliance. Echoing Purachatra's concerns, White warned that "certain Companies may also be in a position to take advantage of the collapse of weaker companies, when restriction is imposed."[81] This was an oblique reference to Howeson's voracious Anglo-Oriental corporation. If participation was inevitable then the Chamber urged the government to secure the highest production quota possible.[82]

From the outset it was clear that British companies in Siam favored participation and objected vehemently to the Australian intervention. Australian tin companies approached the Thai government both collectively through the Chamber and individually. R. J. D. Richardson, a director of Austral-Malay Tin Ltd., wrote personally from his Taiping headquarters to the Director of Mines in Bangkok on behalf of Pungah Tin NL, Austral-Malay's sole dredging company in Siam. Richardson argued that restriction by Malaya, Bolivia, the Netherlands Indies and Nigeria was in itself sufficient to limit world output to a level below anticipated demand. There was thus no need for Siam to join the ITC. Further, restriction would force Pungah Tin to lay off highly trained foreign staff creating long-term difficulties for the company. Richardson also suggested that the government did not have the trained staff necessary to ensure that regulations governing domestic restriction were enforced equitably.[83] The Chamber's petition won approval in Bangkok, Sydney and Melbourne, but caused outrage in

London, while several Anglo-Oriental subsidiaries in Siam lodged protests with the Ministry of Lands and Agriculture.[84] With Chinese mine owners in support, the Thai negotiators and policymakers enjoyed considerable bargaining power which they used to good effect securing a generous production quota in return for its compliance at the expense of larger producing countries.[85]

STERLING BALANCES

Friction between British and Australian business groups further reflected Australian recognition of distinct and separate commercial interests but few Australians wished for complete political and economic independence from Britain. The defeat of Germany's challenge to the British Empire in World War I came at a huge cost to British economic prestige and power. By the 1930s, British primacy faced new challengers in Japan and the United States, and as a consequence, Britain's advocacy of free trade wavered. Australia was by history and sentiment a member of Britain's Sterling Area and the preservation of Britain's global reach was regarded by most Australians as an irreplaceable financial pillar of the Australian Commonwealth. Hence Australia followed Britain's revaluation of sterling and raised the value of the Australian pound. The Greene Tariff of 1921 named after the Minister for Customs in the Hughes Ministry, Walter Massey-Greene, and then the 1932 Ottawa Agreement ensured preferential access for British goods in Australian markets, anchoring Australia within the British commercial sphere. In the 1930s, global and regional geopolitical trends tended to dampen Australian ambitions for greater autonomy in its external relations.

Through the activities of Australian tin-mining companies, Australia was drawn, indirectly at first, into a three-cornered contest between Britain, the United States and Japan for control of supply over what was then considered a vital strategic mineral. Believing the ITC had become the instrument of British tin interests backed by the British government, Purachatra perceptively argued that Britain and the United States were locked in an economic war for control of the world tin industry. The United States annually purchased approximately 50 percent of the world's tin metal production, but Britain had the capacity to neutralize American consumer power by controlling the processing and marketing of tin. If successful the ITC would ensure that tin prices continued to be set by the London Metal Exchange.[86] The prince believed monopolists would exploit the ITC-sponsored control regime to purchase controlling interests in tin companies that faced bankruptcy if forced to cut back production. However, without its own smelting facility, the government was virtually at the mercy of Britain and could expect reprisals against Thai tin ore exports if the government opted to stay outside the ITC.[87]

The degree of dependence upon British tin smelting, tin marketing and price setting on the London Metal Exchange meant Siam had little option other than to join the ITC. Damrong and Purachatra feared that Siam could be prevented from selling ore by virtue of its dependence upon British smelters.[88] Even if Siam could smelt its own ore, it would still be dependent upon British trading companies to market the tin metal. The strong position of Britain in Siam's external trade limited the range of options available. Purachatra perceived that the United States was weak on the issue of international tin control and was unable, due to domestic industrial unrest, to exercise its consumer power to break the cartel.[89]

A lightning *coup d'etat* on June 24, 1932, transformed Siam from an absolute to a constitutional monarchy. Major Australian daily newspapers gave the *coup* limited coverage, relying upon syndicated reports from the Singapore press.[90] There was no panic selling of Thai mining stocks by Australian shareholders and no Australian capital flight from Siam. Pratt was one of the few Australians to take a close interest in these events and reflect upon their significance. He maintained correspondence with people sympathetic to the "Revolution," as he put it, and was thus kept informed of events in Siam during June–August 1932. According to his source the transfer of power was bloodless, smooth and greeted with, if nothing else, dutiful resignation by the general public. Pratt read no challenge to his business interests from civilian *coup* protagonist Pridi Phanomyong, who planned, among many things, to redistribute wealth. Instead Pratt welcomed the end of the absolute monarchy and the creation of a parliamentary government as being in the long-term interest of Siam. While only a few years before Pratt praised the monarchy for its stability and continuity, he was now prepared to denounce it as an "age-old despotism" which the idealistic and unambitious Pridi had successfully transformed into a "democracy."[91] Pratt doubtlessly encouraged similar conclusions among his Collins Street colleagues.

American tin interests attempted to capitalize on the political changes taking place in Siam, appealing to nationalist sentiment in the People's Party with a proposal to build a tin smelter in Siam. The London-registered, but largely American-owned, British-American Mines Ltd. proposed a joint smelting venture to the interim government of *Phya* Mano. Part of an ambitious scheme to secure a share of Siam's tin export market, the approach coincided the company's registration of Siamese Tin Mines Ltd. in London to work a concession at Pinyok in Pattani. British-American Mines was prepared to meet all establishment costs associated with the tin smelter in return for a purchasing monopoly over all tin ore produced in Siam.[92] The Thai government would receive an option over a parcel of preference shares purchasable at par value regardless of market price. In addition to monetary inducements the offer included the appointment of a Thai director of the government's choosing.[93]

British-American Mines estimated that Siam had the capacity to produce as much as 30,000 tons of tin ore. With the nexus between Siam's tin industry and British Malayan smelters broken, Siam could be urged to defect from the ITC. Siamese Tin Mines would be free of quota restrictions and Siam able to supply the burgeoning need for tin metal in the United States. Cook's successor as Financial Adviser, James Baxter, campaigned against the plan on the grounds that Siam's international treaty obligations precluded the granting of an ore-purchasing monopoly. In return for the cancellation of its "unequal" treaties in the 1920s, Siam had entered into treaties of commerce and navigation with Western countries, including Britain, which obliged Bangkok not to hinder the free conduct of trade. The plan to build Siam's first large-scale commercial smelter was therefore rejected on a legal technicality.[94]

Britain's economic sphere in Asia was also subject to increasingly intense pressure from Japan. Japanese plans to secure unhindered access to strategic industrial minerals were encapsulated in a scheme designed to create a new Asian region centered on Japan. Renewed interest in a "southward advance" into the Archipelago emerged at the end of a decade in which the Japanese diaspora in the Netherlands Indies and the Philippines doubled in size.[95] Japanese intellectuals and military and political leaders called for an East Asian Federation to replace the European colonial order. Instrumental to the transformation of Asia was, according to Miyazaki Masayoshi, the development of bonds "of political and economic mutual independence" which would bind East Asia into a liberated and unified region.[96] Idealized as a region of semi-independent Asian and Pacific states, this new framework would foster trade, investment, Japanese migration, and bond Australia and the Archipelago to Japan.[97] The influential non-government Southward Expansion Movement purveyed the logic that race interest was prior to and stronger than economic self-interest, a belief doubtlessly reaffirmed by Australia's resort to punitive trade controls against Japanese and American exporters in the late 1930s.

Plans to expand Japanese influence included the intensification of efforts to secure oil concessions and supplies of tin and rubber from the Netherlands Indies, Malaya and Siam. In August 1936 a delegate from the Japanese Mitsubishi Company was reportedly negotiating with the Thai government to construct a tin smelter.[98] At the same time talks were under way in London in preparation for the Third International Tin Agreement and Siam was steadfastly holding to its demand for an annual quota allowance of 20,000 tons. British negotiators suspected that Siam's position was related to the presence of a Japanese trade delegation in Bangkok.[99] The Phahon government remained attracted to the concept of state-private sector enterprises even if, for the time being, interventionism could not progress far beyond the level of policy discussion. In spite of Baxter's earlier efforts, hopes for a Thai tin smelter endured among the new elite. At the suggestion of the Ministry for Agriculture, the Cabinet again debated the matter in August 1934. The question arose because Japan had expressed an interest in purchasing tin metal from Siam.[100] A tin smelter was thought too risky for the government to develop independently even though the economic and political benefits of breaking the nexus between the tin-mining industry in Siam and British Malayan smelting companies were obvious. Instead terms were outlined for a joint venture between the state and whichever foreign interest was willing to bear the risks of construction.[101]

In October 1936 the *Straits Times* reported the possibility of a Japanese smelter in Siam as "remote."[102] British speculation about Japanese ambitions continued driven by concern over the rising level of Japanese capital investment in Siam and the dominance of Japanese manufactures in Siam's overall import profile by the mid-30s. It was widely believed in the West that Japan wanted to break its dependence upon British Malaya for rubber and tin by diversifying its sources of supply. Foreign capital and a large production quota were essential ingredients for a successful tin-smelting enterprise in Siam. People's Assembly representatives from the south favored a dramatic increase in tin ore output to as much as 23,000 tons per year. British investors and the British government were concerned by Japanese diplomatic overtures towards Siam's military leaders. However, the Council offered Siam a generous compromise quota of 18,500 tons for the Third International Tin Agreement, to run from 1937 until 1940, nearly a 100 percent increase on its previous allowance.[103]

STRATEGIC REAPPRAISALS

The numerical superiority of Australian mining companies continued in Siam through the 1930s. Thai records indicate 22 Australian as opposed to 12 British companies were registered to operate there in 1929. Four out of 10 prospecting companies engaged in exploration work were also Australian. Of the 38 dredges in use in this year 22 were Australian owned and operated. More British Malayan companies gained access to tin deposits in the south. Some, such as Phangna River Tin Dredging Ltd., learned from earlier failures and cooperated with influential local Chinese businessmen. However, the long lead-time between securing a lease and equipping it with a dredge, up to three years in some exceptional cases, meant that British tin interests could not immediately challenge Australian leadership in the Chamber of Mines.

The world economy was contracting, as a consequence of the Depression, but also because of a longer deflationary trend dating from the First World

War. Australian equity markets weakened and tin restriction made it difficult for new companies to obtain production quotas until world tin consumption increased towards the end of the decade. Exposed to traditionally
volatile commodity prices through dependence upon primary industries,
Australian export earnings were slashed. Overseas credit finance, on which
Australian industry and governments were reliant, dried up, creating a
shortage of investment capital. Operating costs for companies engaged in
mining outside Australia increased with a 20 percent devaluation of the
Australian pound against sterling in 1931.[104] Together with a tightening of
mining regulations and growing Australian distrust of Khaw Joo Tok, these
adverse economic conditions prevented new company formations and limited the expansion of existing dredging operations. Inevitably, share prices
suffered, placing any company with cash-flow problems at the mercy of
Howeson's Anglo-Oriental. Furthermore, because the Khaw-Australia syndicate secured extensive rights over high-grade ore deposits in the 1920s,
with only low-grade deposits available to new entrants, Australian companies were attractive take-over targets. Most clung tenaciously to their independence, preferring to ride out the Depression rather than look for an
overseas buyer.[105] The exception was an overcapitalized Tongkah Harbour
which, confronted with crippling debt repayments, was gradually swal-
lowed up by Anglo-Oriental.

Rather than bide its time until prices recovered, Tongkah Harbour raised
additional share capital to fund an ambitious dredge reconditioning program. Although the company received a new twenty-five-year lease from the
Thai government that would have added substantially to shareholder value
in better economic times, by May 1932 the company faced a severe liquid-
ity crisis.[106] The company's financial difficulties were compounded by the
death of director Frank Bond. Acting as a private source of supplementary
operating capital, Bond was responsible for keeping the company afloat
during a period of economic stricture. Indebted to Bond's deceased estate
and exposed to his personally secured bank debts, raised at a time when no
other source of equity or credit was available, the Tongkah board authorized a debenture stock issue in 1933 to raise additional capital, but in so
doing they exposed the company to an aggressive take-over bid.[107]

Major shareholders in Australia were prepared to sell to the highest British
bidder.[108] Anglo-Oriental (Malaya) Ltd., Howeson's eastern subsidiary, took
over management in 1934 and moved slowly to purchase a controlling interest until in 1938 the company's head office was transferred to Kuala Lumpur
and Tongkah Harbour Tin Dredging Ltd. registered in the FMS to acquire the
assets of the old No-Liability company.[109] However, as evidence of strong residual Australian voting power, an Australian, Malcolm Kennedy, was retained as
chairman of the Tongkah Harbour board, and a branch office and share register were kept open in Hobart.[110] Anglo-Oriental (Malaya) Ltd., represented a

potent combination of Australian and British mining capital. By 1934 Sir Walter Massy-Greene, former federal minister turned successful Melbourne businessman, sat on the boards of Anglo-Oriental (Malaya) and Alluvial Tin (Australia).[111] One of the influential "Collins House family," named after the Collins Street building at which were headquartered many of Australia's largest mining companies, Massy-Greene was recruited by the Baillieus after losing his Richmond electorate in the December 1922 federal election.[112] Neither he nor Wilfred Johnson of Sydney, the other Australian director of Anglo-Oriental (Malaya) and Alluvial Tin, could challenge the authority of the London Tin Corporation's Harold Edwards or that of Adolphe Henngeler, Chairman and a director of the Howeson flagship, Anglo-Oriental & General Investment Trust.[113]

Although culture exerted a pervasive influence over Australian trade and investment patterns, the interests of Australian and British capital were never completely aligned. The alliance between Alluvial Tin (Australia), Collins House and Anglo-Oriental reflected the practical financial consideration that Australian investors stood to gain by directly accessing the London capital market. Tongkah Harbour relied upon Anglo-Oriental to raise £187,500 in additional share capital to buy out Siamese Tin Dredging Ltd., in 1934.[114] Australian mining groups could not match the critical mass accumulated by Howeson and thus the benefits of cooperation were too attractive for Tongkah Harbour directors to ignore. However, retreat into the protective arms of British mining capital was only a last resort. Many Australian tin companies clung doggedly to their independence and survived the Depression intact. Australian mining companies operating in Siam represented a capital worth of £2,342,818 in 1936, in which year they returned share dividends totalling £120,023. By then total investor returns over the lifespan of these thirteen remaining companies touched £1.5 million.[115]

The was an underlying British belief, not wholly accepted by Australian state and federal governments, that Australia should not compete with British exporters or investors in Asia nor allow "foreign" competitors to enlarge market share in Australia at Britain's expense. Where Pratt was able to walk a fine line between Empire loyalty and private business interest, others, like those active in the Siamese Chamber of Mines, were quick to assert their competitive advantage. Australian companies in Siam were consequently frowned upon by their British counterparts and by British diplomats. These tensions were mapped out on the broader canvas of Australian trade policy in the 1930s and help to illuminate tensions evident in the contradictory policy directions taken by the United Australia Party government of Joseph Lyons (1932–38). Protected by Commonwealth tariffs, Australian manufacturing expanded significantly in the early 1900s although preferential treatment meant that imports from Britain remained high. The Ottawa Agreement granted privileged access for Australian goods to the

British market and locked Australia more tightly into the British economy. Depressed export markets outside the Empire increased Australian dependence upon Britain and made it all the more imperative for Australia to keep Britain engaged in a system of preferential trade.[116] However, moving in counterpoint to this trend were efforts directed at the federal level towards the promotion of Australian exports in Asia to capitalize upon trade advantages offered by the devalued Australian pound.[117]

Australians both inside and outside government were able to reflect upon their country's place and role in Asia. Jack Shepherd's *Australia's Interests and Policies in the Far East* was, understandably, preoccupied with Japan, but at least balanced discussion of regional security interests and policies with an analysis of commercial priorities.[118] Similar substance is revealed in an anthology edited by Ian Clunies Ross, *Australia and the Far East: Diplomatic and Trade Relations*, which addressed commercial, diplomatic and cultural issues affecting Australian trading relations not just with Japan but also China and the Netherlands Indies.[119] Clunies Ross was at the forefront of debates sponsored by the Honolulu-based Institute for Pacific Relations (IPR) and its Australian affiliate, the Australian Institute for International Affairs (AIIA), addressing Australia's evolving trade and strategic interests in the Pacific.[120] Receptive to these intellectual arguments, Lyons appreciated that reliance upon British markets would not solve Australia's balance of payments problems. Rather than succumb entirely to the lure of financial security through conformity with the interests of the imperial firm, Australian political and business leaders, notably former National Party leader Sir John Latham, Minister for External Affairs and Minister for Industry from 1932–1934, and Ambrose Pratt also believed Australia's economic future was best served by striking out alone in Asia.

Though in semi-retirement due to ill health, Pratt was well connected in conservative political circles and well placed to add an informal voice to government debates about Australia's economic future. With Staniforth Ricketson, head of the stock broking firm, J. B. Were, and the aspiring Victorian politician Robert Menzies, he was one of the so-called "group of six" who founded the United Australia Party and who played a major part in persuading Lyons to resign from Labor and lead the UAP into government.[121] Pratt, who also wrote speeches for Lyons, was an experienced lobbyist at home as well as abroad, evidenced through his work as president of the Australian Industries Protection League in the 1920s.[122] Suspicious of Japan, Pratt's sympathies were with China under Chiang Kai Shek, but Latham attached primary importance to the development of relations with Tokyo. Both exemplified Australian pro-Asia sentiment in the 1930s. They were sympathetic toward Asian nationalism and, in the interests of commercial advantage, prepared to seek accommodation with militaristic Asian elites, be they Chinese, Japanese or Thai.

Three Australian trade delegations were sent out to assess market opportunities in Asia during the first four years of Lyon's tenure. The most significant was John Latham's "Eastern Mission" in 1934, which complemented the earlier findings of Herbert Gepp, a former director of Electrolytic Zinc, and led to the appointment of Australian trade commissioners to China, Japan, the Dutch East Indies and Singapore.[123] Minister for Commerce, F. H. Stewart, found substantial private sector support for an aggressive approach to marketing Australian primary and secondary products across Asia.[124] Advisory committees appointed in state capitals to sustain private sector input into Australia's nascent Asian trade strategy, provided an official forum for business to lobby government.[125] Targeting these markets would inevitably bring Australian businesses into fierce competition with British counterparts.

> Obviously the first duty of the British official is to his own Government and British commercial interests. He cannot be expected to concentrate on Australian interests—more particularly when these interests conflict, as frequently they do, with the interests of British exporters.[126]

If trade efforts in the 1930s were poorly coordinated, Australia's Asia export trade was also affected by an adverse international environment. Governments in Malaya, the Netherlands Indies, and the Philippines were as concerned to develop their industries as was the federal government to protect Australian manufacturing and agriculture. Each enjoyed protected metropolitan markets, trading outside their respective imperial spheres only to disperse surplus produce. World economic conditions were more conducive to expansionary trade policies in the early 1900s than the 1930s. Culturally, Australian export produce was not suited to regional consumer tastes. Contrary to the more optimistic assertions of Latham and Gepp, the Queensland trade delegation sent to undertake market research in the Indies, Malaya, the Philippines and China reported,

> There is apparently in Australia a wide-spread misconception as to the potentialities of these Eastern markets for Australian products, and it was to be regretted that much misleading information and deductions therefrom have been circulated to the public in this regard. In fact the capacity of these markets for Australian products was exceedingly limited. Generally—and this was the unanimous opinion—the Eastern market for Australian foodstuffs was very much over-rated and not only were the possibilities of increasing Australian exports remote, but there was a decided tendency towards decrease.[127]

Australians sought new markets in Asia but were not prepared to let competition run freely where core Empire interests were perceived to be at stake. While no one could escape the reality of Britain's displacement in the interwar balance of power in the Pacific, Australian politicians and officials were anxious that Britain remain committed to the eastern periphery of its Asian empire, and naively believed that preferential treatment of British exporters would guarantee Australia's long-term economic and strategic welfare. Hence, a thriving Japanese market for Australian wool was destroyed by the misguided introduction of trade diversion by the Lyons government in 1937 directed at imported Japanese textiles and American machinery. The measure was designed to protect British manufacturers against cheaper non-Empire imports and, foolishly, pressure Japan and the United States to accept more Australian exports. As to be expected, both countries retaliated against Australia. The Japanese government cut purchases of Australian wool, slashing by nearly two-thirds the proportion of Australian goods exported to Japan.[128] However much Australians appreciated Australia's distinct regional commercial interests, national security was thought inextricably linked to the preservation of the Sterling Bloc, which was then facing a sustained challenge in Asia from Japan and the United States.

Wayne Gobert has convincingly argued that the driving rationale for the establishment of a Commonwealth Trade Commissioner Service was the pressing need to gather political intelligence on Japanese diplomatic and business dealings throughout the Archipelago.[129] While prepared to tolerate Japanese gains in China, Canberra was not convinced by British assurances that Japan posed no threat. Australia's political leaders were also concerned that British preoccupation with events in Europe weakened Britain's resolve to deal effectively with any Japanese military actions in the Pacific.[130] Australia's meager diplomatic resources were directed towards securing a commitment to peace in the Pacific from Britain, the United States and Japan. At the 1937 Imperial Conference Joseph Lyons floated the notion of a Pacific pact to forestall Japanese aggression.[131] During the last days of his prime ministership a decision was made to appoint Australian ministers to the United States and Japan to represent Australia's interests in Washington and Tokyo.[132] A new strategic balance had emerged to force Australia into a more assertive role in regional diplomatic affairs.

The name Australasia now represented a much-truncated sphere but the idea of Australia's wider island region continued to influence official thinking about trade and defense. Yet nearly 70 years after mail steamers regularized contacts with the Archipelago, Australia's diplomatic connections with its northern neighbors remained tenuous. Many thousands of Australians visited the islands but, without the intellectual framework with which to decipher cultural practices or comprehend different world-views, most were blind to the nuances of daily life in the region's tourist havens. The delay in establishing permanent diplomatic posts in Asia in part reflected this intellectual vacuum. Contact with the region, familiarity with its physical and human geography, and acceptance of its proximity and economic possibilities amounted to little without a substantial knowledge base in the region's histories and cultures. Australian businessmen seeking trade and investment opportunities outside the British Empire were largely left to their own devices to obtain market information and to negotiate access arrangements with foreign governments for Australian goods and capital. Where they succeeded, in Siam for example, their success depended upon how quickly managers and investors could assimilate to an Asian business environment.

NOTES

1. *Straits Times*, May 21, 1883, April 15, 1885, July 30, 1889.
2. *Straits Times*, April 26, 1911.
3. "Agreement With Mr. F. Jones, Government Commercial Agent In The East," *Queensland Parliamentary Papers*, vol. 1, 1904, 1325–26
4. F. Jones to F. Denham, April 25, 1904. QSA AGS/N57.
5. F. Jones to Queensland Premier, July 5, 1904, QSA AGS/N57.
6. Attachment to F. Jones to A. Morgan, August 30, 1904, QSA AGS/N57.
7. Attachment to F. Jones to A. Morgan, August 30, 1904, QSA AGS/N57.
8. *North Queensland Herald*, September 3, 1905. *Queenslander*, December 30, 1905.
9. Walker, *Anxious Nation*, 77–78.
10. Trade statistics from George Handley Knibbs, *Official Yearbook of the Commonwealth of Australia, 1901–1919*, no. 13, 1920 (Melbourne: Commonwealth Bureau of Census and Statistics, 1920), 584–89. "Statistics of the State of Queensland for 1910," *Queensland Parliamentary Papers*, vol. 1, part 2, 1911, 25B. "Statistics of the State of Queensland for the Year 1922," *Queensland Parliamentary Papers*, 1697. John B. Trivett, *The Official Yearbook of New South Wales: 1909-1910*, (Sydney: Government Printer, 1911), 114. H. A. Smith, *The Official Yearbook of New South Wales for 1918* (Sydney: Government Printer, 1920), 573.
11. "Address by Frederick Jones to guests of the Guild of Australian, American and Canadian Merchants," *Hong Kong Telegraph*, June 1, 1906. Comments from E. H. Angelo, *Straits Times*, April 26, 1911.
12. David Walker analyzes Suttor's pointedly critical trade reports in Walker, *Anxious Nation*, 76–78.
13. "Report of the Commissioner Senator the Honorable J. J. Long on Java and the East Indies, Singapore and the Straits Settlements," *Commonwealth Parliamentary Papers*, 1917–18–19, vol. 5, 1069.
14. "Report of Commissioner Long," 1073.
15. *Straits Times*, April 26, 1911.
16. "Queensland Delegation to Eastern Countries, Report on Investigations into the Possibilities of New or Extended Trade for Queensland," March 29, 1934, QSA RSI 2641-1.
17. Nelson, *Taim Bilong Masta*, 12.
18. Staniforth Smith, "Report on the Federated Malay States and Java: Their Systems of Government, Methods of Administration, and Economic Development,"

Commonwealth Parliamentary Papers, 1906, vol. 2, 1906, 1157–1232. Staniforth Smith, "The Netherlands East Indies: Report on the Fiscal Policy, Local Government, Civil Service, Native Government, and Economic Development," *Commonwealth Parliamentary Papers*, 1914–15–16–17, vol. 5, 1915, 633–664.

19. Staniforth Smith to Lieutenant Governor of Papua, December 1909, van der Veur, *Documents and Correspondence*, 78–79.

20. Hubert Murray to Gilbert Murray, March 14, 1905, in *Selected Letters of Hubert Murray*, ed. Francis West (Melbourne: Oxford University Press, 1970), 34.

21. Nelson, *Black, White and Gold*, 140–41.

22. Peter Hastings, "The Timor Problem—II: Some Australian attitudes, 1903–1941," *Australian Outlook* (vol. 29, no. 2, August 1975), 182. Meaney, *Security in the Pacific*, p. 210.

23. J. H. P. Murray to George Gilbert Aime, December 18, 1915, in *Selected letters*, ed. West, 91.

24. Copeland, *A Few Weeks*, 15.

25. R. G. Etherage, Secretary, New South Wales Chamber of Mines, to Minister for Agriculture, Bangkok, July 12, 1900, National Archives of Thailand (hereafter NA), R5, MLA, KS 6.9/45. See also Undersecretary for Agriculture's draft response dated 30 August 1900, NA, R5, MLA, KS 6.9/45.

26. J. Praditwan, "Mineralogy of Tin and Niobium-Tantalum-Bearing Minerals in Thailand," in Charles S. Hutchinson (ed) *Geology of Tin Deposits in Asia and the Pacific*, (London: Springer-Verlag, 1988), p. 671. Phuwadol, "Chinese Capital," 82.

27. Yip Yat Hoong, *The Development of the Tin Mining Industry of Malaya* (Singapore: University of Malaya Press, 1969), 147.

28. Prince Thewawong, Minister for Foreign Affairs to R. Paget, British Foreign Office, Bangkok, March 10, 1909, NA, PMO, SR 0201.60.1/19.

29. Thamsook Numnonda, "Negotiations Concerning the Cession of the Siamese Malay States," *Journal of the Siam Society* (vol. 55, part 2, July, 1967), 227–35.

30. Thet Bunnak, *The Provincial Administration of Siam, 1892–1915* (London: Oxford University Press, 1977), 162–65.

31. Birch, "Tropical Milestones," 127.

32. Damrong Rajanuparb, "Extracts from *San Somdet*" in *Prawat Krom Lohakit Khrop Rop 72 Pii* (72 Years of the Department of Mines), (Bangkok: Department of Mines, 1963), 104–5.

33. Birch, "Tropical Milestones," 187.

34. Punee Uansakul, "Kitkaan muang rae dee buk kap kaan plian plaeng thaang sethakit phak tai prathaet thai, BE 2411–2474," (Tin mining and economic change in southern Thailand, 1868–1931), MA Thesis, Chulalongkorn University, Bangkok, 1979, 195–201.

35. *Chaophraya* Wongsanupraphat, Minister for Agriculture, "Memorandum," quoted in full in *Prawat krom lohakit*, 140–43.

36. Wongsanupraphat, "Memorandum," 142.

37. Prince Purachatra, Commissioner for Railways to Phraya Buri, January 24, 1919, NA, Secret Documents: France and Britain, R5, F 36 (1–2).

38. Damrong to Chulalongkorn, 26 July 1906, NA, R5, MLA, KS 6.3/40.

39. Cyril Pearl, Morrison of Peking: The Classic Account of an Australian in China During the Boxer Uprising, (Sydney: Collins Angus and Robertson, 1991), 79, 95, 173

40. Cushman quotes from an interview with Warren Parsons, a former Australian mine manager in Siam in the inter war years. Jennifer Cushman, " 'Dazzled by Distant Fields': The Australian Economic Presence in Southeast Asia," *ASSA Review* (vol. 12, no. 1, July, 1988), 5. Pratt, *Magical Malaya*, 222. F. K. Exell, *Siamese Tapestry* (London: Travel Book Club, 1963), 121.

41. Some companies employed up to 350 laborers in total. Dredges worked 20–24 hours per day 7 days a week. Damrong, *San somdet*, quoted in *Prawat krom lohakit*, 157. See also Pratt, *Magical Malaya*, 219. *Industrial and Australian Mining Standard*, July 21, 1927.

42. Edward T. Miles, "The History of the Tongkah Harbour Tin Dredging Enterprise," in Chatthip Nartsupha and Suthy Prasartset, eds. *Political Economy of Siam, 1851–1910*, (Bangkok: Social Science Association of Thailand, 1981), 262–63. *Industrial and Australian Mining Standard*, July 21, 1927. Pratt, *Magical Malaya*, 219–22. For wage rates and rice farm incomes see Sompop, *Economic Development*, 168.

43. Miles, "History of Tongkah Harbour," 263.

44. Punee, "Kitkaan muang rae," 264–66.

45. *Industrial and Australian Mining Standard*, July 22, 1926. For biographical data on A. J. King see Exell, *Siamese Tapestry*, 119–23.

46. A. J. King to Nai Srisuk Thiensuwarn, April 16, 1924, NA, R5, MLA, KS. 16/826.

47. Nai Srisuk Thiensuwarn, April 21, 1924, NA, R6, MLA, KS. 16/826. Luang Wimol Lohakara to A. J. King, April 25, 1924, NA, R.6, MLA, KS. 16/826.

48. *Chaophraya Phonlatheb* was an honorific title bestowed upon most ministers for agriculture before 1932.

49. Minister for Lands and Agriculture to the Directors, Huey Yot Tin Dredging Co., 2 June 1924, NA, R6, MLA, KS. 16/826.

50. The secretaries, Huai Yot Tin Co. to Minister for Lands and Agriculture, June 10, 1924, NA, R5, MLA, KS. 18/826. A. J. King to Minister for Lands and Agriculture, June 9, 1924, NA, R5, MLA, KS. 16/826.

51. Exell, *Siamese Tapestry*, 121–23. Interview with Richard Miles, Sydney, August 5, 1993.

52. *Industrial and Australian Mining Standard*, October 14, 1926. See reports and correspondence files NA, R7, MLA, KS. 4.1/71, 4.1/72 and 4.1/73. *Industrial and Australian Mining Standard*, June 8, 1926 and July 28, 1927. Damrong, *San somdet* in *Prawat krom lohakit*, pp. 156–58. Philip Pring and Keith Brougham Docker, *A Guide to Eastern Tin Stocks for Australian Investors*, Sydney Stock Exchange, Sydney, 1926, 24.

53. *Industrial and Australian Mining Standard*, July 18, 1927.

54. Paid-up capital for individual companies and an estimate of total Australian mining investment in island Southeast Asia given in Pring and Docker, *Eastern Tin Stocks*, 24–25, 42, 51, 58–59, 64, 68, 76, 78, 83.

55. Yip Yat Hoong, *Tin Mining*, 160–61; Birch, "Tropical Milestones," 229–30. Pring and Docker, *Eastern Tin Stocks*, 14–15, 18–20, 79–84. William Kinglake Garnsey, *Eastern Tin Dredging Companies*, (Sydney: Sydney Stock Exchange, 1937), 33–36. T. A. Miles, typescript on tin dredging, March 31, 1934, Miles Papers.

56. *Industrial and Australian Mining Standard*, July 21, 1927. T. A. Miles, typescript on tin dredging, 31 March 1934, Miles Papers. Garnsey, *Eastern Tin*, 33–34. Yip Yat Hoong, *Tin Mining*. Birch, "Tropical Milestones," 229–30. Pring & Docker, *Eastern Tin Stocks*, 14–15, 18–20, 46, 59, 79–84.

57. *Industrial and Australian Mining Standard*, June 21, 1927. For directors lists see Pring and Docker, *Eastern Tin Stocks*, 42, 58, 64, 79–81

58. Stuart Rosewarne, "Capital Accumulation in Australia and the Export of Mining Capital before World War II," in *The Political Economy of Australian Capitalism*, vol. 5, ed. Ted Wheelwright and Ken Buckely (Sydney: ANZ Book Company, 1983) pp. 188–89. See also E.G. Lee, Royal Department of Mines, to Damrong, July 18, 1928, NA, Damrong Papers, SB 2.49/99.

59. Tongkah Compound NL, *Reports and Statements of Accounts*, no. 6, 1913, 10; no. 7, 1913, 10, no. 19, 1919, 6 VPRO, Corporate Affairs Records, M9444R.

60. *Industrial and Australian Mining Standard*, August 26, 1926. Blainey interpreted the outflow of Australian capital into Malaya and Siam as detrimental to Australia's domestic tin-mining industry. Blainey, *Rush That Never Ended*, 282.

61. Pring and Docker, *Eastern Tin Stocks*, 5.

62. Thewawong to H. G. Dering, British Legation, Bangkok, September 18, 1918, NA, R5, Secret Documents, France and Britain, F 36 (1–2) 4. Minutes of the Board of Commercial Development, December 29, 1926, NA, MLA, KS. 15.2/3/6/5.

63. Minutes of Sub-Committee Appointed to Report on the Subject of Control of Foreign Capital, March 24, 1927, NA, MLA, 15.2/6/5. See also for Cook's identical opinion Minutes of the Board of Commercial Development, December 29, 1926, NA, R7, MLA, KS 15.2/3/6/5.

64. Ambrose Pratt, "An Australian in Malaya No. 6: 'Social Life in the Peninsula,'" handwritten draft, c. 1930, John Kinmont Moir Collection, 51/c, AMC SLV.

65. *Chaophraya* Phonlatheb to Prince Mahidon, February 28, 1928, NA, R7, MLA, KS 4/2.

66. Minutes of the Council of Ministers, March 2, 1928, NA, R7, MCC P5/1.1.

67. Minutes of the Council of Ministers, March 2, 1928, NA, R7, MCC P5/1.1.

68. Minutes of the Supreme Council, March 15, 1928, NA, R.7, MLA, KS. 4.1/71. *Industrial and Australian Mining Standard*, May 3, 1928. *Chaophraya* Phonlatheb to *Chaophraya* Mahidol, Royal Secretariat, September 22, 1928, R7, MLA, KS. 4.1/75. Minutes of the Supreme Council, October 15, 1928, NA, R7, MLA, KS 4.1/75. "Notes on procedures for the granting of mining rights as presently used by the Ministry of Agriculture," c. 1928, NA, R7, MLA, KS 4.1/75, 3.

69. *Government Gazette*, no. 47, 131, August 17, 1930, NA, MLA, KS 4.1/36.

70. *Industrial and Australian Mining Standard*, August 26, 1926, Barrie Dyster and David Meredith, *Australia in the International Economy in the Twentieth Century* (Melbourne: Cambridge University Press, 1991), 117–18.

71. J. K. Eastham, "Rationalisation in the Tin Industry," *The Review of Economic Studies*, (vol. 4, 1936–7), 17. Gillian Burke, "The Rise and Fall of the International Tin Agreements," in *Undermining Tin: The Decline of Malaysian Pre-eminence*, ed. Kwame Sundaram Jomo (Sydney: Transnational Corporations Research Project, University of Sydney, 1990), 48–52. An edited version of Howeson's speech to the annual general meeting of Anglo-Oriental is reproduced in the Stock Exchange of Melbourne *Official Record*, vol. 22, no. 6, June 1929, 304.

72. Yip Yat Hoong, *Tin Mining*, 169.

73. "The Tin Producer's Association Incorporated," NA, R7, MLA, KS 4/5 C. W. Orde, Foreign Offices to Luang Bahiddha Nukara, Siamese Charge d'Affaires, London, 14 May 1930, NA, R7, MLA, KS 4/5. Birch, "Tropical Milestones," 234.

74. Tinsongkhla No-Liability, *Report and Statements of Account for Year Ended 28 February 1929*. VPRO, VPRS 567/P000, 770, M94442. Company reports for the years 1930–1932 are missing from the otherwise complete VPRO collection of Tinsongkhla annual reports to shareholders. The Stock Exchange of Melbourne, *Official Record* (vol. 23, no.s 1–12, 1929) and (vol. 24, no.s 1–5, 1930).

75. *Industrial and Australian Mining Standard*, February 16, 1928.

76. *Industrial and Australian Mining Standard*, February 16, 1928.

77. The Stock Exchange of Melbourne, *Official Record*, vol. 22, no. 6, June 1929, 305. "Draft Agreement for the International Tin Pool," NA, R7, MLA, KS 4.7. Burke, "Rise and Fall," 48–49.

78. *Industrial and Australian Mining Standard*, October 17, 1929.

79. Registered mining company list from Commercial Directory for Siam for 1929 reproduced in Punee, "Kitkaan muang rae," 312.

80. Johnson, *Light and the Gate*, 97.

81. The Chamber had twenty-five members in all. Twenty-two were companies of which fifteen were Australian. An Australian, Tom Miles, mine manager for Ronpibon Tin Dredging NL, was elected as the Chamber's founding president. *Industrial and Australian Mining Standard*, August 16 and October 18, 1928. J. M. White, President, Siamese Chamber of Mines, to Purachatra, May 15, 1931, NA, R7, MLA, KS 4/5. Virginia Thompson, *Thailand: The New Siam* (New York: Paragon Book Reprint Corporation, 2nd edition, 1967), 460.

82. J. M. White to Purachatra, May 15, 1931, NA, R7, MLA, KS 4/5.

83. G. W. Duncan, Secretary, Siamese Chamber of Mines to President of the Board of Commercial Development, Bangkok, May 26, 1931, NA, R7, MLA, KS 4/5. Thewawong Warothaya to Royal Secretary, June 26, 1931, NA, R7, MLA, KS 4/8.

84. R. J. D. Richardson, Director, Pungah Tin NL, to Director General, Department of Mines, Bangkok, May 12, 1931, NA, R7, MLA, KS 4/5.

85. Thamras to Thewawong, May 9, 1931, NA, R7, MLA, KS 4/8. Anglo-Oriental Malaya Ltd. to Minister for Mines, May 27, 1931. Thalerng Tin Dredging Ltd. to Minister for Mines, May 26, 1931. Barkers Agents, Penang tp Chaophraya Phichaiyad, May 29, 1931. Jarvis Eastern Siam to Mines Department, May 29, 1931, NA, R7, MLA, KS 4/5. Thewawong Warothaya to Phichaiyad, June 6, 1931, NA, R7. MLA, KS 4/8. Minutes of the Supreme Council, July 2, 1931, NA, R7, KS 4/7.

86. Yip Yat Hoong, *Tin Mining*, 188–93. Siam's role in the ITC is discussed at length in John Hilman, "The Free-Rider and the Cartel: Siam and the International Tin Restriction Agreements, 1931–1941," *Modern Asian Studies*, (vol. 24, no. 2, 1988), 236–45.

87. Purachatra to Prince Boriphat, Regent, June 25, 1931, (in English) NA, R7, MLA, KS 4/8.

88. Minutes of the Supreme Council, July 7, 1931, NA, R7, MLA, KS 4.7.

89. Board of Commercial Development Minutes, May 13, 1931, NA, MLA, KS 15.2/6/11/1.

90. Minutes of the Supreme Council, July 7, 1931, NA, R7, MLA, KS 4.7.

91. *Sydney Morning Herald*, June 27, 1932.

92. Ambrose Pratt, "The Siamese Revolution," typescript, the Ambrose Pratt Papers in the John Kinmont Moir Collection, 51/2 (b), AMC SLV. See also Richard Aldrich, *The Key to the South: Britain, the United States, and Thailand During the Approach to the Pacific War, 1929–1942*. (Oxford: Oxford University Press, 1993), 94–96.

93. The company was a front for U.S. tin interests. It had four directors in all: one American and three British. The American director, P. K. Horner, took responsibility for negotiating with the Thai government over the establishment of the smelting works. See H. E. Fern, Secretary, British American Tin Mines Ltd., to Minister of the Interior, Bangkok, March 28, 1933, NA, PMO, SR 0201.1/63.

94. Minister for the Interior to Prime Minister, May 13, 1933, NA, PMO, SR 0201.1/63.

95. Cabinet Report, June 28, 1933, NA, PMO, SR 0201.1/63.

96. Frei, *Southward Advance*, 115–118, 136.

97. Extract from Miyazaki Masayoshi, "Theory of East Asian Federation" quoted in *Japan's Greater East Asia Co-Prosperity Sphere in World War II: Selected Readings and Documents*, ed. Joyce Lebra-Chapman (Kuala Lumpur: Oxford University Press, 1975), 6.

98. Wayne Gobert, *The Origins of Australian Diplomatic Intelligence in Asia, 1939–1941* (Canberra: Papers on Strategy and Defence, no. 96, Strategic and Defence Studies Centre, the Australian National University, 1992), 51.

99. *Straits Times*, August 7, 1936.

100. *Industrial and Australian Mining Standard*, June 15, 1936.

101. Cabinet Secretary to Minister for Agriculture, August 18, 1934, NA, PMO, SR 0201.1/63.

102. Cabinet Minutes, August 17, 1934, NA, PMO, SR 0201.1/63.

103. *Straits Times*, October 22, 1936.

104. *Industrial and Australian Mining Standard*, August 15, 1936. Yip Yat Hoong, *Tin Mining*, 238.

105. Dyster and Meredith, *International Economy*, 123–34.

106. The Stock Exchange of Melbourne, *Official Record*, (vol. 26, no. 1, January 1933).

107. Warren Parsons to Tom Miles, September 17, 1961, Miles Papers.

108. The Stock Exchange of Melbourne, *Official Record* (vol. 25, no. 5, May 1932) and (vol. 26, no. 7, July 1933).

109. Miles claimed to have initiated the buy-out from within the Australian mining industry by encouraging fellow Australian shareholders to sell.

110. The Stock Exchange of Melbourne, *Official Record* (vol. 31, no. 3, March 1938).

111. As late as 1941 Ambrose Pratt still considered the new company to be an Australian concern. A. Pratt, to W. R. Hodgson, May 7, 1941, Australian Archives (hereafter AA), 981/1, Thailand 16. *Industrial and Australian Mining Standard*, May 1, 1939. *Tongkah Harbour Tin Dredging Ltd.*, Reports and Accounts, 1939, 1.

112. *Industrial and Australian Mining Standard*, June 1, 1934.

113. Quote is from H. Brain to Kemp, November 27, 1963, C. D. Kemp Collection, MS 1548, National Library of Australia. For further details of Massy-Greene's

business career see also F. Sheddon to C.D. Kemp, September 3, 1963; A. E. Brand to Kemp, July 11, 1963, C. D. Kemp Collection, MS 1548, National Library of Australia. C. J. Lloyd, "Massy-Greene, Sir Walter (1874–1952)." *ADB*, vol. 10, 1891–1939, 437–38.

114. *Industrial and Australian Mining Standard*, June 1, 1934. Anglo-Oriental (Malaya) directors are listed in Garnsey, *Eastern Tin*, 75.

115. Garnsey, *Eastern Tin*, 153.

116. Average share prices calculated from annual highest and lowest prices quoted in Garnsey, *Eastern Tin*, and Research and Statistical Bureau, *Eastern Tin Dredging Companies* (Sydney: Sydney Stock Exchange, 1946).

117. Dyster and Meredith, *International Economy*, 123–159. A. G. L. Shaw, *The Economic Development of Australia*, sixth edition (Melbourne: Longman, 1970), 147–170.

118. See aide-memoire, "Trade Representation," AA, A601/1, 410/12/3.

119. Jack Shepherd, *Australia's Interests and Policies in the Far East* (New York: Institute of Pacific Relations, 1940).

120. Ian Clunies Ross and Stephen Henry Roberts, ed. *Australia and the Far East: Diplomatic and Trade Relations*, (Sydney: Angus and Robertson, 1936).

121. Walker, *Anxious Nation*, 220–224.

122. Johnson, *Light and the Gate*, 93. Allan William Martin, *Robert Menzies: A Life*, vol. 1 (Melbourne: Melbourne University Press, 1993), 83–84. P. Hart, "The Piper and the Tune" in *Australian Conservatism: Essays in Twentieth Century Political History*, ed. Cameron Hazlehurst, (Canberra: ANU Press, 1979), 115. Ambrose Pratt "Speech by J. A. Lyons when he left the Australian Labor Party," Pratt Papers, MS6536, Box 327/5, AMC SLV.

123. Pratt's influence was extensive. He served as the league's president for eight years and vice-president for another three. James Hume-Cook, *The Australian Industries Protection League: A Historical Review* (Melbourne, 1938), 7–10, 16–20, 60. Dyster and Meredith, *International Economy*, 97.

124. Herbert W. Gepp, "Report on Trade Between Australia and the Far East," *Commonwealth Parliamentary Papers*, 1932–33–34, vol. 4, 2343–2379. "Report of the Australian Trade Delegation to India, Burma and Ceylon, October 1935–January 1936," *Commonwealth Parliamentary Papers*, 1937, vol. 5, 2055–2156. John G. Latham, "The Australian Eastern Mission, 1934," *Commonwealth Parliamentary Papers*, 1932–33–34, vol. 4, 437–459. Ruth Megaw, "The Australian Goodwill Mission to the Far East in 1934: Its Significance in the Evolution of Australian Foreign Policy," *Journal of the Royal Australian Historical Society*, (vol. 59, part 4, December 1973), 255–57.

125. Department of Commerce files AA, A601, 410/12/1 part 1 and AA, A601/1, 410/12/3. See also *Industrial and Australian Mining Standard*, November 15, 1932; January 15, 1933, Tweedie, *Trading Partners.*, 87–90.

126. F. H. Stewart, "Advisory Committees on Eastern Trade," Cabinet Submission, October 1933, AA, A601, 410/12/1 part 1. For a list of State Advisory Committee members see "To the Honourable Minister," September 1933, AA, A601, 410/12/1 Part 1.

127. "Trade Representation," AA, A601/1, 410/12/3.

128. "Queensland Delegation to Eastern Countries," QSA RSI 2641–1.

129. Exports declined from 10.5 percent in the period 1931/32–1933/34 to a mere 3.6 percent in 1937/38–1938/39. Dyster and Meredith, *International Economy*, 150.

130. Gobert, *Origins*, 54–59.

131. *Commonwealth Parliamentary Debates*, vol. 167,1937–38–39, 196–199.

132. Minutes of Fifteenth Meeting of Principal Delegates to Imperial Conference, June 8, 1937, in *Documents on Australian Foreign Policy, 1937–49*, vol. 1: 1937–38, (Hereafter referred to as DAFP) ed. Robert George Neale, Australian Government Publishing Service, Canberra, 1975, 141.

133. Joan Beaumont, *The Evolution of Australian Foreign Policy, 1901–1945* (Melbourne: Australian Institute of International Affairs (Victorian Branch), Occasional Paper no. 1, 1989), 21.

6

Arc of Instability

THE COLLAPSE OF IMPERIAL ORDER AND AUSTRALIA'S SEARCH FOR A REGIONAL SECURITY

Australian decision makers were forced to distinguish between Asian allies and enemies as the region spiraled toward war in 1941. Confronted by an Asian power with a clear strategy to dismantle the European colonial order and create a new East Asia, Australian border concerns extended beyond the Netherlands Indies–PNG boundary northwards to Malaya and Indochina. Thoughts of impending invasion focused the minds of military planners and made the close mapping of Australia's northern approaches an exercise in national survival. There were also important Australian business interests to be upheld, in Malaya and Thailand especially. The Archipelago was now viewed as a region into which Australia must be prepared to project military power, albeit under an imperial umbrella and, if necessary, press for revisions to the *status quo*. Australians as soldiers, prisoners of war or guerrilla fighters with Asian "resistance" movements became acutely aware of differences in politics, culture and ethnicity in the countries to the north. The more perceptive, while struggling to come to terms with White disempowerment, sensed the injustices of European colonialism. The Japanese interregnum destroyed the illusion of White invincibility and eroded the foundations of imperial order. In its aftermath there emerged a decolonized region divided by old rivalries pursued in a regional context of new nation-states, new ideological orientations and new political styles to which Australia was painfully slow to adjust.

REGIONAL DIPLOMACY

The stridency of William Morris Hughes's anti-Japanese diplomacy at Versailles in 1919 reflected both his diplomatic inexperience and the depth of Australian fears of a Japanese ascendancy in the Pacific. With the fate of former German Pacific colonies on the negotiating table, Hughes believed Australian security would be substantially diminished were Japan to win possession of the Caroline Islands, which lay within one hour's flight of Australian-controlled German New Guinea. British efforts to build a more substantial security relationship with Japan met with persistent Australian opposition, but Hughes failed to undo a British wartime agreement to support all Japanese claims over former German colonies north of the Equator which included the Carolines. For countries more versed in the art of international diplomacy, flexibility and compromise are recognized as sometimes necessary means to achieve longer-term objectives but Hughes entertained no thought of compromise with Japan. Manning the legislative barricades of White Australia, he campaigned successfully against a racial equality clause that Japanese negotiators wanted written into the Covenant of the League of Nations, and then blocked Japanese demands for commercial concessions and free passage for Japanese nationals in all mandated territories in the Pacific lest this open New Guinea to Japanese migration. Hughes gave possibly the bluntest exposition of the absolutist trinity of sovereignty, territory and race, ever presented by an Australian politician on the international stage.

There was a fundamental difference in Australian and Japanese attitudes towards the Archipelago or, from the Japanese geographical perspective, the South Seas. Australian defense planners viewed the Netherlands Indies, Portuguese Timor, New Guinea, Solomon Islands and New Hebrides, as a single Pacific Island region and a vital defensive outer perimeter. With Singapore seemingly impregnable and the British navy seemingly invincible, Australian naval staff dismissed the possibility of a Japanese invasion through the Archipelago.[1] Australia's political leaders hoped that peace would be buttressed by a Pacific Pact bringing together the region's colonial powers, including Japan. Neither the political allegiances of island peoples nor their attitudes towards their colonial masters remotely entered the equation. Against this narrow alliance-centered view was ranged a more nuanced Japanese vision for a Greater East Asia Co-Prosperity Sphere, superseding earlier ideas for an East Asia Federation. An indication of how advanced Japanese planning was for a new order in Asia, the Japanese military included a statement on cultural diplomacy in their 1939 "Summary Draft of a Policy for the South":

CULTURAL ADMINISTRATION POLICY

Our main aim is good neighborliness and co-prosperity, so it is important to have mutual familiarity and development of our cultures. This point is the greatest lag today. It is impossible to succeed in one day. It will require continuous efforts through the following policies:
  a. introducing the true Japan by means of documents, films, sports, inviting tourists, and goodwill exchanges;
  b. re-educating the Japanese people in the Southern area with the chief aim of appropriate activities in the countries they reside in, and at the same time completing the education of children of Japanese in the Southern area;
  c. doing research relating to the humanities and physical sciences in the Southern area;
  d. making an effort to foster young men who will be active in the Southern area in the future.[2]

Japanese practice deviated wildly from this model in China and during the Japanese interregnum in South East Asia, but the draft policy suggests a comprehensive theoretical grasp of the intricacies of successful regional engagement. Cultural knowledge, common understanding and the bonds of community would open the way for the exercise of Japanese influence through diplomatic and business channels. Another two decades would pass before the idea registered firmly in the minds of Australian policymakers that cultural learning could be a useful avenue through which to pursue closer relations with Asia.

Australian political leaders, before and after Federation, were acutely aware that Australia, though technically a self-governing British dominion, had "national" interests to uphold.[3] Logically, for a small state with limited human and financial resources, Australia relied heavily, far too heavily, upon British naval power and diplomatic resources. When Robert Menzies became Commonwealth Prime Minister in April 1939 he reaffirmed the belief that Australia's most vital strategic interests lay to its "near north." Commensurate with Australia's status as an important Pacific power, he believed, as had Lyons, that Australia should possess more detailed and up-to-date information on political developments in its region of "primary risk":

Little given as I am to encouraging the exaggerated ideas of Dominion independence and separatism which exist in some minds, I have become convinced that in the Pacific Australia must regard itself as a principal providing herself with her own information and maintaining her own diplomatic contacts with foreign powers.[4]

The superstructure of a Pacific diplomatic strategy evolved quickly without the cultivation of any substantial intellectual underpinnings. Like Lyons before him, to Menzies the Pacific encompassed the entire Malay Archipelago extending north to the shores of Mainland Asia, and as such Pacific relations in his usage of the term meant relations with Asia, both colonized and free. Envisaging the expansion of Australia's diplomatic network beyond the existing trade commissioner service, Australian diplomacy would be pursued through Australian legations in Tokyo, Washington and also Chongquing (Chungking).[5] Menzies foreshadowed plans to establish informal relations with other countries on the "fringe of the Pacific."[6] These necessarily involved the utilization of personal contacts between Australians and foreign politicians, bureaucrats, and businessmen.[7]

According to Neville Meaney when the traditional approach to foreign policy failed, as it often did, Australian governments would take policy initiatives of their own in a "personal, disguised and indirect manner."[8] Regional and global networks of Australian businessmen provided the opportunity for Menzies to pursue semi-autonomous security initiatives. In the assessment of Australian connections with Asia, mining companies and their employees surfaced quickly in official thinking. The potential for mining company employees and directors to act as intelligence agents was appreciated in Canberra policy circles. External Affairs explored the possibility of forming an Australian company to explore for oil on some Australian-held mining concessions in the financially vulnerable Portuguese Timor as a cover for intelligence gathering on Japanese business activity.[9] Likewise, Thailand's strategic importance to Australia was becoming ever more evident as scattered reports of Japanese initiatives in Bangkok seeped through to Canberra. With over £2.5 million in Australian capital invested in Thailand alone, there were important Australian commercial and strategic interests to protect.

Thailand was an important element in Menzies' early Pacific strategy. Australians travelling on business to the Peninsula were therefore ideal sources for the surreptitious collection of timely information. Before embarking for Singapore on a business trip to Kuala Lumpur and Bangkok in early August 1939, Ambrose Pratt received a vaguely worded directive from Menzies, a patron of many years standing, to initiate "closer diplomatic relations" with Malaya and Thailand.[10] Though loosely "attached" to the British Legation and the British Minister Sir Josiah Crosby, Pratt used his personal contacts to engineer an appointment with the Thai Prime Minister Phibun Songkhram. Meeting Phibun at a state reception held in Pratt's honor and later in private, Pratt was asked to urge the establishment of an Australia legation in Bangkok "at the earliest possible date."[11] To Pratt, the request signaled a departure from what Britain and Australia presumed a policy of alignment with Japan. Yet the Thai government was committed to a "swing policy" of closer engagement with whosoever appeared to be the most likely future hegemonic power in Asia. From the Thai view, good diplomacy required regular careful readjustments made in the light of new circumstances and new information. This more flexible approach to diplomatic relations made Thai foreign policy much more difficult for Western governments to read and led the more sanguine, like Pratt, to believe that any movement towards the West should be interpreted as a significant change of direction.

Contrasts in diplomatic tradition and style could hardly be greater than between Australia, a Western country incongruously situated between Asia and the Pacific, and Thailand, an independent Asian kingdom with a diplomatic history reaching back 700 years. Unhindered by a history of strategic dependence, the Thai government could afford to entertain both the idea of an East Asian Co-Prosperity Sphere and a Western-brokered regional security framework. Aware that Menzies had revived ideas of a Pacific Pact, Phibun presumed that Thailand would be invited to participate in any future concert of Pacific powers and evidently believed that good relations with Australia could aid Thai diplomacy in Washington and London. The invitation, if accepted, would have placed Australia on an equal diplomatic footing with both Britain and the United States, which operated legations rather than embassies in Bangkok. This undoubtedly piqued Crosby who, while complimentary about Pratt's useful "propaganda work," scotched the idea of an Australian legation in Bangkok lest this interfere with his personal crusade to swing Phibun and the Thai government onto the side of Britain.[12] Ignoring the presence of Australian tin companies, which the British Legation shunned, Crosby argued that bilateral trade was insufficient to justify formal diplomatic relations.

For his anxious company shareholders Pratt also won a personal assurance that the Thai government would not attempt to establish a much-feared state purchasing monopoly over tin. Pratt told Australian investors that Phibun "had no intention of pursuing any policy which would debar the admission of Australian or any other foreign capital."[13] Impressed with the apparent success of Pratt's mission, Crosby suggested a follow-up ministerial visit would be an important expression of goodwill.[14] The immediate step most likely to bring about a greater swing to the West would have been the sale of fuel, materials and military hardware to Thailand but this went against British and American policy. By the time Pratt reported to Menzies in November, Britain and Australia were at war with Germany. The Thai government sent Bisal Sukhumwid from the Ministry of Public Works to finalize contracts for the supply of steel from Broken Hill Proprietary Ltd., but to Bisal's disappointment all available steel supplies and machinery were sequestered for Australia's war effort.[15] Menzies, under intense pressure from the British government, was being lured away from his Pacific strategy back to the old certainties of empire.[16]

THAILAND AND FRENCH INDOCHINA

Japan's swift occupation of northern Indochina in September 1940 both excited and alarmed Phibun. Intoxicated by the defeat of French forces by an

Asian power, he prepared to invade and occupy "lost" territories ceded to
French Indochina.[17] The Tripartite Pact between Germany, Italy and Japan,
signed in late September, confirmed Phibun's belief that Japanese power
was on the ascendant and the British Empire in Asia was doomed. Japanese
diplomatic support for Thai border claims had to be bought with concessions. In October he secretly pledged to allow Japanese forces right of passage through Thailand with the promise of military bases in the event of
war between Britain and Japan. Born of political expediency, it was a promise he had no intention of keeping. Thailand's leaders, in the process of cast-
ing off Western stewardship, had no ambition for Thailand to become a
mere satellite of the Japanese empire. Cabinet ministers, Pridi included,
confessed that a swing towards Japan was a necessary response to the strategic realities faced by Thailand. Such an approach was not thought incom-
patible with neutrality.[18]

Hopes for the creation of a formal regional security regime had not been
abandoned in Canberra, consequently the Australian government responded positively to Phibun's proposal that Britain, France and Japan enter into separate mutual non-aggression pacts with Thailand. Difficulties
arose in negotiations for the Franco-Thai pact. Perceiving French vulnerability in Europe, Phibun pressed for the cession of some small islands on
the Mekong River appropriated by France in 1893. The price, in terms of
lost French prestige, of such a border revision was too high and by November 1939 negotiations had broken down. Britain, unwilling to alienate its
European ally, delayed signature of its agreement with the Thai government
until the impasse was resolved.[19] According a lower priority to France's national pride, Australia suggested that Britain sign immediately and pressure
France to do likewise.[20] Richard Casey, Menzies' Minister for Suppy and Development believed the concessions demanded by Phibun were only
"slight" and that by affirming their intention to respect Thai sovereignty,
Britain and France could draw Phibun closer to the Allies.[21] The Thailand-
Indochina border issue had clear implications for Australian security. Canberra understood from Crosby's dispatches that any Japanese landward assault on Singapore would need to be mounted through southern
Thailand.[22] If Japan were to cajole Phibun into a military alliance then
northern Malaya would be exposed. A short distance across the neck of the
peninsula the integrated communications network of the western Malay
States lay within easy reach of an invading army.

Optimistically, the Menzies government believed that strategic problems
in the Pacific were still amenable to political solutions and adopted a conciliatory attitude towards Phibun's irredentism.[23] The belief and the approach were encouraged by developments concerning the Anglo-Thai and
Franco-Thai non-aggression pacts. Invaded by Nazi Germany in May 1940,
France, anxious to shore up its position in Indochina, softened on the

Mekong River question and consented to the creation of a joint commission to consider border amendments. The back down opened the way for signing of the long-awaited non-aggression treaties on June 12.[24] Five days later France fell to Germany before the Franco-Thai treaty could be ratified, delaying a proposed review of the Thailand-Indochina border issue.[25] Phibun prepared to take full advantage of France's defeat in Europe and press more extensive irredentist claims on the Vichy regime.[26] The opportunity to bolster his personal popularity with a successful requisition of all territory ceded to France was too great for him to overlook. His aims, if not his means, received widespread support in Thailand.[27] Reading plans for the dispatch of a Thai mission to Tokyo as a response to Japanese pressure for closer diplomatic ties, Crosby tried to allay suspicion in London and Canberra. He advised the Foreign Office that "recovery by his [Phibun's] country of the lost provinces ceded to France is probably the dominating factor and in yielding to pressure it may be because he sees in it the best way of realizing his territorial aspirations."[28] Accepting the British Minister's reasoning that Phibun's actions were "inspired largely by fear" and opportunism, the Australian government, convinced of Thailand's "strict impartiality" and "sincere" neutrality, remained sympathetic to Phibun's demands.[29]

THAILAND AND MALAYA

Menzies appreciated that friendly relations with Thailand advanced Australian security interests and was eager to return Thamrong's visit. An opportunity came when the Advisory War Council gave him permission to fly to London and press Winston Churchill to strengthen Imperial defenses.[30] An official visit to Thailand was included on his itinerary of overnight stops. Crosby believed the gesture would be beneficial and was supportive; however, on January 21, 1941, Australian High Commissioner in London, Stanley Melbourne Bruce advised against claiming that the Foreign Office would not approve any act that might antagonize the Vichy regime in French Indochina, against which Thailand was fighting a fierce border war. Furthermore, the Thai government feared an official visit would send the wrong signal to Japan whose help Phibun needed to broker a peace settlement with France. Anxious to tread carefully, Menzies revised his plans, making his visit to Bangkok an unofficial, but nonetheless important, act of Australian regional diplomacy.[31]

Menzies flew out of Sydney on January 24 with many problems and questions on his mind. Australian troops were to sail for Singapore in a few weeks and their role in Imperial strategy was unclear. British plans for a preemptive occupation of the Isthmus of Kra, should a Japanese invasion of Thailand seem imminent, were raised at the Singapore Conference in October at which Australia was represented.[32] He learned more about Operation

Etonian, later renamed Operation Matador, from Singapore governor Sir Sidney Shenton Thomas, Air Chief Marshall Sir Robert Brooke-Popham, the new British Commander in Chief in the Far East, and other high-ranking British officers. Menzies wrote in his diary the following day,

> If Japan is to take over Thailand and moves down the Malay Peninsula, we should push forward to a point already selected, even if it does mean a breach of neutrality.[33]

He omitted a vital detail. It was a breach of Thai neutrality that was contemplated. How deeply Australian troops were to be involved in Operation Matador is unclear. A brigade from the 8th Division of the 2nd AIF (Australian Imperial Force) was to be temporarily stationed in Malaya before re-embarking for the Middle East when British Indian reinforcements arrived. When his plane touched down in Bangkok late in the afternoon of January 29 Menzies had not abandoned hope that political countermeasures against Japan might still be successful. His task was to help Crosby put diplomatic pressure on his Thai counterpart by warning that Australia and Britain were determined to halt Japan, if necessary by force.

Efforts to strengthen relations between Australia and Thailand were again contemplated. Menzies cabled Canberra asking for information on Australian educational institutions to be forwarded to the Thai government advising, "I consider every encouragement should be given to the project of education of Thais in Australia."[34] He also entertained a suggestion by Crosby that John Latham act concurrently as Australian Minister to Thailand and Japan while remaining based in Tokyo, an idea that the War Cabinet later rejected as unworkable.[35] Recognizing the potential effectiveness of Australian diplomacy, he retained the prospect of a future official Australian goodwill mission to Thailand. Senior figures in Australia's foreign policy community were pressing for similar initiatives. Equally convinced of the potential of Australian diplomacy to make an impact in Bangkok, John Latham, Australia's Minister to Japan, advised that

> Australia should actively consider the desirability of taking some prompt action which might operate in the other direction (this is absolutely essential). Most obvious step is to send mission to Thai in return for recent visit of Thai mission to Australia. It should be led by a person of culture and distinction (this is absolutely essential) and should contain army and airmen who can speak of our industry and military strength and an educationalist who could represent the advantages of Australian schools and universities. . . .[36]

Both Latham and Menzies thought that affording educational opportunities for Thai students in Australia would yield diplomatic dividends. They believed that Australian diplomacy could make an impact upon the Thai

government. However, Menzies gave a higher priority to military strategy
and the problems posed by Thailand for the effective defense of Malaya.[37]
A deepening sense of crisis gripped Australian decision makers in February
1941. Minister for the Army Percy Spender, fresh from a fact-finding mission to Thailand, reported to the Advisory War Council that Phibun was being "literally forced into the hands of the Japanese." He reassured them that
the Australian government was now involved in efforts to challenge Japan's
"tremendous influence" over the Thai prime minister and his supporters.[38]
A Japanese attack on Singapore, possibly Australia, was feared imminent.[39]
Latham, observing Australia's current predicament from Tokyo, sketched
out more policy recommendations to External Affairs:

> I think we should decide where we should draw our lines. If, as I believe, it is
> Thailand, I think we should adopt the following policy; we should do what we
> can to strengthen our forces near the Thai border, warn the Thai Government
> against giving footholds to Japan and offer them all aid in our power to resist
> any attempt by Japan to take them by force. We should try to disabuse Thai
> (sic) of any idea they will escape by yielding to Japan.[40]

A growing preoccupation with military affairs hindered any further Australian diplomatic initiatives towards Thailand. Brooke-Popham, in Australia since the beginning of February, had already decided that an invasion
of southern Thailand would go ahead in the event of a Japanese attack. It
was just a matter of exactly when and how far to go; Bangkok was not out
of the question.[41] Japanese troops could reach Penang by train from southern Thai mining districts making a land assault on Singapore unstoppable.
Brooke-Popham recommended that an attack on the Kra Isthmus be regarded as an attack on Australia and pressed for Australian reinforcements
to be sent to Malaya. Australian planners hesitated. Britain was unwilling to
reinforce Singapore and uncertainty lingered over the attitude of the United
States. Yet, the strategic importance of the Isthmus to Malaya and Singapore
was appreciated. Acting Prime Minister Arthur Fadden cabled Menzies in
Cairo to the effect that Australia might consider a Japanese assault on Thailand a *casus belli* urging Menzies to assess London's reaction.[42]

FRIENDS, ENEMIES AND NEIGHBORS

The United States and the Netherlands had, out of fears that Japan was becoming too strong a military and industrial power, ceased supplying tin ore,
rubber and petroleum from their colonies in Asia. Global Rivalry between
British and U.S. tin interests for control of tin resources made the negotiation of a common Anglo-U.S. position on the question of Thailand harder.

The sale of tin metal from Malayan smelters to the United States was an important means for bringing vital dollar-exchange into the Sterling Area. For this reason British financial advisers did their utmost to prevent the construction of a tin smelter in Thailand.[43] Even a suggestion by Crosby for a British-built tin smelter was rejected.[44] Desperate for dollar currency, the Thai Cabinet discussed in October 1940 the possibility of selling tin and rubber direct to the United States.[45] An American-owned rubber and tin trading company, Carl M. Loeb and Co., requested that Thai tin be sold and shipped in its primary state to a smelter in the United States.[46] On the recommendation of William Doll, Baxter's replacement as Financial Adviser to the Thai government, the Straits Trading Company and the Eastern Smelting Company put forward a counter-proposal to build a smelter and included a provision for a portion of the tin metal produced to be allotted for export to the United States.[47] Practical difficulties posed by the cost of shipping tin ore to the United States forced Phibun and Finance Minister Pridi to accept the British offer, which turned out to be nothing more than a tactical ploy. Further, with Australian and British companies already selling their entire ore output under contract to Straits Trading and Eastern Smelting, the British control over the refinement and export of Thai tin ore would be hard to break.[48]

Directly in the line of fire should war break out, Australian tin miners in southern Thailand were already on the front line of the economic war conducted by the British Ministry of Economic Warfare (BMEW) against Japan. Oil, tin and rubber were strategic commodities that the BMEW aimed to deny to countries sympathetic to the Axis powers. Phibun entered into a barter arrangement with Japan under which Japanese aircraft were to be supplied in return for Thai rubber and tin ore. In addition Japan would be allowed to procure as much as 50 percent of Thailand's tin output.[49] To meet its obligations Thailand would have to compel British, Australian and Chinese tin companies to break contracts with British Malayan smelters and sell a portion of their production to Bangkok. With the help of British and Australian tin dredging companies and the Australian government the BMEW planned to shut the Thai State out of the ore purchasing market by shoring up British control over the smelting of tin ore from southern Thailand.[50] Responsibility for ensuring Australian companies complied with the BMEW's tin diversion scheme fell to Canberra. With Australian companies producing over one-third of Thailand's annual tin output, they and the Australian government could not avoid implication in the three-cornered economic struggle developing between Britain, the United States and Japan.[51] Australia's foreign policy would henceforth extend to interference in the domestic affairs of a neighboring state through the agency of Australian business groups.[52]

Unofficially, in early 1941, it was believed in London that Thailand was almost a lost cause. The British and Australian governments knew that the position taken by the United States would be decisive in a war fought in

Asia. Despite a relentless diplomatic onslaught, American policymakers disdained to guarantee Thailand's territorial integrity. To no avail, Menzies asked U.S. President Theodore Roosevelt in May to declare the "point or line beyond which we would all consider similar southward movements a *casus belli.*" President Roosevelt was unwilling even to offer Thailand any economic or military assistance.[53] By August the British War Cabinet was preparing for the eventuality of Japanese occupation of Thailand.[54] What had hitherto been a policy of tin diversion now became a top-secret policy of tin denial. All British and Australian companies in southern Thailand were informed that they should make preparations for the disablement of all mining machinery in the event of a Japanese occupation. The British government suggested that mines refusing to comply would not be evacuated by the Royal Navy should an emergency occur.[55]

Alert Australian mining engineers in southern Thailand might have guessed that an Allied invasion of the Kra Isthmus was "in the air" Commonwealth military activity just across the border in Malaya was increasing. On 26 May two uniformed Australian officers carrying revolvers and cameras crossed into Thailand and were promptly arrested by Thai border police.[56] From May 1941 onwards, southern Thailand was infiltrated by British agents, often military personnel from Malaya in civilian clothes, passing as tourists.[57] Mine company employees were themselves involved in intelligence gathering. There is one documented case of D. Regan being posted by the Australian Army to work on Tongkah Harbour's dredge at Ronpibon on the eastern peninsula near Nakhon Srithammarat.[58] The plight of Australian tin-dredging companies in Thailand was of less concern to the Australian government than the need to shore up inadequate imperial defenses in Malaya. A second AIF brigade, the 27th, was sent to Malaya in August. Four RAAF squadrons were committed to the defense of Singapore; two were stationed close to the Thai-Malay border.[59] Planning for an invasion of southern Thailand, code named Operation Matador, was well advanced. Commonwealth troops would advance to a line stretching from Songkhla on the eastern shore of the peninsula to a point just north of the border on the west coast.[60] The plan would turn southern Thailand into a battlefield and bring much coveted territory under British control.

Though never again venturing into Thailand after his August 1939 visit, Pratt strove to make an impression upon foreign policy formulation in Canberra and Bangkok. He was annoyed with Crosby's distrust of Phibun and the influence that Crosby exercised over decision making in Canberra. The British Minister was increasingly sceptical about Phibun's protestations of neutrality and warned the Australian government not to take Pratt's opinions of the Thai prime minister seriously.[61] In retaliation Pratt determined to break Crosby's hold over Australian policy. He pleaded with Menzies that Phibun, has a strong sentimental leaning towards Australia and is sincerely anxious to acquire "Face" by obtaining our definite recognition of his country as an important Pacific Nationa (sic), via the establishment of an Australian Legation in Bangkok and a Thai Legation in Canberra.[62]

If Menzies was leaning towards Thailand, domestic politics intervened to further delay any move toward independent Australian representation in Bangkok. Country Party leader Arthur Fadden replaced Menzies on 29 August after which Pratt's capacity to influence government was reduced.[63] For Australian policymakers and military planners the defense of Singapore was of much greater moment. At the beginning of September V. G. Bowden, formerly Australian Trade Commissioner in Shanghai, was appointed to Singapore as Australian Government Representative.[64] Bowden was to be Australia's voice and ear at British Far Eastern Command where the crucial decisions affecting Australia's strategic interests in the Archipelago would ultimately be made.

Unwilling or unable to comprehend the worldview of an Asian country, Menzies shied away from institutionalizing diplomatic exchanges with Thailand. Portuguese Timor and the Netherlands Indies were expected to be more cooperative, but shared defense interests in Asia did not guarantee Dutch or Portuguese complicity with Allied plans. Both Portugal and the Netherlands realized that war would most probably spread to Asia and the Pacific but were careful not to antagonize Japan. Their neutral stance was an unwelcome complication for Australia, made harder by Portuguese sensitivity to Australia's "annexationist" tendencies.[65] British and Australian contingency planning for a Japanese attack on Timor and the Netherlands Indies involved preparations to project Australian power across the Archipelago, which constituted "a single political and military line."[66] The logic of stationing Australian forces in the Indies ahead of the expected Japanese assault was obvious, but Dutch and Portuguese prevarication hindered Australian military preparations, inadequate as they were. Hoping Britain could persuade the Dutch to abandon neutrality, Canberra advised Lord Cranbourne that

the arrangements agreed to at the conference contemplate that the movement of Australian troops to Ambon and Koepang is not to take place until hostilities with Japan have commenced. From a military point of view there would be every advantage in moving troops to these localities at once.[67]

Confronted by the gravest ever threat to Australia's national security, Australian defense plans were hampered by the suspicions of its nearest neighbors. Neither Portugal nor the Netherlands welcomed the presence of Australian troops in the far corners of their Asian empires. Dutch sensitivity to the movement of Australian forces elsewhere in the Archipelago suggests that the cordiality of bilateral relations did not necessarily imply that old rivalries were at an end. Dutch objections conveyed through the British government indicate that there was more to their rejection of Australian assistance in the Moluccas than the fear of antagonizing Japan. Although Ambon was one of the oldest and most loyal parts of the Dutch empire in the Indies, Indonesian nationalism had taken hold among some of the islands' Christian and Muslim population.[68] Reluctance to allow the stationing of Australian troops suggests the Dutch were anxious not to give any sign that their imperial grip was loosening. Cranbourne's communiqué to Labor Prime Minister, John Curtin on this matter in late November 1941 contained an explicit warning against any pre-emptive Australian action. Hinting at deeper Dutch concerns, Cranbourne advised,

> Despatch of troops without absolute necessity might lead to undesirable incidents with the population which in turn might have unfavourable repercussions on Netherlands—Australian relations. This applies in particular to the population of Ambon.[69]

By late November British and Australian military planners agreed that an approach toward the coast of southern Thailand by Japanese forces should be considered a *casus belli*. Uncertainty over U.S. reaction to an infringement of Thai neutrality led to a qualification so that only an actual invasion of Thailand would constitute a green light for Operation Matador. On December 5 after peace negotiations between the United States and Japan had clearly stalled, Canberra agreed to the occupation of the Isthmus of Kra with or without Thai consent. Small detachments of Australian infantry were also to be stationed in Dutch-administered West Timor and in Portuguese Timor. The inadequacy of Allied planning and the weakness of Australia's subordinate defense and foreign policies became tragically apparent in the days and months that followed. Phibun intimated to Colonel Tamura Hiroshi, Japan's military attaché in Bangkok, that Thailand would allow Japanese troops free passage through southern Thailand, effectively opening the back door to Malaya.[70] Seizing the initiative, Japanese forces landed along the east coast of southern Thailand early in the morning of December 8.

Japan's invasion of Thailand and Malaya was launched to coincide with the attack on Pearl Harbor and heralded the commencement of hostilities with the Allies across Australia's forward defensive line. The Japanese imperial army encountered fierce Thai resistance at Chumphon and Songkhla where fighting lasted for several days. Brooke-Popham hesitated to implement Operation Matador, but British Indian troops, one division conveyed by units of the Australian Motor Transport Company, eventually crossed into Thailand from forward bases in northwest Malaya only to be fired upon and delayed by Thai border police. The invading Allied force was eventually met by the advancing Japanese and beaten back into Malaya.[71] Australian troops were hurriedly dispersed through the Indies only to be trapped with no prospect of reinforcement or evacuation. In Timor, they faced both the approaching Japanese and the prospect of eviction by Portuguese troops being rushed from Angola in an abortive attempt by Lisbon to forestall either Japanese or Australian annexation.[72] Within weeks the disintegration of Australia's forward defenses was complete, save for a tenuous foothold in southeastern New Guinea.

ON THE OTHER SIDE

The Pacific War drew many thousands of young Australians into a region and in circumstances they would much rather have avoided. As Gavan Mc-Cormack and Hank Nelson write, "They were the first Australians who went en masse into South-East Asia."[73] But theirs was an involuntary exodus. Of these 22,000 were captured by the advancing Japanese, 15,000 alone at the fall of Singapore in February 1942, the remainder mopped-up in Sumatra, Java, Timor and Ambon, where Australia's Gull Force was stationed following the commencement of Japan's assault on the Archipelago. As prisoners of war, they were used as slave labor, tortured and starved. As was evident in the experiences of Australian travelers and tourists to Asia in the nineteenth and early twentieth centuries, Australian wartime encounters with Asian peoples evoked widely differing responses. Japanese guards were hated, but many people outside the camps were also feared and sometimes despised for not doing more to assist the allies of their former colonial overlords. Against this stands the regard and gratitude felt towards Ambonese and Timorese in the islands and towards Thais, Malay, and Chinese who risked their lives to assist escaping POWs or smuggle essential supplies into prison camps along the Thai-Burma Railway.

Japan's swift southward advance destroyed the illusion of European invincibility and dramatically altered power relations between Europeans and Asians. Foreign residents in southern Thailand were thrown into confusion but Thai resistance gave some enough time to flee into Malaya. On the west coast, Australian mines staff and their families were quickly evacuated by the British Navy. For those on the east coast there was no warning. Three mining engineers, D. Reagan and R. Gordon, both employees of Tongkah Harbour, and H. Wright of Ronpibon Tin, were taken prisoner by Thai police. Escaping from the mine manager's bungalow at Nawng Pet Tin, where they were under house arrest, they were captured by the Japanese and shot at Songkhla in December 1941. Robert Farr, manager at Peninsula Tin's Langsuan mine, was shot by Thai border police at La Oon on the Thai-

Burma border, having made his way across the Kra Isthmus with another Langsuan employee, J. H. Hughes. According to Hughes, Farr was shot at close range after an argument with one Thai policeman. Some days after the incident, an official Thai inquiry found that Farr tried to shoot his way out of trouble and that the policeman in question had acted in self-defense.[74]

Four more Australian mine employees, Ken Strafford, H. Moore, A. K. Craigie and J. T. Donnelly, were taken prisoner by Thai police and handed over to the Japanese at Pinyok mine near Yala where they survived the massacre of at least nineteen civilians and eight British Indian soldiers. Donnelly remained a fugitive in the jungle near the Thai-Malay border, dying some two years later. Stafford and Moore were eventually taken prisoner by the Japanese in Malaya. Cragie was not heard of again. Believing himself betrayed by the Thais, Strafford vented his bitterness at the end of the war:

> The Siamese made no attempt to protect or evacuate Europeans resident in their country, which action subsequently led to the atrocity described, which cost the lives of 19 European civilians. The time which elapsed between the outbreak of hostilities and the arrival of the Japanese Forces was adequate for the Siamese administration to inform and arrange for the safe passage of all civilian Europeans in this district over the border into Malaya.[75]

It is impossible to generalize about Australian attitudes towards Thai, Malay and many other peoples engulfed by the Pacific War. The seeming indifference of Thai border police to the fate of European residents contrasts with the sympathetic treatment of civilian internees in the Thai government's charge. Some fifteen or so Australians were taken into custody by the Thai government and interned in Bangkok along with other Europeans for the duration of the war. Allied to rather than conquered by Japan, Thailand retained some vestiges of sovereignty. This factor saved internees from the fate that befell British and Australian soldiers at the hands of the Japanese Army on the Thai-Burma railway, a fate that generated much lasting official bitterness towards Thailand.[76] Edward "Weary" Dunlop's efforts to save the lives of Australian POWs in makeshift hospitals at Tarsau, Hintok, and Chungkai camps on the Thai-Burma railway were materially aided by Boon Pong, a Thai river trader and *Seri Thai* (Free Thai) cadre, who supplied money and precious medicines.[77] At the Mergui rail camp on the Burmese side of the border, Les Hall thought that while local police could not be trusted, Burmese villagers would be willing to help escapees rather than turn them over to the Japanese.[78] In New Guinea, local sympathies often swung according to which army, Allied or Japanese, appeared to be in control. Escaping POWs placed their protectors, whoever they might be, in mortal danger; moreover, colonized peoples had little reason to aid former colonial masters.

Ignorant of the region's history and politics, Australians were perceptive and adaptable enough to quickly come to terms with political realities. Perhaps the first and most bitter lesson was that local sympathies were divided between Australians and advancing Japanese forces. If caught helping Allied prisoners, all villagers, Thai, Malay, Ambonese, Filipino and New Guinean, faced swift and brutal retribution from the Japanese. A member of Gull Force captured on Ambon in 1942, Les Hall acknowledged that Ambonese could not be expected to sacrifice their lives for their Dutch overlords, or aid escaping POWs. Indeed, the KNIL defenders of Ambon, mostly drawn from the local Christian population, melted away unexpectedly and the island was taken within two days. Non-combatants had reason to resent the presence of both Allied and Japanese troops and, as Les Hall said of the Ambonese, tended to "flow with the tide."[79] And yet, some Ambonese fought on, earning the enduring respect and gratitude of Australian soldiers stationed on Ambon who survived the war.

Resistance groups afforded refuge but care was needed to distinguish the enemy. Also many Malay-Chinese and Filipino guerillas that fought against the Japanese did not risk their lives in anticipation of a return to the pre-war imperial *status quo*. Of Australian guerilla fighters Nelson writes, they "entered a world of extremes in physical hardships, cultural differences, and violent political warfare."[80] Several Australian diggers and one civilian tin miner who avoided capture in Malaya joined groups of Chinese Communists fighting with the Malayan People's Anti-Japanese Army only to be revolted by the warrior rituals of their hosts and to find themselves treated with increasing distrust. On the Philippines island of Mindanao escaping Australians stumbled across a centuries-old conflict between the Islamic Moro people and the Christian colonizers, first under the banner of Spain and then the United States. In the north of the country, retreating American forces aided the People's Anti-Japanese Army to resist the Japanese on the island of Luzon, but in the south the Moro were hostile to the Allies. Survival depended upon the ability to distinguish between friend and enemy in a context where historical rivalry and political ideology overlaid the immediate conflict between "pro" and "anti" Japanese groups. In wartime, "ordinary" Australians were capable of extraordinary feats of cultural adaptation.

THWARTED ASPIRATIONS

The Pacific War was fought across a geographical area extending from Burma to the Solomon Islands and from New Guinea to China and Japan. Captured in a lightening Japanese southward push, the Archipelago became the outer perimeter of Japan's enlarged Asian empire and a staging post in air raids on northern Australia. For the colonial powers, Japan included, the war would determine the future economic and political center of Asia and the Pacific. For Japanese strategists, Australia and the Archipelago was part of its South Seas periphery, a valuable source of energy minerals and base metals. For the United States, the Philippines marked the outermost perimeter of its Pacific defensive zone centered on the strategically vital Hawaiian Islands. But the mineral resources of the Archipelago, Malayan and Thai tin being cases in point, beckoned, as did Australian consumer markets. Britain for its part retained the Indian subcontinent as the strategic center of its Asian empire, to which colonies in Burma, Malaya, and the Australasian dominions were important but peripheral elements. At war's end two new regions had formed; South East Asia and the South West Pacific, with the former to supply raw materials to a defeated Japan, reconstructed as a beacon of liberal capitalism for a new and independent Asia and a bulwark against international communism.

Planning the recapture of lost colonies throughout maritime Asia, the Allies experimented with geographical theaters with which to arrange prosecution of the war against Japan. The short-lived Australian British Dutch American Command area (ABDA) encompassed all of modern-day South East Asia and extended north to the China coast. Within this Anglo-American pronounced theater, Darwin Sub-Command tantalizingly suggested an enduring sense that northern Australia, Timor, the Moluccas and New Guinea formed a logical geographical unit, in this instance for strategic rather than economic purposes.[81] Replacing ABDA, Britain and the United States instituted a tripartite strategic division of the South East Asia Command (SEAC), the South West Pacific Area and the South Pacific. SEAC's area of operations encompassed the Indian Ocean rim, British India, Ceylon (Sri Lanka), mainland South East Asia, Malaya and Sumatra. As the former major colonial power, Britain took responsibility for prosecuting the war from the Indian subcontinent to Thailand and Malaya. Out of these administrative constructs emerged the idea of South East Asia, with some significant later adjustments, as a geopolitical entity.

Reflecting the enduring influence of nineteenth-century geography, the South West Pacific Area under U.S. General Douglas MacArthur incorporated the islands east of Sumatra to New Guinea and the New Hebrides in the South Pacific, matching Wallace's Austro-Malayan subdivision of the Archipelago, with the obvious addition of the Philippines.[82] Under Admiral Mountbatten as Supreme Allied Commander for South East Asia, South East Asia Command was primarily a British affair, so much so that it was dubbed "Save England's Asian Colonies" by American cynics and U.S. personnel attached to its operations.[83] The perimeters of both spheres of Allied military command shifted significantly in the period from the end of the Pacific War to the formation of the Cold War alliance, the South East Asian Treaty Organization (SEATO) in 1954 which, marking the transition from an Anglo to an American-centered strategic perspective, excluded Ceylon but included the Philippines.[84]

Questions of inclusion were evident in Australian planning for the post-war order. Locked out of armistice agreements in Europe, the Australian government was determined that it be included as a principal party in negotiations for a peace settlement in its own region. Involvement in the formulation of Allied terms for peace with Japan was, understandably, Australia's prime objective. Japan, a major belligerent, had to be punished and its threat potential neutralized. However, an equally hard line was taken with Thailand, Japan's ally in the Pacific War. The ANZAC Pact, between Australia and New Zealand, signed in January 1944, was designed to add weight to Australia's bargaining position in the inevitable reordering of Australia's island defensive zone.[85] The Australian government generally favored the re-establishment of European colonies, with some qualifications, and advocated for strict oversight of Thailand's rehabilitation into the international community. Australian security was thought better served if Thais were denied the right to govern their own country until qualified to do so in a form acceptable to Australia and the West. Curtin advised the British government that, because of Australia's "direct and vital interest" in peace plans,

> we feel it should always be in mind in any dealings concerning Siam, that there should be no commitments regarding Siam's independent statehood which would hinder or preclude satisfactory arrangements to ensure strategic requirements of security in this region.[86]

A prolonged period of "tutelage" was envisaged by Britain, during which time British political influence would be reinstated and strengthened in Bangkok.[87] Evatt supported Britain's intention to treat Thailand "as a defeated enemy" after the war and urged that a puppet government be established under the control of a Commonwealth occupation force. "We would expect to see Siam pass through a period akin to tutelage, the first stage of which would be the occupation and Allied military control through a Siamese Resistance Government."[88] The British proposal went beyond the restoration of the pre-war regional *status quo* and Evatt's support reflected the Australian government's wish to see the Asian region remade in a manner advantageous to Australian defense interests and post-war development aims. In April 1946 Australia signed a separate peace treaty with Thailand that reiterated British terms but which also specified payment of tin compensation to Australian companies. Here was recognition under international law that Australian and British interests were distinct. Compensation negotiations dragged on for several years however, with Canberra consistently rebuffing Thai diplomatic overtures for an exchange of ministers in spiteful retaliation for what were interpreted as Thai attempts to renege on their treaty obligations.[89]

Evatt failed to appreciate the nuances of Thai politics or foresee Australia's longer-term interests in mainland South East Asia. Australia pressed for harsh punishment to be meted out to Thailand, to secure compensation for Australian tin companies stripped of their assets in 1942, but also to avenge the deaths of Australian POWs. Fearful that Japan might one day be resurgent, the Australian government also wished for the neutralization of elements formerly sympathetic to Japan, lest Thailand again be used as a back door into Malaya. This approach merely aided the spread of American diplomatic and economic influence in a former *de facto* part of the Sterling Area. The toughness of Australia's stand on tin compensation mirrored the assertiveness of Australian foreign policy under the Labor Party in the 1940s.

Attempting to shore up weak points in Australia's outer island perimeter, Evatt pressed for other revisions to the *status quo ante*. Despite Portugal's entry into the war on the Allied side in 1944, Canberra would not accept "an absolute restoration of Portuguese sovereignty without any of the necessary qualifications" to protect Australian defense interests. "We cannot forget" the government advised Cranbourne, "that no assistance whatever was received by us from Portugal at the crucial time."[90] At issue was Portugal's unwillingness to accept the stationing of Australian troops on Timor before the outbreak of war. To guard against a recurrence, Evatt sought Portuguese agreement to future defense collaboration, in effect denying Portugal the option of neutrality. Evatt and Curtin also sought to extend Australian influence into the Netherlands Indies by sending Australian troops to dislodge Japanese forces in the eastern Archipelago. Curtin told the Advisory War Council such a move would

> . . . assist to a considerable degree in the realisation of Australia's general policy of fostering Australian influence and creating conditions for future development of Australian trade in this region.[91]

Nationalists declared Indonesian independence on the heels of the Japanese surrender in August 1945. According to Richard Chauvel, many senior people in External Affairs viewed independence movements in South East Asia with misgiving and in the early months of the Indonesian Revolution Australia's leaders struggled to come to terms which the pace of events in their island region.[92] To make matters more awkward, the Netherlands East Indies maintained a government in exile in Australia. Evatt was no advocate of immediate decolonization but he undoubtedly saw advantages in Indonesian nationalism for the realization of greater Australian influence in the Indies. The dilemma made Australian foreign policy towards Indonesia and the Indies "ambivalent" to say the least.[93]

In the last months of the war Australian troops established Allied control over much of the eastern Archipelago and had assisted the reinstitution of

Dutch authority. However, the revival of Dutch imperial rule promised a return to the controlled trading relations of the pre-war period. The division of the Indies and the creation of an independent Indonesian state might open the way for Australian trade and influence although nationalist sentiment was weakest in the eastern islands. In order to recover their empire, and to weaken the appeal of Indonesian nationalism, the Dutch were willing to consider the idea of devolved political power through a federal structure of government. The Dutch plan envisaged participation by representatives from the traditional and generally loyalist regional aristocracy. Evatt hoped that the Dutch and Indonesian nationalists, led by Sukarno and Mohammed Hatta, could be brought to the negotiating table. Writing in support of a federal system in the Indies, Evatt advised Curtin's successor, Ben Chifley,

> The political forms by which this sovereignty is exercised in any part of the Netherlands territories are not immutable and the principle of development of Self-Government has been publicly recognised by the Netherlands Government.[94]

Armed with weapons left behind by surrendering Japanese troops, Indonesian nationalist forces were, if necessary, capable of waging war against the Dutch in Java and Sumatra. Confronted by the possible disintegration of the Netherlands Indies, Evatt asserted Australia's interest in achieving a resolution to the standoff. He went on,

> Our interest in the region lies in security and also in order provided it is founded on justice, welfare, progress and the satisfaction of legitimate political aspirations. We would hope to see the early beginning of an evolution in *South Eastern Asia and Indonesia* [emphasis added] of a co-operative group of self-reliant states linked with other States of the world by ties of trade, legitimate investments and political co-operation and Mutual Aid.[95]

Evatt's idea of a regional community marked a significant departure from the alliance-centric, realist views that characterized Conservative and Labor approaches to external affairs in the previous half-century. The task of strengthening Australia's outer defenses required delicate diplomacy to bring about the formation of a common "security zone," one that encompassed the Australasia of old, and which included newly independent states on an equal diplomatic footing with the old colonial powers. Evatt's hopes for a sustainable region were strengthened by Australia's inclusion in Philippines president Elpidio Quirino's vision of an Asian Bloc spanning South East Asia and the Western Pacific. Quirino, who appreciated Evatt's attempts to chart an independent course for Australian foreign policy, envisaged the creation of an Asian collective security arrangement similar to the North Atlantic Treaty Organization then being formed in anticipation of future war with the Soviet Union.[96] Evatt embraced Quirino's ideas, and yet, without a commitment to decolonization by all regional colonial powers, Australia included, a Pacific Asia security organization was at best a remote possibility.

There were perhaps too many unresolved political issues relating to identity, sovereignty and territorial boundaries, to permit the early formation of a regional community. New nomenclatures institutionalized during the Pacific War earned currency in negotiations about the future shape of Australia's region, raising a vexing question of which states and which peoples belonged to which part of a bifurcated Archipelago. External Affairs officers involved in deliberations over Australian policy towards the Netherlands Indies, Indonesia, and West New Guinea were divided on the issue. Uppermost in their minds was the question of what criteria, political, economic or anthropological, should be used to establish a precise line of demarcation. The Australian government accepted the division of the Archipelago into South East Asian and South West Pacific areas but the province of Dutch or West New Guinea was left in an ambiguous situation.[97] Informing Evatt on the formation of a South Seas Commission, W. E. Dunk, Secretary to the Department of External Affairs, illuminated the strategic dilemma:

> As far as the geographical situation is concerned the attachment of Dutch to Australian New Guinea makes it difficult to draw the line merely at the Australian-Dutch border. On the other hand there does seem to be some doubt whether Dutch New Guinea falls logically within South Seas area from point of view, of, for example, communications, political interest and economic development. The view is that Dutch New Guinea is rather more directly connected with Java and the islands of the "Indonesian" group.[98]

Dunk was among a group of External Affairs officers who advocated for Indonesian independence and for Indonesian control over more than those Republican enclaves on Java that survived at the end of 1947.[99] In July of that year, the Dutch launched a fierce military assault on all Republican-held territory in Sumatra and Java, inflicting significant defeats upon the independence movement. As the security crisis on Australia's doorstep worsened, Chifley referred the Indonesian conflict to the United Nations against the express wishes of the British government but with support from a newly independent India under the leadership of Jawaharlal Nehru. Both sides were pressed to accept a ceasefire but it took almost another two years and intense diplomatic pressure from the United Nations Security Council, United States and newly independent Asian nations before the Dutch finally released their grip on the East Indies, with the exception of West New Guinea. Australia's intervention was timely and probably prevented the complete rout of Republican forces. After assisting the re-imposition of

Dutch colonial rule in the eastern Archipelago in 1945–1946 the Chifley government played an instrumental part in international efforts to protect the fledgling republic from further Dutch "police actions" until full and formal independence was conferred in 1949.

The Pacific War sharpened Australian awareness of the Archipelago's strategic importance while decolonization hastened the need to cultivate influential allies among newly independent states in this outer island chain. Security rather than diplomatic concerns led Evatt to include West New Guinea in planning for the future management of South and South West Pacific affairs. Anxious to avoid a long land border with Indonesia, the Australian view of the colony's regional location firmed following the election of the Liberal Country Party government in November 1949. The territory, also known as West Papua, was now deemed ethnically and geographically distinct from the rest of the Indonesian Archipelago and therefore to be regarded as part of Melanesia. Policymakers in Canberra quietly expressed the view that West New Guinea might even become Australian mandated territory. This oscillating and contested biogeographical line of division between Asia and the Pacific became a running sore in the Australia-Indonesia relationship until the United States eventually forced Australia to accept the inevitability of Indonesian sovereignty over Irian Jaya in 1962.

DOLLAR CONVERTIBILITY

A strong Anglo-American commitment to underwrite international order at the global and regional level was the strategic base on which rested Australian hopes for a United Nations–sponsored post-war security regime in Asia and the Pacific.[100] Allies in wartime, Britain and the United States were economic and political competitors in peacetime. British post-war aims included the temporary restoration of its Asian empire as a springboard for British business to regain a substantial foothold before decolonization gathered momentum. Yet weakened by war, Britain needed the cooperation of the United States to build a stable international security environment in which to reassert control over its former colonial possessions. The reestablishment of a sterling bloc within which preferential trade could aid Britain's economic recovery did not accord with United States ambitions for a new global trading order. Consequently, Washington challenged restoration of British economic hegemony wherever the opportunity arose, leading to British suspicion of American "political warfare" against the empire.[101] Australia attempted to pursue its regional commercial and strategic interests in a context of intensifying Anglo-American rivalry that extended to divergent views about the appropriate course of decolonization in South East Asia.

Long before the last shots of the Pacific War were fired, Washington determined to pry open the door to American commerce in Thailand, even if this antagonized its principal wartime ally.[102] A swift re-incorporation of Thailand into a global economy founded on the principle of free trade was a major American foreign policy priority, but the country was also clearly targeted as the most vulnerable point in Britain's Malayan tin monopoly.[103] The punitive attitude adopted by Chifley and Evatt gave greater scope for American prestige and influence to continue to rise in Bangkok. After pressuring Britain and Australia to soften peace terms, the U.S. government moved to secure the disbursement of Thailand's wartime tin and future production for American tin interests. Aware of the damage done to Australian-Thai relations by Australian intransigence over the compensation issue, new Secretary to the Department of External Affairs John Burton counseled Evatt: "The time seems past when any useful result would be achieved by approaching the question of Australia-Siamese relations from the position that Siam is a defeated enemy."[104] Burton's implication was that cordial diplomatic relations were essential if Australian exporters were to win a share of the Thai consumer market for manufactured goods ahead of British and American competitors.

The new Menzies government proved more receptive to Burton's advice, but not out of any sense of nascent regionalism, and not to the extent that it embraced Burton's regional vision. Burton, perhaps more than Evatt, saw opportunities for Australian diplomacy to make significant inroads into a slowly evolving regional community of newly independent nations. An invitation to a conference to discuss Quirino's ideas for a regional "Union" of states, to be held in the resort town of Baguio in May 1950, indicated that Australian political stocks were high.[105] They would never reach the same height again until Australia's formal invitation to commence negotiations to join in a free-trade area with the ten-member Association of South East Asian Nations over half a century later. The change of government effected a reorganization of Australian priorities, which included grudging acceptance of U.S. hegemony in Asia. Reversing Evatt's emphasis upon regional community, Menzies reverted to traditional alliance diplomacy within a defense framework defined by an uncomfortable accommodation of British Commonwealth and U.S. strategic interests.

While Australia's treatment of Thailand had engendered animosity, the conciliatory and tolerant approach of the United States paid handsome dividends to American corporations engaged in shipping, smelting, oil refining and manufacturing.[106] Official American military and economic assistance left Thailand awash with dollars. Seeking improved relations with South East Asian countries, Richard Casey visited Bangkok as part of his first regional tour as Minister for External Affairs in 1951 only to find himself apologizing for the previous government's insensitivity. This vital gesture foreshadowed a warming of relations with Thailand, yet, as Casey quickly learned, given the missed diplomatic opportunities of the immediate post-war years, there remained little scope for Australia to exert influence beyond the provision of education aid.[107] In keeping with Casey's intention to build a regional diplomatic network, Australia's consulate in Bangkok, established in 1946 mainly to uphold the financial interests of Australian mining investors, was upgraded to an embassy. The move followed the appointment of Australian ambassadors to the Philippines and Indonesia, and indicated the importance now attached in Canberra to good relations with Australia's nearest neighbors.

The United States cultivated Thailand as a bulwark against the potential southward advance of communism from China and North Vietnam. Australia was compelled by circumstance to accept the exigencies of American foreign policy and the realities of Cold War politics. Closer alignment with American foreign policy under the 1951 Australia, New Zealand, United States Security Treaty (ANZUS) Treaty meant that Australia had to rethink its attitude towards Thailand and regional affairs. In the global war between the West and communism, Australia could not avoid defense cooperation with regional allies, even if these relations were conducted within alliances created by external powers. Under the 1948 Australia New Zealand Malaya (ANZAM) defense agreement, Australia became technically allied to an independent Malaya in 1957. The 1954 South East Asia Treaty Organization (SEATO) brought Australia into alliance with Thailand's military-dominated governments, and, after Australia opposed its inclusion, the Philippines, which hosted the principal U.S. military bases in South East Asia. Although part of the Commonwealth and U.S. strategic frameworks for post-war Asia, these alliances forced Australian policymakers to cooperate with political leaders and military establishments in Thailand, Malaya and the Philippines. Victory in the Cold War against the Soviet Union was Australia's highest international priority, but Australian foreign and defense policies were substantially regionalized as a consequence of these alliances and by the emergence of South East Asia as a key battleground in the global war against communism.

BORDERING ON CHAOS

Australia's confidence in its status as a Pacific power was predicated upon the military support of Britain and increasingly the United States. The Menzies government broadened the scope of Australia's commitment to ANZAM by sending Australian forces to assist Britain in the Malayan Emergency, the name given to the internal war of suppression against the Malayan Communist Party. Casey's alarmist conviction that "Australia's survival may well be involved in what happens in South East Asia for the next decade" defined regional Cold War priorities.[108] Southern Thailand was of crucial importance to the security of Malaya and the country as a whole was a vital front-line state in the Cold War in Asia. Where previously Japanese expansionism was feared, Australia's strategic outlook now envisaged the subversion of Vietnam, Laos and Cambodia by communist forces and communist ideology. As Menzies reported to the Australian Parliament in 1954,

> We would do well, therefore, to consider the significance of Indo-China, not by assuming easily that the frontier of the Vietminh is on the 17th parallel, but by contemplating that before long we may be forced to regard the communist frontier as lying on the southern shores of Indo-China, within a few hundred air miles of the Kra Isthmus.[109]

Australia could at least take heart from the fact that Phibun adopted an unambiguously pro-U.S. foreign policy. Thais were also thought less vulnerable to communist indoctrination because of their devotion to Buddhism, yet, should Thailand become surrounded by hostile communist powers, it was believed a pragmatic revision of Thai foreign policy would follow. Significant political disaffection in north eastern Thailand especially might lead to another uprising similar to the abortive "Palace Coup" of 1949 in which several north eastern politicians figured prominently. An estimated 50,000 Vietnamese refugees living on the Thai-Lao border were thought a potential source of political subversion.[110] Revisiting military scenarios devised during 1940-41, a British Commonwealth plan for the invasion of southern Thailand was prepared. In the event of Thailand falling under communist control, Commonwealth forces would push forward to the "Songkhla Position," roughly equivalent to the point of northernmost advance envisaged for Operation Matador, such was the strength of military opinion that the Isthmus of Kra was vital to the defense of Malaya.[111] The Menzies government opposed the location of SEATO headquarters in Bangkok in preference for Singapore, not out of any lingering hostility to the Thai prime minister but out of a combination of nostalgia for a fast-eroding old imperial order and the implications for Australia's strategic posture.[112] Understandably, the United States was more inclined to back Thailand and preferred the more "neutral" location of Bangkok. Australian wishes were ignored.

Menzies visited Phibun for a second time in 1957 but unlike their previous meeting the occasion was formal recognition of Thailand's new importance as a regional ally. Alliances provided one mechanism through which Australian aid reached non-Commonwealth countries in Asia. A second and much more far-reaching project for strategic intervention in the Archipelago, the Colombo Plan, was spearheaded by Casey's predecessor, Percy

Spender. Initiated at a British Commonwealth conference in Colombo in
January 1950, the plan would see educational and technical aid to newly independent Asian countries used to mute the appeal of international communism by transferring skills with which neighboring peoples could lift
themselves out of poverty.[113] Where only a handful of Asian students had
trickled into Australia before, the plan provided opportunities for thousands to study at Australian colleges and universities. Following the formation of SEATO, Australian Colombo Plan aid to Thailand also increased,
marking the country's inclusion in Australia's defensive outer perimeter.[114]
For the first time since the introduction of race-based immigration restriction, Australians were exposed to the presence of significant numbers of
Asian people in their midst. In the words of Daniel Oakman, the Colombo
Plan "breached the barriers, both geographic and mental, of Australia's
northern frontier."[115] This was the first major peacetime intervention by
Australia in the Asian region. Designed to bolster Western-style parliamentary democracy in neighboring countries, the plan generated far-reaching
consequences for White Australia.

Aside from the struggle for the hearts and minds of regional neighbors,
there were many real and potential South East Asian battlefields in the
global war against communism. By the time the "First" Laos crisis erupted
in 1959, Australia's "line in the sand" had moved northward from the
Songkhla Position to the Thai-Lao border. Concerned by *Pathet Lao* gains
against the American-backed Lao government in a "Second" crisis less than
a year later, the Menzies government provided RAAF air support to its
SEATO ally on its riverine border with Laos to guard against the possibility
of Lao-sponsored communist insurgency in Thailand's northeast.[116] Remote defensive barriers offered little comfort to Australian defense planners
because there could be no clear demarcation between allegedly communist
and non-communist spheres. Indonesia was viewed as a country sinking
further under the influence of the world's third largest communist party, the
Parti Kommunis Indoneisa (PKI), upon which Sukarno relied more and more
for political support. Indeed, the fledgling multi-ethnic nation of Indonesia
appeared in danger of disintegration, first with the declaration of an independent Republic of the South Moluccas centered on Ambon, which survived from April to December 1950 until the islands were forcibly reinte-
grated into the Indonesian state.[117]

The politics of decolonization added more layers of complexity. Differing
visions of nation and region were proposed, discussed and then quickly forgotten. An alternative idea of Indonesia was advanced with the proclamation of *Dar'ul Islam* in West Java, Aceh and south Sulawesi by Muslims committed to the transformation of Indonesia from a secular to an Islamic state.
Military officers concerned about the PKI's growing influence declared their
own short-lived revolutionary countergovernment centered on West Suma-

tra and north Sulawesi.[118] The unwelcome transference of West New Guinea to Indonesian sovereignty gave Australia a common land border with Indonesia, making the cross-border actions of the Free Papua Movement, *Organisasi Papua Merdeka* (OPM) a major Australian security concern. So fragmented were newly independent mainland polities that the actual political reach of governments did not correspond to territorial jurisdictions recognized under international law. In practice, borders were mere frontiers where central power was weak and contested, making any attempt to engineer a regional association extremely difficult.

The short-lived Association of Southeast Asia (ASA), comprising Thailand, the Philippines, and Malaysia, collapsed within two years of its inception because the latter two states maintained intractable territorial grievances. The contemporaneous Philippine proposal for Maphilino, an archipelagic confederation comprising Malaysia, Indonesia and the Philippines, failed to materialize for similar "internal" contradictions.[119] After the formation of the Malaysian Federation in 1963, Malaysia and the Philippines disputed sovereignty over Sabah, formerly British North Borneo, a tension that has yet to be formally resolved. Greg Poulgrain's study of the role of British Intelligence in engineering Indonesia's *konfrontasi* with Malaysia reveals disturbing details about Anglo-American manipulation of regional political rivalries. Poulgrain alleges that Indonesia's brushfire war against Malaysia, into which Australian forces were drawn in 1965, was ignited by British *agent provocateurs* in the face of U.S. diplomatic efforts to foster improved relations with Sukarno to persuade Sarawak and North Borneo to join an enlarged Malaysian Federation.[120] These tensions highlighted the potential for contradictions between Australia's alliance commitments under ANZAM and SEATO and important bilateral relationships. Once deployed, Australian combat troops skirmished with Indonesian army units along the Sarawak-Kalimantan border, but all the while Australian military and development aid flowed to its nearest and most populous Asian neighbor.

The Pacific War represented a major disjuncture in the development of Australian commercial and diplomatic connections with its neighbors, not least because the Japanese interregnum effectively brought the old imperial order crashing down and heralded a new era that required a new attitude towards regional political affairs. The post-war history of state formation in the Archipelago was one of nation-state building within inherited colonial borders but there were significant geopolitical and geo-economic boundary shifts. South East Asia was detached from the Pacific in Australian thinking, although to Australian policymakers the entire Malay Archipelago remained a region still in need of periodic strategic intervention. The Sterling Area slowly disintegrated to make way for corporate America and the U.S. dollar. Wars of decolonization raised the specter of Asian communism and heightened fears of a subterranean communist challenge to the "Australian way of life" that had to be checked by whatever means and as far away as possible from Australia's shores. *Konfrontasi* was a precursor to Australia's involvement in the Vietnam War that lasted from 1965 to 1972. Following the ignominious American withdrawal from Vietnam in 1975, Australia needed a new approach to regional security—one that echoed Evatt's faltering steps towards regional community and one which acknowledged the inescapable significance of Indonesia to Australian security.

NOTES

1. Memorandum prepared for Delegation to Imperial Conference, March 8, 1937, *DAFP*, vol. 1, 1937–38, 38–39.

2. "Summary Draft of a Policy for the South," in *Japan's Greater East Asia Co-Prosperity Sphere in World War II: Selected Readings and Documents*, ed. J.C. Lebra, (Kuala Lumpur: Oxford University Press, 1975), 64.

3. Meaney, *Security in the Pacific*, 1–14.

4. Broadcast speech by R. G. Menzies, Prime Minister, April 26, 1939, *DAFP*, vol. 2, 1939, 97–98. The text of this speech was drafted without prior consultation with the British government. Sir Thomas Inskip, UK Secretary of State for Dominion Affairs to Sir Geoffrey Whiskard, UK High Commissioner to Australia, April 29, 1939, *DAFP*, vol. 2, 1939, 100.

5. Alan Watt, *The Evolution of Australian Foreign Policy, 1938–1965* (London: Cambridge University Press, 1967), 25–26. Thomas B. Millar, *Australia in Peace and War: External Relations Since 1788* (Sydney: Allen & Unwin and ANU Press, 1991), 60.

6. Speech by Menzies, April 26, 1939, *DAFP*, vol. 2, 1939, 97–98.

7. Watt, *Evolution*, pp. 23–28; Casey to F. H. Stewart, November 29, 1940, RGC no. 17, Casey Diaries, vol. 2, June 1940–March 1942, MS6150, Casey Family Papers, National Library of Australia.

8. Neville Meaney, "Introduction" in *Australian and the World: A Documentary History from the 1870s to the 1970s*, ed. Neville Meaney (Melbourne: Longman Cheshire, 1985), 21.

9. Memorandum by Mr. J. K. Waller, Department of External Affairs, July 9, 1937, *DAFP*, vol. 1, 1937–38, 171–174.

10. Sir Josiah Crosby to Viscount Halifax, August 15, 1939. Australian Archives, Canberra, (hereafter AA) A1608/1, J41/1/7.

11. Pratt to Crosby, August 14, 1939, AA, A1608/1, J41/1/7.

12. H. Gullet, Minister for External Affairs, to Robert Menzies, January 14, 1940. AA, A1680/1, J41/1/7 Part 1.

13. *Industrial and Australian Mining Standard*, January 15, 1940.

14. Crosby to Gullet, Minister for External Affairs, August 19, 1939, AA, A981, Thailand 24.

15. Bisal to Menzies, February 26, 1940., AA, A981, Thailand 27. The Melbourne *Age*, January 23, 1940. Bisal Sukhumwid to Pratt, February 1, 1940, MS6590, Box

329/6c, Pratt Papers, AMC SLV. For note on Clem Pratt's occupation see Melbourne *Herald*, April 14, 1944.

16. Churchill convinced Australia to send troops and equipment to the Middle East by guaranteeing the dispatch of naval forces to defend Singapore and Australia against a Japanese attack. David Horner, *High Command: Australia's Struggle for an Independent War Strategy, 1939–45*, (Sydney: Allen & Unwin, 2nd edition, 1992), 28–31.

17. Aldrich, *Key to the South*, 268–269.

18. For the time being Japanese primacy in the Asia-Pacific arena was recognized. However, the outcome of a war between the Allies and Japan was still thought too unpredictable to justify abandonment of diplomatic and economic relations with Britain. Cabinet Minutes, October 23, 1940, NA, PMO, SR 0201.60.1/20.

19. Aldrich, *Key to the South*, 224–230.

20. Gullet to Menzies, January 15, 1940, AA, A 1608/1, J41/1/7 Part 1. See also, Mr. S. M. Bruce, High Commissioner to London, to Mr R. G. Menzies, Prime Minister, Cablegram 70, February 1, 1940.

21. Casey to Menzies, December 21, 1939, AA, A1608/1, J41/1/7 Part 1.

22. Crosby to the High Commissioner for the Malay States, December 18, 1939, AA, A816, 6/301/247. This dispatch was forwarded on to Gullet in External Affairs.

23. Australian political leaders, while afraid of Japanese ambitions, did not want to antagonize Japan nor its potential allies while Britain was embroiled in a war in Europe. Carl Bridge, "Poland to Pearl Harbour," in *Munich to Vietnam: Australia's Relations with Britain and the United States since the 1930s*, ed. Carl Bridge (Melbourne: Melbourne University Press, 1991), 43. Millar, *Peace and War*, 59.

24. Aldrich, *Key to the South*, 230.

25. "Thailand: Territorial Demands on Indochina," *Current Notes on International Affairs*, (vol. 9, No. 7, 1 October 1940)

26. Aldrich, *Key to the South*, 260–66.

27. Aldrich, *Key to the South*, 262. See also Kamon Pensrinokun, "Adaptation and Appeasement: Thai Relations with Japan and the Allies in World War II," in *Thai-Japanese Relations in Historical Perspective*, ed. Chaiwat Khamchoo and E. Bruce Reynolds, (Bangkok: Institute of Asian Studies, Chulalongkorn University, 1988), 130–31.

28. Stirling to External Affairs, Canberra, Telegram no. 649, August 8, 1940, AA, A2937, Thailand 252.

29. Stirling to External Affairs, Canberra, Telegram 649, August 8, 1940, AA, A 2937, Thailand 252. *Current Notes on International Affairs*, (vol. 9, no. 7, 1 October 1940), 197. For the official Australian interpretation of Thai foreign policy and Thai-Japanese relations see also *Current Notes on International Affairs*, (vol. 8, no. 4, 1 March 1940), 92–94. See also Stirling to External Affairs, Telegram 639, August 6, 1940, AA, A 2937, Thailand 252.

30. Advisory War Council Minutes, Minute 39, November 25, 1940, *DAFP*, Vol. 4, Document No. 208, 282–83.

31. Menzies to Crosby, January 21, 1941. "Draft cablegram to High Commissioner, London, from the Prime Minister," undated. Bruce to Menzies, January 21, 1941, Cablegram 63, AA, A1608/1, J65/1/1 Part 1. Menzies to A. Fadden, Acting Prime Minister, February 4, 1941, AA, A1608/1, J41/1/7 Part 1.

32. Lionel Wigmore, *The Japanese Thrust*, (Canberra: Australian War Memorial, 1957), 41.

33. Allan William Martin and Patsy Hardy, eds. *Dark and Hurrying Days: Menzies' 1941 Diary* (Canberra: National Library of Australia, 1993), 24.

34. Menzies to Acting Prime Minister, January 30, 1941, MS 4936, Series 31, World War II, Box 49, Folder 11, Sir Robert Menzies Collection, NLA.

35. Martin and Harding, eds., *Dark and Hurrying Days*, 26. Menzies to Fadden, February 14, 1940, *DAFP*, vol. 4, July 1940–June 1941, 407–8. Acting Prime Minister to Menzies, February 21, 1941, AA, A1608/1, J41/1/7 Part 1.

36. Latham to Prime Minister's Department, January 28, 1941, MS4936, Series 31, World War II, Box 497, Folder 13, Sir Robert Menzies Collection, NLA.

37. Menzies to Acting Prime Minister, February 4, 1941, MS 4936, Series 31, World War II, Box 497, Folder 11.

38. Advisory War Council Minutes, Minute 145, Sydney, February 13, 1941, *DAFP*, vol. 4, 391.

39. Advisory War Council Minutes, Minute 119, Melbourne February 5, 1941, *DAFP*, vol. 4, doc. no. 271, 362–63. Horner, *High Command*, 54–57.

40. Latham to Department of External Affairs, Cablegram 68, February 4, 1941, *DAFP*, vol. 4, doc. no. 272, 366–67.

41. Aldrich, *Key to the South*, 294.

42. Advisory War Council Minutes, Minute 145, February 13, 1941, *DAFP*, vol. 4, July 1940–June 1941, 392. AA, CRS A5954/2, item 730/1, War Cabinet (Sydney) February 12, 1941, 301.

43. "Siam and U.S. Dollars" attached to W. M. Doll, Financial Adviser to Crosby, March 1, 1940, AA, A981/1, Thailand 15 Part 1.

44. Aldrich, *Key to the South*, p. 241. Crosby to Halifax, March 5, 1940, AA, A981/1, Thailand 16.

45. "Banthuk kaan prachum ruang kaan khakhay yaang lae rae dibuk kap prathaet America" (Minutes of a meeting on the sale of rubber and tin to America), September 26, 1940, and covering letter of Minister for Agriculture to Prime Minister October 2, 1940, NA, PMO, SR 0201.60.1/20.

46. Chamnaannitikaset, Director, Department of Lands and Minerals, "Haa ta-laad kaan kha nai america"(Search for markets in America), August 22, 1940, NA, PMO, SR. 0201.60.1/20.

47. "Siam and U.S. Dollars" attached to Doll to Crosby, March 1, 1940, AA, A981/1, Thailand 15 Part 1. See also "Banthuk kaan prachum ruang kaan khakhay yaang lae dibuk kab prathaet america," September 26, 1940, NA, PMO, SR 0201.60.1/20.

48. Cabinet Minutes, October 23, 1940, and Chamnaannitikaset, 'Ruang haa ta-laad kaan kha nai prathaet america,' NA, PMO, SR 0201.60.1/20.

49. Crosby to Anthony Eden, January 16, 1941, AA, A816/1, 6/301/247.

50. Aldrich, *Key to the South*, 323.

51. The Melbourne Stock Exchange *Official Record*, (vol. 33, nos. 1–12, 1940).

52. Crosby to Menzies, January 22, 1941; Secretary of State for Dominion Affairs to Prime Minister's Department, February 21, 1941, AA, A1608, AC 47/1/1. Pratt to Hodgson, April 24, 1941, AA, A981/1, Thailand 16.

53. Diary entry, May 12, 1941, Casey Diary, vol. 1, December 1939–August 1940, MS6150, Casey Papers, NLA.

54. Richard Aldrich, "A Question of Expediency: Britain, the United States and Thailand, 1941–42," *Journal of Southeast Asian Studies* (vol. 19, no. 2, September 1988), 230.

55. W. E. Antrobus, UK High Commissioner in Australia to F. Strahan, Secretary, Prime Ministers Department, September 19, 1941, AA, A1608, AC47/1/1.

56. Wigmore, *Japanese Thrust*, 73.

57. Aldrich, *Key to the South*, 335–36.

58. "Report on Australian Civilians in Siam in December 1941," AA, A431/1, 46/2562.

59. Wigmore, *Japanese Thrust*, 106.

60. See map in Aldrich, *Key to the South*, 338.

61. Cablegram, Crosby to Menzies, June 28, 1941, AA, A1608, AC47/1/1.

62. Pratt to Menzies, July 6, 1941, MS 4936, Series 2, Folder 32, Box 40, Menzies Collection, National Library of Australia.

63. Pratt to Fadden, September 27, 1941, AA, A1608/1, 16/1/689.

64. Melbourne *Age*, September 1, 1941. This was the last overseas appointment to be made by Menzies. Menzies to Lord Cranbourne, August 13, 1941, *DAFP*, vol. 5, 72–73.

65. Hastings, "The Timor Problem – II", 193.

66. Sir Frederick Stewart, Minister for External Affairs, to Mr. R. G. Casey, Minister to the United States, May 23, 1941, *DAFP*, vol. 4, 676.

67. Commonwealth Government to Lord Cranbourne, March 27, 1941, *DAFP*, vol. 4, 516.

68. Richard Chauvel, *Nationalists, Soldiers and Separatists: The Ambonese Islands from Colonialism to Revolt, 1880–1950* (Leiden: KITLV Press, 1990), 168–69.

69. Lord Cranbourne to John Curtin, 27 November 1941, *DAFP*, vol. 5, 231–32.

70. Memorandum on Thailand, A1067/1, PI/46/2/13/2. For British concerns about United States opposition to Operation Matador see Aldrich, *Key to the South*, 344–45.

71. Pratt to McMahon-Ball, October 25, 1942, MS 6587, Box 329/5 (a), Pratt Papers, La Trobe Library. Wigmore, *Japanese Thrust*, 140–46. Phibun's offer of passage is mentioned in Kondhi Suphamongkhon, *Kaan withaetsobaay khong thai rawang pii, 2483–2495 (Thai Foreign Policy, 1940–1952)*, (Bangkok: Post Publishing, 2nd edition, 1994,) 21–22.

72. Peter Hastings, "The Timor Problem – III," *Australian Outlook* (vol. 29, no. 3, December 1975), 328–29.

73. Gavan McCormack and Hank Nelson, "Conclusion,'" in *The Burma-Thailand Railway*, ed. Gavan McCormack and Hank Nelson (Sydney: Allen & Unwin, 1993), p. 153.

74. "Report on Australian Civilians in Siam in December 1941," attachment to R. G. Smith, Lieutenant Colonel, 1 Australian War Crimes Section SACSEA to Australian Army Headquarters, Melbourne, 5 September 1946, AA, A431/1, 46/2562.

75. R. A. Strafford to the Custodian of Enemy Property, Canberra, December 10, 1945, AA, A1066, IC45/33/3/4/8. H. Moore to Undersecretary of State, Foreign Office, London, 28 December 1945, AA, A1067, IC46/33/3/4/5.

76. R. A. Stafford to the Custodian of Enemy Property, Canberra, December 10, 1945, AA, A1066, IC45/33/3/4/8. A. Stirling to External Affairs Officer, London, December 30, 1942, AA, A981/1, 43/235/2/1. "Report on Australian Civilians in Siam in December 1941," AA, A431/1, 46/2562. J. C. R. Proud to Colonel J. Eastman, Australian Consul in Thailand, 12 December 1945, AA, A816, 19/301/1030 Part 1.

77. Edward E. Dunlop, *The War Diaries of Edward "Weary" Dunlop: Java and the Thai-Burma Railway, 1942–1945*, (Melbourne: Nelson, 1986), 279–280, 285, 317, 325.

78. Leslie Hall, *The Blue Haze: POWs on the Burma Railway, Incorporating the History of 'A' Force Groups 3 & 5, Burma-Thai Railway, 1942–1943*, (Sydney: Kangaroo Press, 1996), 50–51.

79. Alisa Rolley, *Survival on Ambon* (Brisbane: self published 1994), 34, 48. Chauvel, *Nationalists, Soldiers and Separatists*, 173.

80. Nelson, *Prisoners of War*, 129.

81. Horner, *High Command*, 148.

82. Horner, *High Command*, 179.

83. Robert M. Hathaway, *Ambiguous Partnership: Britain and America, 1944–47* (New York: Colombia University Press, 1981), 47.

84. Emerson, " What's in a Name," 7–10.

85. The terms of the ANZAC agreement are given under the heading "Thumbing the Nose at Uncle Sam" in *Australia and the World*, ed. Meaney, 488–92. Conference of Australian and New Zealand Ministers, January 17–21, 1944, *DAFP*, vol. 7, 38.

86. Prime Minister's Department to Secretary of State for Dominion Affairs, London, 24 March 1944, AA, A816, 19/301/1030 Pt 1.

87. There were strong suspicions in the U.S. State Department that Churchill planned to occupy the Kra Isthmus after the cessation of hostilities. See Christopher Thorne, "Indochina and Anglo-American Relations, 1942–1945," *Pacific History Review*, (vol. 45, 1976), 75. Sir Josiah Crosby, "Suggestions for a Post-War Settlement with Siam," AA, A2937, Thailand 252.

88. Commonwealth Government to Addison, cablegram 217, Canberra, August 7, 1945, *DAFP*, vol. 8, 299–300; "Armistice Control Machinery," Department of External Affairs, Post-Hostilities Division, December 29, 1944, AA, A1066/H45/1014/2.

89. This course of action was in fact forced upon the Australian government by British negotiators seeking compensation for British-owned companies.

90. Commonwealth Government to Cranbourne, January 2, 1944, *DAFP*, vol. 7, 3.

91. Advisory War Council Submission by Curtin, September 20, 1944, *DAFP*, vol. 7, 541.

92. Richard Chauvel, "West New Guinea: Perceptions and Policies, Ethnicity and the Nation-State," in *Australia in Asia: Episodes*, ed. Anthony Milner and Mary Quilty (Melbourne: Oxford University Press, 1998), 10–16.

93. Bob Catley and Vinsensio Dugis, *Australian-Indonesian Relations since 1945: The Garuda and the Kangaroo*, (Aldershot: Ashgate, 1998), 16–18.

94. Evatt to Makin and Chifley, November 23, 1945, *DAFP*, vol. 9, 636.

95. H. V. Evatt to Makin and Chifley, November 23, 1945, *DAFP*, vol. 9, 635.

96. Rodney Sullivan, "'It Had to Happen': The Gamboas and Australian-Philippine Interactions," in *Discovering Australasia*, ed. Ileto and Sullivan, 104–7.

97. Department of External Affairs to Ballard, September 26, 1946, *DAFP*, vol. 10, 236.

98. Dunk to Evatt, June 30, 1946, *DAFP*, vol. 9, 567–68.

99. Chauvel, "West New Guinea," 22–24.

100. "A Pacific Destiny: Minister for External Affairs Dr. H. V. Evatt Outlines Australia's Post-War Regional Interests and Concerns," in *Australia and the World*, ed. Meaney, 517–20.

101. Thorne, "Indochina and Anglo-American Relations," 83.

102. Secretary of State for Dominion Affairs to External Affairs, Cable D. 1621, 3 September 1945, AA, A1066/1, H45/1014/2.

103. In eager anticipation of an end to Britain's monopoly over the sale of Thai tin, an American company, the Reconstruction and Finance Corporation, was about to send a representative to commence negotiations for the liquidation of Thailand's tin stockpile. Minister for Foreign Affairs to Minister for Commerce, 26 November 1946, NA, MFA, KT 69.2.3/3.

104. "Representation of Siam in Australia," December 2, 1946, AA, A1838/2, 451/3/1/1 Part 1.

105. Sullivan, "It Had to Happen," 104–5. D. Oakman, *Facing Asia: A History of the Colombo Plan*, (Canberra: Pandanus Books, 2004), 28–31.

106. "Siam's New Importance in U.S. Trade Diplomacy," *U.S. News and World Report*, August 20, 1948, AA, A1838/283, 452/6/1.

107. NLA, Casey Papers, MS 6150, Diary 1951, 127.

108. "Extracts from a Parliamentary Statement by R. Casey," August 11, 1954. AA, A4529/2 61/1/1954.

109. "Statement by the Australian Prime Minister, Mr. R. G. Menzies, in the House of Representatives," August 5, 1954. AA, A4529/2 61/1/1954.

110. A. H. Loomes to External Affairs, April 6, 1954, AA, A1838/2 453/2/1 Part 6.

111. Peter G. Edwards, *Crises and Commitments: The Politics and Diplomacy of Australia's Involvement in Southeast Asian Conflicts, 1948–1965* (Sydney: Allen and Unwin with the Australian War Memorial, 1992), 164–66.

112. Alan Renouf, *The Frightened Country* (Macmillan, South Melbourne, 1979), 164.

113. Oakman, *Facing Asia*, 275.

114. Khien Theeravit, *Australian-Thai Relations: A Thai Perspective*, Occasional Paper No. 58 (Singapore: Institute of Southeast Asian Studies, 1979), 8–9.

115. Oakman, *Facing Asia*, 278.

116. Edwards, *Crises and Commitmentss*, 240–48.

117. Chauvel, *Nationalists, Soldiers and Separatists*, 365–92.

118. Werner F. Wertheim, "Fissures in the Girdle of Emeralds," in *Indonesian Politics: A Reader*, ed. Christine Doran (Townsville: Centre for South-east Asian politics, James Cook University of North Queensland, 1987), 63–65.

119. C. Mary Turnbull, "Regionalism and Nationalism," in *The Cambridge History of Southeast Asia, Vol. 2, Part Two: From World War II to the Present*, ed. Nicholas Tarling (Cambridge University Press, Cambridge, 2nd edition, 1999), 285–88.

120. Greg Poulgrain, *The Genesis of Konfrontasi: Malaysia, Brunei, Indonesia, 1945–1965*, (Bathurst: Crawfurd, 1998), 65–75, 288–97.

7

Culture, Region and Economy

THE DEEPENING TIES OF GEOGRAPHY

In the last half of the twentieth century, the dominant image of Australia's region changed from that of a battleground in the war against international communism to a rapidly globalizing marketplace. The shift in Australia's trading patterns after the Pacific War tracked the realignment of global economic and cultural power away from Britain towards a Pacific Asian region dominated by the United States and a reconstructed Japan. Complementarities foreshadowed by Australian business travellers in the nineteenth century materialized as industrialization in the new "tiger economies" of Malaysia, Indonesia and Thailand opened markets for Australian raw materials and foodstuffs. With the end of the Cold War, Asian economic "dynamism" emerged as Australia's principal rationale of regional engagement in an international context where liberal capitalism, in free market guise, assumed the ideological high ground. The gradual reduction of legal barriers to trade, investment and the increased movement of people within South East Asia and between South East Asian states, Australia and New Zealand point towards deeper trends in the regionalization of Australian economic and political relations that temporary shocks and controversies are unlikely to disrupt.

CONTRADICTORY TRENDS

Systemic change stymied the development of closer economic ties between Australia and its island region after the Pacific War. The Bretton Woods system

of international financial regulation was created to prevent another cata-
strophic financial crisis as caused the Depression. Part of a new liberal international order, the system ushered in a period of unprecedented growth in
world manufactures trade, underwritten by American financial and military
power. American foreign investment and American multinationals became
dominant during the first half of this new expansionary phase of globalization. The direct regional impact of these global transformations from an Australian perspective was Japan's rehabilitation and subsequent rapid industrialization, which generated rising demand for Australian minerals. Australia's
place in this new global economy was that of a supplier of primary commodities for manufacturing industries situated elsewhere.

Japanese multinationals made their presence felt in Western electronics
and motor vehicle markets and in the tropical rainforests of South East Asia
and Papua New Guinea, but the emergence of an Asia Pacific–centered
global economy was slow to register in Australian trade with South East
Asian countries. International investment flows, a standard measure of economic globalization, were concentrated between developed countries. Not
until the 1980s, when substantial stocks of U.S. and Japanese foreign direct
investment began to flow towards Australia's nearest neighbors, did Australian exports to South East Asia climb.[1] (figure 7.1)

In the 1950s, macro-economic policies in South East Asia and Australia
also signaled regional divergence rather than convergence. The benefits of
global growth in manufacturing and manufactures trade were not evenly
distributed across the decolonized world. Popular anti-Western sentiment
gave scope for leaders of newly independent states to condemn neo-
colonialism and to propose alternatives to the Anglo-American worldview.
Accepting the logic of *dependencia* theory, which attributed underdevelop-
ment to lingering neo-colonialism, Indonesian, Malaysian and Thai policymakers sought to reduce economic dependence upon Western capital
through state-subsidized import substitution. Economic growth, it was
thought, would naturally follow state-led industrial development. Domestic manufacturing industries were nurtured using a range of policy instruments, including direct state investment in business enterprises or through
the introduction of foreign investment regulations that limited foreign equity in locally registered companies. Tariff walls were erected to protect domestic manufacturers and primary producers and, it was hoped, significant
employment dividends for governments concerned about rapidly expanding numbers of working-age people. Lastly, profits from locally owned enterprises would help to speed the formation of "indigenous" business. In
Australia, tariff protection remained a pillar of the Australian industrial system and welfare state.

In practice, nationalistic economic policies failed to achieve anticipated
results. Of all South East Asian states, the Philippines was the most open

and enjoyed the greatest economic success, registering high-growth rates comparable to those experienced by its neighbors during the boom years of the 1980s. The rise of Ferdinand Marcos to the presidency in 1965, however, ushered in two decades of authoritarian rule and a reversal of the country's economic fortunes.[2] Indonesia, analysts generally agree, went backwards under Sukarno. The crippling effects of rising debt, rising inflation and a trade war with Singapore were compounded by the desertion of the republic's professional managerial class, driven out by anti-Western policies. Nationalization of foreign-owned businesses made economic policy increasingly susceptible to corruption as untrained bureaucrats and army officers took to the reins.[3] In contrast to the political developments in the Philippines, Indonesia's transition from Sukarno's Guided Democracy to Suharto's New Order after 1965 brought a change of attitude towards Western investment in return for much-needed international development assistance.

In Thailand, government promotion of joint ventures between foreign and local companies, often linked to key government ministers, substantially increased the appeal of high office but severely weakened the economy, leaving the country more, not less, dependent upon U.S. support. This dependence upon foreign assistance was perhaps the greatest irony of South East Asian economic nationalism in the 1950s. At independence, Malaysia's import-export trade, mining and plantation industries were largely European controlled, and Prime Minister Tungku Abdul Rahman preferred not to antagonize international investors with threats of nationalization. The Malaysian state failed to break the country's dependence upon foreign capital and technology, but practicalities aside, the strident nationalistic and anti-Western rhetoric voiced in Malaysia and its Asian neighbors nonetheless expressed a popular political wish to chart an independent path to economic modernity.

Local capital formation and industrial skills development were the focus of new foreign investment guidelines for Thailand's mining industry, later generalized under Thailand's Alien Business Law. The Phibun government reserved mineral resources for wholly owned Thai companies and foreign companies with a substantial Thai shareholding. Determined to create a Thai managerial class and to raise the occupational skill levels of the Thai workforce, the government also compelled foreign mining companies to recruit half of their workforce from among Thai nationals. It was also stipulated that any large foreign enterprise should include a Thai on its board of directors.[4] Unlike their Australian competitors, British tin mining companies anticipated the nationalistic mood of Thailand's military leaders and accepted the inevitability of managerial transfer. An official of the Mines Department, Rachan Kanjanawanit, became the first Thai manager of Tongkah Harbour Tin Dredging Ltd., replacing Warren Parsons, the last Australian to manage this famous company.[5] Without government connections and unwilling to promote local expertise, Australian companies could not hope to expand beyond the boundaries of properties acquired in the early 1930s.

Australia's standing in Bangkok suffered from the threatened deportation of a Thai national under the Australian Immigration Restriction Act. Revelations about the insensitive enforcement of Australia's immigration policy in relation to a Jerm Bulgetr (sic) broke in the Bangkok press in April 1949, accompanied by accusations of Australian racism.[6] The case provoked condemnation but not of the same order of magnitude as occurred in the Philippines after the deportation from Australia of Lorenzo Gamboa, a Filipino attached to General McArthur's staff in Australia during the Pacific War, who married an Australian woman only to be denied residency on racial grounds.[7] Australian public sentiment clearly favored Gamboa's case for residency but Calwell's rigid enforcement of the White Australia policy stirred animosity towards Australia throughout Asia. Even so, Thailand's post-war civilian and military politicians pressed for the establishment of formal high-level diplomatic ties. Thai visitors to Australia did not find the Australian people racist. Prince Samosorn Khasem told the Thai newspaper *Liberty* in 1947 that Australians were "frank, friendly and cordial in nature; they are less reserved when compared with Europeans," adding the compliment that "Australia is the best place to live in."[8] What angered Thais and other Asian nationalities was not so much the principle that Australia should be allowed to control immigration in the interests of cultural homogeneity, but rather it was the presumption of racial superiority that the White Australia policy embodied.[9]

Neither Australia's blunt diplomatic treatment of Thailand after the war or the enforcement of Australian immigration policy were connected with the slow decline in Australian mining investment in Thailand. A. W. Palfreyman's Consolidated Tin Dredging Ltd., took control over several large Australian-owned tin-dredging companies in Malaya and Thailand in 1951. Of its issued capital of (Australian currency) £2,730,495, 98 percent was held on Australian share registers.[10] Though there was some Thai shareholding in its subsidiary companies and a residual interest held by the Khaw family, all directors were Australian.[11] Palfreyman remained to oversee the demise of Australian mining enterprise on the peninsula. Of the twenty-five western tin dredging companies left in 1950, ten were Australian owned. Three more were owned by Thai nationals, most probably Sino-Thais, the rest were British. Leases surrounding their operations were instead awarded to Thai and Sino-Thai businessmen, as one by one Australian dredging companies were checkmated and choked out of existence.[12] Over the next sixteen years Australian market share slowly fell away to nothing by 1963, when Consolidated Tin went into voluntary liquidation.

That same year, the U.S.-Thai firm, Eastern Mining Development Company (EMDCo), combining the economic weight of the Union Carbide

Corporation with the political power of Thai Prime Minister Field Marshall Sarit Thanarat, Major General Phao Siyanon and General Thanom Kittika-chorn, obtained exclusive rights to prospect and dredge all off-shore deposits of tin ore laying along the east and west coasts of Thailand. Thailand's first major commercial tin smelter on the island of Phuket incorporated EMDCo and Union Carbide, which together formed the Thailand Smelting and Refining Company (THAISARCO). Sarit died before his dream became a reality but his political allies Phao and Thanom were major shareholders. Of THAISARCO's 150 employees, 144 were Thai nationals. Every scrap of tin metal produced in its first six months went straight to the United States.[13]

Some Australian interest was shown in other sectors of the Thai mining industry, in the development of lignite deposits and the mining of fluorite.[14] Outside the mining industry, a handful of Australian investors exhibited a more adventurous and cooperative spirit. Thai Glass Manufacturers Ltd., formed in 1953 as a joint venture between Australian Consolidated Industries and Thai businessmen, was one example. Capitalizing on the opportunity to both evade import tariffs and secure a supply of cheap labor, the company trained and employed Thai managers and Thai factory workers at its Thonburi plant in accordance with Thailand's evolving foreign investment regime.[15]

The decline in Australian tin-mining activity in Thailand cannot be attributed to a single factor. A federal government decision not to renew the pre-war tax exemption for dividends received from overseas investments was a strong disincentive for anyone planning to invest in a new mining enterprise outside Australia. Yet double taxation did not prevent a major post-war Australian investment spree in Malaya.[16] Also, unlike Malaya, in Thailand at that time there was no general insurgency in the countryside. Stimulated in large part by Japan's "miracle" industrialization, an Australian post-war minerals boom captured the imagination of Australian investors. Mining and prospecting companies became interested in finding and exploiting Australian deposits of iron ore, coal, uranium, lead, zinc and copper. The lesson drawn by the Australian mining industry from the upsurge in post-war nationalist movements throughout Asia was that the mining and smelting of such a strategic resource as tin should take place closer to home. Also, according to mining historian Geoffrey Blainey, the Australian mining community disliked militaristic regimes.[17] In contrast to Australian mining investors before the Pacific War, a new generation of Australian entrepreneurs struggled to comprehend Thai and other South East Asian business elites. Aid and security, not investment, dominated Australia's agenda for relations with its island neighbors.

Trade with South East Asia did not achieve the levels anticipated by Evatt in the immediate post-war era but it would be wrong to attribute this solely to Australian "ambivalence" or to any antagonism felt by South East Asian leaders towards their southern neighbor. In Indonesia, the scarcity of foreign exchange and the lingering dominance of Dutch trading houses restricted access for Australian exporters. Prospects for increased trade with the Philippines were stunted by the adverse economic policies of the Marcos years.[18] On the other side of the ledger, the poor quality of Australian products also allegedly gave Australian brands a bad name.[19] Australia's trade problems were global: its share of world trade fell away after 1950 because of a general failure to take advantage of rapid global growth in manufacturing exports. A specialist exporter of primary commodities, Australia did not excel at the production of manufactured goods for overseas markets. As agricultural and mineral producers, many of Australia's neighbors were economic competitors in key regional markets. Yet Australian exports to Malaysia and Singapore surged, and although a minor trading partner, Australia enjoyed a huge balance of trade surplus with Thailand where Aspro and Akta-Vite became well-known brands.[20] Despite many obstacles, Australian trade with South East Asia grew, but only marginally (figure 7.2).

Australia's racially exclusive immigration policy reinforced a general impression among the region's leaders that Australia was a remnant of British colonialism. There were, however, many systemic impediments to Australia's economic engagement with South East Asia. Firstly, Australia was subject to the directional pull of British and American capital and export markets. Secondly, Australian trade gravitated towards major shipping thoroughfares and global transport hubs in Japan, Sri Lanka (Ceylon), Panama and North America. Thirdly, the cultural orientation of Australia's export commodities remained defined by Northern Hemisphere and predominantly Western consumer tastes. The redirection of Australian trade towards South East Asia needed not just the cultivation of new export products but also a major shift among Australia's closest neighbors, away from inward-looking economic nationalism to a more outward export-orientated version of liberal capitalism.[21] These regional changes did not occur until after the Vietnam War.

STRATEGIC FIT

The end to the Vietnam War marked a watershed in Australia's relations with its island neighbors and in the geopolitical dynamics of the South East Asian region. A reluctant search for economic alternatives to the defunct Imperial preference system followed Britain's decision to seek membership of the European Economic Community in 1963. Then U.S. President Richard Nixon's "Guam Doctrine" and Britain's decision to reduce its military presence "East of Suez" rendered forward defense obsolete as a strategic doctrine, leading to a revival of Evatt's vision of a regional collective security framework. Australia could no longer rely upon Menzies's "great and powerful friends" to buttress Australia's northern defenses or provide export markets for Australian farmers. By the late 1980s Australian economic and strategic interests were officially recognized as being tied to rapid industrialization in Asia.

Forced by the global strategic reappraisals of the major powers, Australian and South East Asian defense thinking temporarily converged during Gough Whitlam's prime ministership (1972–1975). The Association of South East Asian Nations (ASEAN), formed in 1967 to combat the threat of international communism, emerged as a pivotal Asian regional grouping. The five founding member states, Malaysia, Indonesia, Thailand, Singapore and the Philippines, were anti-communist but unwilling to subordinate themselves to U.S. foreign policy. The association's foundation document, the *Bangkok Declaration*, reminded "external powers" that their military bases in South East Asia were temporary and not to be used to subvert the processes of economic and political development in individual states. In announcing a Zone of Peace, Freedom and Neutrality (ZOPFAN) in 1973, a Malaysian idea proposed at a summit of the Non-Aligned Movement in Lusaka in 1970, South East Asian leaders expressed collectively both the nationalist and anti-colonial sentiments that shaped their domestic political agendas, and, equally significant, a concern for regional order in the wake of America's imminent withdrawal from Vietnam.[22]

The association appeared to correspond with Evatt's hopes of a "co-operative group of self-reliant states" sharing regional economic and political aspirations.[23] Australian Prime Minister Gough Whitlam moved ahead of public opinion in expressing his support for the principle of regional neutrality and making Australia an ASEAN dialogue partner in 1974. In a statement that on the surface gave no suggestion that the ANZUS alliance was to be abandoned, he called for "the military and economically dominant powers to cease disruptive intervention in the region, so as to let social and political conflicts work themselves out in truly national solutions." Presaging the Keating government's sponsorship of the ASEAN Regional Forum in the 1990s, Whitlam asserted that traditional alliance diplomacy was to be supplemented by regional common security arrangements and a regional security dialogue. As he told his audience at the University of the Philippines,

> The Australian long-term hope is for regional arrangements which . . . would give all the countries of the area, irrespective of their ideological differences, a forum in which to talk informally together and promote greater understanding and cooperation. [. . .]
> We also wholeheartedly support the ASEAN proposals for a zone of peace ,freedom and neutrality in South-East Asia. We favour co-operation on a regional, as well as a national, basis in facing common security problems. This kind of approach—seeking indigenous solutions to security problems—accords with the attitudes and aims underlying our own foreign policy.[24]

A racially discriminatory immigration policy was no longer tenable in a region of independent states and, thanks to the Colombo Plan, a region of increasingly mobile professional classes. Whitlam abolished the last vestiges of the White Australia policy, but his attempt to write Australia into South East Asia was a bold initiative fraught with political danger. More so than any other event in South East Asia before or since, the Indonesian invasion of East Timor exposed a major contradiction in Whitlam's regional approach. Both the invasion and reports of atrocities against the East Timorese people opened a political and intellectual rift between cosmopolitan universalists committed to uphold global human rights principles and cosmopolitan pragmatists committed to regional engagement. In failing to take a stronger stand against Indonesia's invasion of the former Portuguese colony, Whitlam exposed the dark pragmatism of Australian security policy. He and subsequent Liberal and Labor prime ministers earned the enduring disdain of Australian human rights groups and many ex-servicemen who remembered the assistance given to Australian soldiers stranded in East Timor at the start of the Pacific War. Anger over Australia's tacit acknowledgement of the Indonesian occupation continued unabated until 1999 when East Timorese voted for independence under United Nations auspices and were granted their sovereignty after an Australian-led international force intervened to end a campaign of slaughter and destruction by Indonesian-backed militia.

Both before and after the Pacific War, Australian governments demonstrated that they were prepared to support authoritarian Asian leaders engaged in the suppression of movements deemed hostile to Australian interests. Australia gave tacit approval to the extermination of Indonesian "communists" at the establishment of Indonesia's New Order and looked on as Indonesia attempted to colonize East Timor and exterminate the Timorese revolutionary army, Fretlin. It is not unreasonable to argue that, from the perspective of Australian Conservative and Labor governments, celebrated "Asian dictators," from Chiang Kai Shek to Suharto did much that enhanced Australian security.

At a time when Australian governments struggled to reconcile *Realpolitik* with a commitment to advance human rights abroad, the reassessment of Australian defense pointed unambiguously towards the need to cultivate closer ties with regional neighbors. The search for a more self-reliant defense posture culminated in the *Review of Australia's Defence Capabilities* (1986), a strategic assessment of Australian defense needs by Australian National University academic Paul Dibb, and the subsequent White Paper, *The Defence of Australia* (1987), formulated by Minister for Defence in the Hawke ALP government, Kim Beazley. Dibb's scenario for Australian defense resonated with defense debates of the 1880s and 1890s. Australia's external security environment was, he claimed, benign, and Australia was more vulnerable to tactical raids on Australian territory designed to achieve short-term political advantage. The old idea of Australasia resurfaced as Australia's "area of direct military interest" encompassed island South East Asia and the South West Pacific.[25] The report positioned the Indonesian Archipelago as the most likely route through which a hostile power could mount an attack on the Australian mainland and carried more than a suggestion that Indonesia was a threat.[26]

The multidimensionality of global and regional change in the wake of the Soviet Union's demise was grasped by Labour Minister for Foreign Affairs Gareth Evans in his statement on *Australia's Regional Security* (1989). Echoing Evatt's preference for collective rather than alliance-based security arrangements, Evans envisioned a new multilateral approach to foreign policy at the regional level that attempted to seize opportunities created by the end of the Cold War. Unlike Australian defense policy, which viewed Australia's entire island arc as a single entity, Evans's security strategy retained the distinction between the South West Pacific and South East Asia as two separate spheres requiring two separate policy approaches, an arms length "constructive commitment" towards Australia's South West Pacific neighbors and a more substantial "comprehensive engagement" with South East Asia which included the even greater prioritization of the Australia-Indonesia relationship.

Trade, investment and people-to-people relationships were deemed as crucial to the pursuit of Australian security interests as government-to-government contacts, but principally with South East Asia. Australian foreign and defense policymakers recognized the new challenges posed by non-traditional security

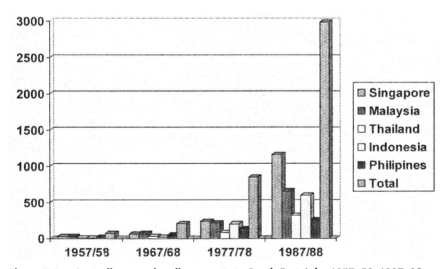

Figure 7.1.   Australian merchandise exports to South East Asia, 1957–58–1997–98.

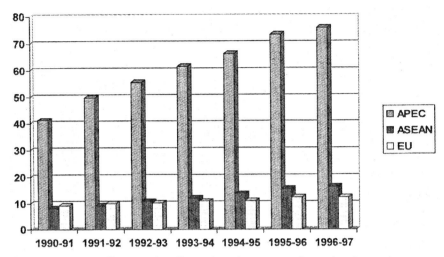

Figure 7.2.   Australian merchandise and services exports by regional grouping.

issues, drug trafficking, authorized and unauthorized cross-border movements of people to the post–Cold War geopolitical status quo.[27] Such practices were obscured by Cold War politics, but with rapid economic growth in countries formerly embroiled by communist insurgency, Thailand in particular, the attractiveness of illicit trade contributed to a dramatic rise in transnational criminal activity between Australia and its region. Recognizing that uneven economic development was a major contributing factor to regional instability, the vehicle by which the ALP sought to improve Australia's regional security environment was trade liberalization.

INCREMENTAL REGIONALISM

Not until the ALP's decision to internationalize the Australian economy in the 1980s was Australian industry forced to attend seriously to international consumer sentiment. At the time of Australia's proposal for the Asia Pacific Economic Cooperation (APEC) forum, economics professor Ross Garnaut declared in his report, *Australia and the Northeast Asian Ascendancy* (1989), that Australia's trading future was irrefutably bound to the economic fortunes of North East Asia and to geostrategic trends in the wider "Western Pacific."[28] Garnaut's report was also a measure of the ascendancy of neo-liberal logic in Canberra policymaking circles. His recommendations accorded with new macro-economic policies introduced by the Hawke government to force structural change by exposing Australian industry to the critical glare of global markets, and the Australian public sector to the scrutiny of global currency traders, financiers and international credit ratings agencies. Paralleling policy shifts in neighboring Indonesia, Malaysia and Thailand, Australia's tariff regime and the country's historical reliance upon traditional exports of primary commodities were viewed with reluctance in some industry circles as outmoded economic policy settings.

The last three decades of the twentieth century witnessed the deepening interconnectedness between South East Asia, Australia and the global economy. Regionally, economic booms in South East Asia's tiger economies, fuelled by Japanese foreign direct investment in electronic components manufacturing, motor vehicle assembly and real estate, gave impetus to Australian exports. But while two-way trade flows have bridged the gap, investment relations between Australia and its neighbors appear marginal by comparison. Peter Dicken questions whether there is a globally discernible trend towards regional economic convergence around three poles, the United States, Japan and the European Union, with Australia harnessed to an industrializing Asia.[29] The measurement of regionality, however, requires recognition of diplomatic and strategic factors, not just economic flows.

ASEAN stands at the forefront of moves towards regional economic cooperation. At its formation, the association was primarily a forum for discussion of common security concerns but at the 1976 Bali Summit member states agreed to a wider agenda under the *Treaty of Amity and Cooperation*, which affirmed the overriding need for regional cooperation in both political and economic affairs. Despite intraregional strategic and economic rivalries for sea-bed resources and foreign investment, for example, the Association exerted considerable policy influence over member states. The centrality of Indonesia within ASEAN and the presence of President Suharto as Asia's then longest-serving political leader explained Australia's increasing courtship of Jakarta in pursuit of economic as well as security ends.

The ASEAN Free Trade Area (AFTA) was proposed at the 1992 ASEAN Summit as a response to economic regionalism in the Americas and Europe at a time when the multilateral trading system appeared to be breaking down. AFTA was intended to give the grouping a new rationale for the post–Cold War era but its scope quickly expanded beyond trade to harmonization of standards, services, trade and regional investment—matching the World Trade Organization's multilateral trade agenda and providing transnational companies with fresh opportunities to rationalize and regionalize their production.[30]

Policy-led regionalism invited scepticism from commentators wedded to a traditional state-centric view of global relations. The American political scientist Samuel Huntington claimed that multi-civilization regional organizations were inherently weak. Arguing that culture led economics, Huntington implied that Australia's attempts to move economically and politically closer to Asia would eventually founder amidst the reefs and shoals of cultural difference.[31]

Despite such pessimistic views, regionalism, if not regional integration, is an established fact in South East Asia. As already discussed, at the level of trade and social interaction, cultural differences can be transcended when neighbors recognize common economic and strategic interests. The geographic extent of ASEAN maritime transport circuits underscores the emergence of a regional economy and the economic attractions of integration. Although Australia is only weakly connected into this maritime world, airline service density between Australia and Asia reflects the rising popularity among Australian travelers of Asian airport hubs in Singapore and Bangkok.[32] Regionalism might not be an antidote to power politics but Australian governments recognize that regional integration is worthwhile pursuing as part of a broader security agenda.

New forms of regional and subregional economic cooperation point to the acceptance of a combination of strategic trade and neo-liberal market theory among ASEAN policymakers. Once suspicious of foreign investment, South East Asia's new industrializers actively courted Japanese and Western investment with a variety of tax and wage incentives. There was wide agreement among ASEAN states that economic growth prospects could be enhanced within geographically smaller sub-regional groupings. South East Asia's key growth zones, the Indonesia-Malaysia-Thailand (IMT) and Singapore-Johore-Riau (SIJORI) triangles, and the Greater Mekong Scheme (GMS), while not directly concerned with the promotion of global trade liberalization, coordinate industry and infrastructure development planning across common borders. Created in the wake of Vietnam's momentous turn to the West following the collapse of COMECON, GMS signaled a new mood of optimism in ASEAN and indicated the degree to which governments of the Mekong six, Thailand, Burma, Laos, Cambodia, China and Vietnam recognized that their economic destinies were substantially interlinked.[33]

Cultural differences slowed but could not halt Australia's general drift towards South East Asia. Regional economic and defense policy initiatives and a general outward reorientation of the Australian economy were hallmark achievements of the ALP governments during the period 1983–1996. The acceptance of Hawke's APEC agenda boded well for the future, despite the abrasive political approach taken by Hawke's successor, Paul Keating, towards Malaysia's Prime Minister Dr. Mahatir. The possibility of a linkage between the Australia–New Zealand Closer Economic Relationship (CER) and AFTA was first floated during Keating's tenure but progress was hindered by Malaysian counterdiplomacy. Although a newly elected Coalition government, in its first term, allayed public concerns about the imagined cultural dangers of Asianization by stripping the rhetoric of engagement from Australian foreign policy, the Howard government recognized that future engagement was both unavoidable and desirable.[34]

Keating's agenda of engagement with Indonesia and the wider South East Asian region was replaced by a sharper focus upon North East Asia, specifically the security situation on the Korean peninsula, the Taiwan Strait and China's booming economy. In South East Asia and the South West Pacific Australian policy became more interventionist. However, even Australia's leading role in the separation of East Timor from an already humiliated Indonesia, which brought bilateral relations to an historic low, has not blocked the path of regional enmeshment. Unregulated cross-border movements of people and narcotics are now an area of bilateral and multilateral law enforcement cooperation between Australia and its neighbors. With Thailand and Indonesia the main thoroughfares for narcotics trafficking into Australia, the Australian Federal Police extended its representation by opening an office in Chiang Mai, on the fringes of the infamous Golden Triangle in 2003 and at Samarang in Indonesia.[35] Australia's police presence in Indonesia confirms the closer cooperation between Australian and Indonesian police following joint efforts to track down those responsible for the Bali bombing. Through police cooperation and intelligence sharing, Australia stepped up efforts to suppress trafficking of drugs and people across South East Asia, changing the dynamics of bilateral and regional relations.

Re-elected in 1998, 2001 and again in 2004, the Coalition shifted emphasis from multilateral to bilateral diplomacy in Asia, partly to circumvent Mahatir, a move that yielded significant results. Australia sealed bilateral free-trade agreements with Singapore (2000) and Thailand (2004). After Mahatir's departure as Malaysian Prime Minister in 2003, ASEAN interest in the AFTA-CER concept revived. At the 2004 ASEAN Summit in Vientiane, Australia and New Zealand were formally invited by Malaysia's new Prime Minister Datuk Seri Abdullah Badawi to join ASEAN in an expanded free-trade area that will one day encompass China, Japan and South Korea. Unthinkable a decade ago, Australia has entered into negotiations for a bilateral free-trade agreement with Malaysia. Canberra's bilateral relations with South East Asian governments are now multifaceted, ranging from trade cooperation to policing and counterterrorism, and are rapidly gaining in importance relative to regional multilateral forums. This said, Australia's signing of the ASEAN *Treaty of Amity and Cooperation* in July 2005 on the insistence, it appears, of Foreign Minister Alexander Downer is further evidence that multilateralism remains an important plank in Australian foreign policy towards the region—not least because ASEAN cooperation is essential to counter the threat of South East Asian Islamic terror networks.

GLOBAL BUSINESS RULES

Australia's accession to the ASEAN Treaty was the price of inclusion in regional trade negotiations. But neither multilateral nor bilateral agreements in themselves generate trade. Although discussed as such in economic literature, trade and investment flows are not impersonal or automatic processes. Without the necessary business interest and people-to-people linkages, trade and investment cannot take place, anywhere. It was evident that the post–Pacific War generation of Australian business leaders lacked the cultural expertise and the persistence with which to benefit more substantially from South East Asia's economic boom.[36] A major impediment to closer trade and investment relations was the common Australian perception of unacceptably high levels of political risk. Reviewing Australia's investment efforts in ASEAN in the 1980s, the East Asia Analytical Unit of the Australian Department of Foreign Affairs and Trade reported Australian "disinvestment" from South East Asia, which it attributed to prior "bad experiences." Faced with unfamiliar legal institutions, and unable to grasp the dynamics of regional business cultures, risk-averse Australian companies worried, not without cause, about intellectual property rights and unpredictable policy environments.[37]

Australian investment was quickly redirected towards the developed world, principally the United Kingdom and the United States where, it was believed, regulatory systems were less prone to political interference and where the legal rights of investors were better protected. Australian direct investment in ASEAN fell as a proportion of the total from a peak of 38.9 percent in 1981 to 4.5 percent in 1991. As a share of total foreign investment, direct and portfolio, the percentage was much smaller, 14 percent in 1981 falling to a mere 2.2 percent in 1987.[38] It should not be forgotten, however, that most Japanese foreign investment, even during South East Asia's boom years, was and remains directed towards more lucrative opportunities in Europe and the United States. But Australian companies have allowed "path dependency" and their cultural inclinations to obscure investment opportunities closer to home.

Where Australian companies feared to tread, Japanese and American companies profited, locating their labor-intensive assembly operations in countries with attractive export investment policies, near rapidly growing markets for new technology consumer products. This proliferation of multinationals and their foreign affiliates has created a market for a new genre of travel guides, the "how to do business in Asia" manual. Written for Western business executives struggling to assimilate to new cultural challenges thrown up by offshore assignments, these guides vary greatly in their level of sophistication.

With the Asia Pacific region recognized as a new center of power in the world economy, American and to a lesser extent European firms had to learn how to survive in Asian business environments if they were to share in this regional dynamism. An industry now exists to cater to this business need for practical training in cross-cultural negotiation and management. Western executives are told how to navigate through highly personalized political systems by forming strategic business relationships with well-connected Asian intermediaries. "How to" advice for Australian business also came from the Keating government. Published at the height of the Keating government's drive for greater Asian engagement, a Department of Foreign Affairs and Trade report advised prospective Australian investors of the practice of "facilitation"—the payment of government officers in return for the speedy consideration of a business application.[39] Such pragmatism in Australian public policy is no longer fashionable.

While many Australian companies, in the mining sector especially, proved adept at working within the constraints of Asian political systems, the "Asian way," it was claimed by Western analysts and delivered too much advantage to governments and Asian business groups and rewarded profligacy and fostered corruption. In the aftermath of the Asian economic crisis, and as a matter of necessity, the climate of opinion in Australia and in the industrialized West shifted away from tolerance of personal connections between Asian politicians and business associates. Campaigns against official corruption, spearheaded by the global anti-corruption watchdog Transparency International and the Organization for Economic Cooperation and Development (OECD), have ushered in a new era where governments and intergovernmental organizations attempt to impose Western standards of ethical business practice. With Australia's ratification of the OECD's Convention on the Bribery of Foreign Officials, facilitation payments are today illegal under Australian law. Advocacy for Anglo-American free-market ideals of a level playing field and government non-interference signaled the capture of the intellectual high ground by market universalists.

A new puritan emphasis upon public sector governance in Australia's foreign aid program aims to proselytize the neo-liberal mantra of efficiency, accountability, and transparency. The practicalities of "sound economic management" in a neoliberal economic system become the moral certainties with which Western political leaders and leading economic professionals proclaimed a new mission to remodernize South East Asia in the wake of the Asian economic crisis. Viewed in this light, Australia's commitment to trade and investment liberalization in the Asian Pacific is as much a measure of its commitment to promote free-market principles and liberal governance bruited by the United States, Britain, the IMF and the OECD than necessarily a major re-orientation of thought and practice.

Table 7.1.   Ownership of equity in Australian enterprise 5 by non-residents, 2000–2003

	June 30, 2000		June 30, 2001		June 30, 2002		June 30, 2003	
	$bn	%	$bn	%	$bn	%	$bn	%
Total	328.4	100	355.4	100	351.8	100	358	100
USA	115.9	33	114.2	32	103.7	29	107.3	30
UK	113.9	36	125.5	35	115.3	33	114.1	32
Japan	15.6	5	16.4	5	19.3	5	18.8	5
Other	83.1	27	99.3	28	113.5	32	117.8	33
OECD	291.4	85	302.7	85	291	83	296.7	83
APEC	153.1	44	162.1	46	162.8	46	168.3	47
EU	141.6	43	148.9	42	141.5	40	142.8	40
ASEAN	5.4	2	8.6	2	16.1	5	17.6	5

Source: ABS.

Australia-ASEAN investment relations deepened in the 1990s. While sources of foreign investment in Australian businesses reinforce the impression of an Anglo-American–centered Australian economy (table 7.1), ABS statistics do not indicate the amount of capital "parked" in Australian real estate. Total Singaporean investment in Australia reached A$22.13 billion in 2003, more than triple that from Malaysia, A$6.1 billion, and dwarfing a mere A $141 million from Thailand.[40] Australian direct investment in South East Asia is difficult to quantify because much of this passes through companies that are headquartered in Singapore or through companies registered in the United States or Europe in which Australians hold a financial stake. Nevertheless, it is clear that in mining, construction, tourism, banking and food and beverages, large and medium-sized Australian companies are establishing a regional presence, with Australian investment in Indonesia alone reaching A$2.1 billion in 2003.[41]

Australian investment is diverse but Australian mining companies attract the most public attention, for the environmental devastation of BHP's Ok Tedi mine in Papua New Guinea to the alleged collusion with Indonesian authorities over human rights abuses. The *Timor Gap Treaty of 1989* between Australia and Indonesia, covering a disputed maritime boundary between Australia and the then Indonesian province of East Timor, was taken by critics as evidence of Australian willingness to subordinate human rights to matters of economic self-interest. The treaty opened a new phase of constructive economic relations between Australia and Indonesia and foreshadowed a new wave of mining interest in South East Asia. Learning to work with local and national politicians and business leaders, Newcrest and the Anglo-Australian company Rio Tinto opened mines on the Indonesian islands of Kalimantan and Sulawesi. Part of the company's Australasian operations, Rio's Kelian gold mine commenced in 1992. As an indication of

Newcrest Mining's confidence in the Indonesian economy after the fall of Suharto, its two mines on the Halemhera Peninsula of Sulawesi, the area where Willie Jack mined gold in the 1890s, commenced operations in 1999 and 2002 respectively.[42] Subject to repeated protests from nearby village communities that the companies are mining on traditional lands without the consent of indigenous owners, both companies stand accused by international human rights and environmental organizations of using the military, police, and private paramilitary gangs to silence protesters.[43]

Rio Tinto and Newcrest stress the employment generating benefits of their Indonesian mining operations, which must also be sold into majority local ownership within a set time frame. Having successfully navigated political and cultural boundaries separating national elites, mining companies are still learning to navigate through the labyrinth of localized "indigenous" cultural boundaries within multi-ethnic states in South East Asia and to come to terms with the intricacies of international human rights law, and, since the Asian financial collapse in 1997, international and localized pressure to respect the natural environment. In the Philippines, during the late 1990s, Western Mining Corporation faced challenges to the legality of government contracts allowing them to own up to 100 percent of their mineral exploration operations. Environmental campaigners allege that the generous foreign investment provision in the Philippine Mining Act of 1995 is unconstitutional.[44]

Demands from the World Bank to implement economic policies that address environmental and social concerns, in return for development assistance, were not well received by the international mining industry. New clauses in Indonesian contracts of work, the basic legal instrument establishing the legal right to possess a mining concession and the duration and extent of mining leases, imposed burdens that Rio Tinto in particular found unacceptable. New mining regulations made royalties payable to provincial governments rather than Jakarta, opening, it was claimed, new avenues for local government officials to impose demands upon mining operations with regard to environmental protection, waste management and community relations. Rio Tinto Indonesia sold off its East Kalimantan coal mine, Kaltim Prima Coal, in 2003, complaining that new mining regulations did not confer security of tenure, and therefore exposed the company to unacceptable political risk.[45]

BORDERED ECONOMIES

Arbitrary colonial borderings remain a source of friction in South East Asia between states and marginalized peoples at their peripheries. Mining on the island of Mindanao is hindered by environmental protest but also ongoing armed conflict between Manila and Moro separatists in the late 1990s. The upsurge in political violence, a consequence of the Asian financial crisis, but more disturbingly, the Islamicization of Islamic separatist groups allegedly linked to Osama Bin Laden's Al-Qaeda network, has increased the personal dangers associated with offshore investments. The killing of over 100 people, allegedly Islamic separatists, in southern Thailand in late 2004 is but one more violent episode that casts a pall over a vibrant "New Asia" At the beginning of the twenty-first century the image of a region rapidly approaching economic modernity was in danger of giving way to an older image of a region in revolt, led not by communist cadres, but by Islamicist terrorists.

Rather than leading to a dissolving of borders, globalization exacerbates tensions between the state, minority ethnic groups and transnational capital. With the demise of the Communist Party of Thailand in the early 1980s, attempts by the Thai military to establish control over its short border with Malaysia saw the Malayan Communist Party (MCP) accorded the niceties of international diplomacy. MCP cross-border operations were a source of diplomatic friction between Bangkok and Kuala Lumpur from the late 1940s. Part of the Thai military's political offensive against the communist movement in Thailand, the MCP agreed to a cease-fire and full demobilization under memorandums of understanding signed between Thailand, Malaysia and the MCP.[46] Declining Cold War tensions in Asia gave the opportunity to resolve longstanding conflicts in South East Asia. However, neither the Malaysian nor Thai governments have succeeded in eliminating the root causes of Islamic separatism in southern Thailand. Cut off from Malay-Muslim neighbors in Malaya under the Anglo-Siamese Treaty of 1909, and economically marginal, Thailand's southern Malay-Muslim provinces of Pattani and Setul have been the focus of political unrest and an ongoing low-intensity separatist campaign. As with longstanding separatist movements in Aceh and Mindanao, the aspirations of Thai Muslims are today tainted by association with Al-Qaeda and the Indonesian-based Jemmah Islamiah network.

If nation statehood is unfashionable, no one told separatists in Pattani, Aceh, Mindanao or West Papua. It would be impossible to persuade East Timorese that their twenty-five-year fight for independence from Jakarta was a futile gesture not of defiance against the Indonesian state but against the global economy. The OPM grew out of the popular movement for West Papuan independence that emerged under Dutch rule and which the Indonesian state has since tried and failed to eradicate.[47] OPM guerrillas have used Papua New Guinea as a sanctuary when fleeing the Indonesian military, creating tensions in the PNG-Indonesia relationship with serious implications for Australia's relations with both countries. As with other border flashpoints, the Thai-Burma border, for instance, many more innocent civilians are caught in the political and military crossfire. To date there has been no border incident serious enough to provoke a war between Indonesia and PNG. Indonesia too has a vested interest in maintaining friendly relations and in insuring internal political stability in PNG. Indeed, Jakarta has from time to time expressed concerns over rioting in Port Moresby, but has never shown any determination to intervene. Echoing the Anglo-Dutch border concerns in relation to the Tugeri a century before, both countries peaceably seek to minimize the risks of conflict by working cooperatively to map their common borders.

Paradoxically, a borderless global economy needs political boundaries because without states or the principal of sovereignty there can be no possibility of global order. Yet the pressure to demarcate territory and regulate commerce also creates or perpetuates conflicts within and between states. Maritime jurisdictions continue to spread outwards into the world's oceans as deep-sea fisheries assume greater economic significance and as seabed mineral resources come within the reach of new extractive technologies. Where once open seas separated Australian from the Archipelago, with the Torres Strait the exception, now Australia and its neighbors patrol common maritime borders. Under the United Nations Convention on the Law of the Sea (1982), the Australian government insists that the "natural prolongation" of Australia's continental shelf permits the delineation of seabed boundaries much closer to East Timor and Indonesia than the Australian mainland. Australia's inheritance of the former British territories of Christmas Island, a mere 186 nautical miles south of Java, and the Ashmore Islands of the Timor Sea adds to the complicated overlay of maritime jurisdictions.[48]

The Torres Strait Treaty (1978) established three overlapping boundaries, a seabed boundary that marks the Australia-PNG maritime border, an Australian fisheries protection line and a protected zone. Australian fisheries jurisdiction extends north of the seabed boundary encompassing fifteen islands adjacent to the PNG coast and mutually recognized as Australian sovereign territory. Freedom of movement is permitted through the protected zone for inhabitants of a small number of designated villages on both sides of the border in recognition of historical cultural ties between communities on the PNG south coast and the Torres Strait islands.[49] The resultant patchwork of zones, boundaries and special transborder "protected areas" aptly illustrates the paradox of territoriality in an allegedly borderless world.

Without a politically stable political environment states cannot provide investors with guarantees and yet it is often competing business interests that exacerbate political tensions between governments. After helping to secure independence for East Timor in 1999, Australia was forced to acknowledge the right of smaller states to extract concessions from larger neighbors. In 2004 East Timor's then Prime Minister Mari Alkatiri raised formal objections to the application of the natural prolongation principle, permitted under UNCLOS but which favored Australian boundary claims in the Timor Sea. The move threatened to impede the development of lucrative oil and gas fields in an area straddling the contested boundary. Estimates at the time put the potential cost to the liquefied natural gas operations of Australian resources company Woodside Petroleum at A$6.6 billion, but also at stake were the potential financial gains for a tiny country whose gross domestic product is dwarfed to a factor of five by Woodside's annual sales turnover.[50] The tenor of bilateral relations with East Timor suffered from this disagreement about the location of a common maritime boundary in the Timor Sea, although presently the matter is deferred by mutual agreement until 2056.

Contested baseline calculations, upon which claims to maritime jurisdiction are made, are not confined to the Timor Sea.[51] Seabed boundary disputes are current between Brunei and Malaysia over the Sabah Trough, China and Vietnam in the Gulf of Tongking, and widely reported and documented claims by the Philippines, Malaysia, Vietnam and China to the oil and gas resources thought to sit beneath the Spratly Islands.[52] All cases involve the interests of nation-states and international resource companies, and have a bearing upon the future of Australian regional relations.

"ORDINARY" COSMOPOLITANS

Heightened fears of Islamicist terrorist attacks have not dampened Australian enthusiasm to travel in South East Asia. Despite Jemmah Islamiah's bombing of the Sari Club on the island of Bali in October 2002 in which 202 people, including 88 Australians, were killed, Australian resident departures for Indonesia jumped appreciably in the financial year 2003-2004. (table 7.2) Today, although tourist demand fluctuates in the face of subsequent if smaller terrorist bomb attacks, southern Thailand, Malaysia, Singapore and Indonesia attract Australians in their tens of thousands. Countless numbers of Australians are as, if not more, familiar with the geographical and cultural attractions of Bali, Phuket or Langkawi than with Cairns or Fremantle. Heightened fears of Islamicist terror aside, increased tourist travel and the ubiquity of Asian imagery and products means that Asia makes a greater impression upon the everyday lives of Australians than at any time previously.

Place recognition defines the significance of travel for Australian conceptions of region at the beginning of the twenty-first century. A new generation of open-minded Australian travelers were crossing into Asia in the 1970s, as cheap travel into exotic Asian destinations became possible and fashionable. Australian author Elizabeth Durack expressed faith in the cosmopolitan potential of modern mass travel. Writing in the 1970s, she con-

Table 7.2. Australian short-term resident departures by calendar and financial year, 2002–2004 ('000)

	Calendar Year		Financial Year	
Main Destination	2002	2003	2002–2003	2003–2004
Oceania				
Fiji	128.3	145.2	129.2	161.4
New Caledonia	17.3	15.3	15.8	15.7
New Zealand	597.3	662.8	615.3	739.2
Norfolk Island	27.4	33.4	30.6	30
Papua New Guinea	33.3	34.6	34.2	34.9
Vanuatu	28.7	27.2	27.2	30
TOTAL	865.9	959.7	888.2	1057
South East Asia				
Indonesia	241.7	186.4	194.4	271.1
Malaysia	109.5	100.9	97.8	126
Philippines	60.3	59.6	55.7	71.2
Singapore	149.2	124.3	119.1	148.4
Thailand	168.9	128.2	150.5	153.8
Vietnam	79.1	76.4	74.1	92.1
TOTAL	839	704	721.9	894.4

Source: ABS.

cluded that travel "is the greatest getting to know you programme," and "nothing less than global."[53] Repositioning Australia in relation to its region, Gough Whitlam alluded to the cultural significance of this tourism in an address at the University of the Philippines in 1974:

> Australians in particular—by force of their history and their geographical isolation in old days of slow and costly travel, unfamiliar, even uneasy, with their own neighbourhood—are getting to know better the region in which they live. The more they get to know it, the more they feel at home in this region; their region; and this region is their home for all time.[54]

Whitlam spoke at a time when Asia was "trendy," and the hippie trail a stimulating detour on a young Australian adult's journey of self-discovery. Australians, he claimed, were shedding cultural orthodoxy to embrace a new geography, and a new sense of "home." Such an awakening was long overdue, though Whitlam's claims were as optimistic as they were premature. London remained the principal destination for Australians seeking new challenges, excitement and fame and fortune and simply because this global city retained its cultural and financial power long after the sun had set on the British Empire. "We Australians can travel ten thousand miles around the big curve of our globe" wrote Elizabeth Durack "and still find ourselves able to relate immediately." But Australians as a people were still ignorant of their own region, and their nearest neighbor, Indonesia,

> the country with which we share a border, whose capital lies fewer air-hours from my Perth home than Sydney, whose insular extremities are within pleas-ant sailing distance of Darwin is one about which we know very little.[55]

For Durack, Australian "Hippies" in Indonesia were "true travelers" marked out by their aspirations, mostly thwarted, to "understand" and win accept-ance by their Asian hosts.[56] Whitlam's image of young Australians "getting-to-know" their region captured the cosmopolitan sentiment evident to the keenly observant Durack. The sharpness with which Australian travellers apparently felt the pain of rejection reflected a naïve expectation of reci-procity for their gestures of friendship, interpreted as condescension by their hosts. Militating against the possibility that international tourism could "bridge cultural divides" was the ongoing commoditization of travel. The reality overlooked or beyond the comprehension of many a would-be cosmopolitan was that for host societies, tourists were merely a source of foreign exchange, and an opportunity for individual local entrepreneurs to earn precious income:

> What the true traveller wants then, it seems, is to be accepted into the hearts of the people whose country he is visiting. This is very difficult today. Both the people themselves and the travel industry have built a wall around him. He is no longer a person, he is simply a statistic on a balance sheet.[57]

A similar naïveté afflicted Australian diplomacy in South East Asia in the 1990s when it was presumed that because of Australia's past generosity with Colombo Plan aid and more and that at a policy level the country was at last ready to befriend its neighbors, regional governments should accept Australian overtures with gratitude and welcome Australia with open arms.[58]

Globalizing processes at a regional level are at least working in such a way as to make possible the acceptance of Australia in the long run. As in the late nineteenth century, global transport "revolutions" boosted Australasian travel in the late twentieth. Both the volume and the velocity of international travel rose dramatically during the 1970s as "space-shrinking" technological ad-vances in jet aircraft design reduced travelling times, increased carrying capac-ity and introduced non-stop "long-haul" flights to and from Europe and America.[59] With the advent of cheap air travel, the airplane supplanted the pas-senger liner as the preferred mode of transport for all categories of Australian traveller drawn towards Java, Bali, Singapore and Manila. This new generation of Australians still, however, based their purchasing decisions on a combina-tion of factors ranging from price and availability to flexibility and interchangeability. The status benefits of having been abroad too were no less significant. Australians passed through new air-conditioned portals of Asia in increasing numbers, with a considerably larger proportion opting for South East Asian destinations than for the United Kingdom.

When they arrived they encountered a region in the throes of rapid modernization. As the fictional character George Hamilton found in Christopher Koch's *Highways to a War*, old colonial Asia was disappearing as a confident "New Asia" leapt into view. More Australian tourists visited South East Asia because there were more tourized places to visit and stay. Recognizing the income and employment generating effects of tourism, Indonesia, Malaysia and Thailand integrated tourism development strategies into their five-year planning cycles in the 1970s. Visitor arrivals to Indonesia rose from 84,100 in 1969 to over five million in 1996.[60] Thailand welcomed 10 million visitors with a smile in 2002. Promotional campaigns like the Thai Tourism Authority's "Amazing Thailand" create alluring national brand images only slightly modified for a more contemporary feel and to reflect a greater diversity of attractions than the exotic images purveyed by shipping companies in the late nineteenth and early twentieth centuries. Tourism infrastructure and service development are today salient features of subregional economic planning, from the SIJORI scheme where Singapore acts as a transport hub servicing resorts in Johore and the Riau Archipelago, to the East ASEAN Growth Area, identified as the next Asian ecotourism playground.[61]

Crafted in advance of the 1988 bicentennial celebrations, Australia's image as an open and tolerant multicultural society suffered greatly in the late 1990s as a consequence of racist public comments from ultra-conservative politicians, tolerated by many more moderate conservative colleagues, about the alleged need to protect the "Australian way of life" from Asian migrants. These comments caused a vein of apprehension among Australians struggling to come to terms with the opening up of the Australian economy and the conspicuous prosperity of neighboring Asian countries. Simon Philpott observed a paradoxical rise in Australian fear of Indonesia in the late twentieth century at a time of thriving bilateral business, tourism and educational exchanges.[62]

The mass migration of Vietnamese refugees in the late 1980s was the single most significant population movement from South East Asia into Australia in the modern era. Many subtler, less visible population transfers, however, point towards deepening engagement at the regional and global level. Regional human mobility is no longer dominated by movements of Vietnamese refugees or the migration of New Zealanders to Australia, but business travelers, tourists, international students, and, exposing the underside of globalization, drug and people traffickers. Demographer Graham Hugo argues that the increasing numbers of South East Asian born

Australians moving into and out of the country are accounted for by cross-border transfers of staff within multinational corporations with branch offices in Australia and the South East Asian region.[63] Australians appear comfortable with the presence of South East Asia's global professionals in their midst and, as Laksi Jayasuriya and Kee Pookong note, Australians are possibly more tolerant of Asian immigration than "shock jock" and opinion pollsters admit. The danger, they say, lies in the political promotion of an idea that nations possess a singular identity which belongs to and must be protected within a geographically defined national space. Cultural chauvinism is a new racism attached to identity markers ranging from language to presumed distinguishing behavioral traits rather than the racial markers used to define national types in the late nineteenth century.[64]

Tens of thousands of fee-paying students from Indonesia, Singapore, Malaysia and Thailand study in Australian schools, colleges and universities. The "Hanson effect," such as it was, barely registered in terms of international visitor arrivals from Asia. In fact, statistics indicate that visitors from the region increased in the year following Hanson's incendiary maiden address to Parliament where she claimed Australia was in danger of being overrun by Asians. A sharp fall in 1998 was attributable to the impact of Asia's financial crisis. (table 7.3) Malaysia and Indonesia were until 2004 the largest sources of international students in Australia but it is too soon to speculate whether declining numbers can be attributed to Australia's support for America's invasion of two Islamic countries, Afghanistan and Iraq, or to the expansion of high quality and relatively cheaper higher education

Table 7.3. International visitors to Australia from Asia (aged 15 years and over) by country of residence, 1994–99

	1995	1996	1997	1998	1999	1999[a]
Japan	737,900	766,600	766,000	704,400	662,500	16
Hong Kong	117,300	137,600	136,600	130,400	127,900	3
Taiwan	138,300	144,800	138,900	135,100	133,600	3.2
Thailand	72,500	80,500	61,800	44,600	55,700	1.3
Korea	160,600	216,200	220,500	62,300	1	2.4
Malaysia	94,400	118,200	125,800	101,800	126,500	3
Singapore	168,500	185,900	201,300	215,600	234,100	5.6
Indonesia	107,600	129,900	138,200	82,600	82,400	1.99
China	n/a	52,300	63,800	73,300	87,500	2.1
Other Asia	102,800	74,400	88,700	92,300	101,800	2.45
All Asia	1,699,900	1,906,400	1,941,600	1,642,400	1,712,100	41
TOTAL	3,422,000	3,829,800	3,974,000	3,859,000	4,143,100	100

[a]Proportion of total visitors for 1999
Source: Commonwealth Bureau of Tourism Research.

programs in South East Asia and the declining competitiveness of an appreciating Australian dollar.

Even if current Australian attitudes towards Asia are yet to be systematically and carefully surveyed, the availability and popularity of Asian products in Australia signal a subtle but general shift away from the Anglo-centricity. While most Australians might not dwell upon the construction or meanings of Balinese or Thai culture, thousands of Australian tourists frequent the resorts of Bali and southern Thailand each year, returning with memories of crowded marketplaces, staged cultural festivals, exclusive hotels, beach parties and possibly some glimpses of poverty. While jet travel made the experiences of people and place potentially more transitory, even the memory of ephemeral trips to Bali or Koh Samui adds new dimensions to popular imaginings of region and place. If they fall short of the cosmopolitan ideal of the culturally informed and sensitive citizen of the world, these packaged tourists expand their horizons and come into contact with local guides and fellow international travelers. The vast majority probably know little about Buddhism or Islam, but then most probably know even less about the Declaration of Independence or the Magna Carta. Living for the enjoyment of the moment, they experience a less pious and less burdensome cosmopolitanism, shallow but not without substance, ephemeral but not without sentiment, sometimes ugly, sometimes thoughtful and inquisitive, but for the most part comfortable and bland.

NOTES

1. Held, McGrew, Goldblatt and Perraton, *Global Transformation,* 248–50.
2. R. J. May, "The Philippines Political Context," in *Natural Partners: North Australia Philippines Relations,* ed. R. J. May (Canberra and Darwin: North Australia Research Unit, Research School of Pacific and Asian Studies, the Australian National University, 1998), 33.
3. Frank Tipton, *The Rise of Asia: Economics, Society and Politics in Contemporary Asia* (Melbourne: Macmillan, 1998), 325.
4. "Thai to Get First-Class Claim on Resources," AA, A1838/1, 3010/10/2. "Thailand:Economic Report," AA, A1838/2, 3010/7/2 Part 1. T. H. Silcock, "Promotion of Industry and the Planning Process" in *Thailand: Social and Economic Studies in Development,* ed. T. H. Silcock, (Canberra: Australian National University Press, 1967), 264.
5. Interview with Rachan Kanjanawanit, Chairman, Mining and General Management Company Ltd., Bangkok, January 19, 1994.
6. *Bangkok Post,* April 20, 1949.
7. Sullivan, "It Had to Happen," 112–14. Sean Brawley, *The White Peril: Foreign Relations and Asian Immigration to Australasia and North America, 1919–78* (Sydney: University of New South Wales Press, 1995), 247.

8. "Australia Best Place to Live In," AA, A1838/280, 3010/10/7 pt 1.

9. Brawley, *White Peril*, 242–51.

10. Consolidated Tin Dredging, VPRS932, 28808H, VPRO. W.R. Skinner, *The Mining Year Book, 1960*, (London: W. E. Skinner and the *Financial Times*, 1960), 267.

11. Return of Allotments of Shares, May 7, 1952; Liquidator's Account of Receipts and Statement of the Position in Winding Up, November 19, 1963, Consolidated Tin Dredging Company, VPRS 932, C28808H LPUB, VPRO.

12. Interview with Arthorn Tongwathana, President of the Mining Industry Association of Thailand, Phuket, January, 1994.

13. *Tin International*, March, 1966.

14. The Stock Exchange of Melbourne, *Official Record* (vol. 43, nos. 1–12, January–December, 1950). R. G. Taylor, "The Mmining Industry in Thailand," *Australian Mining* (vol. 62, no. 4, April 1960), 63.

15. "Thai-Australian Industries," *Investor Supplement* (March 1972), 23, 25–26.

16. *Industrial and Mining Standard*, September 6, 1951. Edwards, "Crises and Commitments," 38.

17. Blainey, *Rush That Never Ended*, 355.

18. May, "Philippines Political Context," 33.

19. Tweedie, *Trading Partners*, 181–93.

20. "Thai-Australian Industries," *Investor Supplement*, (March 1972), 23, 25–26. *Bangkok Post*, September 10, 1959, AA, A1838/1, 3010/10/2 "Welcome Message to the Australian Trade Mission from the Officials of the Ministry of Economic Affairs," April 1958, AA, A1838/1, 3010/10/2.

21. Cumberland, *Southwest Pacific*, 45.

22. Turnbull, "Regionalism and Nationalism," 292.

23. ASEAN member states and date of entry: Singapore, Indonesia, Thailand, Malaysia, the Philippines (1967), Brunei (1986), Vietnam and Laos (1995), Myanmar (1998), Cambodia (1999).

24. Address by the Prime Minister of Australia, Mr. E. G. Whitlam, at the University of the Philippines, February 11, 1974, *Australian Foreign Affairs Record* (vol. 45, no. 2, 1974), 86–87.

25. *Review of Australia's Defence Capabilities*, Report to the Minister for Defence by Mr. Paul Dibb, March 1986 (Canberra: AGPS, 1986), 3.

26. Gary Smith, "Australia's Political Relationships with Asia," in *Australia and Asia*, ed. Gary Smith and Mark McGillivray (Melbourne: Oxford University Press, 1997), 110.

27. *Australia's Regional Security*, Ministerial Statement by the Senator the Hon. Gareth Evans QC, Minister for Foreign Affairs and Trade, December 1989.

28. Ross Garnaut, *Australia and the Northeast Asia Ascendancy* (Canberra: AGPS 1989), 6–7.

29. Peter Dicken, *Global Shift: Reshaping the Global Economic Map of the 21st Century*, (Thousand Oaks: SAGE, 2003), 73–74.

30. K. Kesavapany and Rahul Sen, "ASEAN's Contribution to the Building of an Asian Economic Community," in *Towards an Asian Economic Community: Vision of a New Asia*, ed. Nagesh Kumar (Singapore: Institute of Southeast Asian Studies and New Delhi: Research and Information Service for Developing Countries, 2004), 43–49.

31. Samuel P. Huntington, *The Clash of Civilizations and the Remaking of World Order* (New York: Touchstone, 1997), 151–53, 218–21.

32. Peter J. Rimmer, "Spatial Impact of Innovation in International Sea and Air Transport" in *Southeast Asia Transformed: A Geography of Change,* ed. Chia Lin Sen, (Singapore: Institute of Southeast Asian Studies, 2003), 312–13.

33. James Parsonage, "Trans-State Developments in South-East Asia: Subregional Growth Zones," in *The Political Economy of South-East Asia: An Introduction,* ed. Gary Rodan, Kevin Hewison and Richard Robison (Melbourne: Oxford University Press, 1997), 248–49.

34. Department of Foreign Affairs and Trade, *In the National Interest: Australia's Foreign and Trade Policy,* White Paper, (Canberra: Commonwealth of Australia, 1997), 1–3. Department of Defence, *Defence 2000: Our Future Defence Force,* (Canberra: Commonwealth Government, 2000), x.

35. AFP media release, June 11, 2003 <http://www.afp.gov.au/afp/page/media/2003/0611/postsoutheastasia.htm>

36. East Asia Analytical Unit (hereafter EAU), *Changing Tack: Australian Investment in South-East Asia* (Canberra: Department of Foreign Affairs and Trade, 1994), 58–59.

37. EAU, *Changing Tack,* 58–59.

38. EAU, *Changing Tack,* 30. Dyster and Meredith, *International Economy,* 289.

39. EAU, *Australia's Business Challenge: Southeast Asia in the 1990s* (Canberra: AGPS, 1992).

40. Department of Foreign Affairs and Trade (hereafter DFAT), Country Information: Singapore, Malaysia, Indonesia and Thailand, <http://www.dfat.gov.au/geo>

41. Department of Foreign Affairs and Trade, Indonesia Country Information, <http:www.dfat.gov.au/geo/Indonesia/Indonesia_brief.html> (Accessed January 4, 2005)

42. Rio Tinto Worldwide Operations <http://riotinto.com/aboutus/worldwideoperations> (Accessed January 5, 2005) Newcrest Mining, Operations Overview <http://newcrest.com.au/operations.asp?> (Accessed January 5, 2005)

43. Igor O'Neill and Cam Walker, "Newcrest Slammed for Collusion with Military," *Green Left Weekly,* Online Edition, January 21, 2004 <http://www.greenleft.org/back/2004> (Accessed January 5, 2005)

44. DFAT, Philippines Country Brief, <http://www.dfat.gov.au/geo/philippines/philippines_brief.html> (Accessed January 25, 2005) *Manila Times,* February 4, 2004.

45. *The Australian,* July 25, 2003. AFX Asia, July 30, 2003. Platts International Coal Report, June 21, 2004.

46. Kitti Ratanachaya, *Dap fai tai kab phak kommunist malaya (The Malayan Communist Party and the Suppression of Communism in the South),* (Bangkok: Duang Kaew, 1995), 56–61, 255–57.

47. Peter King, *West Papua & Indonesia since Suharto: Independence, Autonomy or Chaos?* (Sydney: UNSW Press, 2004), 20–25, 27–51.

48. Joint Standing Committee on Treaties, Australia-Indonesia Maritime Delimitation Treaty, 12th Report, (Canberra: Commonwealth of Australia, November 1997), 11–13.

49. Treaty between Australia and the Independent State of Papua New Guinea concerning Sovereignty and Maritime Boundaries in the area between the two Countries, including the area known as Torres Strait, and Related Matters (Sydney, December 18, 1978), *Australian Treaty Series*, 1985, no. 4, (Canberra: Department of Foreign Affairs, AGPS, 1985).

50. *Sydney Morning Herald*, October 26, 2004. Australia-East Timor Maritime Arrangements http://www.dfat.gov.au/geo/east_timor/fs_maritime_arrangements .html

51. R. R. Churchill and A. V. Lowe, *The Law of the Sea*, 4th ed., (Manchester: Manchester University Press, 1999), 31–56.

52. *Petroleum Intelligence* Weekly, November 29, 2004.

53. Elizabeth Durack, *Seeing Through Indonesia: An Artist's Impressions of the Republic*, (Melbourne: Hawthorn, 1977), 90.

54. Address by the Prime Minister of Australia, Mr. E. G. Whitlam, at the University of the Philippines, February 11, 1974, *Australian Foreign Affairs Record* (vol. 45, no. 2, 1974), 86–87.

55. Durack, *Seeing Through Indonesia*, iii.

56. Durack, *Seeing Through Indonesia*, 92.

57. Durack, *Seeing Through Indonesia*, 93.

58. Address by the Hon. Dr. Surin Pitsuwan, Minister for Foreign Affairs in the Government of Thailand, Asialink Conference, James Cook University, Cairns, May 1997.

59. Rimmer, "Spatial Impact," 290, 294–97, 302–10.

60. Myra P. Gunawan, "Indonesia's Tourism: Development Policies and the Challenge for Research and Education," in *Asia-Pacific Tourism: Regional Co-operation, Planning and Development*, ed. Kee Pookong and Brian King (Melbourne: Hospitality Press, Victoria University of Technology, 1999), 149.

61. Ernesto Pernia, "Tourism and Development in the East ASEAN Growth Area (EAGA)," in *Asia-Pacific Tourism*, ed. Pookong and King, 47–53.

62. Simon Philpott, "Fear of the Dark: Indonesia and the Australian National Imagination," *Australian Journal of International Affairs* (vol. 55, no. 3, November 2001), 379.

63. Graham Hugo, "Demographic Change and Implications," in *Southeast Asia Transformed*, ed. Chia Lin Sien, 123.

64. Laksri Jayasuriya and Kee Pookong, *The Asianisation of Australia?* (Melbourne: Melbourne University Press, 1999), 77–78.

8

Conclusion

Terra Australis was once part of the imagined exotic Orient, but then British colonizers built White enclaves along its eastern and southern shores, subdued indigenous Australasians and then expelled non-White settlers and guest-workers in their drive to make Australia and its surrounds safe for White civilization. In the hazy geography of the popular Australian imagination, the islands were as much a potential staging post for invasion by the Netherlands, Germany or Japan as they were a platform for the projection of Australian interests into Asia. They formed a distant moral frontier and defensive barrier, along and beyond which lived the unclean, barbaric, teeming hordes of Asia who were to be kept out by a racially exclusive immigration policy. European colonization of Asia and the Pacific generated economic and social dynamics that both frightened and excited colonial Australians. The formation of a federated White Australia stymied the development of closer social, cultural and economic ties to Australia's region, but the rupture was incomplete.

In the heroic age of the nineteenth and early twentieth centuries, fear, covetousness and brutality characterized much of White Australia's interaction with the indigenous peoples of the Archipelago and Australia. Extensive evidence of popular engagement with South East Asia through business interactions, tourism and consumer culture from the early nineteenth century, however, begs a revision of this dominant reading of Australia's past. Many Australians were able to escape, however temporarily, entrenched orthodoxies to envisage a different future for an independent Australia linked closely to its natural geographical region. This repositioning of Australian ideas of place, region and belonging over the last two centuries forms the central concern of this book. As much the consequence of wider global economic and political changes as the result of conscious decisions by Australian political leaders, this regional coalescence was foreshadowed by Marcus Clarke, whose grasp of systemic processes was accurate, even if his prediction of cultural intermingling leading to a new Australasian civilization has yet to be realized.

AN INSULAR NATION

Given Australia's history of racism and xenophobia, a persistently inward-looking island mentality and a national cultural inclination towards the Anglo-Saxon world, it is surprising to find any historical evidence at all of Australian interaction with what we know today as maritime or island South East Asia. The global currents that carry Australia into closer alignment with regional neighbors have travelled undetected beneath the surface of Australian history over the last two hundred years. The orthodox view that Australians only awakened to the importance of Asia after the outbreak of the Pacific War carries with it the weight of numbers. Before the advent of mass communications, the number of Australians directly or indirectly exposed to Asia was small. Encounters with peoples and places were relatively individualized affairs, mostly private, sometimes reproduced in a newspaper article or a travelogue, sometimes registering in a mining company share price, but of insufficient magnitude to rank as collective experiences. Where colonial, state and federal governments took an interest in developing regional links, they did so in an uncoordinated and often particularistic manner. It is important, however, not to be deceived by numerical superiority into presuming that historical significance only attaches to majority experience or opinion.

British colonizers were a minority on the Australian continent until the 1850s if not later. In terms of the indigenous Australian historical memory, the arrival of a few hundred convicts and their gaolers at Sydney Cove was a relatively insignificant affair until, as the British population grew, land was increasingly expropriated from traditional owners. European colonization of the Archipelago began with only a handful of merchant adventurers and Catholic missionaries. Even in the era of high colonialism, Europeans comprised a tiny minority, no more than a few thousand in British Malaya and perhaps twenty thousand in the Indies. The rapid expansion and increasing sophistication of transport and communications technology elevated the colonial powers to a position of material superiority over Asian and Pacific peoples, creating possibilities for a much stronger Australian minority presence. Australian expansionism was, however, deliberately confined by British imperial policy to the Australian continent. Nonetheless, the Australian colonies, Queensland and New South Wales especially, were aggressive imperial competitors in the eastern Archipelago.

Unchecked, the material processes that buoyed Western imperialism in the nineteenth century might have produced a differently configured Australasia. Colonial Australians looked expectantly towards the eastern Archipelago, probed for Dutch weaknesses and contemplated the abandonment of Dutch claims to the western portion of New Guinea. According to Simon Winchestor, Krakatoa's eruption fuelled religious militancy among peoples already chaffing under Dutch rule and for whom natural disasters were traditionally interpreted as portents of millennial change. Throughout the 1880s and the 1890s, the Dutch waged war against the Muslim Sassak inhabitants of Lombok and the Hindu animists of Bali and persuaded hundreds of independent rajahs to accept Dutch overlordship, including those on the northern arm of Sulawesi whom Sydney traders had sought to engage before the celebrated *Costa Rica Packet* case. It is not unreasonable to propose that businessmen-politicians in New South Wales and Queensland were aware of the centrifugal forces at work in the Indies and coveted more territory than they were prepared to make public for fear of losing a strategically vital corridor to Britain's Asian empire.

The expansion of maritime connections with Asia opened opportunities for trade, investment, and travel, but migratory waves from the north promised to alter the composition of colonial Australian society to a degree that was unacceptable to political leaders for whom race pride and the ideal of racial exclusivity were potent instruments of self-advancement. The smallness of Australia's population worked in favor of politicians willing to orchestrate support by fuelling public fear and loathing of anyone or anything that deviated from an idealized Australian way of life. Clinging to Australia's coastal fringe, White Australians were easily frightened into demanding that the flows of money, goods and people across their borders be filtered of all impurities. Comfortable with the economic advantages of regional trading ties, white Australians were less prepared to accept the inevitable social consequences of uncontrolled movements of people across Australia's vast northern maritime frontier. Nationalistic opposition to Asian immigration in the 1890s mirrored popular debates about the consequences of intensified regional economic and social interactions a century later.

The faintly voiced notion that Australians might share a common humanity with neighboring peoples, originating from the romantic idealisation of nature and of the simple rural life, was not, however, widely held. Clarke's belief that Australians would one day find common ground and live peacefully alongside Chinese, Indian, Malay or Kanaka migrants barely survived the poisonous but attractive amalgam of commercial self-interest and Darwinian race theory that added potency to a nascent

Australian nationalism. However, the circular transmission of influences between Australia and Asia could never be entirely choked off by racism and immigration restriction, not least because there were so many willing White Australia carriers. In the early years of Federation, when the White Australia policy was adopted as an article of national faith, a large minority of Australians were excited by the opportunities afforded by their proximity to Asia, and, if they could afford it, willing to travel the Archipelago as holidaymakers, prospectors and commercial agents. Australian travel and tourism overseas has from its beginnings contributed to the formation of a consciousness of nation and home that more accurately reflected geographical reality. Australians might not like or necessarily understand what they see in their island world, but they seem predisposed to travel there in steadily increasing numbers.

DEGREES OF OPENNESS

Colonial Australians venturing into Asia were cosmopolitans within an imperial system, travelling the extremities of the British Empire, many with ideas about how the Empire could expand beyond Malaya and the Australian continent into the intervening islands. For the majority of Australian transit passengers pausing briefly in Batavia or Singapore, transient encounters with Asian peoples confirmed preformed ideas of Oriental despotism and decadence. Rather than looking for proof of ingrained race-pride in every traveller's thought and act, however, this study is more concerned with instances where White Australians abroad in the nineteenth century dared to publicly transgress racial taboos. Paralleling broader movements observed by Tony Ballantyne in British "imperial cosmopolitanism" at the end of the nineteenth century, Australians became more racially chauvinistic—and less cosmopolitan in the cultural sense of the word.[1]

Australians travelled to destinations in the Indies, Malaya and the Philippines in much greater numbers in the early twentieth century. At a basic level, their geographical imaginations positioned the islands, island peoples, hotels, hotel food and service in relation to Australia and not Britain. Conventions of speech and imperial geography ensured that the Far East remained so in name, but Australian perceptions of exotic scenery, bustling Asian ports, hotels, streets and marketplaces were written into biographies and mapped into the imaginary terrain of Australia's island region. Though usually lacking the intellectual polish of the literary traveller, ordinary Australians were capable of thoughtful reflection. One Western Australian tourist declared "Java was a life-long study" and a place possibly never fully comprehensible "for one of Western birth."[2] Australians viewed Oriental others through the lens of British race pride, but those like Pratt sensed the need to revise their preformed impressions if they were to take advantage of commercial opportunities.

Commercial cosmopolitans could be found in every Australian colony and every port city. Admittedly, blackbirders were beyond the pale, prospectors and miners in New Guinea, too, distinguished themselves by their brutality, yet mining entrepreneurs were prepared to collaborate with Malay and Chinese businessmen, and, in Thailand, subordinate themselves to the aims of the Thai royal elite and their Sino-Thai clients. While Australians with the power of life and death over indigenous peoples exhibited the worst aspects of Australian society, in contexts where power was more evenly distributed Australians acted with restraint. Those engaged in regional trade believed it advantageous to seek closer political and commercial relations with the Chinese merchant classes of Malaya and the Indies and with the independent Asian kingdom of Siam. They were considerably outnumbered, of course, by those comfortably wedded to the imperial firm, but their openness to the possibilities of Asian engagement needs to be acknowledged.

Historically, Conservative and Labor politicians recognized the value of regional ties, albeit with different policy emphases. Two contending views of regional political engagement appeared in Australian foreign policy thinking after the Pacific War. Evatt's vision of an archipelagic regional association committed to collective security grew out of his active involvement in shaping regional affairs and his gradual abandonment of discredited colonial modes of thought. During the Menzies era, foreign policy was directed more towards the export of Australian values into the wider Asian region to combat the challenge of international communism. The Chifley government pursued partnership and Menzies, guided by Spender and then Casey, pursued diplomacy within a traditional alliance framework. Under Labor, political engagement was actively sought, but Asian migrants remained pointedly unwelcome. Menzies was much more concerned with developing regional ties than he receives credit for in Australian history. In addition to overseeing the expansion of Australian diplomatic representation, he established the Australia-Indonesia Institute to foster greater awareness by Australians of their largest South East Asian neighbor. Under Menzies, the Colombo Plan opened Australian society to limited temporary migration from Asia—with major consequences for the ideology of White Australia and the practice of racial exclusion.

Asian modernization endures as both an explanation and justification for the pursuit of South East Asian engagement. Government reports and policy statements emphasize the growth of market opportunities for Australia among South East Asia's bourgeoning middle classes, echoing earlier assumptions of regional convergences around Westernized tastes and lifestyles. Embracing the fashionable neoliberal rhetoric and logic of globalization, Gareth Evans argued that a pattern of cultural convergence was reshaping the Asian Pacific, driven by modern information communication technologies, rising economic interconnectedness and the acceptance of global consumer brands. Seeking all the trappings of corporate success, and the prestige of partaking in global consumer culture, regional elites savor the delicacies of *Pizza Hut*, *KFC* and *McDonalds*, but these are superficial fashionable adoptions that signal local penetration by global corporations rather than the immediate and uncontested triumph of Anglo-American capitalism.

In its mundane or everyday sense, regional engagement is not so much sought as served up in tropical holiday brochures, restaurant menus and a supermarket Asian food section. Diversifying consumption patterns mean that South East Asian food brands are absorbed into Australian suburban spaces, ranging from packets of Indofoods egg noodles to Ayam condiments and coconut cream, or generic Thai, Malaysian or Singapore-style sauce mixes. Reflecting the new regional division of labor, electrical goods retailers stock Hewlett-Packard printer/scanners in cartons bearing the Thai script and containing bilingual assembly instructions.

Millions of Australians say yes to telephone services provided through a through a local subsidiary of the Singaporean Singtel corporation, Optus, or elect for surgery, respite and recovery in private hospitals owned by the Singapore Investment Corporation. Tasmanians drink a local beer brand owned by the Philippine brewing company, San Miguel, a company controlled by the influential Cojuangco family. Australian penetration of Asian cultural spaces extends to the marketing of education services, dairy produce, wine and beef. The federal government is even seeking to promote Australian investment in the production of *halal* foodstuffs in Malaysia.[3] These interconnections evidence the accelerating detachment of production, consumer culture and place, but it is more likely that they are interpreted in Australia and South East Asia as elements of global economic change rather than signifying nascent regional integration.

WHAT KIND OF REGION?

Two centuries after the British colonization of the Australian continent began, Australians are still unsure of where they belong. Paul Keating took a quantum leap towards defining Australia as part of an emerging regional community, although neither he nor Gareth Evans seemed quite sure what this community was. Keating defined Australia as no longer a cultural misfit, but part of a dynamic region characterized by its cultural diversity and interdependence. But what was this region to which Australians purportedly belonged? Was it Asia? Was it the Asian Pacific? Was it an East Asian hemisphere community? Was this new region defined by a harmony of economic interests that would negate the possibility of war, or did stability hinge upon the maintenance of a regional power balance involving the United States? The ALP government under Keating anticipated a drawing down of the American presence in Asia but the Howard government views the engagement of U.S. power in Northeast Asia as of pivotal importance for regional stability.

Australia's future is unquestionably tied to the fortunes of its nearest northern neighbors and the historical record suggests that this is a future that Australians can be persuaded to accept. Paradoxically, the greater the intensity of exchanges or movements across frontiers, the greater the political pressure to delineate and police terrestrial and maritime space and to harden the protective outer membranes of nation.[4] It is tempting to interpret the nascent AFTA-CER as representing a sudden Australian rediscovery of Australasia, but this new state-led convergence is part of a much wider phenomenon of region formation encompassing South, South East and East Asia, and includes the significant rediscovery of Australia by its regional neighbors. From the Australian point of view, however, the prospect of an Australia-ASEAN free-trade area represents the persistence of a regional idea dating back into the early years of British colonization.

Even though the name went out of currency after 1900, Australasia never really left the Australian geographical imagination and may be realized through the further expansion of ASEAN. Perhaps a new grouping of states encompassing South East Asia, the South West Pacific and Australia is a logical step in an intensely competitive global economy. What remains to be seen is the extent to which liberal ideology and liberal economic policies can deliver the levels of development needed to subdue political challenges to this new regional economic order, both within Australia and in the nations to Australia's north. Free trade is not a universally accepted good. Critics of Australia's bilateral free-trade agreement with Thailand point to the likely economic disenfranchisement of Thailand's rural poor who depend upon agriculture for their livelihood.[5]

ADRIFT IN THE PACIFIC

Even though the complacent Western triumphalism of the 1990s is somewhat muted, the sterile neoliberal discourse of harmonization, efficiency, productivity and transparency still sets the agenda for regional diplomacy—terms that are hardly universal. Reflecting the tenor of the times, engagement across borders is increasingly negotiated in terms of managed processes, subject to international regulatory regimes for oceans governance, trade, investment, social control and the control of migration. With the hubris of those wedded to economic liberalism, there is a presumption in policy circles that if economic settings are correct, and the appropriate legal and moral controls are in place at a national and regional level, then subterranean political challenges to Australian interests will be subdued—a dangerous presumption founded on the shaky logic of generic management. The application of liberal economic principles cannot neutralize nor dilute culture, nor politics for that matter, as factors in Australia's regional relations, even though Australia's political leaders have abandoned the acquisition of strategically vital cultural knowledge and skills to the vicissitudes of consumer choice.

The politics of Australian nationhood still revolve around popular fears of invasion, fears intensified by television images of social anarchy from the Middle East to South Asia and Indonesia and embodied in the harrowing images of Afghan boatpeople on Australia's doorstep or the images and sounds of Islamic devotional practice.[6] Images of mass Islamic worship were used as code for a global terrorist threat on early morning infotainment news following the attacks on the Twin Towers on September 11, 2001. New waves of people from South Asia and the Middle East, including women and children, unarmed and travelling in leaky boats, were used by the Coalition Party government to personify an Islamic threat to the Australian way of life, and to win a third election in 2001. Pandering to popular xenophobia, John Howard echoed Billy Hughes in declaring that the government alone would decide who had the right to seek asylum in Australia. Strident Australian political statements about border protection and police actions to defend Australia's northern maritime borders against the infiltration of asylum seekers are legitimated at home if not in Asia by the stridency of anti-Western rhetoric emanating from Asian Imslamicists. Border protection is today the catchcry for anyone desiring political credibility in a deliberately cultivated climate of fear.

The "Bali Bombing" and the "Asian Tsunami" mark out the range of contradictory impressions of South East Asia in the Australian imagination. Within the space of little more than two years, Australians were presented with two sharply different collective images of their region—one image of an arc of instability subject to the machinations of Islamicist terrorists plotting to attack Australians as they had done at the Sari Club, the other of a maritime region devastated by a natural disaster and urgently in need of humanitarian assistance. The first image served the global agenda of the American-led war on terror, the second a more localized agenda to promote a favorable image of Australia to Indonesian Muslims.

There are new dynamics in regional relations, arising partly from the Australian response to the events of Boxing Day 2004. At a time when Australia is increasingly perceived as part of a Western assault on traditional Islamic values, Australian generosity towards tsunami survivors in Indonesia has undoubtedly helped to heal some of the damage done to bilateral relations by Australia's role in bringing about East Timor's independence. The Howard government moved quickly to negotiate a new defense relationship with Indonesia, encouraged by comments made by Susilo Bambang Yudhoyono before Indonesian presidential elections in 2004. Having downgraded the security relationship with Indonesia in 1997, Canberra sought to revive the Australia-Indonesia security agreement which the Indonesians tore up in protest in 1999 and which was subsequently renegotiated and signed in 2006.[7] Yet, Australian public support for a reinvigorated Australia-Indonesia relationship remains fragile at best.

Amidst the justifiable self-congratulation for the significance of Australia's tsunami relief effort there lies a danger that Australians could easily find their generosity used to downplay the abuse of human rights at home, legitimate unequivocal support for another American-led global police action or validate a unilateral Australian military assault on suspected terrorist bases in the Archipelago to protect Australia and to uphold Australian values. Popular Australian patriotism, assiduously promoted by shock-jocks and conservative politicians alike, counters the so called "Black Armband" narrative of Australian racism and oppression by cultivating images of the idealized Australian: egalitarian, caring, generous, proudly Anglo-Celtic but tolerant of all peoples. The net effect is to dull the public appetite for critical reflection and replace secret misgivings about past and present wrongs with a somnolent warm inner glow.

Australian foreign policy is today more assertive and interventionist than at any time since the Vietnam War. Intervention to end the anarchy in the Solomon Islands and the dispatch of Federal Police to New Guinea are responsible steps towards strengthening states in Australia's region. Yet the Howard government was reluctant to give an unequivocal commitment to a collective regional approach prior to signing the ASEAN Treaty, a precondition for attending the ASEAN Summit. Publicly the prime minister asserted Australia's reasonable right of unilateral hot pursuit in response to terrorist acts on Australian soil perpetrated from within South East Asia. Perhaps to save the prime minister's face, Foreign Minister Downer signed the treaty while John Howard visited London, no doubt to discuss the war in Iraq with his British counterpart but also to take in some test cricket. The episode suggested a foreign policy dilemma for the Howard government: to acknowledge the ongoing regionalization of Australia's economic and political interests, yet remain seen as a global player at home and abroad. In the absence of a clear regional policy, Australia will continue its slow drift into Asia, but it will require more time and some careful persuasion before neighboring states offer anything more than formal, if not grudging, acceptance of Australia as a regional partner.

NOTES

1. Ballantyne, "Empire, Knowledge and Culture," 134.

2. *Straits Times*, June 10, 1911.

3. *Australian Financial Review*, July 31, 2002.

4. Lim Joo-Jock, *Territorial Power Domains, Southeast Asia and China: The Geo-Strategy of an Overarching Massif* (Singapore: Institute of Southeast Asian Studies and Canberra: Strategic and Defence Studies Centre, Australian National University, 1984), 67–76.

5. Ben Moxham, "Milking Thailand: The Thai-Australia Free-Trade Agreement," November 18, 2004, http://www.focusweb.org/main/html/PrintArticle537.html (Accessed July 6, 2006)

6. As discussed at length in Anthony Burke, *In Fear of Security: Australia's Invasion Anxiety* (Sydney: Pluto Press, 2001).

7. *Australian Financial Review*, March 29, 2005.

Bibliography

PRIMARY SOURCES

Unpublished Government Records

AUSTRALIAN ARCHIVES

Prime Minister

A461: Correspondence files, multiple number, third system (series range 1934–50)
A1209: Correspondence files, annual single number series (classified) (series range 1957–)
A1608: Correspondence files, multiple number series with variable alphabetical prefix and general prefix "sc" (fourth system) (series range 1939–1947)
CP290: Papers from records of the Prime Minister's Office (series range 1930–1942)

Defense

A816: Correspondence files: Department of Defence Coordination prefixes (1939–42), Department of Defence (1942–57) multiple number system (class 301), classified (series range 1935–57)
A816: Correspondence files: Department of Defence Coordination prefixes (1939–42), Department of Defence (1942–57) multiple number system (class 301), classified (series range 1935–57)
AA1974: Correspondence files (date range 1939–1940)
A5954: Sir Frederick Sheddon Collection, collected Defense records, 1937–79

Defence Committee

A5799: Defence Committee agenda, annual single number series (series range 1932-)

External Affairs

A981: Correspondence files, alphabetical series (series range 1925-42)

A989: Correspondence files, multiple number series with year prefix (series range 1943-44)

A1066: Correspondence files, multiple number series with year and letter prefix (series range 1943-44)

A1067: Correspondence files, multiple number series with year and letter prefixes (series range 1946)

A1068: Correspondence files, Central Office, multiple number series with year and letter prefixes (series range 1947)

A1838: Correspondence files, multiple number series (series range 1948-)

A3317: Correspondence files, Department of External Affairs Office, London, annual single number series (series range 1945-47)

A4311: "Cumpston Collection, " Australian foreign policy documents (series range 1901-1969)

Trade and Customs

CP529: General correspondence (Trade information and trade relations) (series range 1939-56)

Commerce

A601: Correspondence files, multiple number series (series range 1935-43)

Governor General

A6662: Miscellaneous correspondence relating to local (non-Imperial) matters (series range 1900-1911)

CP78: Correspondence files relating to the war of 1914-1918 ("War Files") (series range 1914-1919)

Australian High Commission, London

A2910: Correspondence files, multiple number series (class 400) (series range 1930-52)

Australian Legation, Washington

A3300: Correspondence files, annual alphabetical series (series range 1939–48) alphabetical prefix (series range 1930–1952)
A5460: Secret/top secret correspondence files, multiple number series, (first system) (series range 1949–1951)

Australian Consulate General, Bangkok

A5019: Correspondence files, multiple number series (second system) (series range 1949–56)

NATIONAL ARCHIVES OF THAILAND

Ministry of Lands and Agriculture

Board of Commercial Development
KS 15.2: Correspondence files (R6–7)
Council of Ministers
KS 15.1: Correspondence files (R6–7)
Department of Mines and Geology
KS.16:   Correspondence files (R6–7)
KS 6.1–6.8: Correspondence files (R6)
KS 4–4.1: Correspondence files (R7)

Ministry of Commerce and Communications

P3, P5–5.1: Correspondence files (R7)

Ministry of Foreign Affairs

T4.2, T6.8: Correspondence files (R7)

Ministry of Communications

Department of State Railways
KK5–5.2: Correspondence files (R7)

Secret Documents: France and England

F.36: Miscellaneous correspondence, maps and reports (R6)

Royal Secretariat

RL 6, RL 11, RL 17: Correspondence files (R7)

Cabinet Secretary

SR 0201.28.3; (2)SR 0201.60: Correspondence files (date range 1932+)

Committee for the Control and Management of Alien Business and Property

KKhThD: Correspondence files (Date range 1942–1948)

QUEENSLAND STATE ARCHIVES

Colonial Secretary's Office

PRV 8112: Executive Council Minutes
PRV 8226: Letterbooks and despatches to the Secretary of State for the Colonies
PRV 7192: Correspondence re annexation of New Guinea and the administration of the protectorate
PRV 8231: Confidential dispatches from the Secretary of State for the Colonies
PRV 8235: Correspondence and reports on defense
SRS 5384: Batch files (inwards correspondence) and related correspondence and papers
RSI 128481: Miscellaneous correspondence

Office of the Governor of Queensland

PRV 8235: Correspondence and reports on defense

Creating agency unknown

RSI 2641: Report of Investigations into the possibilities of new or extended trade for Queensland

VICTORIAN PUBLIC RECORDS OFFICE

Australian Securities Commission

VPRS 567: Mining Company Registration Files
VPRS 932: Trading Company Registration Files
VPRS 8273: Register of Mining Companies
VPRS 8275: Index to Defunct Mining Companies and Prospecting Syndicates

GOVERNMENT REPORTS AND STATISTICS

Queensland

Queensland Census. 1886, 1891, 1901.

"Queensland Committee on Settlement at the Gulf of Carpentaria, " *Queensland Legislative Council Journals*. vol. 1, 1860.

"Report from the Joint Select Committee on Existing and Proposed Lines of Steam Communication." *Queensland Legislative Assembly Votes and Proceedings*. 3rd Session, 2nd Parliament, 1865.

"Report of the Board Appointed to Inquire into the Alleged Cases of Cholera Among Passengers on Board the SS *Dorunda* on the Voyage Between London and Brisbane." *Queensland Legislative Assembly Votes and Proceedings*. 1886, vol. 3, 1886.

"Report of the Royal Commission Appointed to Inquire into the General Condition of the Sugar Industry in Queensland Together with Minutes of Evidence." *Queensland Legislative Assembly Votes and Proceedings*. vol. 4, 1889.

"Statistics of the State of Queensland for the Year 1910." *Queensland Parliamentary Papers*. Vol. 1, Part 2, 1911.

Statistics of the State of Queensland for the Year 1901. Brisbane: Government Printer, 1902.

Statistics of the State of Queensland for the Year 1912. Brisbane: Government Printer, 1913.

Statistics of the State of Queensland for the Year 1920. Brisbane: Government Printer, 1921.

Statistics of the State of Queensland for the Year 1922. Brisbane: Government Printer, 1923.

New South Wales

Minutes of Proceedings, Intercolonial Convention. *New South Wales Legislative Assembly Votes and Proceedings*. vol. 11, 1883–84.

"Report from the Select Committee on the 'Costa Rica Packet' Case together with the proceedings of the Committee and Minutes of Evidence." *New South Wales Legislative Council Votes and Proceedings*. vol. 51, 1893.

"Statistics of New South Wales from 1848 to 1857." *New South Wales Legislative Council Journals*. vol. 3, 1858.

Smith, H. A. *The Official Yearbook of New South Wales for 1918*. Sydney: Government Printer, 1920.

Trivett, J. B. *The Official Yearbook of New South Wales: 1909–1910*. Sydney: Government Printer, 1911.

Commonwealth

Department of Foreign Affairs and Trade. *In the National Interest: Australia's Foreign and Trade Policy*. White Paper, Canberra: Commonwealth of Australia, 1997.

Dibb, Paul. *Review of Australia's Defence Capabilities*. Report to the Minister for Defence by Mr. Paul Dibb, March 1986, Canberra: Australian Government Publishing Service (hereafter AGPS), 1986.

East Asia Analytical Unit, Department of Foreign Affairs and Trade. *Changing Tack: Australian Investment in South-East Asia*. Canberra: AGPS, 1994.

———. *Australia's Business Challenge: Southeast Asia in the 1990s*. Canberra: AGPS, 1992.

Evans, Gareth. *Australia's Regional Security*. Ministerial Statement by the Senator the Hon. Gareth Evans, QC, Minister for Foreign Affairs and Trade, December 1989.

Garnaut, Ross. *Australia and the Northeast Asia Ascendency*. Canberra: AGPS, 1989.

Gepp, Herbert W. "Report on Trade Between Australia and the Far East." *Commonwealth Parliamentary Papers*. Session 1932–33–34, vol. 4.

Joint Standing Committee on Treaties. *Australia-Indonesia Maritime Delimitation Treaty*. 12th Report, Canberra: Commonwealth of Australia, November 1997.

Knibbs, George Handley. *Official Yearbook of the Commonwealth of Australia Containing Authoritative Statistics for the Period 1901–1907*. Melbourne: McCarron, Bird and Co., 1908.

———. *Official Yearbook of the Commonwealth of Australia, 1901–1913*. no. 7, 1914, Melbourne: McCarron, Bird and Co., 1914.

———. *Official Yearbook of the Commonwealth of Australia, 1901–1919*. no. 13, 1920, Melbourne: Commonwealth Bureau of Census and Statistics, 1920.

Latham, John G. "The Australian Eastern Mission, 1934." *Commonwealth Parliamentary Papers*. Session 1932–33–34, vol. 4.

Long, James J. "Java and the East Indies, Singapore, and the Straits Settlements." *Commonwealth Parliamentary Papers*. Session 1917–18–19, vol. 5.

"Report of the Australian Trade Delegation to India, Burma and Ceylon, October, 1935–January, 1936, " *Commonwealth Parliamentary Papers*. Session 1937, vol. 5.

Smith, Staniforth. "Report on the Federated Malay States and Java: Their Systems of Government, Methods of Administration, and Economic Development." *Commonwealth Parliamentary Papers*. Session 1906, vol. 2, 1906.

Smith, Staniforth. "The Netherlands East Indies: Report on the Fiscal Policy, Local Government, Civil Service, Native Government, and Economic Development." *Commonwealth Parliamentary Papers*. Session 1914–15–16–17, vol. 5, 1915.

Wilson, R. *Official Yearook of the Commonwealth of Australia*. 31, 1938, Canberra: Commonwealth Government Printer, 1939.

PARLIAMENTARY DEBATES

Commonwealth

Commonwealth Parliamentary Debates. vol. 165, Senate and House of Representatives, Session 1940, Canberra: Commonwealth Government Printer, 1941.

Commonwealth Parliamentary Debates. vol. 167, Senate and House of Representatives, Session 1940–41, Canberra: Commonwealth Government Printer, 1941.

Commonwealth Parliamentary Debates. vol. 188, Senate and House of Representatives, Session 1945–46, Canberra: Commonwealth Government Printer, 1946.

Commonwealth Parliamentary Debates. vol. 189, Senate and House of Representatives, Session 1946, Canberra: Commonwealth Government Printer, 1946.

Commonwealth Parliamentary Debates. vol. 211, Senate and House of Representatives, Session 1950, Canberra: Commonwealth Government Printer, 1951.

Queensland

Queensland Legislative Assembly, *Parliamentary Debates.* vol. 55, 1888.

PUBLISHED OFFICIAL DOCUMENTS

Commonwealth Parliament. *Historical Records of Australia, Series 3, Despatches and Papers Relating to the Settlement of the States,* vol. 5. Sydney: Government Printer, 1922.

Dorling, Philip and David Lee, eds. *Documents on Australian Foreign Policy, 1937–49.* Vol. 13, Indonesia, 1948. Canberra: AGPS, 1996.

———. ed. *Diplomasi: Australia & Indonesia's Independence. Documents, 1947.* Canberra: AGPS, 1994.

Department of External Affairs. *Current Notes on International Affairs.* 1939–1962.

Neale, Robert George et al, eds. *Documents on Australian Foreign Policy, 1937–1949.* Vol. 1–10, Canberra: AGPS, 1975–83.

Jodmaihaet wa duai Karn Tham Muang Rae nai Prathaet Syam (Documents on Mining in Siam). Bangkok: Royal Department of Mines and Geology, 1925.

Prawat Krom Lohakit Khrop Rop 72 Pii (72 Years of the Department of Mines). Bangkok: Department of Mines, 1963.

Treaty between Australia and the Independent State of Papua New Guinea concerning Sovereignty and Maritime Boundaries in the area between the two Countries, including the area known as Torres Strait, and Related Matters (Sydney, 18 December 1978), Australian Treaty Series, 1985, no. 4, Department of Foreign Affairs, Canberra: AGPS, 1985.

UNPUBLISHED MANUSCRIPTS

National Library of Australia

Miles, Tom. "The Life Story of Captain Edward Thomas Miles, Master Mariner and Pioneer of Tin Dredging." National Library of Australia.

John Oxley Library

Deeney, Jack C. "Round the World in a School Vacation (30, 000 miles in 50 Days) The Story of a Holiday trip." Unpublished manuscript, John Oxley Library, OM 78–16.

PRIVATE PAPERS
Casey, Richard G. National Library of Australia.
Kemp, C. D. National Library of Australia.
Menzies, Robert G. National Library of Australia.
Pratt, Ambrose G. H. Australian Manuscripts Collection, State Library of Victoria.

INTERVIEWS

Arthorn Tongwathana, January 1994, Phuket.
Rachan Kanjanawanit, January 1994, Bangkok.
Richard Miles, August 1993, Sydney.
Somsakdi Xuto, January 1994, Bangkok.
Wicha Sethabut, March 1995, Bangkok.

UNPUBLISHED PUBLIC LECTURES

Address by the Hon. Dr. Surin Pitsuwan, Minister for Foreign Affairs in the Government of Thailand, Asialink Conference, James Cook University, Cairns, May 1996.

NEWSPAPERS AND MAGAZINES

Australian, 1991–2005.
Australian Financial Review, 1991–2005.
Bangkok Chronicle, 1940–41.
Bangkok Daily Mail, 1930.
Brisbane Courier, 1866–1926.
Brisbane Telegraph, 1889.
Cairns Argus, 1890, 1910–1912
Far Eastern Survey, 1938–41.
Industrial and Australian Mining Standard, 1909–1911, 1924–1957.
Mackay Mercury, 1882–1892
Mackay Standard, 1886.
Melbourne *Age.* 1938–1942.
Melbourne *Argus.*1938–1942.
Melbourne Stock Exchange, *Official Record.* 1929–1958.
North Queensland Herald, 1895, 1910–1911.
North Queensland Register, 1888–1896.
Petroleum Intelligence Weekly, 2003–2004.
Queenslander, 1874–1926.
Straits Times, 1874–1914, 1936.

Sydney Morning Herald, 1901, 1927–1941.
Times, 1883.
Tin International, 1959–1963, 1965–1970.
Townsville Daily Bulletin, 1912.
Townsville Herald, 1888–1895.
Walkabout, 1928–1941.
West Australian, August 1883.

BOOKS, BROCHURES AND MONOGRAPHS

Australian Handbook and Almanac and Shippers and Importers Directory for 1875. Melbourne: Gordon and Gotch, 1875.
Australian Handbook and Almanac and Shippers and Importers Directory for 1884. Melbourne: Gordon and Gotch, 1884.
Australian Institute of International Affairs. *Australia and the Pacific.* vols. 1 & 2, Papers delivered to the Eighth Conference of the Institute of Pacific Relations, Mont Tremblant, Canada, December, 1942.
Barme, Scott, trans. and ed. *Kulap in Oz: A Thai View of Australian Life and Society in the Late 1940s.* Clayton, Victoria: Centre for Southeast Asian Studies, Monash University, 1995.
Bird, Isabella. *The Golden Chersonese and the Way Thither.* London: Century, 1983.
Cairns, James F. *Living with Asia.* Melbourne: Lansdowne Press, 1965.
Callis, H. G. *Foreign Capital in South-east Asia.* New York: Institute of Pacific Relations, 1942.
Carrington, Dorothy. *The Traveller's Eye.* London: Readers Union, 1949.
Clarke, Marcus. *The Future Australian Race.* Melbourne: A. H. Massina and Co., 1877.
Clune, Frank. *To the Isles of Spice.* Sydney: Angus and Robertson, 1944.
Clunies-Ross, Ian, and Stephen Henry Roberts, ed. *Australia and the Far East: Diplomatic and Trade Relations.* Sydney: Angus and Robertson in conjunction with the Australian Institute of International Affairs (New South Wales Branch), 1936.
Conrad, Joseph. *Almayer's Folly.* London: Penguin, 1988.
———. *Lord Jim.* London: Penguin, 1989.
Copeland, Henry. *A Few Weeks with the Malays.* Singapore: Straits Times Press, 1883.
Department of Mineral Resources. *100 pii krom saphayakorn thoranee: khawsarn kaan thoranee chabab phiset,* (100 Years of the Department of Mineral Resources: Mining and Mineral Information Special Edition). Bangkok: Department of Mineral Resources, 1991.
De Wit, Augusta. *Facts and Fancies about Java.* London: Luzac & Co, 1900.
Dunlop, Edward E. *The War Diaries of Edward "Weary" Dunlop: Java and the Thai-Burma Railway, 1942–1945,* Melbourne: Nelson, 1986.
Durack, Elizabeth. *Seeing through Indonesia: An Artist's Impressions of the Republic.* Melbourne: Hawthorn, 1977.
Evatt, Herbert V. *Australia in World Affairs.* Sydney: Angus and Robertson, 1946.
Excel, F. K. *Siamese Tapestry.* London: Travel Book Club, 1963.
Flinders, Matthew. *A Voyage to Terra Australia,* Vol. II. London: G&W Nicol, 1814.

Garnsey, William Kinglake. *Eastern Tin Dredging Companies.* Sydney: Sydney Stock Exchange, 1937.

Gilmore, Robert J., and David Warner, eds. *Near North: Australia and a Thousand Million Neighbours.* Sydney: Angus and Robertson, 1948.

Hall, Leslie. *The Blue Haze: POWs on the Burma Railway: Incorporating the History of "A" Force Groups 3 & 5, Burma-Thai Railway, 1942–1943.* Sydney: Kangaroo Press, 1996.

Harrison, Cuthbert Woodville. *An Illustrated Guide to the Federated Malay States.* London: The Malay States Information Agency, 1911.

Hill, Ernestine. *The Territory.* Sydney: Angus and Robertson, 5th edition, 1968.

Hume-Cook, James. *The Australian Industries Protection League: A Historical Review.* Melbourne, 1938.

Java the Wonderland. Weltevereden (Batavia): Netherlands East Indies Official Tourist Bureau, c. 1907.

Kitti Ratanachaya. *Dap fai tai kab phak kommunist malaya* (The Malayan Communist Party and the Suppression of Communism in the South). Bangkok: Duang Kaew, 1995.

Mackenzie, Eneas. *A New and Complex System of Modern Geography.* London: Mackenzie and Dent, 1817.

Macmillan, Alister. *Seaports of the Far East.* London: W. H. Allen, 2nd edition, 1925.

Makepeace, Walter, Gilbert E. Brooke, and Roland St. John Braddell, eds. *One Hundred Years of Singapore,* Vol. II, London: John Murray, 1921.

Martin, R. M. *British Possessions in Europe, Africa, Asia and Australasia.* London: W. H. Allen, 1847.

McMahon, Thomas J. *The Orient I Found.* London: Duckworth, 1926.

Meaney, Neville, ed. *Australia and the World: A Documentary History from the 1870s to the 1970s.* Melbourne: Longman Cheshire, 1985.

Meudell, George. *The Pleasant Career of a Spendthrift and His Later Reflections.* Melbourne: Wilke and Co., 1936.

Picturesque Travel under the Auspices of Burns Philp and Company Ltd. no. 3, 1913, Sydney: Burns Philp and Company, 1912.

Picturesque Travel under the Auspices of Burns Philp and Company Ltd. Sydney: Burns Philp and Company, 1920.

Pratt, Ambrose. *Magical Malaya.* Melbourne: Robertson and Mullens, 1931.

———. *The Big Five.* London: Ward Lock and Company, 1910.

Pratten, Herbert. *Through Orient to Occident.* Sydney: Ferguson, 1911.

———. *Asiatic Impressions: A Collection of Articles by H. E. Pratten.* Sydney: Ferguson, 1908.

Prawat krom lohakit khrop rop 72 pii (72 Years of the Department of Mines). Bangkok: Department of Mines, 1963.

Pring, Philip, and Keith Brougham Docker, eds. *A Guide to Eastern Tin Dredging Stocks for Australian Investors.* Sydney: Sydney Stock Exchange, 1926.

Raffles, Thomas S. *The History of Java:* vol. 1. Melbourne: Oxford University Press, 1978.

———. *The History of Java:* Vol. 2. Melbourne: Oxford University Press, 1978.

Rolley, Alisa. *Survival on Ambon*. Self-published: Queensland, 1994.

Roush, G. A. *Strategic Mineral Supplies*. New York: McGraw-Hill, 1939.

Rydge, N. B. The Australian Stock Exchange: Being an Explanation of the Functions of the Australian Stock Exchanges, a Consideration of the Principles Involved in Speculation and Investment, and a Commentary Upon Essential Features in the Selection of Sound Investments." Sydney: *Rydges Business Journal*, 1934.

Shepherd, Jack. *Australia's Interests and Policies in the Far East*. New York: International Secretariat, Institute of Pacific Relations, 1940.

Simkin, Tom, and Richard S. Fiske (with the collaboration of Sarah Melcher and Elizabeth Nielsen). *Krakatau, 1883: The Volcanic Eruption and Its Effects*. Washington DC: Smithsonian Institution Press, 1983.

Statistical Yearbook of the Kingdom of Siam, 1919. Bangkok: Department of Commerce and Statistics, Ministry of Finance, 1919.

Stewart, R. *Australasia*. London: W. Tweedie, 1853.

Swettenham, Frank A. *British Malaya: An Account of the Origin and Progress of British Influence in Malaya*. London: George Allen and Unwin, 1948.

Sydney Stock Exchange Research and Statistical Bureau. *Eastern Tin Dredging Companies*. Sydney: Sydney Stock Exchange, 1947.

van der Veur, Paul W. ed. *Documents and Correspondence on New Guinea's Boundaries*. Canberra: Australian National University Press, 1966.

van Dyke, John C. *In Java: And the Neighbouring Islands of the Dutch East Indies*. Charlers Scribner's and Sons: London, 1929.

Visit Malaya, Singapore, c. 1938.

Wallace, Alfred, R. *The Malay Archipelago: The Land of the Orang-Utan and the Bird of Paradise*. Singapore: Oxford University Press, 1986.

———. *Australasia*, vol. 1. *Australia and New Zealand*. Stanford's Compendium of Geography and Travel, London: Edward Stanford, 1893.

———. *Australasia*. London: Edward Stanford, 1879.

Warner, David. *Wake Me If There's Trouble: An Australian Correspondent at the Front Line—Asia at War and Peace, 1944–1964*. Melbourne: Penguin, 1995.

Wildey, William B. *Australasia and the Oceanic Region*. Melbourne: George Robertson, 1876.

Wilkins, W. *Australasia: A descriptive and Pictoral Account of the Australian and New Zealand Colonies, Tasmania, and the Adjacent Lands*. Blackie: London, 1888.

Worsfold, William Basil. *A Visit to Java with an Account of the Founding of Singapore*. London: Richard Bentley and Son, 1893.

SECONDARY SOURCES

Books and Monographs

Abeyasekere, Susan. *Jakarta: A History*. Singapore: Oxford University Press, 1989.

Akira Iriye. *The Origins of the Second World War in Asia and the Pacific*. London: Longman, 1987.

Aldrich, Richard. J. *The Key to the South: Britain, the United States, and Thailand during the Approach to the Pacific War, 1929–1942.* Oxford: Oxford University Press, 1993.

Allen, Charles. *Tales from the South China Seas: Images of the British in South-East Asia in the Twentieth Century.* London: Futura, 1983.

Andaya, Barbara W., and Leonard Y. Andaya. *A History of Malaysia.* London: Macmillan, 1982.

Anderson, Benedict. *Imagined Communities: Reflections on the Origin and Spread of Nationalism.* New York: Verso, 2nd edition, 1991.

Anderson, J. *Political and Commercial Considerations Relative to the Malayan Peninsula and the British Settlements in the Straits of Malacca.* Singapore: Malaysian Branch of the Royal Asiatic Society, 1965.

Andrews, Eric M. *Australia and China: The Ambiguous Relationship.* Melbourne: Melbourne University Press, 1985.

Andrews, Malcolm. *The Search for the Picturesque: Landscape, Aesthetics and Tourism in Britain, 1760–1800.* Aldershot: Scholar Press, 1989.

Appleyard, R. T., and C. B. Schedvin. *Australian Financiers: Biographical Essays.* Melbourne: Macmillan, 1988.

Bach, John. *A Maritime History of Australia.* Sydney: Thomas Nelson, 1976.

Baliant, Ruth. *Troubled Waters: Borders, Boundaries and Possession in the Timor Sea.* Sydney: Allen and Unwin, 2005.

Beaumont, Joan. *The Evolution of Australian Foreign Policy, 1901–45.* Melbourne: Australian Institute of International Affairs (Victorian Branch), Occasional Paper No.1, 1989.

Begbie, P. J. *The Malayan Peninsula.* London: Oxford University Press, 1967.

Bell, Coral, ed. *Agenda for the Nineties: Australian Choices in Foreign and Defence Policy.* Melbourne: Longman Cheshire, 1991.

Bell, Roger J. *Unequal Allies: Australian-American Relations and the Pacific War.* Melbourne: Melbourne University Press, 1977.

Blainey, Geoffrey. *The Rush That Never Ended: A History of Australian Mining.* Melbourne: Melbourne University Press, 4th edition, 1993.

———. *The Tyranny of Distance.* Melbourne: Macmillan, 2nd edition, 1988.

Bolton, Geoffrey. C. *The Oxford History of Australia: The Middle Way, 1942–1988.* vol. 5, Oxford: Oxford University Press, 1993.

———, and B. K. de Garis (ed.) *University Studies in History.* University of Western Australia Press, Perth, 1966.

Boyce, P. J. and J. R., Angel, eds. *Diplomacy in the Marketplace: Australia in World Affairs, 1981–90,* Melbourne: Longman Cheshire, 1992.

Brawley, Sean. *The White Peril: Foreign Relations and Asian Immigration to Australasia and North America, 1919–78.* Sydney: University of New South Wales Press, 1995.

Bridge, Carl, ed. *Munich to Vietnam: Australia's relations with Britain and the United States since the 1930s.* Melbourne: Melbourne University Press, 1991.

Brinnin, John Malcolm. *The Sway of the Grand Saloon: A Social History of the North Atlantic.* New York: Delacorte Press, 1971,

Broinowski, Alison. *About Face: Asian Accounts of Australia.* Melbourne: Scribe, 2003.

———. *The Yellow Lady: Australian Impressions of Asia,* Oxford: Oxford University Press, 1992

Buckley, Ken, and Kris Klugman, *The History of Burns Philp: The Australian Company in the South Pacific*, Sydney: Burns, Philp and Company, 1981.

Burke, A. *In Fear of Security: Australia's Invasion Anxiety*, Sydney: Pluto Press, 2001.

Burton, John. *The Alternative: A Dynamic Approach to Our Relations with Asia*, Sydney: Morgan Publications, 1954.

Capling, Anne. *Australia and the Global Trade System: From Havana to Seattle.* Cambridge: Cambridge University Press, 2001.

Carter, Paul. *Living in a New Country: History, Travelling and Language.* London: Faber and Faber, 1992.

Catley, Bob, and Vinessension Dugis. *Australia-Indonesian Relations since 1945: The Garuda and the Kangaroo.* Aldershot: Ashgate, 1998.

Chai-Anan Samudavanija, Kusuma Snitwongse, Suchit Bunbongkarn. *From Armed Suppression to Political Offensive.* Bangkok: Institute of Security and International Studies, Chulalongkorn University, 1990.

Chai Hon Chan. *The Development of British Malaya*, London: Oxford University Press, 2nd edition, 1967.

Chaiwat Khamchoo and E. B. Reynolds, eds. *Thai-Japanese Relations in Historical Perspective.* Bangkok: Institute of Asian Studies, Chulalongkorn University, 1988.

Chaiyan Rachagool. *The Rise and Fall of the Thai Absolute Monarchy: Foundations of the Modern Thai State from Feudalism to Peripheral Capitalism.* Studies in Contemporary Thailand, vol. 2, Bangkok: White Lotus, 1994.

Chandran Jeshurun. *The Contest for Siam, 1889–1902: A Study in Diplomatic Rivalry.* Kuala Lumpur: Penerbit Universiti Kebangsaan Malaysia, 1977.

Chathip Nartsupha and Suthy Prasartset, eds. *The Political Economy of Siam, 1851–1910,* Bangkok: The Social Science Association of Thailand, 1981.

Chauvel, Richard. *Nationalists, Soldiers and Separatists: The Ambones Islands from Colonialism to Revolt, 1880–1950.* Leiden: KITLV Press, 1990.

Chia Lin Sen, ed. *Southeast Asia Transformed: A Geography of Change.* Singapore: Institute of Southeast Asian Studies, 2003.

Churchill, R. R., and A.V. Lowe. *The Law of the Sea.* Manchester: Manchester University Press, 4th edition, 1999.

Clark, Manning. *A History of Australia*, vol. 1: *From the Earliest Times to the Age of Macquarie.* Melbourne: Melbourne University Press, 3rd edition, 1988.

Craig, Robin. *The Ship: Steam Tramps and Cargo Liners, 1850–1950.* London: National Maritime Museum, 1980.

Cumberland, Kenneth B. *Southwest Pacific: A Geography of Australia, New Zealand and Their Pacific Island Neighbourhoods.* Christchurch: Whitcombe and Tombs Limited, 2nd edition, 1968.

Cumpston, I. M. *History of Australian Foreign Policy, 1901–1991.* vols. 1 & 2, Canberra: Self-Published, 1995.

Cushman, Jennifer. *Family and State: The Formation of a Sino-Thai Tin-Mining Dynasty, 1797–1932.* Oxford: Oxford University Press, 1991.

Day, David. *Menzies and Churchill at War.* Melbourne: Oxford University Press, 1993.

———. *The Great Betrayal: Britain, Australia and the Onset of the Pacific War, 1939–42,* Oxford University Press Australia, Melbourne, 1992.

Dalrymple, Rawdon. *Continental Drift: Australia's Search for a Regional Identity.* Aldershot: Ashgate, 2003.

Davidson, Jim, and Peter Spearritt. *Holiday Business: Tourism in Australia since 1870.* Melbourne: Miegunyah Press, 2000.

D'Cruz, J. Vin, and William Steele. *Australia's Ambivalence Towards Asia.* Melbourne: Monash University Press, 2003.

Dicken, Peter. *Global Shift: Reshaping the Global Economic Map of the 21st century.* Thousand Oaks: SAGE, 2003.

Dixson, Miriam. *The Real Matilda: Woman and Identity in Australia, 1788 to the Present.* Melbourne: Penguin Books Australia, 2nd edition, 1987.

Dobell, Graham. *Australia Finds a Home: The Choices and Chances of an Asia-Pacific Journey.* Sydney: ABC Books, 2000.

Downs, Roger M., and David Stea. *Maps in Minds: Reflections on cognitive mapping.* London: Harper & Row, 1977.

Dyster, Barrie, and David Meredith. *Australia in the International Economy in the Twentieth Century.* Cambridge: Cambridge University Press, 1991.

Edwards, Peter G. *Crises and Commitments: The Politics and Diplomacy of Australia's Involvement in Southeast Asian Conflicts, 1948–196.,* Sydney: Allen and Unwin in association with the Australian War Memorial, 1992.

———. *Prime-Ministers and Diplomats: The Making of Australian Foreign Policy, 1901–1949.* Melbourne: Oxford University Press, 1983.

———. and David Goldsworthy, eds. *Facing North: A Century of Australian Engagement with Asia,* vol. 2, 1970s to 2000, Melbourne University Press, Melbourne, 2002.

Esthus, Raymond A. *From Enmity to Alliance: US-Australian Relations, 1931–1941.* Melbourne: Melbourne University Press, 1965.

Evans, Gareth, and Grant Bruce. *Australia's Foreign Relations in the World of the 1990s.* Melbourne: Melbourne University Press, 1992.

Fernandes, Clinton. *Reluctant Saviour: Australia, Indonesia and the Independence of East Timor.* Melbourne: Scribe, 2004.

FitzGerald, Stephen. *Is Australia an Asian County?* Sydney: Allen and Unwin, 1997.

Foley, John C. H. *Reef Pilots: The History of the Queensland Coast and Torres Strait Pilot Service.* Sydney: Banks Bros. and Street, 1982.

Frei, Henry P. *Japan's Southward Advance and Australia: From the Sixteenth Century to World War II.* Melbourne: Melbourne University Press, 1989.

Fry, Greg, ed. *Australia's Regional Security.* Sydney: Allen and Unwin, 1991.

Fussell, Paul. *Abroad: British Literary Traveling Between the Wars.* New York: Oxford University Press, 1980.

Gobert, Wayne. *The Origins of Australian Diplomatic Intelligence in Asia, 1933–1941.* Canberra Papers on Strategy and Defence, no. 96, Canberra: Strategic and Defence Studies Centre, Research School of Pacific Studies, The Australian National University, 1992.

Greenhill, Basil, and Anne Giffard. *Travelling by Sea in the Nineteenth Century: Interior Design in Victorian Passenger Ships.* London: Adam and Charles Black, 1972.

Greenwood, Gordon, ed. *Approaches to Asia: Australian Post-War Policies and Attitudes.* Sydney: McGraw-Hill Book Company, 1974.

Guirdham, Mary. *Communicating Across Cultures.* London: Macmillan Business, 1999.

Gunn, John. *Challenging Horizons: QANTAS, 1939–1954.* Brisbane: University of Queensland Press, 1987.

Hainsworth, David R. *The Sydney Traders: Simeon Lord and His Contemporaries, 1788–1821*. Melbourne: Melbourne University Press, 1981.

Harper, Norman. *A Great and Powerful Friend: A Study of Australian-American Relations Between 1900 and 1975*. Brisbane: University of Queensland, 1987.

Harry, R. *The North Was Always Near.* Australians in Asia, no. 13, Brisbane: Centre for the Study of Australian-Asian Relations, Griffith University, 1994.

Hasluck, Paul. *The Government and the People, 1939–41*. Canberra: Australian War Memorial, 1965.

Hathaway, Robert M. *Ambiguous Partnership: Britain and America, 1944–47*. New York: Colombia University Press, 1981.

Hazlehurst, Cameron, ed. *Australian Conservatism: Essays in Twentieth-Century Political History*, Canberra: Australian National University Press, 1979.

Held, David, Anthony McGrew, David Goldblatt and Jonathan Perraton. *Global Transformations: Politics, Economics and Culture*. Cambridge: Polity Press, 2000.

Higgott, Richard, Richard Leaver, and John Ravenhill, eds. *Pacific Economic Relations in the 1990s: Cooperation or Conflict?* Australian Fulbright Series, Sydney: Allen and Unwin, 1993.

———. and J. L. Richardson, eds. *International Relations: Global and Australian Perspectives on an Evolving Discipline*. Canberra: Department of International Relations, Research School of Pacific Studies, The Australian National University, 1991.

Hobsbawm, Eric. *Age of Extremes: The Short Twentieth Century, 1914–1991*, Abacus, London, 1994.

———. *The Age of Capital, 1848–1875*. London: Abacus, 1985.

Hogue, Cavan, ed. *Thailand, Australia and the Region: Strategic Developments in Southeast Asia*. Proceedings of the Thai Update, 2001, 26–27 April 2001, Canberra: National Thai Studies Centre, The Australian National University, 2002.

Hopkins, A. G., ed. *Globalization in World History*. London: Pimlico, 2002.

Horner, David. *High Command: Australia's Struggle for an Independent War Strategy, 1939–45*. Sydney: Allen and Unwin, 2nd edition, 1992.

Howe, K. R. *Nature, Culture, and History: The Knowing of Oceania*. Honolulu: University of Hawai'i Press, 2000.

Hudson, William J. *Australia and the New World Order: Evatt at San Francisco, 1945*, Canberra: Department of International Relations, Research School of Pacific and Asian Studies, The Australian National University, 1993.

———. *Towards a Foreign Policy, 1914–1941*. Melbourne: Cassell, 1967.

Hulme, Peter, and Tim Youngs, eds. *The Cambridge Companion to Travel Writing*. Cambridge: Cambridge University Press, 2002.

Huntington, Samuel. P. *The Clash of Civilizations and the Remaking of World History*. New York: Touchstone, 1997.

Hutchinson, C. S, ed. *Geology of Tin Deposits in Asia and the Pacific*. New York: Springer-Verlag, 1988.

Ileto, Reynaldo C., and Rodney J. Sullivan, eds. *Discovering Australasia: Essays on the History of Australian-Philippines Relations.* Townsville: Department of History and Politics, James Cook University of North Queensland, 1993.

Ileto, Reynaldo C. *Filipinos and their Revolution: Event, Discourse and Historiography*. Manila: Ateneo de Manila University Press, 1998.

Ingram, James C. *Economic Change in Thailand, 1850–1970*. Stanford, CA.: Stanford University Press, 1971.

Johnson, Ross C. *The Light and the Gate*. London: Hodder and Stroughton, 1964.

Johnson, Robert D, ed. *On Cultural Ground: Essays in International History*. Chicago: Imprint Publications, 1994.

Jagjit Singh Sidhu. *Administration in the Federated Malay States, 1896–1920*. Oxford: Oxford University Press, 1980.

Keating, Paul. *Engagement: Australia Faces the Asia-Pacific*. Sydney: Macmillan, 2000.

Kelley, Colleen, and Judith Meyers, *CCAI (Cross-Cultural Adaptability Inventory) Manual*. Minneapolis: National Computer Systems, 1995.

Keyes, Charles F. *Thailand: Buddhist Kingdom as Modern Nation-State*. Duang Kamol, Bangkok, 1989.

Keylor, W. R. *The Twentieth-Century World: An International History*. Oxford: Oxford University Press, 2nd edition, 1992.

Khien Theeravit. *Australian-Thai Relations: A Thai Perspective*. Occasional Paper No. 58, Singapore: Institute of Southeast Asian Studies, 1979.

King, Peter. *West Papua & Indonesia since Suharto: Independence, Autonomy or Chaos?* Sydney: UNSW Press, 2004.

Kobkua Suwannathat-Pian. *Thailand's Durable Premier: Phibun through Three Decades, 1932–1957*. Oxford: Oxford University Press, 1995.

———. *Nayobaay Tang Prathaet Khong Rathabaan Phibun Songkhram, 2481–2487* (The Foreign Policy of the Phibun Songkhram Government, 1938–1944). Bangkok: Thai Khadi Research Institute, Thammasat University, 1989.

———. *Thai-Malay Relations: Traditional Intra-Regional Relations from the Seventeenth to the Early Twentieth Centuries*. Singapore: Oxford University Press, 1988.

Kondhi Suphamongkon. *Kaan Witaetsobaay Khong Thai, 2483–2495* (Thai Foreign Policy, 1940–1952). Bangkok: Postbook Publishing, 1994.

Kumar, Nagesh, ed. *Towards an Asian Economic Community: Vision of a New Asia*. Singapore: Institute of Southeast Asian Studies and New Delhi: Research and Information Service for Developing Countries, 2004.

Laksri Jayasuriya, and Kee Pookong. *The Asianisation of Australia?* Melbourne: Melbourne University Press, 1999.

Lebra-Chapman, Joyce, ed. *Japan's Greater East Asia Co-Prosperity Sphere in World War II: Selected Readings and Documents*. Kuala Lumpur: Oxford University Press, 1975.

Levi, Werner. *Australia's Outlook on Asia*. Sydney: Angus and Robertson, 1958.

Lim Joo-Jock. *Territorial Power Domains, Southeast Asia and China: The Geo-Strategy of an Overarching Massif*. Singapore: Institute of Southeast Asian Studies and the Strategic and Defence Studies Centre, Australian National University, 1984.

Macintyre, Stuart. *The Oxford History of Australia: vol. 4, The Succeeding Age, 1901–1942*. Oxford: Oxford University Press, 1990.

Macknight, Charles Cambell. *The Voyage to Marege': Macassan Trepangers in Northern Australia*. Melbourne: Melbourne University Press, 1976.

Manich Jumsai. *History of Anglo-Thai Relations*. Bangkok: Chalermnit, 1970.

Martin, Allan W., and Patsy Hardy, eds. *Dark and Hurrying Days: Menzies' 1941 Diary*. Canberra: National Library of Australia, 1993.

May, R. J. ed. *Natural Partners: North Australia-Philippines Relations*. Canberra and Darwin: North Australia Research Unit, the Australian National University, 1998.

McCormack, Gavan, and Hank Nelson, eds. *The Burma-Thailand Railway.* Sydney: Allen and Unwin, 1993.

McKernan, M., and M. Browne, eds. *Australia: Two Centuries of War and Peace.* Canberra: Australian War Memorial, 1988.

McPherson, Naomi, ed. *In Colonial New Guinea: Anthropological Perspectives.* Pittsburgh: University of Pittsburgh Press, 2001.

McQueen, Humphrey. *Japan to the Rescue: Australian Security Around the Indonesian Archipelago During the American Century.* Melbourne: William Heinemann Australia, 1991.

———. *A New Britannia: An Argument Concerning the Social Origins of Australian Radicalism and Nationalism.* Melbourne: Penguin Books Australia, 1986.

McVey, Ruth, ed. *Southeast Asian Capitalists.* New York: Cornell University, Ithaca, 1992.

Meaney, Neville. *A History of Australian Defence and Foreign Policy 1901–1923: vol. 1, The Search for Security in the Pacific, 1901–1914.* Sydney: Sydney University Press, 1976.

———.ed. *Under New Heavens.* Melbourne: Heinemann Educational Australia, 1989.

Mercer, Patricia. *White Australia Defied: Pacific Islander Settlement in North Queensland.* Townsville: James Cook University, 1995.

Millar, Thomas B. *Australia in Peace and War: External Relations since 1788.* Sydney: Australian National University Press, 2nd edition, 1991.

———. ed.. *Australian Foreign Minister: The Diaries of R. G. Casey, 1951–60.* London: Collins, 1972.

———. *Foreign Policy: Some Australian Reflections.* Melbourne: Georgian House, 1972.

———. *Australia's Foreign Policy.* Melbourne: Angus and Robertson, 1968.

Milner, Anthony, and Mary Quilty, eds. *Australia in Asia: Episodes.* Oxford: Oxford University Press, 1998.

Morrison, Charles Edward, ed. *Threats to Security in East Asia-Pacific: National and Regional Perspectives.* Lexington MS: Lexington Books, 1983.

Moses, John A., and C. Pugsley, eds. *The German Empire and Britain's Pacific Dominions, 1871–1919: Essays on the Role of Australia and New Zealand in World Politics in the Age of Imperialism.* Regina: Claremont, 2000.

Mullins, Steve. *Torres Strait: A History of Colonial Occupation and Culture Contact, 1864–1897.* Rockhampton: Central Queensland University Press, 1994.

Murray, Tim, ed. *Archaeology of Aboriginal Australia: A Reader.* Sydney: Allen and Uniwn, 1998.

Nelson, Hank. *Prisoners of War: Australians under Nippon.* Sydney: ABC Books, 2000.

———. *Taim Bilong Masta: The Australian Involvement in Papua New Guinea.* Sydney: ABC Books, 1982.

———. *Black, White and Gold: Goldmining in Papua New Guinea.* Canberra: Australian National University Press, 1976.

———. *Papua New Guinea: Black Unity or Black Chaos?* London: Penguin, 1972.

Nicholson, Ian H. *Via Torres Strait: A Maritime History of the Torres Strait Route and the Ships' Post Office at Booby Island.* Nambour: Roebuck Society, 1996.

Oakman, Daniel. *Facing Asia: A History of the Colombo Plan.* Canberra: Pandanus, 2004.

Parsons, Ronald. *Steamers in the South.* Sydney: Rigby, 1979.

Paul, Erik. *Australia and Southeast Asia: Regionalisation and Democracy*. Copenhagen: Nordic Institute of Asian Studies, 1998.

Pearl, Cyril. *Morrison of Peking: The Classic Account of an Australian in China During the Boxer Uprising*. London: Collins Angus and Robertson, 1991.

Pimlott, J. A. R. *The Englishman's Holiday: A Social History*. London: Faber and Faber, 1947.

Poulgrain, Greg. *The Genesis of Konfrontasi: Malaysia, Brunei, Indonesia, 1945–1965*. Bathurst: Crawfurd, 1998.

Rees, Judith. *Natural Resources: Allocation, Economics and Policy*. London: Routledge, 2nd edition, 1990.

Reid, Anthony. *Southeast Asia in the Age of Commerce, vol. 2, Expansion and Crisis*. New Haven: Yale University Press, 1993.

———. *Southeast Asia in the Age of Commerce, 1450–1680, vol. 1, The Lands Below the Winds*. New Haven: Yale University Press, 1988.

Renouf, Alan. *The Frightened Country*. Melbourne: Macmillan, 1979.

Reynolds, E. Bruce. *Thailand and Japan's Southern Advance, 1940–1945*. London: Macmillan, 1994.

Reynolds, Henry. *North of Capricorn*, Sydney: Allen and Unwin, 2003.

———. *Race Relations in North Queensland*. Townsville: Department of History and Politics, James Cook University of North Queensland, 1993.

Ricklefs, Merle. *A History of Modern Indonesia Since c. 1200*. Stanford CA.: Stanford University Press, 2001.

Robison, Richard, ed. *Pathways to Asia: The Politics of Engagement*. Sydney: Allen and Unwin, 1996

Rodan, Gary, Kevin Hewison, and Richard Robison, eds. *The Political Economy of South-East Asia: An Introduction*. Melbourne: Oxford University Press, 1997.

Rolls, Eric. *Sojourners: The Epic Story of China's Centuries Old Relationship with Australia*. Brisbane: University of Queensland Press, 1992.

Rojek, Chris. *Capitalism & Modern Leisure Theory*. London: Tavistock Publications, 1985.

Savage, Victor R. *Western Impressions of Nature and Landscape in Southeast Asi*. Singapore: Singapore University Press, 1984.

Schwartz, Adam. *A Nation in Waiting: Indonesia's Search for Stability*. Sydney: Allen and Unwin, 1999.

Shann, Edward. *An Economic History of Australia*. Melbourne: Georgian House, 1967.

Shaw, A. G. L. *The Economic Development of Australia*. Melbourne: Longman Australia, 6th edition, 1970.

Sheridan, Greg. *Asian Values, Western Dreams: Understanding the New Asia*. Sydney: Allen and Unwin, 1999.

Shermer, Michael. *In Darwin's Shadow: The Life and Science of Alfred Russel Wallace*. Oxford: Oxford University Press, 2002.

Shnukal, Anna, Guy Ramsay, and Yuriko Nagata, eds. *Navigating Boundaries: The Asian Diaspora in the Torres Strait*. Canberra: Pandanus, 2004.

Silcock, T. H., ed. *Thailand: Social and Economic Studies in Development*. Canberra: Australian National University Press, 1967.

Smith, Gary, and Mark McGillivray, eds. *Australia and Asia*. Melbourne: Oxford University Press, 1997.

Smith, Valene L., ed. *Hosts and Guests: The Anthropology of Tourism*. Oxford: Basil Blackwell, 1978.

Sompop Manarungsan. *Economic Development of Thailand, 1850–1950: Response to the Challenge of the World Economy*. Bangkok: Institute of Asian Studies, Chulalongkorn University, 1989.

Souter, Gavin. *Lion and Kangaroo: The Initiation of Australia*. Sydney: Pan Macmillan, 1992.

Stargardt, A. W. *Australia's Asian Policies: The History of a Debate, 1839–1972*. Hamburg: Institute of Asian Affairs, 1977.

Stowe, Judith A. *Siam becomes Thailand: A Story of Intrigue*. London: Hurst and Company, 1991.

Stuart, Francis. *Towards a Coming of Age: A Foreign Service Odyssey*. Brisbane: Centre for the Study of Australian-Asian Relations, Griffith University, 1990.

Sullivan, Rodney J. *Exemplar of Americanism: The Philippine Career of Dean C. Worcester*. Ann Abor: Center for South and Southeast Asian Studies, University of Michigan, 1991.

Tarling, Nicholas. *The Fall of Imperial Britain in South-East Asia*. Oxford: Oxford University Press, 1994.

———. ed. *The Cambridge History of Southeast Asia, vol. 1, From Early Times to c. 1800*. Cambridge: Cambridge University Press, 1992.

———. ed. *The Cambridge History of Southeast Asia, vol. 2, The Nineteenth and Twentieth Centuries*. Cambridge: Cambridge University Press, 1992.

Temple, R. C. *The World Encompassed by Sir Francis Drake*. Amsterdam: N. Israel, 1926.

Terwiel, Bas, J. *A History of Modern Thailand, 1767–1942*. Brisbane: University of Queensland Press, 1983.

———. *Field Marshall Plaek Phibun Songkhram*. Brisbane: University of Queensland Press, 1980.

Thet Bunnak. *The Provincial Administration of Siam, 1892–1915*. Kuala Lumpur: Oxford University Press, 1977.

Thompson, Virginia. *Thailand: The New Siam*. New York: Paragon Book Reprint Corporation, 2nd edition, 1967.

Tipton, Frank. *The Rise of Asia: Economics, Society and Politics in Contemporary Asia*. Melbourne: Macmillan, 1998.

Tomlinson, John. *Globalization and Culture*. Cambridge: Polity, 1999.

Tregonning, Kennedy. *Under Chartered Company Rule: North Borneo, 1881–1946*. Singapore: University of Malaya Press, 1958.

Turner, Victor, and Edith Turner. *Image and Pilgrimage in Christian Culture: Anthropological Perspectives*. Oxford: Basil Blackwell, 1978.

Tweedie, Sandra. *Trading Partners: Australia & Asia, 1790–1993*. Sydney: University of New South Wales Press, 1994.

Vandenbosch, A., and M. B. Vandenbosch, *Australia Faces Southeast Asia: The Emergence of a Foreign Policy*. Lexington: University of Kentucky Press, 1967.

van Oosterzee, Penny. *Where Worlds Collide: The Wallace Line*. Melbourne: Reed Books, 1997.

Veblen, Thorstein. *The Theory of the Leisure Class*. London: Penguin, 1994.

Vickers, Adrian. *Bali: A Paradise Created*. Melbourne: Penguin, 1989.

Walker, David. *Anxious Nation: Australia and the Rise of Asia, 1850–1939*, Brisbane: Queensland University Press, 1999.

Wang Gungwu, ed. *Community and Nation: China, Southeast Asia and Australia*. Sydney: Asian Studies Association of Australia and Allen and Unwin, 2nd edition, 1992.

Ward, Russel. *The Australian Legend*. Oxford: Oxford University Press, 1977.

Warr, Peter G., ed. *The Thai Economy in Transition*. Cambridge: Cambridge University Press, 1993.

Watt, Alan. *The Evolution of Australian Foreign Policy, 1938–1965*. London: Cambridge University Press, 1967.

West, Francis, ed. *Selected Letters of Hubert Murray*. Melbourne: Oxford University Press, 1970.

Wheatley, Paul. *The Golden Khersonese: Studies in the Historical Geography of the Malay Peninsula before AD 1500*. Westport CT.: Greenwood Press, 1961.

Wheelwright, Ted, and Ken Buckley, eds. *The Political Economy of Australian Capitalism*. vol. 4, Sydney: ANZ Book Company, 1980.

White, Richard. *On Holidays: A History of Getting Away in Australia*. Sydney: Pluto Press, 2005.

Wigmore, Lionel. *The Japanese Thrust*. Canberra: Australian War Memorial, 1957.

Wilson, Thomas M. and Hastings Donnan, eds. *Border Identities: Nation and State at International Frontiers*. Cambridge: Cambridge University Press, 1998.

Winchester, Simon. *Krakatoa: The Day the World Exploded, 27 August 1883*. Melbourne: Viking, 2003.

Wolters, Oliver W. *History, Culture, and Region in Southeast Asian Perspectives*. Singapore: Institute of Southeast Asian Studies, 1982.

Wong Lin Ken. *The Malaysian Tin Industry to 1914*. Texas: University of Arizona Press, 1965.

Wright, J. J. *The Balancing Act: A History of Modern Thailand*. Bangkok, Asia Books, 1991.

Wyatt, David K. *Thailand: A Short History*. New Haven: Yale University Press, 1984.

Yip Yat Hoong. *The Development of the Tin Mining Industry of Malaya*. Kuala Lumpur: University of Malaya Press, 1969.

CHAPTERS IN BOOKS

———. "Diggers and Diplomats: Australian Mining Entrepreneurs and the Evolution of the Australia-Thailand Bilateral Relationship, 1901–1941." in *Australia-Thailand Relations in the Twentieth Century*, edited by Michael Hayes and Steve Smith, Bangkok: Australian Studies Centre, Kasetsart University, Thailand, 2000 <http://www.asc.ku.ac.th/Thai-Australia%20CD-ROM/Thai-Oz%20Homepage.htm> [Inactive].

———. "Influential Circles: The Philippines in Australian Trade and Tourism, 1840–1926." Pp. 47–69 in *Discovering Australasia: Essays on Philippine-Australian Interactions*, edited by Reynaldo C. Ileto, and Rodney J. Sullivan, Townsville: James Cook University, 1993.

Ballantyne, Tony, "Empire, Knowledge and Culture: from Proto-globalization to Modern Globalization." Pp. 115–40 in *Globalization in World History*, edited by A. G. Hopkins, Pimlico, London, 2002.

Battersby, P. "Mapping Australasia: Reflections on the Permeability of Australia's Northern Borders." Pp. 13–30 in *Navigating Boundaries: The Asian Diaspora in the Torres Strait*, edited by Anna Shnukal, Guy Ramsay, and Yuriko Nagata, Canberra: Pandanus Books, 2004.

Burke, Gillian. "The Rise and Fall of the International Tin Agreements." Pp. 43–70 in *Undermining Tin: The Decline of Malaysian Pre-eminence*, edited by Kwame Sundaram Jomo, Sydney: Transnational Corporations Research Project, University of Sydney, 1990.

Campo, J. A., "Steam Navigation and State Formation." Pp. 11–30 in *The Late Colonial State in Indonesia: Political and Economic Foundations of the Netherlands Indies, 1880–1942*, edited by Robert Cribb, Leiden: KITLV Press, 1994.

Carr, Helen. "Modernism and Travel, 1880–1940." Pp. 70–86 in *The Cambridge Companion to Travel Writing*, edited by Peter Hulme and Tim Young, Cambridge: Cambridge University Press, 2002.

Chauvel, Richard. "West New Guinea: Perceptions and Policies, Ethnicity and the Nation State," Pp. 10–36 in *Australia in Asia: Episodes*, edited by Anthony Milner and Mary Quilty, Melbourne: Oxford University Press, 1998.

Fox, James. J. "Reefs and Shoals in Australia-Indonesia Relations: Traditional Indonesian Fishing." Pp. 111–39 in *Australia in Asia: Episodes*, edited by Anthony Milner and Mary Quilty, Melbourne: Oxford University Press, 1998.

Gunawan, Myra P. "Indonesia's Tourism: Development Policies and the Challenge for Research and Education." Pp. 147–64 in *Asia-Pacific Tourism: Regional Cooperation, Planning and Development*, edited by Kee Pookong and Brian King, Melbourne: Hospitality Press, Victoria University of Technology, 1999.

Hopkins, A. G. "The History of Globalization – and the Globalization of History." Pp. 11–46 in *Globalization in World History*, edited by A. G. Hopkins, London: Pimlico, 2002.

Hugo, Graham. "Demographic Change and Implications." Pp. 95–42 in *Southeast Asia Transformed: A Geography of Change*, edited by Chia Lin Sien, Singapore: Institute of South East Asian Studies, 2003.

Ileto, Reynaldo C. "Philippine-Australian Interactions: The Late Nineteenth Century." Pp. 10–46 in *Discovering Australasia: Essays on Philippine-Australian Interactions*, Reynaldo C. Ileto and Rodney J. Sullivan, Townsville: James Cook University, 1993.

Ingleson, John, and David Walker. "The Impact of Asia." Pp. 287–324 in *Under New Heavens*, edited by Neville Meaney, Melbourne: Heinemann Educational Australia, 1989.

Jones, R. "The Fifth Continent: Problems Concerning the Human Colonization of Australia." Pp. 102–18 in *Archaeology of Aboriginal Australia: A Reader*, edited by Tim Murray, Sydney: Allen and Unwin, 1998.

Kamon Pensrinokun. "Adaptation and Appeasement: Thai Relations with Japan and the Allies in World War II." Pp. 125–60 in *Thai-Japanese Relations in Historical Perspective*, edited by Chaiwat Khamchoo and E. Bruce Reynolds, Bangkok: Institute of Asian Studies, Chulalongkorn University, 1988.

Kesavapany, K. and Rahul Sen. "ASEAN's Contribution to the Building of an Asian Economic Community." Pp. 43–56 in *Towards an Asian Economic Community: Vision of a New Asia*, edited by Nagesh Kumar, Singapore: Institute of Southeast Asian Studies and New Delhi: Research and Information Service for Developing Countries, 2004.

Miles, Edward Thomas. "The History of the Tongkah Harbour Tin Dredging Enterprise." Pp. 252–64 in *Political Economy of Siam, 1851–1910*, edited by Chatthip Nartsupha and Suthy Prasartset, Bangkok: The Social Science Association of Thailand, 1981.

Nash, Jill. "Paternalilsm, Progress, Paranoia: Patrol Reports and Colonial History in South Bouganville." Pp. 111–50 in *In Colonial New Guinea: Anthropological Perspectives*, edited by Naomi McPherson, Pittsburgh: University of Pittsburgh Press, 2001.

Overlack, Peter. "Australian Reactions to German Interests in the Netherlands Indies and Timor prior to 1914: A Strategic Imperative." Pp. 277–308 in *The German Empire and Britain's Pacific Dominions, 1871–1919: Essays on the Role of Australia and New Zealand in World Politics in the Age of Imperialism*, edited by John Moses and Christopher Pugsley, Regina: Cleremont, 2000.

Parsonage, James. "Trans-State Developments in South-East Asia: Subregional Growth Zones." Pp. 248–83 in *The Political Economy of South-East Asia: An Introduction*, edited by Gary Rodan, Kevin Hewison, and Richard Robison, Melbourne: Oxford University Press, 1997.

Pernia, Ernesto. "Tourism and Development in the East ASEAN Growth Area (EAGA)." Pp. 47–54 in *Asia-Pacific Tourism: Regional Co-operation, Planning and Development*, edited by Kee Pookong and Brian King, Melbourne: Hospitality Press, Victoria University of Technology, 1999.

Philipps, Lorraine. "Plenty More Little Brown Man: Pearl Shelling and White Australia in Queensland, 1901–18." Pp. 58–83 in *The Political Economy of Australian Capitalism*, vol. 4, edited by Ted Wheelwright and Ken Buckley, Sydney: ANZ Book Company, 1980.

Rimmer, Peter J. "Spatial Impact of Innovation in International Sea and Air Transport." Pp. 287–316 in *Southeast Asia Transformed: A Geography of Change*, edited by Chia Lin Sen, Singapore: Institute of Southeast Asian Studies, 2003.

Rosewarne, Stuart. "Capital Accumulation in Australia and the Export of Mining Capital before World War II." Pp. 181–220 in *The Political Economy of Australian Capitalism*. vol. 5, edited by Ted Wheelwright and Ken Buckley, Sydney: ANZ Book Company, 1983.

Searle, Peter. "Recalcitrant of Realpolitik: The Politics of Culture in Australia's Relations with Malaysia." Pp. 56–84 in *Pathways to Asia: The Politics of Engagement*, edited by Richard Robison, Sydney: Allen and Unwin, 1996.

Shnukal, Anna. "They Don't Know What Went on Underneath": Three Little-known Filipino/Malay Communities of Torres Strait, Pp. 81–121 in *Navigating Boundaries: The Asian Diaspora in the Torres Strait*, edited by Anna Shnukal, Guy Ramsay, and Yuriko Nagata, Pandanus Books, Canberra, 2004.

Silcock, T. H. "Promotion of Industry and the Planning Process," Pp. 258–88 in *Thailand: Social and Economic Studies in Development*, edited by T. H. Silcock, Canberra: Australian National University Press, 1967.

Smith, Gary. "Australia's Political Relationships with Asia." Pp. 100–119 in *Australia and Asia*, edited by Gary Smith and Mark McGillivray, Melbourne: Oxford University Press, Melbourne, 1997.

Staples, A. C. "Maritime Trade in the Indian Ocean, 1830–1845." Pp. 84–120 in *University Studies in History*, edited by Geoffrey C. Bolton, G. C. and B. K. de Garis, Perth: University of Western Australia Press, 1966, pp. 84–120.

Sullivan, Rodney J. " 'It Had to Happen': The Gamboas and Australian-Philippine Interactions." Pp. 98–116 in *Discovering Australasia: Essays on Philippine-Australian Interactions*, Reynaldo C. Ileto and Rodney J. Sullivan, Townsville: James Cook University, 1993.

Swan, William. "Aspects of Japan's Prewar Economic Relations with Thailand." Pp. 59–124 in *Thai-Japanese Relations in Historical Perspective*, edited by Chaiwat Khamchoo and E. B. Reynolds, Bangkok: Institute of Asian Studies, Chulalongkorn University, 1988.

Turnbull, C. Mary. "Regionalism and Nationalism." Pp. 257–317 in *The Cambridge History of Southeast Asia, volume 2, Part 2: From World War II to the Present*, edited by Nicholas Tarling, Cambridge: Cambridge University Press, 2nd edition, 1999.

Vickers, Adrian. "Indonesia in Australian Writing Before C. J. Koch." Pp. 21–30 in *Representations of Indonesia in Australia*, edited by Natalie Monbini-Kesheh, Melbourne: Monash Asia Institute, 1997.

Wang Gungwu. "Trade and Cultural Values: Australia and the Four Dragons." Pp. 301–13 in *Community and Nation: China, Southeast Asia and Australia*, edited by Wang Gungwu, Sydney: Australian Asian Studies Association and Allen & Unwin, 1992.

Wertheim, Werner F. "Fissures in the Girdle of Emeralds." Pp. 59–73 in *Indonesian Politics: A Reader*, edited by Christine Doran, Townsville: Centre for South-East Asian Politics, James Cook University of North Queensland, 1987.

Wilson, Thomas M., and Hastings Donnan, "Nation, State and Identity at International Borders." Pp. 1–30 in *Border Identities: Nation and State at International Frontiers*, edited by Thomas M. Wilson and Hastings Donnan, Cambridge: Cambridge University Press, 1998.

PUBLISHED CONFERENCE PROCEEDINGS

Battersby, Paul. "Over the Top: Writing Australia into South East Asia." *Asia Examined: Proceedings of the 15th Biennial Conference of the Asian Studies Association of Australia*, 29 June–2 July 2004, edited by Robert Cribb, <http: //coombs.anu .edu.au/ASAA/conference/proceedings/asaa-2004-proceedings.html>

Battersby, Paul. "Peaks and Troughs: Risk, Regionalization and Australia's Rediscovery of Its East Asian Future." *Proceedings of the Second Oceanic Conference of International Studies*, 6–9 July 2006, University of Melbourne, 2006. <http: //www .politics.unimelb.edu.au/ocis/refereed.html>

Cushman, Jennifer. "A Marriage of Convenience: Australian Mining Investment and Its Thai Sponsors in Early Twentieth-Century Siam." in *Rural Thai Society/*

Development of the Thai Economy, Proceedings, International Conference on Thai Studies, Bangkok, 1984, 1–22.

AUSTRALIAN DICTIONARY OF BIOGRAPHY

Bennet, Scott. "Miles, Edward Thomas (1849–1944)." Pp. 500–501, *ADB*, vol. 10, 1891–1939, Melbourne: Melbourne University Press, 1986.

Borchart, D. H, "Tenison-Woods, Julian Edmund (1832–1889)," Pp. 254–55, *ADB*, 1851–1890, vol. 16, Melbourne: Melbourne University Press, 1976.

Burke, Keast. "Kerry, Charles Henry (1857–1928)." Pp. 577–578, *ADB*, vol. 9, 1891–1939, Melbourne: Melbourne University Press, 1983.

Kennedy, B. E. "Gepp, Sir Herbert William (1877–1954)." Pp. 640–642, *ADB*, vol. 8, 1891–1939, Melbourne: Melbourne University Press, 1981.

Langmore, Diane. "Pratt, Ambrose Goddard Hesketh (1874–1944)." Pp. 274–75, *ADB*, vol. 11, 1891–1939, Melbourne: Melbourne University Press, 1988.

Lloyd, C. J. "Massy-Greene, Sir Walter (1874–1952)." Pp. 435–438, *ADB*, vol. 10. 1891–1939, Melbourne: Melbourne University Press, 1986.

Mercer, Patricia. "Clark, James (1857–1933)." Pp. 9–10, *ADB*, vol. 8, 1891–1939, Melbourne: Melbourne University Press, 1981.

Pope, David. "Pratten, Herbert Edward (1865–1928)." Pp. 277–78, *ADB*, vol. 11, 1891–1939, Melbourne: Melbourne University Press, 1988.

Poynter, J. R. "Baillieu, William Lawrence (1859–1936)." Pp. 138–45, *ADB*, vol. 7, 1891–1939, Melbourne: Melbourne University Press, 1979.

Richardson, Peter. "Robinson, William Sydney (1876–1963)." Pp. 428–433, *ADB*, vol. 11, 1891–1939, Melbourne: Melbourne University Press, 1988.

Rutledge, Martha. "Copeland Henry (1839–1904)." Pp. 458–459, *ADB*, vol. 3, 1891–1939, Melbourne: Melbourne University Press, 1969.

JOURNAL ARTICLES

Aldrich, Richard. "A Question of Expediency: Britain, the United States and Thailand, 1941–42." *Journal of Southeast Asian Studies.* vol. 19, no. 2, September 1988, 209–45.

Battersby, Paul. "Border Politics and the Broader Politics of Thailand's International Relations: From Communism to Capitalism." *Pacific Affairs.* Winter 1998–99, 473–88.

———. "An Uneasy Peace: Britain, the United States and Australia's Pursuit of War Reparations from Thailand, 1945–1952." *Australian Journal of International Affairs.* vol. 54, no. 1, 2000, 15–31.

———. "Journeys of an "Amateur Orientalist": Australia and Asia through the Eyes of Ambrose Pratt." *Journal of the Royal Australian Historical Society.* December 2000, 159–75.

Broeze, Frank. "Australia, Asia and the Pacific: The Maritime World of Robert Towns, 1843–1873," *Australian Historical Studies.* vol. 24, no. 95, October, 1990, 222–40.

Brown, Nicholas. "Australian Intellectuals and the Image of Asia: 1920–1960." *Australian Cultural History*. no. 9, 1990, 80–92.

Buest, T. N. M. "Australian Citizenship and British Nationality." *Australian Outlook*. vol. 3, no. 2, June 1949, 109–16.

Chandran, Jeshrun. "Britain and the Siamese Malay States, 1892–1904: A Comment." *The Historical Journal*. vol. 15, no. 3, 1972, 471–92.

Cushman, Jennifer. " 'Dazzled by Distant Fields': The Australian Economic Presence in Southeast Asia." *Asian Studies Association of Australia (ASAA) Review*. vol. 12, no. 1, July, 1988, 1–5.

———. "The Khaw Group: Chinese Business in Early Twentieth-Century Penang." *Journal of Southeast Asian Studies*. vol. 17, no. 1, March, 1986, 58–79.

Denoon, Donald. "Re-Membering Australasia." *Australian Historical Studies*. 122, 2003, 290–304.

Eastham, J. K. "Rationalisation in the Tin Industry." *The Review of Economic Studies*. vol. 4, 1936–37, 13–32.

Emerson, Donald K. " 'Southeast Asia': What's in a Name?" *Journal of Southeast Asian Studies*. vol. 15, no. 1, March 1984, 7–21.

Gurry, Meg. "Identifying Australia's Region;: From Evatt to Evans." *Australian Journal of International Affairs*. vol. 49, no. 1, May, 1995, 17–32.

Hamilton, Annette. "Fear and Desire: Aborigines, Asians and the National Imaginary." *Australian Cultural History*. no. 9, 1990, 14–36.

Hastings, Peter. "The Timor Problem – II: Some Australian Attitudes, 1903–1941." *Australian Outlook*. vol. 29, no. 2, August 1975, 180–96.

———. "The Timor Problem – III." *Australian Outlook*. vol. 29, no. 3, December 1975, 323–34.

Hillman, John. "The Free-Rider and the Cartel: Siam and the International Tin Restriction Agreements, 1931–1941." *Modern Asian Studies*. vol. 24, no. 2, 1990, 297–321.

———. "Malaya and the International Cartel," *Modern Asian Studies*. vol. 22, no. 2, 1988, 236–45.

Horne, J. Ann. "The Practical Man as Hero? Technical Education in New South Wales in the 1870s and 1880s." *Australian Cultural History*. no. 8, 1989, 62–77.

Howard, Dora. "The English Activities on the North Coast of Australia in the First Half of the Nineteenth Century." *Proceedings of the Royal Geographical Society of Australasia, South Australian Branch*. vol. 33, 1931–32, 56–57.

Keating, Paul. "Australia and Asia: Knowing Who We Are." *Backgrounder*. vol. 3, no. 7, April 1992, 2–15.

Kenichi Ohmae. "The Rise of the Region State." *Foreign Affairs*. vol. 72, no. 2, Spring 1993, 78–87.

Kiernan, Victor G. "Britain, Siam and Malaya: 1875–1885." *The Journal of Modern History*. vol. 28, no. 1, March, 1956, 1–20.

MacLeod, Ray. "The 'Practical Man': Myth and Metaphor in Anglo-Australian Science." *Australian Cultural History*. no. 8, 1989, 24–49.

McCarthy, John. "The 'Great Betrayal' Reconsidered: An Australian Perspective." *Australian Journal of International Affairs*. vol. 48, no. 1, May, 1994, 53–60.

McCulloch, R. "New Directions in Australian Trade." *Business in Thailand*. January 1983, 73–78.

Meaney, Neville. "The End of "White Australia" and Australia's Changing Percep-
  tions of Asia, 1945–1990." *Australian Journal of International Affairs*. vol. 49, no. 2,
  November, 1995, 171–89.
Megaw, Ruth. "The Australian Goodwill Mission to the Far East in 1934: Its Signifi-
  cance in the Evolution of Australian Foreign Policy." *Journal of the Royal Australian
  Historical Society*. vol. 59, part 4, December 1973, 255–57.
Nash, D, and V. L. Smith. "Anthropology and Tourism." *Annals of Tourism Research*.
  vol. 18, 1991, 12–25.
Pearson, M. N. "Pilgrims, Travellers, Tourists: The Meanings of Journeys." *Australian
  Cultural History*. no 10, 1991, 125–33.
Philpott, Simon. "Fear of the Dark: Indonesia and the Australian National Imagina-
  tion." *Australian Journal of International Affairs*. vol. 55, no. 3, November 2001,
  371–88.
Reed, Robert. "Remarks on the Colonial Genesis of the Hill Station in Southeast Asia
  with Particular Reference to the Cities of Buitenzorg (Bogor) and Baguio." *Asian
  Profile*. vol. 4, no. 6, December 1976, 551–589.
Richardson, Peter. "The Origins and Development of the Collins House Group,
  1915–1951." *Australian Economic History Review*. 27, 1987, 3–29.
Spencer, J. E., and W. I. Thomas. "The Hill Stations and Summer Resorts of the Ori-
  ent." *Geographical Review*. vol. 38, 1948, 637–651.
Swan, William L. "Thai-Japanese Relations at the Start of the Pacific War: New In-
  sight into a Controversial Period." *Journal of Southeast Asian Studies*. vol. 18, no. 2,
  September 1987, 270–93.
Taylor, Roger G. "The Mining Industry in Thailand." *Australian Mining*. vol. 62, no.
  4, April, 1960, 62–64.
"Thai-Australian Industries." *Investor Supplement*. March 1972, 23–29.
"Thai-Australian Trade: Price Is the Problem." *Business in Thailand*. January 1983,
  62–66.
Thamsook Numnonda. "Negotiations Concerning the Cession of Siamese Malay
  States, 1907–1909." *Journal of the Siam Society*. vol. 55, pt. 2, July 1966, 227–35.
Thio, E. "Britain's Search for Security in North Malaya, 1886–97." *Journal of South-
  east Asian History*. vol. 10, no. 2, September, 1969, 279–303.
Vickers, Adrian. "Kipling Goes South: Australian Novels and South-East Asia." *Aus-
  tralian Cultural History*. no. 9, 1990, 65–80.
———. "Racism and Colonialism in Early Australian Novels about Southeast Asia."
  ASSA Review. vol. 12, no. 1, July 1988, 7–12.
Walker, David. "Survivalist Anxieties: Australian Responses to Asia, 1890s to the Pre-
  sent." *Australian Historical Studies*. 120, 2002, 319–30.
———. "Travellers to the Orient." *ASAA Review*. vol. 12, no. 1, July 1988, 12–17.

THESES

Battersby, Paul. "Tourists of Substance: Australian Travellers and Tourists in Island
  Southeast Asia, 1866–1913." Honours Thesis, Department of History and Politics, James Cook University of North Queensland, 1992.

Birch, Francis D. "Tropical Milestones: Australian Gold and Tin Mining Investment in Malaya and Thailand, 1880–1930." MA Thesis, University of Melbourne, 1976.

Copeland, Matthew P. "Contested Nationalism: The 1932 Overthrow of the Absolute Monarchy in Siam." PhD Thesis, The Australian National University, 1993.

Cornish, Richard A. "Malays and Thai Officials: Relations Between Malay Rubber Producers and Thai Government Officials in a Development Project in Southern Thailand." PhD Thesis, The Australian National University, 1989.

Legarda y Fernandez, B. F. "Foreign Trade, Economic Exchange and Entrepreneurship in the 19th-Century Philippines." PhD Diss., Harvard University, 1955.

McCarty, J. W. "British Investment in Overseas Mining, 1880–1914." PhD Thesis, University of Cambridge, 1960.

Neher, Arlene Becker. "Prelude to Alliance: The Expansion of American Economic Interest in Thailand During the 1940s." PhD Diss., Northern Illinois University, Illinois, 1980.

Phuwadol Songprasert. "The Development of Chinese Capital in Southern Siam, 1868–1932." PhD Thesis, Monash University, Victoria, Australia, 1986.

Punee Uansakul. "Kitkaan muang rae dee buk kab kaan plian plaeng thaang sethakit phak tai prathaet thai, BE 2411–2474" (Tin mining and economic change in southern Thailand, 1868–1931). MA Thesis, Chulalongkorn University, Bangkok, 1979.

INTERNET SOURCES

Department of Foreign Affairs and Trade, Country Information: Singapore, Malaysia, Indonesia, and Thailand, <http://www.dfat.gov.au/geo>

Moxham, Ben. "Milking Thailand: The Thai-Australia Free Trade Agreement." Focus on the Global South <http://www.focusweb.org/main> (Accessed 30 August 2005)

Newcrest Mining, Operations Overview <http://newcrest.com.au/operations.asp?> (Accessed January 5, 2005)

O'Neill, Igor, and Cam Walker, "Newcrest slammed for collusion with military," *Green Left Weekly*, Online Edition, 21 January 2004 <http://www.greenleft.org/back/2004> [Accessed January 5, 2005]

Rio Tinto Worldwide Operations <http://riotinto.com/aboutus/worldwideoperations> (Accessed January 5, 2005)

Index

Abeyasekere, Susan, 53
Alluvial Tin, 122, 129
Ambon. *See* Netherlands Indies
Angelo, Edward Houghton, 56–57, 107
Anglo-Oriental: Anglo-Oriental and
General Investment Trust, 129;
Anglo-Oriental (Malaya) Ltd.,
120–29; Anglo-Oriental Mining
Corporation, 120, 128.
Arafura Sea, 47, 75–76
Aru Islands. *See* Netherlands Indies
Asian Tsunami, 1–2, 220
Association of Southeast Asian Nations
(ASEAN): ASEAN expansion, 187;
ASEAN Free Trade Area (AFTA), 185;
ASEAN Regional Forum (ARF), 181;
ASEAN Summit, 187, 209;
Association of Southeast Asia (ASA),
167; Australia-New Zealand Closer
Economic Relationship (CER),
186–87, 209; Australian policy
towards, 183, 187, 208, 211;
Bangkok Declaration, 181;
Diplomatic and investment relations
with Australia, 188–90; Indonesia-
Malaysia-Thailand growth area
(IMT), 186; Singapore-Riau-Johore
growth triangle (SIJORI), 186, 197;

Treaty of Amity and Cooperation
(1976), 185, 187, 211; Zone of
Peace Freedom and Neutrality
(ZOPFAN), 181. *See also* Australian
foreign and defence policy;
Indonesia
Australasia. *See* Malay Archipelago
Australian Army, 148, 151, 154, 156
Australian Consolidated Industries, 179
Australian foreign and defence policy:
ANZAC (Australia New Zealand
Army Corp) Pact, 158; ANZAM
(Australia New Zealand and
Malaya), 164, 167; ANZUS
(Australia New Zealand and the
United States) treaty, 164; ASEAN,
184–88, 209; Asia Pacific Economic
Cooperation (APEC), 185; Australia
Indonesia security agreement, 211;
Britain, 37–38, 129–31, 142–54,
157–64, 180; East Timor, 144, 182,
193–94, 211; Indonesia, 159–62,
182, 211; Malaysia, 167, 186–87,
208; Netherlands Indies, 149–54;
Pacific Pact, 132; Philippines, 160,
163; regional security, 132, 142–68,
180–87, 191–94, 208–11; South
East Asia Treaty Organization

94, 118–19, 125; Sarit Thanarat, 179; South East Asia Treaty Organization, 165; Thailand Australia Free Trade Agreement, 187; United States interests, 124–26, 150–51, 163, 165, 178–79; *See also* Australian foreign and defence policy; Chalerm Na Nakhon; Pratt, Ambrose
Thursday Island, 24, 31, 37
Tin Producers' Association (TPA), 120–23
Tomlinson, John, 50
Torres Strait, 17, 22, 29–30, 37, 47
Turner, Edith, 75
Turner, Victor, 75

United Australia Party, 130
United States: ANZUS, 164; and Australia, 150–51, 163–64; and Britain, 124–26, 132, 150, 153, 157, 162–64; "Guam Doctrine," 180; MacArthur, General Douglas, 157; SEATO, 164–66; South West Pacific Area, 157; and Thailand, 124–26,

150–51, 153, 157, 162–64, 179; van Gennep, Arnold, 75

Vickers, Adiran, xv, 6, 8
Victoria, 18, 25, 104. *See also* Melbourne

Wakefield, Edward Gibbon, 22
Wallace, Alfred Russel, 3, 6, 32, 76, 83, 86–87, 157
Weld, Frederick, 59
Wentworth, William Charles, 5
West Australian Steam Navigation Co., 50, 52
White Australia policy, 33, 34, 38, 97, 107
Whitlam, Gough, 181–82
Wildey, William Brackley, 79
Wilkins, W., 6–7
Wongsanuprapat, *Chaophraya*, 113
Worcester, Dean, 61, 84
Worsfold, William Basil, 55, 77

Zone of Peace Freedom and Neutrality (ZOPFAN). *See* ASEAN

About the Author

Paul Battersby was born in the United Kingdom and migrated to Australia in 1985. He completed his Ph.D at James Cook University in 1996 after which he lectured in history and politics at universities and colleges in Australia and Thailand before joining the International Studies program at RMIT University in 2000. He was written book chapters and journal articles on issues ranging from Australia Asia relations to international project based learning. He is currently writing a book with Joseph Siracusa on globalization and human security.

Paul Battersby has led the International Studies program for the last five years and has made a major contribution to the internationalization of RMIT through his work in Asia and Latin America. He has served on the Executive Committee of the Australia Thailand Business Council Victoria and is currently a council member for the Australian Institute of International Affairs Victoria.